D0217629

Playing the Race Card

Playing the Race Card

MELODRAMAS OF BLACK AND WHITE FROM

UNCLE TOM TO O.J. SIMPSON

Linda Williams

PRINCETON UNIVERSITY PRESS   PRINCETON AND OXFORD

Copyright © 2001 by Princeton University Press
Published by Princeton University Press, 41 William Street,
Princeton, New Jersey 08540
In the United Kingdom: Princeton University Press,
3 Market Place, Woodstock,
Oxfordshire OX20 1SY

Third printing, and first paperback printing, 2002
Paperback ISBN 0-691-10283-X

The Library of Congress has cataloged the cloth edition of this book as follows

Williams, Linda, 1946–
Playing the race card : melodramas of Black and white from Uncle Tom
to O.J. Simpson / Linda Williams.
p.   cm.
Includes bibliographical references (p.) and index.
ISBN 0-691-05800-8 (alk. paper)
1. Afro-Americans in popular culture. 2. Racism in popular culture—United States.
3. Melodrama, American—Social aspects. 4. Mass media and race relations—
United States. 5. Afro-Americans in mass media. 6. Afro-American men—Race identity.
7. White women—United States—Race identity. 8. United States—Race relations—
Psychological aspects. 9. Popular culture—United States—Psychological aspects. I. Title.
E185.625   .W523   2001
305.8—dc21   00-058467

British Library Cataloging-in-Publication Data is available

This book has been composed in Electra LH Twelve and
Futura Condensed typefaces.

Printed on acid-free paper. ∞

www.pupress.princeton.edu

Printed in the United States of America

10 9 8 7 6 5 4 3

Dedicated to Paul Fitzgerald

and to the memory of

Lorelle Williams

Contents

Illustrations

List of Illustrations

Preface

Like many people who watched the October 3, 1995, verdict in the trial of O. J. Simpson, I felt deeply implicated in its drama. The verdict in what some would call "the trial of the century,"[1] viewed by more Americans than any other event in the history of television, resonated profoundly with the earlier verdict in the trial of the police accused in the beating of Rodney King. And that verdict, in turn, resonated with a long history of racial villains and victims. This book is my attempt to understand how that long history came to inform these trials. Sometime between the verdict in the police beating of Rodney King on April 29, 1992—a verdict that sparked a major race riot—and the 1995 verdict in the Simpson trial—a verdict that sparked unprecedented white resentment—I realized that a book I had been writing on the American melodramatic imagination as played out in "moving pictures" would have to become a book about black and white racial melodrama. It would need to reach back to the moving picture of the violent beating death of Uncle Tom at the hands of the white slave driver Simon Legree in countless stage melodramas and forward to the Rodney King beating and the O. J. Simpson murder trial. In other words, to understand the collision of these two contemporary "trials in black and white," it would be necessary to trace the mass culture genealogy of black and white racial melodrama over the last hundred and fifty years. It would not be sufficient to limit the "moving pictures" of this study to "the movies" alone. Rather, it would be necessary to study a set of racially resonant music and pictures that have moved the American public to feel sympathy for racially beset victims and hate for racially motivated villains across a wide range of mass media.

If, as Robyn Wiegman (1991, 325) has argued, the commodified appearance of the black body became "a representational sign for the democratizing process of U.S. Culture itself," and if, as Michael Rogin (1996, 14) has argued, the black body has had a "surplus symbolic value," then it is important to determine what *form* that democratizing, commodified, symbolic value has taken. I will argue that this form is melodrama, conceived not as a genre, as many film critics have thought, but as a central *mode* of American popular culture. In narrowing my topic from melodrama in general to "black and white" racial melodrama in particular, in taking what seemed at first to be a "detour" through race, I believe I ultimately found a more direct route to the heart of melodrama itself. In racial melodrama we discover the generation of "moral legibility" (Brooks 1995) through the spectacle of racialized bodily suffering.

Melodrama will be understood in these pages not as an aberration, archaism, or excess, but as the fundamental mode by which American mass culture has "talked to itself" about the enduring moral dilemma of race. I hope we will come to understand how two key icons—the suffering black male body and the threatened white female body—have generated such highly charged racial feelings over so much time. Why, for example, have the iconography and music (melos) of black male suffering been so enduring in mainstream American culture even at those moments when, as in *The Jazz Singer* or *Gone With the Wind*, black people themselves were shunted to the periphery or evacuated entirely from the story? And why has the counter-icon of white female suffering at the hands of hyper-sexualized black men been the focus of white resentment against the gains of African Americans since Reconstruction?

Working backward from my confused and outraged response to the verdict in the O. J. Simpson trial, I have sought to understand the reasons for my own raced and gendered resentment—not to vindicate it, but to better understand the deep-seated racial and sexual fantasies that fuel it. The genealogy that I offer in this book traces back to *Uncle Tom's Cabin*, the first widely popular moment in the melodrama of black suffering, and its key icon of the beaten black slave, played to a white public as commodified mass entertainment. This icon has not ceased to resonate in contemporary American culture. Looking back at Uncle Tom from the vantage point of Rodney King and O. J. Simpson, I began to see that the emotionally charged "moral legibility" that we shall see to be so crucial to the mode of melodrama is intrinsically linked to a "racial legibility"[2] that habitually sees a Manichaean good or evil in the visual "fact" of race itself—whether it is the dark male victim of white abuse or the dark villain with designs upon the innocent white woman. This genealogy has enabled me to take a longer and deeper look at the psychic investments in these archaic, yet ever-modernizing forms of racial victimization and vilification.

While the spectacle of Uncle Tom's suffering at the whip of the white slave driver once functioned progressively to "humanize" the figure of the slave, the romantic racialism of this negrophilia humanized him in his very blackness as a figure of racialized suffering. By the same token, the sympathy I felt for Nicole Simpson, and which I wanted to believe was "race neutral"—

uncontaminated by any preexisting scripts of racial pity or antipathy—could not be extricated from a virulent strand of negrophobia that was inextricably connected to a cycle of racial melodrama begun by the antebellum Uncle Tom and "answered" by the Progressive Era's *Birth of a Nation*. Leslie Fiedler (1979, 1982) has provocatively dubbed the dialectic between these two (negrophilic and negrophobic) scenarios "Tom" and "anti-Tom." I have adopted elements of Fiedler's terminology and dialectic in the following study, keeping his sense that these works speak to some of the culture's most utopian hopes as well as its most paranoid delusions about race and gender, but adapting it to my strong belief that these works are not epics, as Fiedler calls them, but melodramas, a form that has been insufficiently understood as a major force of moral reasoning in American mass culture.[3]

The O. J. Simpson murder trial, and the earlier trial of the police in the beating of Rodney King that so informed it, were such galvanizing experiences for Americans of all races, genders, and ethnicities because there was no race-neutral—no unmelodramatic, no non-Tom or non-anti-Tom—way of seeing them. Morally, one had to put one's finger on the scales and decide who was the victim and who was the villain of these racially saturated scripts. This is not to say, however, as have many critics of the Simpson verdict, that a pure "colorblind" justice was perverted by the calculated invocation of racialized ways of seeing. Rather, it is to say that from the very beginning of this tradition, the quest for justice has depended upon the application of a melodramatic "Tom lens," with a habit of seeing virtue in the suffering of the black male body at the hands of white villains and white female bodies suffering at the hands of black male villains. In the trial of the police in the beating of Rodney King this "Tom" lens collided with an equally melodramatic "anti-Tom lens" capable of seeing every movement of the black body as a potential assault on white law and order and as lust for the endangered white woman. Similarly, in the Simpson trial, the alleged attack on the blond white woman by the jealous black ex-husband invoked an "anti-Tom" lens that immediately racialized the case, as in the infamous darkening of the mug shot of O. J. Simpson as soon as he became a suspect. This racial vilification then collided, in its turn, with a predominantly "black" jury's perception that every movement of the white police was an effort to frame the black defendant.

For good reason, many intellectuals have done their best to resist the lurid confluence of these two trials, to resist being sullied by the commodified frenzy that was O. J. and to resist the paranoid fantasies that have fueled black and white responses to these trials. My approach, on the contrary, has been to delve deeper into the paranoid nature of these fantasies, to pursue the logic of racial victimization and vilification that fuels them. At times this has meant writing a book from inside the logic of white supremacy, for even the "Tom lens," for all its romantic racialist sympathy for the suffering African, is undeniably white supremacist and deeply violent. I realize that in doing so I run the risk of making legible that which might better be excoriated and refused. Nevertheless I hope to trace the genealogy of black and racial melodrama from a time when white (and male) meant American to a time when American has come to include diverse races, genders, and ethnicities—not to celebrate a progress of inclusion, but to show instead how basic the melodramatics of racial suffering has been to the very process of inclusion.[4]

Acknowledgments

Only gradually and with a certain trepidation did the necessity of writing about racial melodrama dawn on me. Only gradually did I expand an original study on film melodrama into a larger study of many media. I could not have done this without a great deal of help and encouragement. A deep debt of gratitude goes to the friends, colleagues, and fellow scholars who have patiently read and generously advised me in the overlong process of writing this book. Eric Lott and Michael Rogin were very helpful readers of early drafts; Carol J. Clover and Lauren Berlant gave especially important guidance at a middle stage; and Valerie Smith and Susan Gillman were generous readers of a near-final draft. If I have not realized all that these readers wished, I hope that I have at least not betrayed their interest. I especially want to acknowledge how deeply I have been influenced by the examples of each of their work. I also owe thanks to no fewer than two editors at Princeton University Press: Deborah Malmud, whose interest initiated the book and whose enthusiasm for an "American Studies" project at first intimidated and later fully engaged me, and Mary Murrell, whose wise advice and steady follow-through toward the end encouraged me to prune a great deal of extraneous material. In addition, thanks are due Donna Kronemeyer and Anne Reifsnyder, who shepherded the manuscript through the production process, and Eric Schramm, whose skillful and knowledgeable editing greatly improved the final manuscript.

A President's Fellowship while at the University of California–Irvine and a Guggenheim while at UC-Berkeley provided invaluable time, the first for research and the second for writing. An early formulation of my thinking about genre and melodrama was made possible during a wonderfully congenial research seminar at the University of California's Humanities Research Institute in Irvine, for which I thank Leo Braudy, Nick Browne, Carol J. Clover, George Lipsitz, David Russell, Nita Rollins, Thomas Schatz, and Vivian Sobchack. Collegiality doesn't get much better than that. Students at UC-Irvine (Farid Mattuck, Fiona Ng, and Betinna Soest Wohner) and UC-Berkeley (Scott Combs, Kiersten Johnson, Melissa Riley, Steve Sun, and Domietta

Acknowledgments

Torlasco) have contributed invaluably to this project. I am especially grateful to Misa Oyama, who coined the term "racial legibility"; to Maria St. John, who taught me much about Mammy; to Mark Mullen, who prepared the way with his remarkable dissertation on antebellum melodrama; and to Despina Kakoudaki, who understands the mysterious workings of mass culture better than I ever will. Other helpful interlocutors have included Elizabeth Abel, Carroll Blue, Susan Courteny, Marilyn Fabe, Alice Fahs, Paul Fitzgerald, Jane Gaines, Judith Gardiner, Christine Gledhill, David Mayer, Russell Merritt, Roddy Reid, Kate Sibley, Ben Singer, and Vivian Sobchack. Sincere thanks to all.

Linda Williams
Berkeley, California
March 2000

Playing the Race Card

Introduction
Playing the Race Card

The "race card" was invoked as a term during the first O. J. Simpson double-murder trial when the prosecution accused Johnny Cochran's team of cheating by introducing evidence of detective Mark Fuhrman's racism. This evidence—of Fuhrman's prior use of the word "nigger"—was called an "ace of spades" by prosecutor Christopher Darden: "Mr. Cochran wants to play the ace of spades and play the race card. . . . If you allow Mr. Cochran to use this word and play this race card, not only does the direction and focus of the case change, but the entire complexion of the case changes. It's a race case then. It's white versus black" (Bugliosi 1996, 66). According to Darden, evidence of Fuhrman's racism, which permitted the defense to put the Los Angeles Police Department on trial, should have been irrelevant to the question of Simpson's guilt. Behind this statement stands a moral assertion that within American jurisprudence—and indeed in many other areas of contemporary American popular culture—race should be unmentionable. As Peggy Pascoe (1999, 482) puts it, "In a society determined to be colorblind, granting public recognition to racial categories [seems] to be synonymous with racism itself."

In the Simpson trial the term "playing the race card" became a frequently invoked mantra. It would be invoked again by defense attorney Robert Shapiro after the verdict to distance himself from an overtly raced defense. Once again, the term was invoked with no sense of the history behind it, or even the short-term memory that it was Shapiro himself who first introduced the evidence of Fuhrman's racism; his criticism thus smacked of hypocrisy. As it became **4** possible for some whites to say that one extremely privileged African-American male may have "gotten away with murder" by deploying the disadvantage of race to make the jury see him as a racial victim, it also became possible to say that the address of past African-American grievances through affirmative action and othe programs no longer deserved priority.[1] In effect, then, one race card of racial grievance was being used to trump another.

Instead of accusing racialized persons of playing the race card, I argue that it might be more useful to consider how extensively race cards have been in play in the racial power games of American culture. If the very accusation of playing the race card has now become a way of disqualifying the attempt to discuss past and present racial injury, then we need to understand the history that has led up to that disqualification—a history in which both blacks and whites have repeatedly played the race card. We need, further, to understand the metaphor of the cheating card game itself. As Anne Cheng (2000, 103–104) has noted, the rhetoric betrays a peculiar logic by which what constitutes a winning hand has been identified with a handicap. To win at the "game" of race is to lose the larger game of life in which unraced competitors already play with a full deck. Liability is transformed to asset and reformed again as liability. Thus the metaphor of the race card attempts to discredit any racialized suffering that can be turned to advantage now that colorblindness is supposedly in effect. It acknowledges, and simultaneously condemns, what Wendy Brown (1995) has called a politics of identity grounded in injury. Yet if offers no alternative means to the redress of injury beyond the injunction to get over it, to not drag the baggage of past injury into the present.

How, then, shall we understand the term race as it figures in this study of black and white racial melodrama? One lesson that the Simpson trial teaches is that even if race is a fiction, even, if, as Anthony Appiah and Amy Gutman (1996, 37) put it, race does not exist as an essential, biological category upon which identity is based, it is equally the case, as Hazel Carby (1992, 193) notes, that it constructs "racialized subjects" in the political imagination. In the Simpson trial, for example, we saw its famous defendant and his ex-wife racialized before our very eyes. If race as an essential entity does not exist, racialization does; it gives meaning to the visible signs of difference and that meaning has long been embedded in popular culture in such icons as the beaten black man or the endangered white woman. The race card is best viewed, then, not as a cheating, marked card. It needs to be seen, rather, as an integral process of the gaining of rights through the recognition of injury. It was in play when Americans first recognized the virtue of black victims in the beating of Uncle Tom; it was in play when Americans first perceived the white woman endangered by the black man. The study of black and white melodrama affords an opportunity to see just how frequently racialized claims of injury have been in play and how they are linked with that other familiar history of embodied difference: gender. For example, prosecutor Darden himself could not help but play a gender-inflected version of the race card when he showed pictures of the battered face of the blond Nicole Brown Simpson during the trial, or when, in objecting to the very deployment of the "race card," he mentioned how "outrageous" it would be were he to insist, in turn, that the "defendant has a fetish for blond-haired or white women."[2] Indeed, the very fact that the accusation of playing the race card was made by a black attorney—whom some believed was chosen as a prosecutor in the case at least partly because of his race[3]—demonstrates how futile the quest for race neutrality and "color blindness" was, and how deeply a melodramatic ethos of race and gender permeated all judgments.

I will argue in the following pages that Harriet Beecher Stowe played the first mass-culture version of the race card when she pictured the sufferings of Tom and Eliza at the hands of white masters. Early in the next century in the Progressive Era, Thomas Dixon and D. W. Griffith trumped Stowe's race card by inverting its racial polarities to show white women threatened by emancipated black men in *The Clansman* and *The Birth of a Nation*. The card has been in play whenever racial abuse is invoked to cast one racially constituted group as the victim of another. It would seem, then, that there is no single race card; rather, there is a history of mutually informing, perpetually trumping, race cards animating a long tradition of black and white racial melodrama. One of the purposes of this book is to trace the moments of emergence of new versions of racial victimization and vilification through the mode of melodrama.

Like the mode of melodrama, the race card has been vilified as an archaic evil, a throwback to a distant era beyond which modern, and postmodern, American citizens have long since "progressed." And yet, like melodrama, the race card finds unsuspected relevance and appeal with each new configuration of racial victims and villains, with each new stage of American racial politics. In the painfully long and slow movement toward and beyond civil rights, and no matter how each "bad" old melodrama is vehemently rejected by whites or blacks, these two central and opposed "moving pictures"—the vision of a black man beaten by a white and the responding "counter" vision of the white woman endangered or raped by the emancipated and uppity black villain—have endured even as they have transmuted. The power of *Uncle Tom's Cabin* "to convulse a mighty nation," as literary historian George Whicher (1963, 583) once said Stowe's novel had done, thus needs to be seen not simply as the power of a single work to convulse viewers into sympathy with racial victims, but as the inauguration of an extended cycle of racial melodrama seeking to give "moral legibility" to race.

The Leaping Fish

Henry James once described Harriet Beecher Stowe's *Uncle Tom's Cabin* as a "wonderful 'leaping' fish" alighting first in one medium and then in another. Recalling in particular an actress from a P. T. Barnum production with a memorable "swelling bust" whose portrayal of Eliza's flight across the ice blocks of the Ohio River was particularly graceful, James took a somewhat condescending view of the phenomenon's disconcerting inability to remain in its original literary form.[4] But he importantly reminded his readers that for his generation *Uncle Tom's Cabin* had ceased to be a novel and had become a more general "state of vision, of feeling and consciousness" (James 1941, 159–60), leaping about the American cultural landscape. I will argue that this "leaping" quality that James observes in *Uncle Tom's Cabin* can be applied to an entire tradition of black and white racial melodrama that often leaps out of literary incarnations to more visual (or musical) media. Black and white racial melodrama as a whole leaps from medium to medium, functioning, whether on page, stage, screen, or courtroom as "a state of vision, of feeling and of consciousness." The works we will examine in this book include novels, plays, films, Broadway musicals, and televised events, yet even though they inhabit some of these media quite vigorously, they often exceed any one of them. I have done my best to do justice to the myriad and multiple nature of the forms while focusing on the versions that were most moving in their own day. In the case of *Uncle Tom's Cabin* this has meant focusing on several of the Tom plays rather than the more canonical novel, while in the case of the *Birth of a Nation* it has meant giving equal attention to Dixon's novels and play as well as the more canonical film. In all cases, however, I have tried not to slight the multiplicity of the forms taken by all these works, since in many cases the real point of the importance of the melodrama is not only a particularly memorable media incarnation but its ubiquitous cross-media influence. The melodramatic playings of the race card will be best understood, then, as a story cycle brought to life by a circulating set of transmuting icons and melos pointing sometimes to the virtue of racially beset victims and sometimes to the villainy of racially motivated villains.

Each new incarnation of this negrophilic/negrophobic cycle cites a previous version of the Tom or anti-Tom story of racial victims and villains, sometimes reversing the moral polarities, sometimes simply appropriating old polarities in new ways. Each version is a partial attempt to explain the secret of American national identity in relation to that racial "Other" whose enslaved presence in the nation precipitated an original crisis of moral legitimacy. In all cases, however, the old melodrama is made new through a shift of moral valence and through an animation of new media. Indeed, one of the greatest fascinations of the American melodramas of black and white is the way they have brought to life new forms of media even as they have seemed to have a ubiquity that transcends individual media form.

To have been a white American who saw a "Tom show" in the 1850s or the film *The Birth of a Nation* on its first release in 1915 was to be converted to the new power, unprecedented length, and legitimacy of media that had not previously been taken seriously: the morally serious stage melodrama in the case of *Tom*, the "two-dollar movie" in the case of *Birth*. In both instances the thrill to the power of a new medium and the thrill to the experience of new racial sympathy are linked. Both became integral to the very formation of national identity. On stage in the mid-nineteenth century, *Uncle Tom's Cabin* broke with minstrel stereotypes (even as it created new forms of blackface minstrelsy) and embraced moral reform melodrama, by discovering the suffering humanity of slaves. On screen in the early twentieth century, the "anti-Tom" reversal of the Tom story in *The Birth of a Nation* gave power and moral seriousness to the new medium of film. Once again a novel object of sympathy—in this case the racially threatened white woman—gave moral legitimacy to a new medium. The melodramatic theater and the melodramatic film thus became distinctly American with the "leap" of the thematics of raced and gendered suffering into their midst.

Each animation of a new form of melodrama has constituted a new wrenching of the signs of racialized virtue: *The Jazz Singer* (1927) and *Show Boat* (1927) would confer importance to the stage and filmic form of the musical and would borrow elements of the Tom melodrama of suffering slaves to lend virtue and seriousness to assimilating white ethnicities. *Gone With the Wind* (1936, 1939) would confer importance on the new producer-system epic blockbuster novel transformed into film while rewriting both the Tom and the anti-Tom narratives to suit the travails of a Depression-era and New Deal southern belle hero. *Roots* (1976, 1977)—both the bestseller family saga and the subsequent television miniseries—would rewrite all of the above from an Afrocentric post–civil rights perspective. Finally, as we have begun to see, racial melodrama would find its most recent form in the televised "race trial." Through the close study of these works in relation to one another, I hope to show how differently raced and gendered persons have played the race card and parlayed victimization into melodramatic forms of moral power.

The Home "Space of Innocence"

One of the key ways of constructing moral power is the icon of the good home. The icon of home helps establish the "space of innocence" of its virtuous victims (Brooks 1995, 29). Black and white racial melodrama originates in the homey virtues of Uncle Tom's cabin, which renders familiar the American "family values" of the African slave. In an era when even many abolitionists

8

(Stowe included) preferred Liberia to Kentucky as the proper home for emancipated African slaves, the humble cabin of Uncle Tom worked, against official ideology, to make Tom and his cabin seem quintessentially American. The icon of home is thus essential to establish the virtue of racially beset victims. It comes as no real surprise, then, that Dixon and Griffith's "former enemies of North and South" would find themselves uniting in "common protection of their Aryan birthright" within the confines of this symbol of humble virtue borrowed from the tradition of Uncle Tom. Nor is it surprising that the cabin as space of innocence is reworked in the Jazz Age for assimilating whites as a Lower East Side Jewish home in *The Jazz Singer* and as a kind of floating plantation in *Show Boat*. The home is refunctioned again in the next decade in *Gone With the Wind*, where the plantation itself becomes a paradoxical icon of land and people tailored to a post–Jazz Age New Deal.

In post–civil rights America, however, the plantation home could no longer serve as the locus of virtue. Once African Americans finally took on the full mantle of citizenship and became themselves the authors of the master narrative of racial melodrama, home sweet home began to be figured as home sweet Africa. Because nostalgia for the good home could not be, for African Americans, the place of slavery, yet because nostalgia for the "good home" continued to function as it had in both the Tom and the anti-Tom traditions, an exotic and idealized Africa took on that function, leaving the ongoing melodrama of black and white without a homegrown icon. At its deepest level the icon of O. J. Simpson's Brentwood mansion, known familiarly as Rockingham, resonated with this problem of good home versus Gothic mansion, taking on an iconic significance, as Uncle Tom's home had before, out of all proportion to its actual importance in the story.

This study opts to focus exclusively on a very limited cycle of works whose unquestioned popularity and importance gives them an almost mythic dimension and cultural ubiquity. Authorship matters, of course, and there are some very important authors in this study. However, I will be less interested in individual vision and personality than I will be in the interpenetrating cycle of "Tom" and "anti-Tom" in which these authors participate. Many familiar and important African-American writers have engaged with the dialectic of Tom and anti-Tom, from Harriet Jacobs to Toni Morrison, to produce works of great brilliance and importance. Nevertheless, these works have often not deeply affected the more popular, subliterary realm of mass culture addressed here. Instead, I have treated African-American authorial intervention with the tradition only at the point at which, as in the media events of *Roots* or the O. J. Simpson trial, it has registered as part of the mass-culture mainstream.

My goal in what follows will neither be to rehabilitate the mode of melodrama nor to weigh in on one side or the other of the "black and white" resentments about race. Rather I consider it sufficient to recognize melodrama's almost incalculable influence on American attitudes toward race and to trace the genealogies of an influence that, whether because it is too obvious or because it is too embarrassing, has been relatively ignored. The study of melodrama has the potential to explain why it is that in a democracy ruled by rights, we do not gain the moral upper hand by saying simply that rights have been infringed. We say, instead, much more powerfully: "I have been victimized; I have suffered, therefore give me rights." To understand racial melodrama is to see why repeated calls for more accurate, or more "realistic," representations of racially marked characters are powerless to overturn deeply embedded racial stereotypes that seem hopelessly outmoded yet live on in the culture. Until we understand the melodramatic imagination that these stereotypes serve, and the historical dynamic of its popular cycles, we will never grasp why we are compelled to feel for the raced and gendered sufferings of some and to hate the raced and gendered villainy of others.

1 The American Melodramatic Mode

As a modality, melodrama organizes the disparate sensory phenomena, experiences, and contractions of a newly emerging secular and atomizing society in visceral, affective and morally explanatory terms.

—*Christine Gledhill*

"Melodramatic, Melodramatic, Terribly So!"

In 1853, the year after she had become a celebrity with the publication of her novel *Uncle Tom's Cabin*, Harriet Beecher Stowe embarked upon a tour of Europe. In a book of letters describing her travels, she narrates a visit to Windsor Castle. Passing unmoved before a succession of paintings by such masters as Van Dyke and Caneletto, she suddenly finds herself transfixed before a marble monument by an unnamed sculptor. It is a scene depicting the death of the Princess Charlotte, daughter of King George IV. Stowe describes the sculpture in great detail. On the terrestrial side, the princess has just "thrown herself over in a convulsion, and died" (Stowe 1854, 2:45). Around her are four figures bowed in mute despair. On the celestial side, however, the princess's spirit is seen to rise toward heaven. "Two angels, one carrying her infant child and the other with clasped hands of exultant joy, are rising with her, in serene and solemn triumph" (45).

Stowe and her party shed tears before the "unutterable pathos and beauty" of a monument depicting the sorrow of death and the triumph of afterlife (46). Soon after, however, she finds her taste challenged by precisely the kind of refined cultural authority she has come to England to encounter. A cultivated artist, the sort who "knows all that is proper to be admired," informs her that the statue is a "shocking thing" in "miserable taste" (46).

Alarmed, Stowe inquires what is wrong with it; the artist informs her, as if there could be nothing more to say, that it is "melodramatic, melodramatic, terribly so!" (47)

In midcentury England, a cultivated artist would indeed have condemned the histrionic pathos of such a statue as "melodramatic." In invoking this term he would have meant very much what we mean by it today: a seemingly archaic excess of sensation and sentiment, a manipulation of the heartstrings that exceeds the bounds of good taste.[1] No doubt if this same artist had read Stowe's *Uncle Tom's Cabin*, or seen any of its stage productions already sweeping Stowe's home country, he would have deplored a similar "miserable taste" encountered in the terrestrial pathos and celestial triumph in the deaths of her Little Eva and Uncle Tom.

What interests me in this anecdote is not only the familiar high culture contempt for the presumed "excesses" of the "melodramatic," but Stowe's desire to present herself as not quite comprehending what it means. She first reports that she is "so appalled by the word, of whose meaning I had not a very clear idea, that I dropped the defence at once and determined to reconsider my tears. To have been actually made to cry by a thing that was melodramatic was a distressing consideration" (2:45–47). At the same time, however, she vehemently defends the unsophisticated cultural consumer against the judgment of experts: "A thing may be melodramatic, or any other *atic* that a man pleases; so that it be strongly suggestive, poetic, pathetic, it has a right to its own peculiar place in the world of art" (47). Without specifically taking up the defense of the term, Stowe nevertheless defends the right of an artist to break the "classical" rules of unity and decorum even if it means "being melodramatic." After all, where would "Shakespeare's dramas have been, had he studied the old dramatic unities?" (48).

Stowe's folksy and democratic defense of such a "melodramatic" "moving" picture is typical of the ad hoc nature of many attempts to defend melodrama. While unwilling categorically to defend the word, Stowe nevertheless defends an art of strong pathos and action that recognizes the virtues of suffering victims. Her gesture of disavowing participation in a mode of representation that has been universally condemned as manipulative and spurious but which, in this unique case, seems justified has been frequently repeated by popular artists and critics from Stowe's day to the present. Typically, when an emotionally powerful work is deemed good it is seen to "transcend" melodrama; when not, it is inevitably the melodrama that prevents it from being so. According to this system it is rarely possible to invoke melodrama as the source of a work's power unless this melodrama is judged ironic or what film scholars like to call "Sirkian."[2]

Today, as in the mid-nineteenth century, the word melodrama seems to name an archaic form—what vulgar, naive audiences of yesteryear thrilled to, not what we sophisticated realists and moderns (and postmoderns) enjoy today. Yet melodrama remains the most accurate name for what all these and many, many more moving pictures do, and melodrama is, in the eyes of most critics who have studied it closely, fundamentally modern. Indeed, melodrama perpetually arises from the ashes of critical disrepute to demand an ad hoc defense of its popular appeal, yet it never quite receives the full description and analysis that its sheer power to move generation after generation warrants. Sometimes, as with Stowe, these ad hoc defenses operate against the classical and neoclassical strictures of good taste and high art in the name of sentiment; sometimes they operate against the values of realism in the name of stylistic "excess." Within the field of cinema studies, a field that will concern us in this chapter, the defense of melodrama has often been marshaled against something that has been called both classical and realist, as in the eminently confusing category "classical realist" cinema.[3]

It is the primary thesis of this chapter that melodrama is neither archaic nor excessive but a perpetually modernizing form that can neither be clearly opposed to the norms of the "classical" nor to the norms of realism. Melodrama, in fact, is precisely what most people mean when, like Stowe, they rise to the defense of "pictures"—whether literal or metaphorical—that move them to powerful sentiments. Only the disrepute of the term has prevented, and still prevents, the categorization of "moving pictures" as melodrama, and the categorization of melodrama as modern.

By what better name, however, shall we refer to those novels, stories, stage plays, movies, songs, and media events that move us to sympathy for the sufferings of the virtuous? I argue that melodrama is still the best, and most accurate, description of the serious narrative and iconic work performed by popular American mass culture, broadly conceived. Melodrama endures not only as an archaic holdover of the nineteenth-century stage play (and its virtuous victims and leering villains) and not only in soap operas and disease-of-the-week TV movies, but as an evolving mode of storytelling crucial to the establishment of moral good.[4]

A corollary thesis to be explored later is that while it is possible to study melodrama as it has evolved in a single medium—as, for example, in the nineteenth-century stage or the twentieth-century film—it may be more appropriate to its dynamic and protean nature to see it as a broad aesthetic mode existing across many media and in certain interpenetrating narrative cycles. Once again, however, Harriet Beecher Stowe can instruct us and lead us into that place in American culture where melodrama has been paramount. When Henry James described Stowe's *Uncle Tom's Cabin* as a "wonderful 'leaping' fish," effortlessly flying from one medium to another, he was evoking a version of the play produced by P. T. Barnum, one of whose set pieces pictured the fleeing mulatta slave Eliza, incarnated by an actress with a memorable "swelling bust," whose flight across the ice of the Ohio River was "intrepidly and gracefully performed." James recalls how "we lived and moved at that time, with great intensity, in Mrs. Stowe's novel." Yet he also insists that it was not in the novel alone that this intense living and moving took place but in all manner of derivative pictures, exemplified for us by this image of Eliza's flight reproduced on a late-nineteenth-century cigar box (Fig. 1.1). As James explains, for an immense number of people Uncle Tom was "much less a book than a state of vision, of feeling and of consciousness" (James 1941, 159–60). As we shall see in Chapter 2, this "state of vision" and "feeling" was inseparable from an incendiary revolutionary sympathy felt by whites toward the sufferings of blacks.

James's insight about this most important American melodrama of the nineteenth century can be extended to the whole of the melodramatic tradition. Melodrama, too, is a "wonderful 'leaping' fish," reformulating itself as a configuration of "moving pictures" alighting first in one medium, then another, functioning, whether on the page, stage, or screen as "a state of vision, of feeling and of consciousness." Like Uncle Tom's Cabin, melodrama "leaps" from one spectacular, popular manifestation to another. Although it can be and has been viewed as a genre, for the purposes of this book it will be best understood as a fundamental mode of popular American "moving pictures." Sentimental novels painted metaphorical pictures of pathos and action that moved readers to strong emotions and occasionally even to action.[5] The melodramatic stage, in contrast, delighted in the construction of literal moving pictures and even found a powerful emotional emphasis in the freezing of these pictures into still tableaux of the narrative's most intense moments. In the twentieth century, the predominant moving pictures before the arrival of television are, of course, "the movies" themselves—pictures that literally move and that move their viewers emotionally in turn. Today, the heritage of moving picture melodrama shapes not only fictional films and television but the media representation of war, athletic competitions, and courtroom trials. These diverse forms of melodrama have moved American readers and audiences throughout the last century and a half of American popular culture to feel for the virtue of some and against the villainy of others.

The goal of this first chapter will be to represent some of the most familiar and recognizable features of a melodramatized media in the twentieth century through an overview of the form of moving pictures with which we are most familiar today: popular American movies. I begin my discussion of melodrama in this chapter with the movies because they represent some of the most accessible examples of American popular culture and because the movies are, as Nicholas Vardac long ago showed, the twentieth-century inheritors of the stage melodrama (Vardac 1949).

Studies of the nineteenth-century stage in France, England, and the United States have established the international existence of an amazingly protean theatrical form that dominated the popular theater and offered a crucial means of "resolving" the many contradictions of modern life.[6] While the

UNCLE TOM'S CABIN

14

ELIZA'S ESCAPE

Figure 1.1 Eliza flees with her child over the ice of the Ohio River with slave-catchers and hounds at her heels. (Harriet Beecher Stowe Center, Hartford, Conn.)

study of the melodramatic stage proper has been crucial to the understanding of the importance and reach of melodrama, there is a danger in locating it too firmly on the stage and in the too-far-distant past. Henry James's somewhat condescending memory of Eliza's "swelling bust" as she negotiated the theatrical ice blocks is a case in point. Melodrama is often referred to as occupying the childhood of the nation, or, as in the case of James, the childhood of individual readers or viewers. Yet as Peter Brooks's study of the melodramatic imagination of James's own fiction has shown, melodrama does not reside in any essential way in the theater, and it can often be found in works, such as those of James, otherwise thought to represent the height of subtlety and psychological realism. I will have much to say in the next chapter about the specifically melodramatic theatrical tradition that reigned supreme in American popular culture in a wide variety of forms from the 1820s through the 1870s. It would be a mistake, however, to perceive a form as contemporaneously vital and adaptable as melodrama as only a reprise of the supposedly archaic emotional forms of the nineteenth-century stage. If emotional and moral registers are sounded, if a work invites us to feel sympathy for the virtues of beset victims, if the narrative trajectory is ultimately concerned with a retrieval and staging of virtue through adversity and suffering, then the operative mode is melodrama.[7] The kind of novelistic, theatrical, or cinematic realism that introduces the look and feel of real city streets, contemporary social problems, or more complex psychological motives is perfectly compatible with what needs to be regarded as an ever-modernizing melodrama.

Consider the case of the 1996 Olympics, whose reporting by NBC may well prove to be a landmark in the contemporary melodramatization of American sports. In these Olympics, as many commentators have remarked, the story was not only in the (time-delayed) presentation of the action of competition, but in the way that action combined with the pathos of each athlete's story of overcoming adversity. Swimmer Tom Dolan did not just swim a terrific 400-meter individual medley; the action of that competition was combined in the NBC coverage with the pathos of the much-publicized fact that his asthma gave him much less oxygen than other swimmers. Gymnast Kerri Strug did not just perform a great vault to push the U.S. women's gymnastic team to victory; she landed in great pain on an injured leg and attempted to overcome that pain with a smile. This "vault over adversity" would come to be called the "defining moment" of the whole games (as seen from a certain U.S.-centric, melodramatic point of view). Another such "defining moment" occurred when former heavyweight boxing champion Muhammad Ali overcame the adversity of his mute, Parkinson's-afflicted body to light the Olympic flame and become, in dramatic contrast to his once defiant, anti-mainstream politics, everybody's favorite American.

Although many "pure" sports lovers objected to this emotional "feminization" of the Olympics—not to mention the feminization of a once super-macho black nationalist—the astronomical ratings won many nonpurists, especially women, to the spectacle.[8] If the form of melodrama was old and familiar, recognizable as a cliché to all, NBC had nevertheless succeeded in applying pathos to realms of action that made an old form seem new. Something of the same kind of novelty was at work, I suspect, when Henry James encountered the melodramatic "moving picture" of a maiden in distress in

Uncle Tom's Cabin.[9] The cliché was hardly new, even to James's "small boy." What was new, however, was its novel object of sympathy: not simply the conventional maiden-in-distress of melodrama, but a mulatta slave escaping bondage. This sympathy for another grounded in the manifestation of that person's suffering is arguably a key feature of all melodrama.[10] Here again, however, we find melodrama modernizing and renewing itself with new objects of sympathy embedded within new social problems, new contexts for pathos and action, and new media. We should not be fooled, then, by James's nostalgic memories of the quaint features of the mode into thinking that melodrama itself is passé. Though its roots are in the theater, melodrama exceeds the limits of the theatrical. Its genius lies in its protean ability to "leap" across centuries and media, to make jaded readers, audiences, and viewers thrill to ever new forms of pathos and action.

"Classical" Cinema vs. Melodrama

In the field of film studies melodrama has often been regarded as a genre, or subgroup of films, situated within the larger film style called variously "classical" Hollywood or "classical realist" cinema. In this field, melodrama has rather consistently been characterized as a narrow and particular exception to the "classical" norm, either in its emotional and scenic "excesses" or in its peculiar address to female audiences. Further specified into subcategories of melodrama known as "women's films," "weepies," and "family melodramas," melodrama has not been viewed, as I wish to see it here, in its more general and pervasive operation as a mode of representation with a particular moralizing function operating across many genres. Thus film critics have tended to establish a rigid polarity between, on the one hand, bourgeois, classical realist (often masculine) "norms" and, on the other hand, anti-realist, melodramatic (often feminine) "excesses."[11] One problem with this approach is that it defines melodrama in opposition to a cinematic "classicism" that quickly evaporates under close scrutiny.[12] The generic category of melodrama has been so consistently identified in recent years with women's concerns that its central relation to what Christine Gledhill has called the "great tradition of humanist realism" was never investigated except as an oppositional excess.[13]

Missing in many of these previous approaches to cinematic melodrama is the sense in which it has been the norm, rather than the exception, of American cinema. American movies, like most forms of popular storytelling, have been popular because of their ability to seem to resolve basic moral contradictions at a mythic level—whether conflicts between garden and civilization typical of the western, or between family-love and ambition-career typical of the biopic, the "family melodrama," and the gangster film.[14] Film critics have often not seen the forest of melodrama—the sense in which all these genres, and many more, partake of a basic melodramatic mode—for the trees of these individual genres. They have not seen the way in which melodrama constitutes the larger cultural mode driving the articulation of specific genres. In a related way, they have also been blinded to the larger entity of melodrama in their concern to distinguish it from realism. We need, as Christine Gledhill (1987, 2000) has urged, a general study of melodrama as a broadly important cultural mode inherited from the nineteenth-century stage, in tension with and transformed by infusions of realism—whether of content or form—yet best understood *as melodrama*.

Melodrama can be viewed, then, not as a genre, an excess, or an aberration, but as what most often typifies popular American narrative in literature, stage, film, and television when it seeks to engage with moral questions. It is the best example of American culture's (often hypocritical) attempt to construct itself as the locus of innocence and virtue. If we want to confront the centrality of melodrama to American moving-picture culture, we must first turn to the most basic forms of melodrama, and not, as many feminist critics— myself included—have previously done, to a ghetto subgenre of "women's films."[15] Rather, we must seek out the dominant features of an American melodramatic mode. For if melodrama has been classified in film studies as a sentimental genre for women, it is partly because other melodramatic genres, for example the western and gangster films that received early legitimacy in film study, had already been constructed, as Christine Gledhill notes, in relation to supposedly masculine cultural values (1987, 35).

Narrative cinema as a whole has been theorized as a realist, inherently masculine medium whose "classical" features were supposedly anathema to its melodramatic infancy and childhood. Thus, while narrative silent cinema has always been recognized as melodrama at some level, the "essential" art and language of cinema has not. Melodrama has been viewed either as that which the "classical" cinema has grown up out of, or that to which it sometimes regresses. However, as Gledhill notes, well into the sound era, industrial exhibition categories continued to assert the melodramatic base of most genres. The names of these categories are themselves revealing: western melodrama, crime melodrama, sex melodrama, backwoods melodrama, romantic melodrama, and so on. (Gledhill 1987, 35).[16] What is striking in the above examples is the way the noun *melodrama* functions to denote a certain form of exciting, sensational, and, above all, moving story that could then be further differentiated by more specifications of setting or milieu and/or genre. It is this basic sense of melodrama as a modality of narrative with a high quotient of pathos and action to which we need to attend if we are to confront its most fundamental appeal.

Perhaps the most influential work contributing to the understanding of melodrama as a vital cultural form has been Peter Brooks's *The Melodramatic Imagination: Balzac, James and the Mode of Excess*. Brooks offers a valuable appreciation of the historical origins of the nineteenth-century melodramatic project. This appreciation is still the best grounding for an understanding of its carryover into twentieth-century mass culture. Brooks takes melodrama seriously as a quintessentially modern (though not modernist) mode. He sees it arising historically out of a "post-sacred" world where traditional imperatives of truth and morality had been violently questioned and yet in which there was still a need to forge some semblance of truth and morality (Brooks 1976, 15). Brooks's central thesis is that the quest for a hidden moral legibility is crucial to all melodrama. In the absence of a traditional moral and social order linked to the sacred, and in the presence of a reduced private and domestic sphere that has increasingly become the entire realm of personal significance, a theatrical form of sensation developed that carried the burden of expressing what Brooks calls the "moral occult"—"the domain of operative spiritual values which is both indicated within and masked by the surface of reality" (Brooks 1996, 5).[17]

The theatrical function of melodrama's big sensation scenes was to be able to put forth a moral truth in gesture and picture that could not be fully spoken in words. Brooks interestingly shows, in fact, that the rise of melodrama was linked to the ban on speech in unlicensed French theaters, which originally turned to pantomime as a more powerful and direct form of communication.[18] Typically the "unspeakable" truth revealed in the sensation scene is the revelation of who is the true villain, and who the innocent victim, of some plot. The revelation occurs as a spectacular, moving sensation. That is, it is felt as sensation, and not simply registered as ratiocination in the cause-effect logic of narrative, because it shifts to a different register of signification, often bypassing language altogether. Music, gesture, pantomime, and, I would add, most forms of sustained physical action are the elements of these sensational effects most familiar to us today in film, television, and musical theater.[19]

Despite the fact that Brooks's study works hard to give melodrama its due, rather than to treat it as failed tragedy or as realism manque, his subtitle, *The Mode of Excess*, betrays the sense in which it is seen as a deviation from more "classical" realist norms. "Excess" for Brooks is ultimately the triumph of desire over reality, "a plenitude of meaning" that restores melodramatic subjects to a fullness of expression. As in the psychoanalytic theory that serves as his ultimate model of melodrama, the payoff is in the final ability of the mode to speak the unspeakable, to express the inexpressible, even in novelists with realist reputations like Balzac and James.

Adapting Brooks, Christine Gledhill has argued that melodrama typically seizes upon the social problems of everyday reality—problems such as illegitimacy, slavery, racism, labor struggles, class division, disease, nuclear annihilation, genocide. All the afflictions and injustices of the modern post-enlightenment have been dramatized in melodramatic form. Part of the excitement of the mode is the genuine turmoil and timeliness of the issues it takes up and the popular debate it can generate when it explores controversies not yet placed on the agenda of liberal humanism. Thus melodrama differs from realism in its will to force the status quo to yield signs of moral legibility within the limits of the "ideologically permissible," even as it builds upon genuine social concerns (Gledhill 1987, 38). The French, of course, have a long tradition of classical tragedy which led them to believe that the "norms" of literature and theater are antithetical to melodrama. Americans, however, have a very different set of norms. Whether we look at the novelistic romances of Hawthorne, Stowe, or Twain, the popular theater of David Belasco, George Aiken, Augustin Daly, or Dion Boucicault, the silent films of D. W. Griffith, Cecil B. DeMille, or Frank Borzage, the sound films of John Ford, Francis Ford Coppola, Steven Spielberg, or James Cameron, the most common thread running through them is not simply a lack of realism or an "excess" of sentiment, but the combined function of realism, sentiment, spectacle, and action in effecting moral legibility. Hawthorne's Hester Prynne, Stowe's Uncle Tom, Twain's Jim and Huck, Ford's searcher, Spielberg's E.T., Elliot, and Schindler, and Cameron's Rose and Jack all share the common function of revealing moral good in a world where virtue has become hard to read.

The bad reputation of melodrama in American popular culture derives, like the derision of the "cultivated artist" who deplored Harriet Beecher Stowe's taste, from the sense that such emotional displays of virtue necessarily cheapen a more stoical (and sternly masculine) morality. Ann Douglas's (1977) study of nineteenth-century American culture, for example, traces the long process by which a rigorous Calvinist morality was supplanted by what she views as a cheaply sentimental "feminization" of American culture carried out by ministers and lady novelists. Using Little Eva's death in Harriet Beecher Stowe's *Uncle Tom's Cabin* as her melodramatic touchstone, Douglas argues that a wholesale debasement of American culture took place in the idealization of feminine qualities of piety, virtue, and passive suffering. Douglas opposes a popular literature of "excessive" feminine sentimentalism to a high canonical literature—Melville, Thoreau, Whitman—that was masculine and active but never fully popular. Her study of the feminization of nineteenth-century American culture is a study of how a masculine "high" culture was feminized and degraded. Douglas thus blames the increased anti-intellectualism and consumerism of American culture on a facile cultural feminism.

Rather than blame the excesses of a feminizing melodrama, however, we need to investigate the reasons for its popularity: the search for moral legibility in an American context that was increasingly unattainable in the belief system of Calvinist election. We need also to recognize that melodrama is only in some of its manifestations an exclusively sentimental, feminine form. The sensationalism of which it partakes can be seen as part of a larger phenomenon by which sensational pathos *and* action—the sufferings of innocent victims *and* the exploits of brave heroes or monstrous criminals—become the focus of cultural attention. Karen Halttunen has shown, for example, that the rise of sensational accounts of crime in American culture in the early nineteenth century was the result of a shift that took place once the manifestation of good or evil could no longer be attributed to God's providential power (Halttunen 1998, 47). Where crime, murder, and excruciating suffering had once been explicable as proof of the inherently sinful nature of the human soul and were thus unworthy of detailed attention, new interest developed in the sensational details of pain, suffering, and crime in early nineteenth-century America. Where previously the accounts of sensational incidents had been offered in the form of "execution sermons" interested only in the state of the soul of condemned prisoners on the way to meet their makers, in the early nineteenth century, secular narratives routinely invoked liberal humanist explanations for violent acts that just as routinely failed to understand the deeper mysteries of why crimes were committed. Halttunen argues that in this period sensational, horrifying details were increasingly invoked in place of explanation for the acts of criminals. In place of the religious understanding of the "common sinner," modern secular American culture produced new conventions for the account of lurid, sensational crime. These conventions of sensationalism produced a popular culture fascinated with pain and suffering. Murder narratives increasingly sought, Halttunen argues, not only to report intense excitement and horror, but to incite [them] in readers of the news (73).

Gothic horror, as we shall see, is the flip side of melodramatic pathos. In the American context the end of Calvinist moral and religious certainty about the power of God and the sinning nature of the human soul gave rise to a modern fascination with, on the one hand, the spectacle of the good person who suffers and, on the other hand, the evil person who creates suffering. Mass culture melodrama and mass culture horror (not to mention the simultaneous rise of mass culture pornography) would prove to be the quintessential modern forms created to fill the void opened up by the loss of religious certainty. There are important gender issues to bring to bear upon all three of these sensational genres, considered *as* genres—most significantly the traditional feminization of the suffering body (Williams 1991). It is clear, however, that "feminization" does little to explain the deeper cultural reasons for the rise of sensationalism in American mass culture in general and the rise of the particular appeal of melodrama as a means to establish a compensatory moral legibility. So while the historical waning of Calvinist morality in America might be seen to function much like the end of the sacred in Brooks's French-based model, it is important to recognize the differences between American sensationalist melodrama and that produced by the French. In a country with a much less established tradition of high art and letters than Europe, it is not surprising that sensationalist melodrama in the United States became so popular. However, while England had Dickens, and France had Hugo—both melodramatists who were also in some sense "great" writers—America had

Stowe, a writer who has never been given much credit as a writer. Writing, however, has never been the essence of melodrama. Its sensations are the means to something more important: the achievement of a felt good, the merger—perhaps even the compromise—of morality and feeling into empathically imagined communities forged in the pain and suffering of innocent victims, and in the actions of those who seek to rescue them.

Recent American film scholars have attempted to recuperate emotionality and sensationalism from the status of excess. Tom Gunning, for example, has rehabilitated the term "attraction" in order to address the emotional and sensational side of cinema spectatorship. Gunning borrows the term from Sergei Eisenstein's celebration of spectacles with particularly strong sensual or psychological impact and the ability to aggressively grab and move spectators. The acknowledgment of the existence of a "cinema of attractions" different from the linear narrative of the "classical realist text" has fruitfully called attention to the spectacle side of cinematic visual pleasures in early cinema.[20] However, when the term simply posits the existence of some ideological "other" that "escapes" the dominant ideology of the classical, it remains implicated in the putative dominance of the "classical."[21]

Another film critic to argue for the importance of melodrama is Rick Altman. Questioning a long tradition of film theory and criticism that, ever since Bazin, has described mainstream sound cinema as "classical," Altman ponders the very "classicism" of the classical. Arguing in particular against Bordwell, Thompson, and Staiger's notion of an enduring classical tradition of rule-bound invisible storytelling, self-effacing craftsmanship, and causality motivated by character, Altman points out that this description cannot accommodate much of the spectacle, "flagrant" display, showmanship, and "artistic motivation" of melodrama.[22]

The notion that the "classical" Hollywood narrative subordinates spectacle, emotion, and attraction to the logic of personal causality and cause and effect assumes that the "action" privileged by the classical mode is not in itself spectacular. However, we have only to look at what is playing at the local multiplex to realize that the familiar Hollywood feature of prolonged climactic action is, and I would argue has always been, a melodramatic spectacle fully consonant with Gunning's notion of "attraction," and with Altman's notion of "flagrant" display, no matter how goal-driven or embedded within narrative it may be. Indeed, nothing is more sensational in American cinema than the infinite varieties of rescues, accidents, chases, and fights. These "masculine" action-centered climaxes may be scrupulously motivated or wildly implausible depending on the film. While usually faithful to the laws of motion and gravity, this realism of action should not fool us into thinking that the dominant mode of such films is realism. Nor should the virility of action itself fool us into thinking that it is not melodrama.

Altman argues that film scholars have not attended to the popular theater of melodrama as the original sources of these spectacles. He rightly chides film historians and scholars for skipping over theatrical melodramas in their rush to link the emerging film to the realist novel. He also points out that this repression of popular theater has the effect of denying Hollywood cinema its fundamental connection to popular melodramatic tradition. "Unmotivated events, rhythmic montage, highlighted parallelism, overlong spectacles— these are the excesses in the classical narrative system that alert us to the existence of a competing logic, a second voice" (Altman 1989, 346). To Altman these "excesses" give evidence of an "embedded melodramatic mode" within the classical (347). He thus sees popular American cinema—which he nevertheless calls classical—as proceeding from a dialectic between a submerged, nondominant, melodrama and a dominant classicism. Thus, like Brooks, Altman too easily cedes to the dominance of the classical, and to melodrama as its excess.

More recently, Ben Singer (2000) has also challenged Bordwell's assertion of the dominance of the classical style with a study of stage and film melodrama's relation to modernity. Focusing exclusively on those films that in the first two decades of film history were actually called melodrama, Singer importantly establishes what others have challenged—the stable existence of melodrama as a coherent genre—a genre with a specific relation to the hallmarks of modern life: urbanization, cultural discontinuity, increased mobility, and sensory complexity.[23] Also, Miriam Hansen recently has questioned the ahistorical, antimodernist tendencies in the term *classical cinema*, suggesting that the very category of the classical verges on anachronism when we are using the term to refer to "a cultural formation that was, after all, perceived as the incarnation of *the modern*" in its methods of industrial production and mass consumption (Hansen 2000, 337). Like Singer, Hansen wants to keep in mind the inherent modernism of cinema—the fact that it was the first mass-based, international, modernist idiom to offer a cultural horizon in which the traumatic effects of modernity were negotiated. But after a slight hesitation, Hansen, like Altman, retains the term classical, albeit with some qualification.[24] It seems that even those critics who question the totalizing and universalizing nature of the term still hold on to it, despite the fact that it gives us no way to account for the more destabilizing effects of the modern world so important to the cinema.

For years I have held on to the term too, laboring under the impression that the "nonclassical" cinematic forms that have been my particular interest—pornography, horror, melodramas—were simply exceptions to classical norms (Williams 1984, 1991). Now, however, I recognize that these binaries, whether between classical and excess, or classical and modern, or classical and nonclassical, are simply too crude to perform much analytical work. They perpetually relegate the sensational, affective, destabilizing, spectacular, haptic, exciting, and moralizing dimensions of cinema to some kind of deviation from a more "harmonious" "norm."

It is time, then, to make a bolder claim: not that melodrama is a submerged, or embedded, tendency, or genre, within classical realism, but that it has more often itself been the dominant form of popular moving-picture **23** narrative, whether on the nineteenth-century stage, in twentieth-century films or, as we shall explore in the last chapter of this book, in contemporary media events. The emotional content and vivid style regarded as excess, in other words, much more often constitutes the mainstream even as it continues to be perceived as excess. And most important in this mainstream are the entertainment needs of a modern, rationalist, democratic, capitalist, industrial, and now post-industrial society seeking moral legibility under new conditions of moral ambiguity. In other words, the ongoing loss of moral certainty has been compensated for by increasingly sensational, commodified productions of pathos and action.

This is certainly not to say that all popular cinema is dominated by melodrama. But it is to say that the mode of melodrama drives the production of a great variety of familiar film genres. As Christine Gledhill writes, "The success of melodrama lies partly in its heterogeneity, arguably producing a greater variety of genres than its close modal neighbor, comedy, and able, moreover, to draw into its articulation the other dominating modes of contemporary popular culture: comedy, romance, realism" (Gledhill 2000, 235).[25] The mainstream of melodrama is often not acknowledged as such, however, since melodrama consistently decks itself out in the latest trappings of realism in order to command recognition of the world it represents. We need to see, however, that melodrama is the name of the cultural force that, beginning in the nineteenth century, supplied story materials about race, gender, and class already organized into visually compelling forms of pathos and action, already performable in pictures through a system of gesture and demeanor, and already given musical accompaniment on the stage. The melodramatic mode of narrative in American popular culture is thus nothing less than the process whereby melodrama sheds its old-fashioned values, acting styles, and ideologies to gain what Gledhill calls the "imprimatur of 'realism'" (Gledhill 1992, 137).[26]

Suffering and Suffrage[27]

Feminist critic Lauren Berlant has written insightfully about the role of pain and suffering in the construction of American citizenship. In the liberal, Constitutional model of citizenship, a citizen's value is secured through the notion of an abstract personhood protected equally under the law. But since this juridical notion of abstract personhood often fails to provide equal protection to all citizens, a second model of citizenship has emerged around the visible emotions of suffering bodies that, in the very activity of suffering, demonstrate worth as citizens. In this model, pioneered by abolitionists and feminists of the nineteenth century, and continued in contemporary identity politics, citizenship is paradoxically established not through reason, nor the acquisition of wealth and power, but through "the trumping power of suffering" (Berlant 2000). Manifestations of pain—or what Wendy Brown calls "states of injury" (Brown 1995, 67)—become, in themselves, evidence of a subjectivity worthy of recognition. Uncle Tom, as we shall see in Chapter 2, is the prototypical American mass-culture example of such a "state of injury." His suffering at the hands of Simon Legree confers upon him the eventual right to recognition as a person—if not yet in Stowe's ideology to citizenship proper.

There is every reason to be critical of the manipulations of these forms of "sentimental politics." Like Ann Douglas (1977) before her, Lauren Berlant critiques a culture that grounds the construction of citizenship in channels of affective identification and empathy. She points out that the eradication of pain does not necessarily equate with the achievement of justice. Unlike Douglas, however, Berlant recognizes the seriousness and complexity of what she calls "sentimental politics" (Berlant 2000). Such a politics tends toward climaxes that offer a feeling for, if not the reality of, justice. Melodramatic climaxes that end in the death of a good person—Uncle Tom, Princess Charlotte, Jack Dawson (in *Titanic*)—offer paroxysms of pathos and recognitions of virtue compensating for individual loss of life. But if we persist in calling these paroxysms of pathos sentimental, we relegate them to a realm of passivity that misses the degree to which sentiment enables action. For melodrama— the term that I believe can best encompass both pathos *and* action—can also channel the paroxysm of pathos into the more action-centered variants of the rescue, the chase, and the fight (as in the action genres).

Melodrama, as in our examples of NBC's Olympics, the statue of Princess Charlotte, and the diverging stories of Eliza and Uncle Tom, most typically offers combinations of pathos *and* action. Virtuous sufferer and active hero may be divided into conventional male and female roles or combined in the same person. "Women's film" heroine Stella Dallas, for example, throws herself quite actively into the self-sacrificial task of alienating her daughter's affections. In the film's pathos-filled ending she also physically pushes through the crowd in order to see her daughter's wedding. While such action is hardly thrilling in the manner of male action films, within the more circumscribed realm of action available to women it may seem quite thrilling. On the other hand, Rambo—to cite a stereotypically masculine, action- oriented, example—endures multiple indignities and pathetically suffers in ways that elicit audience empathy before he begins his prolonged rescue-revenge. [28]

Big "sensation" scenes, whether of prolonged "feminine" pathos or prolonged "masculine" action, do not interrupt the logical cause-effect progress of a narrative toward conclusion. More often, it is these spectacles of pathos and action that are served by the narrative's cause-effect. As American melodrama developed from nineteenth-century stage to screen, and from silent movie to sound, it frequently instituted more realistic causations and techniques for the display of pathos and action, but it never ceased to serve the primary ends of displaying both in the service of moral legibility.[29] To study the relation between pathos and action is to see that there is no pure isolation of pathos in woman's films nor of action in the male action genres. For if, as Peter Brooks argues, melodrama is most centrally about being able to read an occulted moral truth, and the assigning of guilt and innocence in a "post sacred," post-Enlightenment, modern world where moral and religious certainties are no longer self-evident, then pathos and action are the two most important means to the achievement of moral legibility.

D. W. Griffith's *Broken Blossoms* (1919) is an excellent early model for this pathos-filled, self-sacrificing side of melodrama, as well as for its racialization. Griffith's feminized Chinese victim-hero proves his virtue by not taking sexual advantage of the waif he befriends. His attempt to save her from the clutches of her brutal father comes too late, however, and in the pathos-filled ending, in which a virtuous heroine in need of rescue does not get saved "in the nick of time," he can only lay out her body and join her in death. Pathos predominates in a range of sad-ending melodramas: in most "women's films," in many "family melodramas," and sad musicals in which song and dance do not save the day—such as *Applause* (1929), *Hallelujah* (1929), *A Star Is Born* (1954, 1976), and in "social problem" films without optimistic endings, such as *I Am a Fugitive from a Chain Gang* (1932) or *You Only Live Once* (1937). It also continues in biopics such as *Silkwood* (1983) or *Malcolm X* (1992). In these films victim-heroes, following in the footsteps of the nineteenth-century melodrama's Uncle Tom and Little Eva, achieve recognition of their virtue through the more passive "deeds" of suffering and/or self-sacrifice.

The action side of the melodramatic mode finds its silent cinema prototype in Griffith's *The Birth of a Nation* (1915) and *Way Down East* (1920). It is continued in most of the male action genres—westerns, gangster films, war films, cop films, Clint Eastwood films, as well as happy musicals and social problem films. In these films active victim-heroes either solve problems through action—such as *Salt of the Earth* (1953) or *Norma Rae* (1979)—or are themselves rescued from some fix. The suffering of the victim-hero is important for the establishment of moral legitimacy, but suffering, in these examples, is less extended and ultimately gives way to action. Similarly, the recognition of virtue is at least partially achieved through the performance of some deed. Here pathos mixes with other emotions—suspense, fear, anxiety, anger, laughter, and so on—experienced in the rescues, chases, gunfights, fistfights, or spaceship fights of the various action genres.

Westerns, war films, and Holocaust films, no less than women's films, family melodramas, and biopics thus participate, along with any drama whose outcome is the recognition of virtue, in the long-playing tradition of American melodrama.[30] We do well, then, to shift our critical gaze from the often superficial coherence of specific genres with their familiar costumes, locales, and themes, toward the deeper coherence of melodrama. Of course, we may still rail at the simplification and obfuscation of melodrama; we can regret the absence of moral ambiguity in the "solutions" posed to the problems of race, class, gender, ethnicity, and disability; we can criticize the perverse location of moral power in the role of victims; but even as we note all limitations of the mode we need to recognize that it is in ever-modernizing forms of melodrama—not epic drama, not "classical realism"—that American democratic culture has most powerfully articulated the moral structure of feeling animating its goals of justice.

Typical Melodrama: The Case of *Way Down East*

"Every discussion of film should begin with Griffith." Jean-Luc Godard's famous advice to the student of cinema derives from the fact that the art and technique of the "first author" and "father" of film is often equated with the art and technique of "the movies" themselves. This advice is all the more pertinent if the goal in discussing film is to determine the significance of melodrama to popular moving-image culture. Griffith's reputation as "father" of film was established by an influential first generation of film historians and scholars as that which not only grew out of, but also outgrew, the more "infantile" and "primitive" form of stage melodrama.[31] In the rest of this chapter I will counter this tendency with an attempt to articulate what is typical, and typically melodramatic, about one of D. W. Griffith's most popular and familiar films, *Way Down East* (1920). I choose this film because of its status as a well-loved, enduringly popular example of the American silent cinema, and because it has obvious roots in the American melodramatic stage. When Griffith announced he was making this film he was laughed at for reviving a "horse and buggy melodrama" already considered past resuscitation (Gish 1969, 229). He surprised everyone with the viability of the hoary material in what was to be his last truly popular film. My point about this viability is the same as my point about the melodramatic mode: it is not the transcendence of melodrama to which we should attend, but its forms of revitalization. In what follows I undertake the obvious, but oddly neglected task of situating *Way Down East* as a melodrama, and, by extension, melodrama itself as a basic mode of American moving pictures.[32] In order to suggest the ways in which popular American cinema is still, *mutatis mutandis*, melodrama, I will supplement this discussion with a somewhat briefer comparison of

James Cameron's *Titanic* (1997), a film whose ability to excite and move audiences and critics who, like Griffith's, thought they knew better is typical of the way the power of melodrama continually takes its audiences and critics by surprise. Like *Way Down East*, *Titanic* has been acknowledged to be melodramatic by its supporters and detractors alike. Yet as with Griffith's film, its critics have usually moved on to peg its appeal to other elements—in this case the disaster genre, historical romance, and the techniques of spectacular special effects—without first considering the framework that holds them all together.

27

Another reason for examining Griffith's film is that, unlike some of his earlier, more controversial, racially based melodramas—most significantly *The Birth of a Nation* (1915) and *Broken Blossoms* (1919), but also many of the early Biograph films—*Way Down East* allows an investigation into some of the primary, and enduring, features of melodrama without the added complication of racist stereotyping. Although we will pursue the way the melodramatic mode has shaped the controversies of race and gender in American popular culture in the following chapters, for the moment in order to be as clear as possible about what a typical melodrama is, let us investigate the simpler case of a popular silent melodrama of gender and class and its end-of-the-millennium parallel.

Way Down East is a 1920 film adaptation of Lottie Blair Parker and Joseph Grismer's popular stage melodrama first performed in 1898 under that title. This play was itself an adaptation of Parker's play of 1896 called *Annie Laurie*. All versions tell the story of Anna, a poor country girl who goes to the city to claim help from rich relations. There an aristocratic cad tricks her into a mock marriage and leaves her pregnant. The baby dies soon after birth and a destitute Anna finds work on a New England farm. However, when the farm's stern squire learns that Anna has had a child out of wedlock, he expels her from his house in the middle of a blizzard. His son, David, then rescues her from the storm. Both versions of the play begin with Anna arriving at the farm, a woman with a secret. The story of her pregnancy and the death of the child only comes out when the villain, Sanderson, encounters Anna at the farm.

Griffith altered the play by telling the story of Anna from the beginning. He shows her domestic life with her mother; her trip to the big city where she is ridiculed by female cousins, elegantly decked out by an eccentric aunt, then seduced into a fake marriage by the suave villain. One of the most moving scenes in the film is also a Griffith "invention"—though actually one freely borrowed from Thomas Hardy's 1891 novel *Tess of the D'Urbervilles*: Anna's baptism of her dying baby.[33]

What, then, are the key melodramatic qualities of this film that can be applied to the melodramatic mode as a whole? I will isolate five features drawn from the previous discussion of melodrama, some of them adapted from Peter

Brooks's seminal study. These features will prove useful touchstones for understanding melodrama throughout the rest of this book. Each of these features was significantly modernized by Griffith from the stage melodrama and is further modernized in Cameron's *Titanic*. Each will be seen to be central to the racial melodrama that constitutes the rest of this study. And in each case I will connect the now "hoary" example of Griffith's film to a recent example, James Cameron's eleven-Oscar, all-time highest-grossing film.

Home: Melodrama begins, and wants to end, in a "space of innocence." Peter Brooks (1995, 29) notes that while tragedy usually begins at a moment of crisis and proceeds to the fall, classic stage melodrama usually begins by offering a moment of virtue taking pleasure in itself. Gardens and rural homes are the stereotypical icons of such innocence. Melodrama seizes upon the icon of a home with which to figure this innocence. Uncle Tom's "Old Kentucky Home" is a key icon in the melodramas of black and white we will soon engage. The narrative proper usually begins when the villain intrudes upon this idyllic space. The narrative then ends happily if the protagonists can, in some way, return to this home, unhappily if they do not. It is not necessary that the space of innocence be an actually realized, pre-lapsarian garden. Uncle Tom's cabin (see Fig. 2.1, 2.8) or the carefree revels of the innocents in the steerage of the Titanic are cases in point. Both are fragile and fleeting spaces of innocence and freedom embedded within larger corrupt social orders: chattel slavery in the first instance, a class system that will only provide sufficient lifeboats for first-class passengers in the second. Even if this space is not literally represented, and the narrative cannot begin there, even if it has never been possessed, the most enduring forms of the mode are often suffused with nostalgia for a virtuous place that we like to think we once possessed, whether in childhood or the distant past of the nation.

The beginning of *Way Down East* is emblematic: Anna (Lillian Gish) performs household tasks, sews with her mother; and plays with a puppy. In Gish's girlish performance she is the perfect example of what Brooks calls innocence "taking pleasure in itself" (69). The pleasure, however, is momentary. When Anna is compelled to visit the big city in search of rich relations, she encounters the feminine antithesis of the original space of innocence: the decadent city where New Women with bobbed hair slink about in low-cut gowns. After she is similarly decked out by an eccentric aunt, Anna catches the eye of the villain, Lennox Sanderson (Lowell Sherman), and is seduced and abandoned. Later, finding work at the farm of Squire Bartlett, she encounters a second rural haven and a second mother in the squire's wife. The melodramatic climax of her rescue from the raging torrent of an icy river will finally restore Anna to this substitute home. *Way Down East* is thus a happy-ending melodrama that regains the space of innocence with which it began, ending in a three-way marriage between all eligible couples. But the final kiss is not between any of the heterosexual couples but instead between the two moth-

ers—Anna and Mrs. Bartlett—who represent a restoration of the original innocence of the mother-daughter "space of innocence" of the film's beginning.

Titanic, too, offers a restoration of innocence even though its male hero,
unlike Anna, is not rescued in time from the icy waters that become his grave.
In this case, his embrace of life lives on in the person of Rose and makes
nostalgia for the doomed ship a viable structure of feeling by the film's end.
At the very end of Titanic, the happy ending that parallels the double wedding
of Way Down East, is Rose's dream of a resuscitated ship restored magically
from present wreck to past glory. In this depiction of glory, Jack in his humble
clothes greets Rose in elegant attire on the grand staircase of the "ship of
dreams." Surrounding them are rich and poor passengers mingled promiscu-
ously in a kind of curtain call that recognizes the virtue of the democratic
romantic couple against the evil of class division and separation. The very
class-based grandiosity that made a ship like the Titanic possible in the first
place is thus denied in this final image of the "ship of dreams."

*Melodrama focuses on victim-heroes and on recognizing their virtue. Rec-
ognition of virtue orchestrates the moral legibility that is key to melodrama's
function.* Thomas Elsaesser (1975, 86) argues that a characteristic feature of
melodrama is its concentration on "the point of view of the victim." One
of the reasons Elsaesser privileges fifties family melodrama as the "genre's"
quintessential form is the tendency for these films to "present *all* the characters convincingly as victims" (86), but just as melodrama needs a home as its
locus of innocence, it needs a victim whose visible suffering transmutes into
proof of virtue.[34] The key function of victimization is to orchestrate the moral
legibility crucial to the mode, for if virtue is not obvious, suffering—often
depicted as the literal suffering of an agonized body—is. The suffering body
caught up in paroxysms of mental or physical pain can be male or female,
but suffering itself is a form of powerlessness that is coded feminine. Of course
the transmutation of bodily suffering into virtue is a topos of western culture
that goes back to Christian iconography. I shall be arguing in the next chapter
that the "Christian passion" of death on the cross carried special weight in
American melodrama through its importation via Harriet Beecher Stowe's
anti-slavery appeal in *Uncle Tom's Cabin*. The American variant of melodrama was thus invested, from the mid-1850s on, in the iconographic display
of passionate suffering of a feminized, if not feminine, body. Even happy-
ending melodramas are heavily invested in displays of bodily suffering as the
means to the recognition of virtue. Indeed, the happy ending dramatic outcome that is often derided as the most unrealistic element of the mode—the
reward of virtue—is only a secondary manifestation of the more important
recognition of virtue in a world in which such recognition is not obvious.
Virtue can be recognized through suffering alone, or in the action variants of
melodrama by suffering that calls for deeds.

In stage melodrama, the moment of recognition is often the classic theatrical tableau used at the ends of scenes to offer a concentrated summing up of and punctuation for the tensions of the whole act. Peter Brooks points to a moment in *La Fille de l'exilé* when evil tartars fall down on their knees before a virtuous Siberian girl. In such theatrical tableaux the actors would move into a held "picture," sometimes self-consciously imitating existing paintings or engravings. The tableau was used theatrically as a silent, bodily expression of what words could not fully say. It was also a way of crystallizing the dramatic tensions within a scene and of musically prolonging their emotional effects. The sustained close-up of a character's prolonged reaction to some dramatic news before the cut to commercial in soap opera is the contemporary inheritor of this tradition adapted to the needs of commercial interruption.

In *Way Down East* the recognition of Anna's virtue takes place in the sugar shack after her climactic rescue from the ice when first Sanderson, then the squire, ask her forgiveness. In *Titanic*, Jack's virtue is most fully recognized as he tells Rose, even as he himself freezes, that she must promise to survive and go on to make "lots of babies." In both cases the victim-hero's virtue is initially misrecognized—as when Squire Bartlett "names" Anna as an unwed mother and as when Cal Haukley "names" Jack a thief after planting a diamond in his pocket.

The astonishment that typically follows the misrecognition of virtue enhances the tension of establishing female virtue in *Way Down East* and male virtue in *Titanic*. For Anna *is* the unwed mother named by the squire, and Jack, if not an actual thief, *is* the low-class interloper who has painted Rose in the nude. Both films thus need their victim-heroes to suffer in order to purge them of the taint of selfish ambition. The final and full recognition of virtue will not take place, in Anna's case, until she receives the apology of both the squire, who had condemned her as a fallen woman, and Sanderson, who had wronged her in the first place. It will not take place in Jack's case until the aged Rose tells the world the many ways this man has rescued her. In both cases, a climactic rescue from icy water—rescue that occurs either too late (Jack) or in the nick of time (Anna)—proves crucial. But just how such exciting climaxes enable the recognition of virtue cannot be explained without a discussion of the phenomenon of melodramatic timing in the following section.

Melodrama's recognition of virtue involves a dialectic of pathos and action—a give and take of "too late" and "in the nick of time." We have seen that pathos is not the only emotional note sounded by melodrama. However, pathos is crucial, and even in happy-ending action melodramas there is tension between the paroxysm of pathos and the exhilaration of action. Franco Moretti (1983) is one of very few critics to analyze the phenomenon of crying in response to "moving literature."[35] Moretti writes not about melodrama, but about what might be called a particularly melodramatic form of Italian boys' fiction. Perhaps because it is about boys' literature, the essay does not spend too much time worrying about the "excess" femininity of tears. Instead, Moretti notes the vast literature on what makes for the somatic response of laughter and the paucity of literature on the response of tears. Setting out to be for tears what Bergson was for laughter, Moretti ventures an explanation connected, like Bergson's, to temporality: we cry when we recognize that something is lost and cannot be regained. Time is the ultimate object of loss; we cry at the irreversibility of time. We cry at funerals, for example, because it is then that we know, finally and forever, that it is "too late" (Moretti 1983, 159–62).

Moretti borrows the rhetorical term "agnition"—the resolution of a clash between two mutually opposed points of view—as the key "moving" device in the stories he discusses (161–62). He argues that the precise trigger to crying occurs at the moment when agnition reduces the tension between desire and reality: e.g., it is too late for the father to make amends to his dying son, so he cries. The tension ends, according to Moretti, because desire is finally shown to be futile. When we let go of this desire the sadness that results is also a paradoxical kind of relief. Tears can thus be interpreted, Moretti argues, as both an homage to the desire for happiness and the recognition that it is lost. Hence tears are always a kind of false consciousness, released, hypocritically as it were, when it is already too late. But Moretti also notes that tears at least acknowledge that in this sad reconciliation with the world, something important has been lost (180).

It is this feeling of loss that is crucial to crying's relation to melodrama. A melodrama does not have to contain multiple scenes of pathetic death. What counts is the feeling or threat of loss suffused throughout the form, the sense that something has, as one of our later racial melodramas will put it, "gone with the wind," and the imagination of a loss that is not normally spoken. Audiences may weep or not weep, but the sense of a loss that implicates readers or audiences is central. And with this feeling of "too late," suspenseful time and timing become all-important.

In an adaptation of Moretti's thesis to film melodrama, Steve Neale suggests that in practice we do not cry just when it *is* too late, we cry even in happy-ending melodrama, out of the desire that it *not* be too late. Happy-ending melodramas can move us to tears, Neale explains, when, hope against hope, desire is fulfilled, and time is defeated. In these cases—he cites *The Big Parade* (1925), *Only Yesterday* (1933) and *Yanks* (1979) as examples; I would cite *Way Down East* (1920), *Rambo* (1985), *Schindler's List* (1993), and *Titanic* (1997)—Neale argues that we cry because we fulfill an infantile fantasy that on some level we know is infantile and fantastic (Neale 1986, 8).

Neale thus explains psychoanalytically the pleasurable tears of the happy-ending and sad-ending melodrama: crying is a demand for satisfaction that can never be satisfied, yet tears sustain and express the fantasy that it can.

However, if the pathos of tears derives from the knowledge of loss, and if what is lost is ultimately time itself—our connection to the lost time of innocence—then we need to examine the timing of the relation between the pathos of lost time and the action that sometimes regains it.

Moretti argues that a key element of "moving literature" occurs when what one character knows is reconciled with what another knows, but "too late." In death scenes, for example, tears unite us, not to the victim who dies, but to the survivors who recognize the irreversibility of time (Moretti 1983, 179). For example, in the pathetic scene of the death of Anna's baby, we see an example of Moretti's agnition played out when Anna's desire to believe that her baby is merely cold comes into conflict with her suspicion, and the doctor's certainty, that her baby is dead. When Anna hears this news, so Moretti would say, the discrepancy between her and the doctor's point of view is reconciled; tension is released and at this point, Anna, and we, can cry. We have seen above, however, how the powerlessness of tears that flow too late can be the proof of a virtue that, at another point in the narrative, can give moral authority to action. Both Moretti and Neale note that tears are a product of powerlessness. It seems to me, however, that if tears are an acknowledgment of a hope that desire will be fulfilled then they are also a source of future power; indeed, they are almost an investment in that power. The pathos of suffering thus not only ensures virtue, but also seems to entitle action. Let us see how this works in *Way Down East* by turning again to the climactic scene of astonishment that precedes the famous rescue from the ice.

Wronged by the upper-class villain Sanderson but silenced by his power throughout the bulk of the film, Gish's Anna is forced to serve Sanderson as a guest in the home of the family that has taken her in. But she cannot speak of his wrong to her because of the double standard that would shame her more than him. It is only when a busybody gossip reveals what all believe to be her sexual taint that she is forced into action—to name Sanderson as her seducer.

This naming of the villain, which occurs in both the stage play and film, is Anna's big moment of action before throwing herself out into the snowstorm. It is well earned by her many earlier moments of silent pathos, which the audience, but none of the other characters, has been able to appreciate. Our tension mounts as we await this long-wished-for and equally long-delayed "nomination" of the guilty villain. But nomination is only a first step; it is not yet an achieved and public recognition of her virtue and his villainy. For this recognition to really work the film must move from pathos to action and from the tears that pay homage to "too late" to a rescue that is "in the nick of time."

We are so familiar with the "in the nick of time" rescue of the happy-ending melodrama that we take its seemingly facile effects for granted. Popular criticism will often praise the effective direction of such scenes.[36] In a famous appreciation of Griffith's melodrama, V. I. Pudovkin has noted that Anna's ordeal is in three stages: "First the snowstorm, then the foaming, swirling river in thaw, packed with ice blocks that rage yet wilder than the storm, and finally the mighty waterfall, conveying the impression of death itself. . . . This harmony—the storm in the human heart and the storm in the frenzy of nature—is one of the most powerful achievements of the American genius" (Pudovkin 1970, 129). **33**

Each of these stages of Anna's ordeal, intercut with David's (Richard Barthelmess) painfully delayed pursuit, increases our sense of her helplessness (Fig. 1.2). Yet the very investment of film time in the detailing of the different stages of the ordeal provides the counter "hope-against-hope" for her rescue. David's last-minute capture of Anna's body at the very last moment before she and he plummet over the falls has been seen as an unrealistic heroic exploit saved by the beauty and power of the natural elements that form its context, as well as by the device of parallel montage. Because some of the best appreciations of Griffith's editing come from Soviet directors, American critics have often seen Griffith's melodrama through the lens of what it might have become had Griffith been able to transcend, as Eisenstein wished, the "Dickensian [read melodramatic] limits" of his montage. Eisenstein cites this rescue to fault the lack of unity between the race of the ice break and the race of David to the rescue, accusing the film of not becoming the human flood that Pudovkin's *Mother* becomes (Eisenstein 1949, 235). In effect, both Eisenstein and Pudovkin laud the technique of parallel montage but fault the rescue itself as an intrinsically hokey outcome, a product of dualistic thinking in which "reconciliation" is hypothetical wish fulfillment. If rescue as unrealistic reconciliation is ideologically flawed, especially from a Soviet perspective, this same Soviet perspective calls attention to temporal, rhythmic elements that make Griffith, and by extension American action melodrama, an effective manipulator of audience response.

There is still a need, however, for a better understanding of these temporal and rhythmic elements on their own, melodramatic, terms. To watch a last-minute rescue—whether of Anna from the ice, of American P.O.W.'s from the Vietnamese prison in *Rambo*, of the women prisoners from Auschwitz in *Schindler's List*—is to feel time in two contradictory ways. Although a rapid succession of shots specifying the physical danger gives the effect of speed, of events happening extremely fast, the parallel cutting between the breaking ice, David's pursuit, Anna's unconscious body, and the churning falls prolongs time beyond all possible belief. Actions *feel* fast, and yet the ultimate duration of the event is retarded. We are moved in both directions at once in a contradictory hurry-up and slow-down. The effect is to propel events into the future while insisting on the continued reminder of the past pathos of "too late." However, often if a film invests too much time in suspenseful delays that enhance the effect of the "in-the-nick-of-time" rescue, it cannot then convincingly revert to the pathos of "too late" in the end. Paradoxically, it is as if the

Figure 1.2 Anna freezes on the ice, suffering as David attempts a painfully de-layed rescue. (*Way Down East*, D. W. Griffith, 1920, Museum of Modern Art Film Stills Archive)

more the temporal prolongation of suspense builds, the more sure we can be that this investment of time will have a successful outcome.

If and when a film moves to the fast-paced register of suspenseful action, we experience enormous relief from the constant repetition of loss. Exhila-rated, we are caught up in the physical logic, one might even say the physics, of time and space. But this exhilaration does not progress linearly. Whether in stage melodrama's episodic "cutting" back and forth between endangered heroine, and pursuing hero, or the film melodrama's cross- cut editing, we encounter an intensely rhythmic tease whose core question is melodramatic: will we ever get back to the time before it is too late? Only the teasing, suspenseful retardation of the outcome, constantly threatening that it must by now, certainly, be too late, permits the viewers felt acceptance of the fantasy that it is not.

This teasing delay of the forward-moving march of time has not been sufficiently appreciated as basic to the cinematic application of theatrical melodrama.[37] Nor has it been appreciated as an effect that cinema realized more powerfully than stage or literary melodrama. As suggested above, it needs to be linked with melodrama's larger impulse to reverse time, to return to the time of origins and the space of innocence that can musically be felt in terms of patterns of anticipation and return. The original pattern—whether of melody, key, rhythm, or of physical space and time—thus takes on a visceral sort of ethics.[38] They are a form of somatic knowledge, *felt* as good. The "main thrust" of melodramatic narrative, for all its flurry of apparent linear action, is thus actually to get back to what *feels* like the beginning.

Melodrama offers the hope, then, that it may not be too late, that there may still be an original locus of virtue, and that this virtue and truth can be achieved in private individuals and individual heroic acts rather than, as Eisenstein wanted, in revolution and change. For these reasons the prolonged play with time and timing so important to the last-minute rescue should not be attributed to the linear cause-effect outcome of classical realism or to the naturalism of scenery, sets, or acting. The rescue, chase, or fight that defies time, and that occupies so much time in the narrative, is the desired mirror reversal of the defeat by time in the pathos of "too late."

The physical "realism" of this climax, so devoted to convincing viewers of the reality of the material forces that combine to make the victim-hero suffer, so little concerned with the plausibility of their implementation, is thus inherent to its melodrama. At its deepest level melodrama is thus an expression of feeling toward a time that passes too fast. This may be why the spectacular essence of melodrama seems to rest in those moments of temporal prolongation when "in the nick of time" defies "too late."

Titanic offers an interesting '90s revision of the gendered convention of active male hero rescuing a passive heroine "in the nick of time." In this case, the failure of all but one of the twenty lifeboats full of survivors to come to the rescue of the passengers immersed in the icy water after the ship's sinking represents a manifestly class-based victimization, a rescue that is definitively "too late" for the vast majority of victims. Jack Dawson, without life jacket and immersed, freezes while aiding Rose, with life jacket and partially above water. In the process, however, repeating the rescue he effected at the beginning of the film, he passes his masculine virtue and energy onto Rose. Rose, we are meant to understand, will henceforth live her life as an independent woman freed from the classed and gendered prison that had made the supposed "ship of dreams" a "slave ship" for her. Thus Rose is rescued from her gendered and class-based exploitation as chattel in a loveless marriage, even as the brutal class system that will only rescue the "better half" of the passengers kills Jack. Jack's own death is nevertheless redeemed by the will to live that he passes on to Rose. When the lone lifeboat finally does appear, "too late" to rescue all but a few survivors, Rose severs the death grip of Jack's frozen hand, paradoxically recognizing that it is through her will to live that she will "never let go" of him. She then calls for help and is rescued. The rescue that was "too late" for Jack is "in the nick of time" for Rose. Through a sleight of hand typical of melodrama, we morally condemn the class system that kills so many poor passengers yet feel good about the rescue that will permit Rose—an upper-class heroine now properly identified with the déclassé poor—to live free. What is rescued, in the end, is not only the individual victim-hero, but the memory of the Titanic as a "ship of dreams," despite the class-crime that failed to rescue so many of the poorer passengers. Here too, the melodramatic narrative recovers, like the explorers probing the wreck of the doomed ship, the virtue of a lost past.

Melodrama does not always move, then, toward a new future; very often it moves to restore some semblance of a lost past. To this degree melodrama can be considered an inherently conservative and backward-looking form even as it progressively tackles basic problems of social inequity. Consider, for example, how Anna's rescue from the ice functions as much to restore the virtue of the beginning as it does to imagine a new society at the end. We have seen that just before she runs out into the storm, Anna "nominates" Sanderson as the villain. This nomination produces astonishment, but it does not produce the public recognition of Anna's virtue. Her guilt remains in the eyes of a patriarchal status quo that the film does not directly confront. Yet somehow the snowstorm of the play and the snowstorm and ordeal on the ice of the film eradicate this guilt and make possible the final denouement that not only recognizes, but actually restores, Anna's innocence.

Why is this recognition only possible after the rescue on the ice? How does the in-the-nick-of-time rescue function to solve the problem of Anna's sexual guilt in the eyes of the stern patriarch? To answer we need to realize that what is at stake in the rescue is much more than Anna's and David's lives. At stake is the viability of the patriarchal law that has more harshly blamed the unwed mother than the man who seduced her for sexual misconduct, and that is therefore, at least technically, allied with the villain. Indeed, if any work of Griffith's deserved to be called *The Mother and the Law*—the title of the modern sequence of his 1916 film *Intolerance*—it is this one.

When David saves Anna from the icy river and waterfall, he also saves the system that has so harshly expelled her. He tempers his father's law with his mother's love, saving the patriarchal family from casting out the maternal figure of love capable of tempering its stern law. He is able to do so, however, precisely because at this moment it is no longer the villain, nor even his father, who endangers Anna but instead the icy river. We have seen how Griffith's use of these natural elements have been praised as transcending melodrama and yet falling back into it. I have been arguing, however, for the need to recognize such moments as fully melodramatic. One of the key features of melodrama noted above is its compulsion to "reconcile the irreconcilable"— that is, its tendency to find solutions to problems that cannot really be solved without challenging the older ideologies of moral certainty to which melodrama wishes to return. By posing the problem of injustice to the unwed mother, Griffith set himself the impossible task of reconciling the double standard with a culture and an ideology that did not, in fact, grant equality to women.

When the good-hearted but stern patriarch, Squire Bartlett, learns that Anna has been an unwed mother, he feels his moral duty is to expel her from his home. Though he has grown to love Anna, "the law is the law." The film is thus not simply about a "good" woman victimized by a "bad" man, but about what happens when a "good" man condemns, according to his code of ethics, an otherwise "good" woman. The happy-ending resolution of this conflict must reconcile a maternal empathy that feels for Anna with the stern, paternal law that cannot, within the limits of conventional ideology, be fundamentally challenged.

When David rescues Anna from the river, the fight that could easily be with his father is displaced onto a battle with the river. At this point in the film the natural elements take on the role of the villain. What, then, does the perilous ice accomplish that a personal villain does not? I believe it affords a covert satisfaction of the punishing law that unjustly accuses Anna. Ice, icy water, and snow are frigid elements that counter the sexual fires that produced the illegitimate child whose brief existence still haunts her. They cool and wash Anna metaphorically clean of the crimes she technically did commit and which the patriarchal double standard still believes stain her. The "moving picture" of the frozen heroine passed out on the ice, hair and hand trailing in the water, rushing toward the falls—enhanced by extratextual legend that Lillian Gish suffered acutely from frostbite during the shooting of the film— moves us not only because it combines the pathos of her suffering with the action of David's rescue; it also punishes the heroine in the most appropriate manner for a sexual crime that the melodrama both believes and does not believe she is guilty of committing. Anna's flight into the storm is a suicidal, self-punishing gesture. But Anna is melodramatically saved by this punishing instrument of her near destruction.

Operating here in the more optimistic vein of American melodrama, Griffith wanted, like the stage play on which his film was based, to save his victim-heroine not only from the falls, but from her taint as a fallen woman. But, unlike the theatrical melodrama on which his film was based, he wanted realistically to show the pathos of her sexual victimization. Griffith therefore had to devise a rescue that could save Anna from the more vivid sins he had realistically insisted on showing. He thus needed a better resolution of Anna's sexual "guilt" than had been offered by the brief mechanical snowstorm of the original play. In other words, he needed a realistic *and* melodramatic resolution. This resolution was, in effect, to prolong what had been an offstage rescue into an on-screen ordeal that was itself a form of punishment.[39]

Where Griffith's 1920s update of an already ancient melodrama deployed icy water to covertly punish his heroine for sexual crimes he and his film cannot fully ignore, James Cameron's deployment of icy water has no such function with respect to Rose's sexual adventure with Jack Dawson. Anachronistically for the era it represents, but appropriately for the postmodern era of its audience, Rose's virtue is actually established by her willingness to pose nude for, and engage in steamy sex with, a poor man. Yet as we have seen, the melodramatic reconciliation of the irreconcilable still operates through the mechanism of the icy water that kills Jack to free Rose.

The dialectic of pathos and action can be viewed as a crucial feature of melodrama. It was a melodramatic staple long before *Way Down East* and it will continue to be so long after *Titanic*. It controls the structures of feeling that animate the form. It combines a fear of loss with the excitement and suspense of action. The study of melodrama has often suffered from the misperception that it was either one or the other of these poles. One of melodrama's greatest interests as a form is in the dialectic between them.

Melodrama borrows from realism but realism serves the melodrama of pathos and action. Theater history, no less than film history, has tended to posit melodrama as a crude retrograde form out of which a more modern realism (and in film studies "classical realism") has developed. Theater historian Jeffrey Mason, for example, argues that theatrical "melodrama is a means of affirming a belief in a reductive perception of reality" (Mason 1993, 93). Film historians, too, have tended to follow the model of Nicholas Vardac (1949) to see the rise of cinema as quickly transcending theatrical melodrama. More recently, however, theater historian Thomas Postlewait has argued that melodrama did not come to an end or evolve into something else at the beginning of the twentieth century. Historically, melodramatic and realistic dramas developed during the same period in the nineteenth and twentieth centuries. They have been mutually influential. Although theater history has most commonly been written as the victory of realism over melodrama, a more careful history observes the mutual borrowings and lendings of the two forms (Postlewait 1996, 46–50).

Consider, for example, Richard Schickel's praise for the realistic qualities of *Way Down East* in contrast to the archaic melodrama of the classic casting-out scene, inspiration since of a thousand cartoons and parodies. . . . It is the ability to show real sleigh rides and spacious barn dances, to place Gish and Barthelmess in a real blizzard, and on a real river as the winter ice breaks, that gives the film an insuperable advantage over the stage. Whatever reservations one entertains about the motives and psychology of these characters, whatever strain has been placed on credibility by the coincidences on which the story so heavily depends, they are (almost literally) blown away by the storm sequence, so powerfully is it presented. (Schickel 1984, 431)

I argue in contrast that an accurate account of D. W. Griffith's version of *Way Down East* would see these realistic touches as a way of modernizing stage melodrama into a popular cinematic form rather than as the triumph of realism over melodrama. Indeed, without the "classic casting-out scene" that Schickel ridicules, none of the realistic background would come into play to purify Anna and permit the recognition of her virtue.

To understand just how the climax of *Way Down East* achieves the happy-ending issue-in-action of the familiar melodramatic rescue, we have seen that what really victimizes Anna is not simply the personal villain Sanderson, but the patriarchal double standard that permits men to sow wild oats and then punishes women for the consequences. One of Griffith's inimitable, preachy titles directly states the problem: "Today woman brought up from childhood to expect ONE CONSTANT MATE possibly suffers more than at any moment in the history of mankind, because not yet has the man-animal reached this high standard, except perhaps in theory." As Virginia Wright Wexman has noted, in the same year that American women won suffrage, *Way Down East* realistically posed the problem of a woman with no rights and with no proper place in the public sphere. This woman is sexually deceived by a powerful, aristocratic man and then condemned by the stern patriarchy that does not grant her equal rights (Wexman 1993, 43–63). Griffith graphically portrayed this victimization in several ways: in a highly realistic scene of Anna's seduction; in another scene showing—unprecedentedly even in discrete long shot—the travail of childbirth; in the wrenching scene, mentioned above, of the baby's death; and finally in the last-minute rescue from the breaking ice of an unmistakably real river and waterfall. None of these scenes appeared in the stage melodrama. All are usually cited as examples of Griffith's realism "transcending" melodrama.

Christine Gledhill notes that the mode of realism pushes toward renewed truth and stylistic innovation, while melodrama's search for something lost, inadmissible and repressed, ties it to the past (Gledhill 1987, 31–32). *Way Down East* does both. While the film is undeniably more realistic than its turn-of-the-century stage version, its solution to the problem of out-of-wedlock maternity is fundamentally melodramatic. That is, rather than directly address the double standard as a social problem, the narrative works to retrieve Anna's personal innocence so that she can return to the rural happiness of her original bond with her mother. Thus the more profound, patriarchal causes of her suffering are never addressed.

40

In this way, the film thus "solves" the problem of the persisting double standard by avoiding its source in flawed patriarchal law.[40] Rather than argue, then, that Griffith took a melodramatic stage play and made it realistic by confronting the harsh realities of Anna Moore's victimization, we can say that having realistically brought up the pressing social problem of out-of-wedlock motherhood, and having presented the dilemma of the stern patriarch who condemns the woman for crimes for which she is not responsible, the narrative then entirely evades this problem by retrieving Anna's innocence through its climax of pathos and action.

Titanic can be seen to observe much the same deployment of realism in the interest of melodrama. In this case the realism consists of the special effects that recreate the experience of a famous historical shipwreck and the social criticism of class privileges that doomed the poorer passengers to a watery grave. At the same time, however, as we have already seen, this very same social critique depends upon the resurrection of the splendor and elegance of the very class system it condemns. The fantasy of the transcendence of class embodied in the love story between vagabond Jack and aristocrat Rose thus relies entirely upon the resurrection of an elegance that belonged exclusively to a class-bound world. The fantasy of the transcendence of class—the sense in which the ship does become for Rose the "ship of dreams"—depends upon the meticulous depiction of class distinction, the Titanic as "slave ship."

The final key feature of melodrama is the presentation of *characters who embody primary psychic roles organized in Manichaean conflicts between good and evil* (Brooks 1995, 2–4). This feature is melodrama's infamously simplistic moral stereotyping: Anna is the good daughter, David the good son, the squire the stern father, Sanderson the selfish cad. The drama operates to reveal simple, but "true," moral identities; characters are "monopathic," lacking the more complex mixes of feelings and the psychological depths of realism.[41] It is easy to view the primary psychic and Manichaean characters of melodrama as archaic features of crude theatricalism lacking the depth and social texture of more realistic, and psychologically nuanced, characters. However, such a view perpetuates the antagonism between melodrama and realism, casting realism as the modern and melodrama as the archaic form of characterization.

When Peter Brooks (1995, 160) writes that evil is a "swarthy cape-enveloped man with a deep voice," he notes that moral forces are viewed in melodrama as expressions of personality embodied in physical being and gesture. However, one era's swarthy cape-enveloped villain is another era's smiling one. Evil, like virtue, can be differently embodied and differently revealed. It is the constant goal of melodrama to make visible occulted moral distinctions through acts and gestures that are felt by audiences to be the emotional truths of individual, but not too individualized, personalities. What is truly modern about melodrama, then, is its reliance on personality—and on the revelation of personality through body and gesture—as the key to both emotional and moral truth.

41

Christine Gledhill argues that the entire Hollywood star system, including the tradition of method acting, is a more sophisticated development of the traditions of melodramatic character and performance (Gledhill 1991, 208). Adapting Brooks's notion that amid the collapse of the sacred as the standard of value, the individual ego became "the measure of all things," Gledhill argues that this reduction of morality to an individual embodiment of ethical forces prepared the way for the psychologization of character and the performance orientation of twentieth-century popular culture (Brooks 1995, 16; Gledhill 1991, 209). Faced with the familiar dilemmas of modernity—the decentered self, the failure of language to say what is meant—melodrama responded with a heightened personalization and expression of the self. The cult of the star fed into this personalization. The contemporary phenomenon of the commodified star whose task is not so much to act as it is to embody a "truthful" "presence"—an authentic performance of his or her "self"—is simply another example of the melodramatic attempt to articulate what Brooks calls "full states of being" (Gledhill 1991, 216–218).

The "method" acting popularized by Lee Strasberg on the American stage and in film in the fifties became known as a means of increasing performative realism, but Gledhill convincingly shows that it actually drew realism toward melodramatic concerns by dissolving the boundaries between acting and psychotherapy and by providing the melodramatic imagination with a new form of the articulation of the moral occult: only now it was the very existence of an individual self that was at stake. The pathos of melodrama becomes the pathos of the assertion of self in the face of encroaching meaninglessness and nonentity (Gledhill 1991, 221–25). In a very real sense, then, melodrama has evolved in the direction of expressing ever more primary psychic roles, not just in the silent cinema's typage—of the father, mother, son, daughter—but in the primary psychic resources drawn upon by actors to express the very pathos of their being.[42]

In the early-nineteenth-century melodramas cited by Brooks, the villain would thus indeed be the swarthy cape-enveloped man with a deep voice and the victim-hero would be a young man and/or woman whose goodness was equally manifested in visible bodily signs. As we shall see in the next chapter, however, a remarkable reversal of these coded stereotypes of good and evil occurred in the forging of a new type of victim-hero in the swarthy complexion of Uncle Tom, whose blackness flew in the face of previous conventions of the representation of good, and the forging of a new type of villain who was not the least "swarthy" and whose whiteness contrasted with the blackness of Uncle Tom.

By the 1920s and the advent of an advanced silent cinema typified by *Way Down East*, victim-heroes became part of a cinematic star system that not only codified goodness in blond innocence (for Gish) or earnest handsomeness (for Barthelmess), but also through close-ups that isolated and privileged these features as part of the discourse of the star. The villain was in this case a sophisticated variation of what was by now the too-easily deciphered swarthy, cape-enveloped man. Lennox Sanderson, for example, is a suave man of the world who hesitates before committing his villainous seduction and abandonment and who even apologizes for his wrongdoing afterward.

Black and white Manichaean polarities simplify and twist the real social and historical complexities of the problems addressed by melodrama. The melodramatic solution to the very real social and political issues raised by the form can only occur through a perverse process of victimization. Virtuous suffering is certainly, and quite literally, a pathetic weapon against injustice, but we need to recognize how frequently it has been deployed as the melodramatic weapon of choice of American popular culture from Lillian Gish to the newly feminized hero personified by Leonardo DiCaprio, from Uncle Tom to Rodney King.

These, then, are five key features of melodrama isolated in a single 1920 silent film, but applicable, I believe, to a wide range of "moving pictures" existing across many genres and media. Not all melodramas begin and end in a space of innocence; not all melodramas successfully recognize the virtue of victim heroes; not all melodramas modernize by borrowing from realism. Certainly some melodramas may have a less complex dialectic of pathos and action than does *Way Down East*. And certainly the tendency toward primary psychic roles may range from purely Manichaean forms of good and evil to more complex, psychoanalytically motivated combinations of symptoms. Nor do these five key features exhaust the definition of melodrama. They are a start, however, in our attempt to grasp the basics of a mode that has been so fundamental to American popular culture that it has often been taken for granted. It is my hope that these five categories will serve us, in the chapters to come, as we pursue the most influential melodramatic story of all American culture: the story of black and white racial victims and villains.

Melodramas of Black and White

I have attempted to introduce the mode of melodrama through the relatively innocent examples of a well-loved silent film and a more recent blockbuster partly because I want to offer a sense of the typicality of the melodramatic mode as it has operated and continues to operate in cinema before turning, in the rest of this book, to a very specific tradition of black and white racial melodrama. If we can now entertain the notion that melodrama is a fundamental mode by which American culture has dealt with the problem of "moral legibility," and if we can also accept that race and ethnicity (in complex intersections with gender and class) represent a primary and enduring moral dilemma of American culture, then the importance of investigating racial melodrama—of understanding the dynamics of melodrama in relation to the stories about race that American popular culture has long been telling itself—becomes clear.

American racial melodrama deploys the paradoxical location of strength in weakness—the process by which suffering subjects take what Nietzsche calls *ressentiment*, a moralizing revenge upon the powerful achieved through a triumph of the weak in their very weakness. In contemporary political terms this is what feminist political scientist Wendy Brown has called the overvaluation of the "wound" in the political rhetoric of liberal identity politics (Brown 1995, 67). As we have already seen, Lauren Berlant has further investigated the process by which pain and suffering confers moral power on "wounded" subjects (Berlant 1998, 637; Berlant 2000). Ever since the abolitionist and suffrage movements, Berlant argues, individual citizens have been most compellingly identified with the national collectivity not through a universalist rhetoric of abstract citizenship but through a "capacity for suffering and trauma" viewed as the core of citizenship (Berlant 1998, 636). "It would not be exaggerating to say that sentimentality has long been the more popular rhetorical means by which pain is advanced, in the United States, as the true core of personhood and political collectivity. It operates when relatively privileged national subjects are exposed to the suffering of their intimate Others, so that to be virtuous requires feeling the pain of flawed or denied citizenship as their own pain" (Berlant 2000).

Nowhere has this advancement of pain as the true core of personhood and political collectivity been more in evidence than in the "big" melodramas of racially beset victims that have galvanized American audiences over the past century and a half—on stage, in film, and on television. From the moment Simon Legree's whip first lent Uncle Tom a paradoxical visibility and dignity as a suffering, and thus worthy, human being, the political power of pain and suffering has been a key mechanism of melodrama's rhetorical power. But who has the franchise on being represented as suffering victims? Not only the racial minorities who found themselves at the wrong end of a whip or gun. Consider this compelling description of performances of Buffalo Bill's Wild West Show depicting wagon trains attacked by Indians toward the end of Ric Burns's PBS documentary *The West*: "This is a show about . . . the conquest of the West. Yet everything that the audience sees is Indians attacking whites. This is the strange story of an inverted conquest in which the conquerors are the victims. . . . What is going on when you celebrate a conquest and you only show yourself being victimized?" (*The West*, episode 8). What is going on, we should immediately recognize, is melodrama: the generation of sympathy for the position of suffering victims, in this case white settlers victimized by marauding "redmen." It is a peculiarly American form of melodrama in which virtue becomes inextricably linked to forms of racial victimization. The white settlers are not just victims in this scenario; they are racially beset victims who acquire moral legitimacy through the public spectacle of their suffering. Racial melodrama takes on enormous importance as the engine for the generation of legitimacy for racially constituted groups whose very claim to citizenship lies in these spectacles of pathos and action. Racial melodrama is the popular form that gives permission to these racially constituted groups to carry out actions that they could not carry out in the name of bald self-interest. In terms of our third feature of melodrama, the pathos of the suffering of white settlers victimized by marauding Indians in Buffalo Bill's Wild West Show ultimately authorizes the action of the conquest of the West. As Ric Burns's commentator puts it, it gives the impression of a conquest won without any intentional quest: "They attacked us and when we ended up, we had the whole continent."

How, then, should we go about grasping the importance of these stories in which racialized suffering trumps conventional attributes of power? This is where genre criticism, of the Western, or the "race problem" film, for example—while it may trace important traditions of the construction of racial victims and villains—fails to grasp the full measure of the phenomenon because it does not confront the mode of melodrama centrally. Recourse to a broader melodramatic mode can more fully grasp the complex networks and recombinations of racial victimization and vilification in American culture.

The rest of this book argues that since the mid-nineteenth century, melodrama has been, for better or worse, the primary way in which mainstream American culture has dealt with the moral dilemma of having first enslaved and then withheld equal rights to generations of African Americans. It argues that melodrama is the alchemy with which white supremacist American culture first turned its deepest guilt into a testament of virtue. But, as we shall see, it is also the alchemy by which African Americans would themselves eventually reframe both the Tom tradition of white sympathy for blacks and the anti-Tom tradition of sympathy for beleaguered whites to their own ends. Melodrama is therefore much more than an embarrassing, excessive leftover of popular Victorian theater; if the works we are about to examine are "melodramatic, melodramatic, terribly so," then we do well to do more than lament the "terribly so." Melodrama may prove central to who we are as a nation, and black and white racial melodrama may even prove central to the question of just who we mean when we say "we" are a nation.

2 "A Wonderful, 'Leaping' Fish": Varieties of *Uncle Tom*

"[*Uncle Tom's Cabin*] knew the large felicity of gathering in alike the small and the simple and the big and the wise, and had above all the extraordinary fortune of finding itself, for an immense number of people, much less a book than a state of vision, of feeling and of consciousness, in which they didn't sit and read and appraise and pass the time, but walked and talked and laughed and cried. . . . Letters, here, languished unconscious, and Uncle Tom, instead of making even one of the cheap short cuts through the medium in which books breathe, even as fishes in water, went gaily roundabout it altogether, as if a fish, a wonderful 'leaping' fish, had simply flown through the air. . . . If the amount of life represented in such a work is measurable by the ease with which representation is taken up and carried further, carried even violently furthest, the fate of Mrs. Stowe's picture was conclusive: it simply sat down wherever it lighted and made itself, so to speak, at home."

—Henry James

When Henry James called *Uncle Tom's Cabin* a "wonderful 'leaping' fish," he meant to describe the almost unfathomable popularity and ubiquity of a work that once seemed to leap freely about the American cultural landscape. "Leaping" beyond its original literary incarnation, Uncle Tom made itself "at home" in so many places that it was hard to pin down to any particular text or form. Following James's insight, this chapter assumes that we must attempt to understand these "leaps" into new forms of media if we are really to understand the power of "Mrs. Stowe's picture" and the variety of its ways of making itself "at home" in the culture. This means that, although we will certainly begin with Stowe's written "picture," it will only be as the starting point.

How, then, shall we approach the myriad, ephemeral performances of a "work" with no fixed text, with songs and dances that attached to certain versions and disappeared in others, over the course of eighty years, through the Civil War, the Spanish-American War, World War I, and beyond? Where do we find our text amid so many variations?[1] And how do we fathom the diverse racial feelings generated by a work that was once a revolutionary defiance of the presumed inhumanity of the black race but which now has become the very term for black servility?

A first step toward answering some of these questions will be to follow Eric Lott and diverge, at least initially, from the now-familiar path of feminist criticism that has been so crucial in locating the "sentimental power" of Stowe's novel. Feminist critics have been influential rehabilitators of Stowe's sentimental fiction, pointing out that the feelings generated by the novel ultimately were a major factor in inducing the nation to go to war over slavery. Jane Tompkins (1985, 134) notes that this sentimental power resides in the novel's retelling of the "culture's central religious myth of the crucifixion in terms of the nation's greatest political conflict—slavery—and of its most cherished social beliefs—the sanctity of motherhood and the family." But as we shall see, the varieties of Uncle Tom—as manifested in stage and film versions—have not been terribly respectful of those parts of the novel most revered by feminist critics, especially Rachel Halliday's idyllic Quaker kitchen, Miss Ophelia's brave overcoming of her own racial prejudices, or Cassy's moral and physical triumph over Simon Legree. Nor have they always been respectful of the novel's religious warnings and abolitionist politics.

Feminist and other literary critics have understandably shown little interest in the later, "watered-down" versions of Stowe's novel. Eric Sundquist (1986, 5), for example, views these versions as eviscerations of Stowe's power, verging in many cases on the grotesque excesses of blackface.[2] Though he may be right that these stage versions lost much of the emotional, religious, and political power of Stowe's jeremiad, it is a mistake to assume that Uncle Tom in blackface had no cultural power. To consider Uncle Tom apart from its blackface embodiments on stage and screen is to misunderstand the complex workings of racial sympathy that grounded all future melodramas of black and white. Following the lead of Eric Lott, I will argue that it is precisely in the confrontations and confluences of Stowe's Christian jeremiad against slavery with minstrelsy that we shall be able to grasp the full extent of this work's influence on national racial feeling. We will therefore examine the novel's relation first with blackface minstrelsy—in the ways the work was sung, danced, paraded, performed, and illustrated throughout the second half of the nineteenth century and well into the twentieth—and second (in the following chapter) as it began to mutate into a negrophobic response in the work of Thomas Dixon and D. W. Griffith. For it is as racial melodrama, played to the broadest American audience, alternating the melodramatic pathos of bondage and the action of escape, and not simply as a sentimental novel "written by, for, and about women" (Tompkins 1985, 125), that we shall grasp the infinite variety and vast influence of the work across decades. Let us begin, then, with Stowe's novel, so often opposed to minstrelsy, but also profoundly influenced by it.

The Novel

The claims for this work's influence and power are the strongest made for any novel in American history. The abolitionist senator Charles Sumner once declared that had there been no *Uncle Tom's Cabin,* there would have been no Lincoln in the White House (Whicher 1963, 563). Even more famously, Abraham Lincoln himself is reported to have said to Harriet Beecher Stowe, upon meeting her early during the Civil War, "So this is the little lady who made this big war" (Adams 1989, 8–9). And, finally, after the Civil War, no less an authority than Frederick Douglass wrote that Stowe's novel had been "a flash to light a million camp fires in front of the embattled hosts of slavery" (Adams 1989, 144).[3] What was the extraordinary power of this novel to "convulse a mighty nation" (Whicher 1963, 563)?

Stowe's novel tells the story of a "kindly" Kentucky slave owner, George Shelby, who, despite good intentions, sells two of his best slaves to pay a debt to a slave trader. The first slave, Uncle Tom, accepts his fate and goes unprotestingly; the second is Harry, the young son of Eliza, the mulatta wife of George Harris. Eliza escapes with Harry across the frozen Ohio River, where she is protected by Quakers and eventually joined by her escaped husband, George Harris. The novel alternates between the story of Eliza, heading north to freedom, and the story of Tom, heading south to even greater bondage. The "southern bondage story" tells of Tom as he is sold down the river, first to a kindly New Orleans master, St. Clare, where he encounters the angelic Little Eva, then to the demonic Simon Legree, where he is eventually beaten to death. The "northern escape story" tells of Eliza and George's escape, passing for white, first to the Quakers in Ohio, then to Canada, eventually to Africa.

The key to the novel's convulsive power is Stowe's interweaving of a conventional sentimental story of youthful female suffering on the model of Dickens (Little Eva's death by consumption) with a more distinctively American, story of a racialized Christlike passion (Tom's death by beatings from his white master). The combination created an unprecedented opportunity for melodramatic crossracial recognitions of virtue. Though Little Eva is the stereotyped tubercular child of countless sentimental novels and European- and British-derived stage melodramas, her suffering becomes newly powerful once it becomes clear that tuberculosis is simply the outward symptom of a much deeper ailment: the wrongs of slavery that the young girl takes to heart. Each time Eva learns more of the sufferings of slaves, she sickens a little more. Eventually, she uses her own dying as a kind of emotional blackmail to force her father to promise to free his slaves.

48

Throughout Eva's illness and death, Tom bears witness to her suffering; more than any member of her immediate family, he is the key "recognizer" of her virtue. When St. Clare dies suddenly thereafter (before freeing his slaves), Tom is sold even further down the proverbial river. Like Eva, he too takes on the moral weight of the sufferings of slavery, pitying his fellow slaves, refusing to beat them when ordered, praying for them. When Tom resists the moral authority of his evil master, insisting on the higher authority of Christ, Simon Legree beats him to death. Once again, as with Tom's witness to Eva's suffering, an empathic crossracial witness in the person of his former master's son, George Shelby, Jr., is there to recognize his virtue.

These two racially victimized deaths, one white but recognized as virtuous by a black, one black but recognized as virtuous by a white, function as black-and-white mirror reversals. White readers are effectively "set up" in the first half of the novel, by the more conventional display of docile African grief for the death of Eva, for the (then) much more revolutionary display of white sympathy for virtuous black victims in the second half. African (Americans) whose primary depiction in popular American culture had previously been as objects of fun, suddenly became, in and through this work, new objects of sympathy by whites. While there was nothing particularly novel about a melodramatic story of a lost "space of innocence" created by the separation of families, the premature deaths of innocent children, or the martyrdom of a devout Christian, the application of these familiar tropes of both sentimental fiction and stage melodrama to African characters achieved, almost overnight, a "moral reframing" of the issue of slavery by northern readers (Hanne 1994, 89). The novel's first publication in serial form in 1851 appeared at a transitional moment of white northern opinions of slavery, and became a catalyst of change over the next decade solidifying, by 1861, into irreconcilably antagonistic blocs of North and South (Hanne 1994, 93). But this is only to consider the novel's influence on those who read it. From the very beginning, and even from its conception, Stowe's novel was something more than literature; its most emotionally resonant components were melodramatic moving pictures.

"Mrs. Stowe's Picture"

According to her son, Charles Stowe, the genesis of Stowe's novel came to her in a melodramatic vision of a beaten and bleeding slave. Like D.W. Griffith's similarly apocalyptic description of the genesis of *The Birth of a Nation* out of an image of his earliest memory—his father's sword, "the sword [that] . . .

became a flashing vision" (Geduld 1971, 13–14; Rogin 1984, 215)—this "moving picture" represented a deeply felt solution to the previous impasse of Stowe's own life.

Charles Stowe informs us that as Stowe sat in the First Parish Church in Brunswick, Maine, in the winter of 1851, she was haunted by both moral and **49** religious doubt: the recent suicide of her brother George, a devoutly religious man who felt he had failed to achieve the "perfection" his millennial creed demanded of him; doubts about her own perfection as wife, housewife, mother, and quasi-citizen; and doubts about the immoral compromises of the Fugitive Slave Act, which called for the return of escaped slaves to their owners, suddenly making even abolitionists complicit with the sins of slavery. During the Eucharistic celebration of the body and blood of the suffering Christ, a vivid picture of a whipped and bleeding male slave appeared before her eyes: "It seemed as if the crucified, but now risen and glorified Christ was speaking to her through the poor black man, cut and bleeding through the blows of the slave whip" (Stowe 1911, 145). According to her son, she could hardly keep from weeping aloud. On returning home "she wrote out the vision which had been as it were blown into her mind as by the rushing of a mighty wind" (Stowe 1911, 48).

This hyper-visual icon of racial victimization proved to be Stowe's way out of the impasse of elitist Calvinist doctrines of perfectionism. Instead of striving, as she had previously striven, for personal perfection in an imperfect world, Stowe found a way to synthesize an interest in the common and the "lowly"—whether slave, woman, or child—with evangelical exaltation (Hedrick 1991, 353). The black imitation of the life of Christ allowed her to see similarities in the lowly realities of primitive Christianity, the contemporary lives of slaves, and her own life as a woman and mother. Everyday sinners and sufferers thus became for her an important new source of moral and creative energy. Replacing the unrealistic and impossible-to-emulate doctrine of Calvinist perfection (which had only brought her brother to suicide) with a new gospel of suffering that united her experiences as a woman and mother with that of an oppressed male slave, Stowe found a way out of her spiritual impasse. That way out was an infusion of democratic religious fervor, grounded in the linked suffering of an innocent child with an adult male slave, into the popular mode of melodrama. Thus was assimilated the preexisting abolitionist figure of the "Christian slave" to the preexisting mode of melodrama—that crass popular word Stowe had at least pretended not to know (see chapter 1) but whose mode was quite familiar to her through her reading of Dickens.[4]

On June 5, 1851, Stowe published the first installment of *Uncle Tom's Cabin* in a Washington, D.C., weekly abolitionist magazine, the *National Era*. Although this first periodized version of the novel would have no illustrations, Stowe wrote to her editor, "My vocation is simply that of a painter, and my object will be to hold up in the most lifelike and graphic manner possible

Slavery, its reverses, changes, and the negro character which I have had ample opportunities for studying. There is no arguing with *pictures* and everybody is impressed by them, whether they mean to be or not" (Hedrick 1994, 208).

On March 20, 1852, this thirty-nine-year-old mother of six, wife of theologian Calvin Stowe, and daughter of the famous preacher Lyman Beecher published the whole of *Uncle Tom's Cabin, or Life among the Lowly* in two volumes. This first edition, published by John Jewett, included six full-page illustrations from engravings drawn by Hammatt Billings, an illustrator with abolitionist sympathies who had designed a masthead for William Lloyd Garrison's abolitionist newspaper, the *Liberator*. The most frequently reproduced of these depicted the interracial amity of Tom and Eva sitting in the garden reading the bible and communing about the life to come. The book's cover, however, immediately literalized Stowe's "picture" of Tom's cabin, depicting the doorway of the cabin with Chloe standing in it, the children milling about, and Tom approaching with a hoe (Fig. 2.1). It is significant, however, that despite the generative importance of the beating icon in Stowe's imagination, that this particular incendiary image is omitted (as it would frequently be omitted from many of the early stage adaptations of the novel). It would seem that the "pictures" that were most immediately extracted from the novel were initially those of home, family, and interracial amity.

The novel abounds with moving pictures in a Dickensian tradition that would prove to be almost instantly reproducible the world over. The authenticity of Stowe's picture of slavery would be much challenged, both by its defenders and by later critics who wondered at how much opportunity this New Englander who had lived for a while in Cincinnati had really had for studying the conditions of slavery. (The answer, of course, is that she had no more direct opportunity than did her minstrel predecessors who rubbed elbows with free blacks but actually had no direct southern experiences.) However, Stowe's appeal to the automatic truth of pictures, like her vision of the whipped and bleeding slave who appeared to her in church, was never a matter of faithful photographic record but of impassioned vision—a vision with the power to move readers or viewers to sympathy with newly racialized, victims. An invigorated and evangelized American racial melodrama was born in this vision, and its power was measured in tears.[5] As Stowe later wrote in her 1879 preface to the novel, the beating death of Uncle Tom convulsed her in tears and did the same to two of her young sons when she read it to them. Thus the novel that would eventually "convulse a mighty nation" first convulsed a mother and her children through the moving picture of a beaten and bleeding black man *recognized* as a racial victim by empathic white readers.

It was not until the second, 1853, edition of the now-runaway bestseller that Stowe's beating vision was included in a group of expanded illustrations. These drawings were again by Hammatt Billings for what was now a single-volume edition.[6] The picture of Tom's beating condenses separate moments

UNCLE TOM'S CABIN;

OR,

LIFE AMONG THE LOWLY.

BY

HARRIET BEECHER STOWE.

VOL. I.

BOSTON:
JOHN P. JEWETT & COMPANY.
CLEVELAND, OHIO:
JEWETT, PROCTOR & WORTHINGTON.
1852.

Figure 2.1   Title page illustration by Hammatt Billings for the first edition of *Uncle Tom's Cabin*, showing the eponymous cabin. (Harriet Beecher Stowe Center, Hartford, Conn.)

from the novel. The first moment is Tom's beating by Sambo and Quimbo as punishment for failing to flog a slave woman who did not pick enough cotton. This beating is ordered by Legree. When Tom refuses to accept his authority ("my soul an't yours Massr!"), Legree has him whipped. But Stowe, for all her inspiration taken from the vision of a beaten slave, does not depict the whipping itself.[7] In the next two instances of beating, Stowe devotes a single sentence to Legree's action, first: " 'D—n you!' said Legree, as with one blow of his fist he felled Tom to the earth" (330); and even more simply for the final blow: "Legree, foaming with rage, smote his victim to the ground" (358; all subsequent references to the novel are from Ammons 1994).

Stowe almost apologizes in the next paragraph for her lack of graphic detail: "Scenes of blood and cruelty are shocking to our ear and heart. What man has nerve to do, man has not nerve to hear. What brother-man and brother-Christian must suffer, cannot be told us, even in our secret chamber, it so harrows up the soul!" (358). But having started down the path of pictorialism, having ventured to say what this "brother Christian must suffer," Stowe's second illustrator finally depicts what she herself "has not nerve to show." In a half-page illustration found on page 517 of the 1853 edition, a strong and virile Tom (not at all the doddering elderly man of later stage and film versions) crouches before a post to which his hands are tied while two slaves (Sambo and Quimbo in the text) whip his back. Legree urges them on from the right background and a Christ figure, only half drawn, holds a cross up to Tom on the left (Fig. 2.2). The figure of Christ derives from yet another moment of Tom's suffering when he lies dying after receiving Legree's fatal blow: "Was he alone, that long night, whose brave, loving spirit was bearing up, in that old shed, against buffeting and brutal stripes? Nay! There stood by him ONE,—seen by him alone,—'like unto the Son of God' " (358).

In these illustrations we see how an iconographic tradition grounded in Stowe's "moving pictures" begins to take on a life of its own. Billings's illustration of the beating depicts the vision that inspired Stowe to write but to which her novel only alludes elliptically. Stowe's eschatological vision seeks to demonstrate the Christlike suffering of Tom and his salvation. Billings chooses to illustrate the moment Sambo and Quimbo beat Tom rather than the two other moments when Stowe—however briefly—shows Legree beating him. It is possible that at this early moment in the developing iconography of the Tom story—an iconography that would eventually flood the world—that outright violence between the races, unlike interracial amity, was still too incendiary. However, this image of white-on-black beating would eventually become a staple of the Tom iconography in the more explicitly abolitionist works mounted before the Civil War as well as in most works presented in the North in the postwar era. Consider, for example, figure 2.3, a fully conventionalized postbellum advertisement for the play. In this image, the suffering of an elderly black man at the hands of a conventionalized stage villain emerges as

Figure 2.2 Half-page illustration from the 1853 edition. The beating of Tom, by Hammatt Billings. (Harriet Beecher Stowe Center, Hartford, Conn.)

the key element of pathos. Black suffering—not black suffering leading to spiritual struggle and resistance—is paramount, and Tom has become the old uncle of conventional stage representations.

Interracial Sympathy: Weeping and Wailing

Weeping is the agency of the recognition of virtue in Stowe's novel. It is never a merely passive wallowing in powerless tears. Early in the novel, when Mrs. Shelby arrives at Tom's cabin to bid him goodbye after her husband has sold him to a slave trader, she weeps with Tom, Aunt Chloe and the children: "And in those tears they all shed together, the high and the lowly, melted away all the heart-burnings and anger of the oppressed. O, ye who visit the distressed, ye know that everything your money can buy . . . is not worth one honest tear shed in real sympathy" (167). To a Dickensian class tradition of rich and poor weeping together, Stowe adds the dimension of race. As Mrs. Shelby weeps with Tom and his family, an initial bond of sympathy between the races is forged. It will be the business of the novel to multiply and intensify

Figure 2.3   A conventional depiction of Tom's beating from a postbellum advertisement for the play. (Harriet Beecher Stowe Center, Hartford, Conn.)

its forms. Stowe's much-noted asides to mothers, usually asking them to take action against the "patriarchal institution" of slavery, are thus grounded in an emotional bond between white mother and black.[8]

What was new in Stowe's novel were thus not the tears of the powerless—which had long been staples of sentimental fiction by lady novelists, and of stage melodramas like *The Drunkard* (1844)—but the use of tears to cross racial barriers, to create new pictures of interracial amity and emotional intimacy. The racial dimension of these "sympathetic vibrations"[9] was new. In the case of Eva's death, this picture occurs twice: first when Eva, knowing she is about to die, distributes locks of her hair to her father's assembled slaves, and second on her deathbed proper. In the first instance, Eva announces her imminent departure to the assembled slaves, eliciting initial "sobs, and lamentations." She then preaches to them about the care of their souls, admonishing them to pray and read the bible, but when she suddenly realizes that they can not read, it is her turn to sob for them. Thus black and white weep for one another. The slaves weep for Eva who dies because of slavery and she, in turn, weeps for their enslaved state.[10] Even Topsy succumbs to this tearful recognition of a white virtue overcome by the oppression of black suffering. Thus the novel asks its white readers to empathize with black suffering initially through the medium of its white angel.

When Eva finally dies, St. Clare, unable to bear Eva's "mortal agony," turns to Tom for comfort:

> "O, God, this is dreadful!" he said, turning away in agony and wringing Tom's hand, scarce conscious what he was doing. 'O, Tom, my boy it is killing me!'
>
> Tom had his master's hands between his own; and, with tears streaming down his dark cheeks, looked up for help where he had always been used to look. (257)

Thus Tom and St. Clare, slave and master, bond in mutual sympathy for the racially motivated death of Evangeline. This scene would become a set piece of all subsequent stage and film versions embellished by ever-more elaborate tableaux of Eva's ascent into heaven and of swelling black choruses lamenting her death. As we shall see, while many subsequent theatrical versions of the novel might omit Tom's death or Eliza's escape, Eva's death was the one essential scene (Fig. 2.4). Tom's death is its much more incendiary mirror reversal. In place of Eva's opulent bedroom and crowd of mourners, Tom lies for two days dying on a bed of dirty cotton. But Tom too requires an interracial witness to his glory. Though his young master, George Shelby, arrives "too late" to rescue him, he is "in the nick of time" to recognize his suffering: "Tears which did honor to his manly heart fell from the young man's eyes, as he bent over his poor friend" (362). And thus, for the first time in popular American culture a white man weeps over the racial suffering of a slave (Fig. 2.5).

Sympathy between black and white is thus made possible by the initial perception that Eva's death is a refusal to live in a world where a romantically racialized black virtue must suffer. Little Eva's own (entirely incommensurate) "racialized" suffering enables a black reflection in that of Uncle Tom.

Figure 2.4   Death of Eva. (*Uncle Tom's Cabin*, Universal, Harry Pollard, 1927).

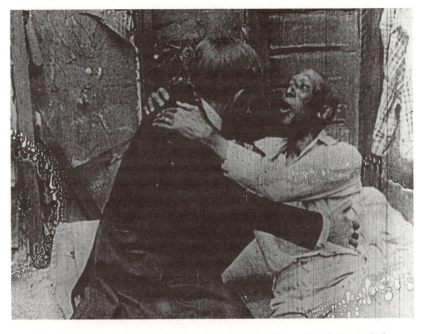

Figure 2.5   George Shelby, Jr., embraces the dying Tom. (*Uncle Tom's Cabin*, World Producing Corporation, Robert Daly, 1914)

Much as Little Eva seems today extraneous to a contemporary appreciation of the horror of slavery, her function in the novel and on stage in the 1850s was a crucial preparation for audiences unused to taking black suffering seriously. With *Uncle Tom's Cabin*, Africans had become, in Philip Fisher's (1985, 98) words, "novel objects of feelings." While the melodramatic sympathy for the virtue of a beset victim was not new, the racialized object of these feelings was.

But how novel exactly? Certainly, as Eric Lott has shown, Africans had long been constructed as "creatures of feeling" in popular American consciousness and by white men in blackface on the minstrel stage (Lott 1993, 33). Abolitionists as well had long employed what George Fredrickson (1994, 433) calls "romantic racialism"—the belief in the special docility and emotionality of Africans—to argue that Negroes were unjustly enslaved.[11] Indeed, Stowe did not invent the beating vision; it had long been a topos of antislavery literature in the United States and England. What Stowe invented was a way to make even those not susceptible to abolitionist politics feel its melodramatic pathos and action. Romantic racialism asserted the moral superiority of feeling over intellect, of affection, docility, and patience over Anglo-Saxon coldness, will, and impetuosity. It could be used to assert the moral—if not the intellectual—superiority of Negroes over Anglo-Saxons. To argue for the humanity of slaves on the basis of the Negro's childlike, feminine innocence was obviously a two-edged sword, leading, on the one hand, to the assertion of permanent differences between blacks and whites, and, on the other hand, to the politically radical awakening to a common humanity before God. While exhibition of Negro sympathy for Little Eva's death did little to challenge the status quo of racial hierarchy, it prepared the way for the more revolutionary challenge of Tom's death. The demonstration of white sympathy for this death leads, first, in the novel, to George Shelby's weeping, next to the freeing of his slaves, and, finally, in American history, to Civil War.

Home, Bondage, and Escape

Leslie Fiedler (1982, 157) has noted that Harriet Beecher Stowe's novel contains "the most compendious gallery of homes in all American literature," ranging from the good "old Kentucky" home through the elegant but decadent villa of the St. Clares's, to the squalid, Gothic mansion of Simon Legree. Here is Stowe's description of the eponymous cabin home from a chapter entitled "An Evening in Uncle Tom's Cabin."

> The cabin of Uncle Tom was a small log building, close adjoining to "the house," as the negro *par excellence* designates his master's dwelling. In front it had a neat garden-patch, where, every summer, strawberries, raspberries, and a variety of fruits and vegetables, flourished

under careful tending. The whole front of it was covered by a large scarlet bigonia and a native multiflora rose, which, entwisting and interlacing, left scarce a vestige of the rough logs to be seen. Here, also, in summer, various brilliant annuals, such as marigolds, petunias, four-o'clocks, found an indulgent corner in which to unfold their splendors, and were the delight and pride of Aunt Chloe's heart. (16)

Several more paragraphs establish the idyllic homeyness of the neat cabin: Aunt Chloe's corn cakes, hoe cakes, dodgers, and muffins; the neat "drawing room" corner of the cabin, complete with a portrait of General Washington, drawn and colored in a way that "would have astonished that hero" (16). At a table covered with a cloth and already set for dinner, Uncle Tom is seated at a reading lesson offered by his master's thirteen-year-old son. From the very beginning the special virtue of Uncle Tom's cabin (both novel and home) lies in its representation of interracial sympathy: a humble black man is taught to read scripture by his white master's son.

Melodrama is fueled by nostalgia for a lost home. We saw in the first chapter how basic the longing to return to a "space of innocence" is to the form and how central this innocence is to the function of recognizing virtue. In American culture this quest for a lost childhood was already fatefully linked to the South and to the southern plantation—sometimes euphemistically called a "farm"—in minstrel songs. These songs, as we shall see below, cemented the connection between the rural southern home of what in the postbellum period would come to be called "the old South." With *Uncle Tom's Cabin*, the humble iconography of the slave cabin was introduced as a figure of virtue and nostalgia. Though this nostalgia would often open up troubling associations with the plantation myth—its insistent humbleness, coupled with the fact that Tom, Eliza, and her son Harry could never regain its idyll— meant that this home constituted a particularly poignant and elusive "space of innocence."

For the good home is perpetually deferred in this novel. Indeed, both Eva and Tom decide that heaven is preferable. As Tom tells George: "O, Mas'r George, ye're too late. The Lord's bought me, and is going to take me home,— and I long to go. Heaven is better than Kintuck" (362). Both Eliza and Tom encounter a succession of substitutes for their original "old Kentucky home." In the southern bondage story, Tom encounters a "good" master but never a real home. Sold down the river, he encounters its Gothic antithesis.

For Stowe—and indeed for the entirety of black and white racial melodrama—the topos of home is particularly fraught. Home raises the question of whether, or how, the races so melodramatically entwined within the novel in their mutual sorrows shall live together when the sorrows of slavery have passed. Like Tom, Eliza and her family also reject "Kintuck" as home. Nor, after the enforcement of the Fugitive Slave Law, could home be a free state like Ohio. Nor could it be Canada or France, where they live for a while until political troubles send them back to the "free states." In a chapter entitled "Results," Stowe grapples with the question of where her reunited slave family will live out the putative "happy ending" she has provided them.

In the end, Stowe's deeply unsatisfying "solution" is to have the group embrace Africa (specifically Liberia) as their "true" home. George's reasons are worth examining. Acknowledging that his race has "equal rights to mingle in the American republic as the Irishman, the German, the Swede" (375), he spurns these rights to argue for what Arthur Riis calls racial nationalism: "I want a country, a nation, of my own. I think that the African race has peculiarities yet to be unfolded in the light of civilization and Christianity, which, if not the same with those of the Anglo-Saxon, may prove to be, morally, of even a higher type" (375–6). Though he can pass as white, George chooses Africa, casting his lot with the African race. Yet unlike Alex Haley's later quest for his African roots, this identification with the oppressed is also a clear identification with the maternal feminine: "My sympathies are not for my father's race, but for my mother's. To him I was no more than a fine dog or horse: to my poor heart-broken mother I was a *child*. . . . When I think of all she suffered, of my own early sufferings, of the distresses and struggles of my heroic wife . . . I have no wish to pass for an American, or to identify myself with them" (374).

Choosing to identify with his racially marked mother-home rather than with that of his father, George's choice also conveniently "solves" the problem of any future black-white alliances by creating separate (and not very equal) homes. Stowe's narrative argues for the humanity of black slaves by placing them in close contact with whites—whether in the comic Topsy/Ophelia relation, the cruel Tom/Legree relation, or in the sympathetic intergenerational and intergender Tom/Eva relation. The melodrama of escape and bondage thus places the races in emotional contacts of both kindness and cruelty. But the "happy" ending of the novel posits the recovery of a racially pure "mother-home" that challenges the law of paternity and the foregoing lessons of racial sympathy. Thus Stowe intellectually constructs a notion of family grounded not simply in relations of blood, but more importantly in relations of race. As Arthur Riis (1994, 534) argues, Stowe's notion of the integrity of the family is based not only on the fact that the children are related to the parents, but on the fact that the parents are biologically related to one another. Rather than conflating the category of the family and the notion of race, she imagines that ascriptions of race actually replace paternity as the ultimate mark of belonging to a family. Race thus serves as the only legitimate sign of the family.

For George Harris and the other survivors from "mother Africa," this highly feminized figure of race thus also becomes the figure of home. The problem with this formulation is that while it is powerfully argued by George, it is not powerfully felt or imagined either in the novel or in the larger melodra-

Figure 2.6 Illustration by Hammatt Billings for the 1853 edition of *Uncle Tom's Cabin*: "Freedom to Africa." (Harriet Beecher Stowe Center, Hartford, Conn.)

matic pictorial tradition of the Tom material. Significantly, neither Stowe nor her first illustrator can manage to "picture" this African home with any "homey" detail. Stowe herself never even tries a depiction. She simply has George make the argument cited above. Billings, her first illustrator, attempts to offer a picture, but he too can only accomplish an abstraction: a broken manacle in the foreground and a large crowd of mostly undifferentiated slaves with arms raised in the direction of a rising or a setting sun where the words "FREEDOM TO AFRICA" are inscribed (Fig. 2.6). It is not clear from this final illustration of the book whether Africa itself is being wished freedom or whether the freed slaves are projecting themselves toward a free Africa. One thing is clear, however: neither Stowe nor her illustrator has a clear icon of it as home.

Almost by default, then, Kentucky goes on functioning, narratively, iconically, and musically as the locus of virtue both in the novel and in its popular stage versions. None of the myriad stage versions of the novel even hints at this "back to Africa" solution. Familiar yet exotic, Kentucky, not an utterly alien Africa, continues to function emotionally as the good southern home. The question of how blacks and whites shall live together in this home is thus very much on the agenda from the beginning of black and white racial melodrama.

While the feminized disempowering of the African male has been much noted in the entire Tom tradition, the concomitant masculinized empowerment of the African woman has not. We have only to contrast Eliza's active, self-propelled escape across the ice with Anna's passive fainting on, and rescue from, the ice in Griffith's *Way Down East* (1920) to appreciate the difference. Griffith's white Victorian maiden-in-distress was rescued by a chivalrous white hero. In contrast, Stowe's mulatta maidens — Eliza, Cassy, and Emmeline — cannot rely upon "their men" as rescuers and so save themselves.[12]

Throughout the first half of the nineteenth century, the popular melodramas that dominated the American stage were about charismatic male heroes seeking, as Bruce McConachie puts it, "freedom, revenge, or death" (McConachie 1992, 91). Edwin Forest's roles as Spartacus in *The Gladiators* (1831) and as a seventeenth-century Wampanoag chief in the Native American melodrama *Metamora* (1829) are typical. Both these heroes seek freedom, fail, and become heroic martyrs. Contemporary abolitionist accounts of slavery differed very little from these masculine heroic models. Stowe's biographer has noted that prior to *Uncle Tom's Cabin*, the conventional "Freedom narrative" of the period, like the resistance to the Fugitive Slave Law, was primarily cast as a heroic "male plot." Male slaves told stories of leaving behind wives, mothers, and children to seek freedom. Even if they managed to bring along family in their escape, as did Josiah Hensen, the central story remained theirs (Hedrick 1994, 212–13).

Frederick Douglass's versions of this story, told most familiarly in his first autobiography (1845) as well as his short story, "The Heroic Slave" (1853), are cases in point. In both, the black male slave escapes, leaving behind a woman whose own story is ignored. In the fictional short story, Madison Washington is a slave who escapes to Canada but returns to rescue his wife. She is killed in the effort and he is recaptured. Later, however, he leads a successful revolt of slaves aboard a ship, proving his heroism a second time. In the autobiography, which has by now eclipsed Stowe's as the canonical slave narrative, Douglass himself does much the same thing: he escapes to New York and sends for his "intended wife" — a woman who has not previously appeared in the narrative.[13] Douglass attributes his ability to escape to an initial recognition of his condition of slavery and then to his acquisition of a heroic masculine identity that transcends it. In both cases, this recognition occurs when he sees female slaves — most memorably his aunt Hester — beaten by their white masters. His own heroic identity is grounded in a sympathetic recognition of the suffering of these women as slaves. But at the same time, as recent feminist critics have argued, he disidentifies with the femininity of the slave condition. Throughout his autobiography, and despite the fact that Douglass informs us that he himself was frequently beaten, the significant beatings are enacted on women, with Douglass looking on. In melodramatic fashion, Douglass sympathizes deeply with the beaten bodies of the slave women. But he also gains his own sense of difference from these suffering female bodies. As Gwen Bergner has argued, "manhood" and "freedom" become linked, as do "womanhood" and "bondage." It is not that Douglass is complicit with his master's power, or even that he identifies with his power, but his own freedom and manhood seem to need this image of female bondage as a measure of his own difference (Bergner 1998, 255–56).

Thus before the publication of Stowe's novel the story of female bondage and male escape was the convention for slave narratives; Harriet Jacobs's *Incidents in the Life of a Slave Girl*, which broke this mold, would not be published until 1861. Stowe's great melodramatic innovation was thus her *feminization of the freedom narrative* through the characters of Eliza, Cassy, and Emmeline—and her *masculinization of the bondage narrative and the beating vision* through the character of Uncle Tom. By this simple reversal, Stowe reenergized what were already, by 1852, stale gender conventions of melodramatic pathos and action even in slave narratives. Tom's (passive, feminine) story of patient bondage, going against the grain of more conventional heroic melodramas of oppressed slaves, is thus sandwiched between (active, masculine) stories of self-rescue by two brave and adventurous female slaves, going against the grain of conventional portrayals of women as helpless victims: Eliza's harrowing escape with baby Harry over the ice would become a staple icon of the tradition, immediately picked up by Billings, her first illustrator, and embellished in subsequent forms (see Fig. 1.1). Cassy's ingenious haunting of Legree, which permits her to walk boldly down the road to freedom with fellow slave Emmeline dressed as a ghost, was also significant although much less pictorialized in the later tradition.[14]

No white, middle-class heroine in a melodrama of this period is capable of such masculine heroic action as Eliza.[15] And no white hero demonstrates such passive feminine virtue as Uncle Tom. Upon this basic gender reversal, so despised by contemporary black male critics, rests much of the power of all subsequent performances of the work as melodramatic pathos and action. Influential African-American critics, like James Baldwin, who have understandably deplored the emasculation of Tom in Stowe's novel, have not always noted the accompanying empowerment of black women in the same tradition. Baldwin vehemently rejected the "excessive and spurious" dream of black martyrdom in the stereotype of an Uncle Tom "robbed of his humanity and divested of his sex" (Baldwin 1949, 578). This condemnation of Uncle Tom was in its own time a politically and artistically empowering rejection of the stereotype of black (male) servility. Published almost a hundred years after the novel, it marked the definitive end of the popular appeal, to blacks or whites, of a novel whose martyred main character's name had now become an epithet of servility. After this essay, to be moved by the Tom story would be considered racially retrograde by most progressive thinkers.[16] It would take no less than a feminist reorganization of literary history itself—in the form of Jane Tompkins's 1978 throwing down the gauntlet to white male critics and the white male canon—before the novel would again gain cultural capital among progressive (this time white feminist) thinkers.

But here we might pause to ask what both Baldwin and Tompkins leave out of the novel in order to make their different claims. In order to defend the project of sentimental fiction's "monumental effort to reorganize culture from the woman's point of view" (Tompkins 1985, 124) Tompkins, must, every bit as much as Baldwin, neglect the novel's exciting action and its active empowerment of (light-skinned) black women. While she importantly permits us to value the passive feminine Christian ethic of sacrifice that underlies the novel, and while she notes that it "retells the culture's central religious myth— the story of the crucifixion—in terms of the nation's greatest political conflict—slavery" (Tompkins 1985, 134), she misses the equally important point that this story goes in two directions at once. If what I have been calling the bondage story enacted by a black man is the passive acceptance of suffering on the model of Christ, the escape story enacted by women represents a much overlooked active resistance to bondage. And this resistance occurs not only in the story of Eliza, at the beginning, but in the story of Cassy and Emmeline at the end.

In a remarkably playful chapter immediately following the death of Tom, called "An Authentic Ghost Story," Stowe shows Cassy carrying through a "stratagem" of exploiting Legree's superstition and guilt by haunting the garret at the top of his house. Having previously complained to Legree that the garret made ghostly sounds in the middle of the night, Cassy now places a bottle neck in a knothole to ensure that ghostly sounds are produced by the wind. Soon she has linked Legree's guilt over past crimes committed in this garret to its apparent ghosts. The last place Legree would ever go now to look for an escaped slave is this garret. Cassy and Emmeline boldly escape into the night, but circle back from the swamps, where the dogs will follow them, to hide in the garret right under Legree's nose. From this hiding place they later escape undetected, with no dogs following, well provided with Legree's own money. Stowe reports the events in the following playful manner:

> Authorities were somewhat divided, as to the outward form of the spirit, owing to a custom quite prevalent among negroes,—and, for aught we know, among whites too—of invariably shutting the eyes, and covering up heads under blankets, petticoats, or whatever else might come in use for a shelter. . . . There were abundance of full-

length portraits of the ghost, abundantly sworn and testified to, which, as is often the case with portraits, agreed with each other in no particular, except the common family peculiarity of the ghost tribe,—the wearing of a *white sheet*." (365)[17]

Thus does a "tall figure in a white sheet" avenge the death of Tom by walking "at the most approved ghostly hours, around the Legree premises," shattering Legree's nerves (366). And thus, finally, do the Negroes on the place see "two white figures gliding down the avenue towards the high-road" (367). In this episode, leisurely extended over the last few chapters of the novel, and "cross-cut" with the pathetic death in bondage of Tom, Stowe offers a remarkably humorous variation and expansion on the novel's earlier, and much briefer, escape of Eliza. Yet neither Eliza's escape nor the remarkable revenge-escape—with which Cassy not only avenges Tom but rescues Legree's new concubine, Emmeline—receives any note in Tompkins's account. She places her emphasis, instead, on the matriarchal epiphany of white Rachel Halliday's kitchen.

The problem with Tompkins's reading of the novel is thus not unlike Baldwin's: both see the work as an exclusively female form. For Baldwin it is a scold, for Tompkins it is a maternal "eschatological vision." Tompkins's claim that the genre of the sentimental novel to which it belongs is "written by, for, and about women" is an unwitting ghettoization of a novel that had precisely moved beyond such gender-limited appeal. Baldwin's claim that Tom is "desexed" by a feminized Christianity also fails to appreciate the vigorous empowerment of Eliza, Cassy, and Emmeline. It is striking, in fact, that the novel that begins its exciting action with Eliza inviting Tom to flee also ends with a similar appeal by Cassy. In this novel, if not always in the stage and film versions that follow, light-skinned black women act while the dark-skinned black man suffers.[18]

I do not wish to detract either from Tompkins's just celebration of white female sentimental power, or from Baldwin's just anger at black male disempowerment. But I do want to channel both of these concerns into a longer range view of what is at stake in the entwined issues of race and gender in the "Tom," and the subsequent "anti-Tom," popular traditions. Baldwin, for example, is silent about the function of Tom's "desexing" as a counter to another, perhaps even more insidious stereotype of the comically oversexed, lazy Zip Coon of minstrel caricature. His argument against "Everybody's Protest Novel" is ultimately against its schematic, "black and white" stereotypes and its endorsement of a "cause" at the expense of novelistic truth. However, the "desexed" black male stereotype must be understood, not in the context of novelistic truth, but in the context of the stereotype it, in turn, overturns: in this case, that of the comically virile, "oversexed" caricatures of blackface minstrelsy. The "Tom" material's revolutionary consequences in the antebellum period were a direct result of its historically unprecedented recognition of the humanity of slaves. It is thus quite true that the novel could only create this humanity by "divest[ing Tom] of his sex" and, in effect, feminizing him. However, the black and white, Manichaean stereotypes of melodrama need to be judged, not in relation to authentic and objective historical "truths" apparent to all, but in relation to previous, and subsequent, stereotypes.   **65**

Consider, for example, two icons of Uncle Tom used as advertisements for stage productions taken from a much later era, *Stetson's Double Mammouth Uncle Tom* (Fig. 2.7 and **2.8**). Double Mammouth productions of *Uncle Tom's Cabin* were a phenomenon of the 1880s modeled vaguely on the practice of combining two circus companies into one Mammouth show. In this case, two Tom shows would double the performers in the key roles: two Toms, two Topsies, and so on. Harry Birdoff (1947, 310–12) notes that in some shows these doubled characters could be played as alter egos. *The Stetson Double Mammouth Uncle Tom* was performed under a giant canvas that seated four thousand. In figure 2.7, the first Tom is pictured as a grotesquely comic figure based on minstrel stereotype; in figure 2.8, he is an older version of the domestic paterfamilias of Stowe's opening chapters.

The point is that Stowe's "ennobling" feminization of Uncle Tom, so empowering to Tompkins's (white) feminism and so disempowering to Baldwin's (black male) modernism, needs to be seen first in the context of popular representations of blackness contemporary with Stowe's novel, and later on a stage strongly influenced by minstrelsy, and then again in relation to its "anti-Tom" reaction. Indeed, all of these representations were deeply informed by American stage traditions of blackface minstrelsy that projected comically grotesque forms of virility onto black male bodies but that were also simultaneously beginning to imagine the pathos of suffering slaves. We thus need to better understand the blackface minstrel tradition upon which the Tom material drew, from which it diverged, and to which it also, eventually, contributed, before we can tackle what *Uncle Tom's Cabin* became when it began to be embodied on stage.

Blackface Minstrelsy and Melos/Drama

Once *Uncle Tom's Cabin* "leaped" from the pages of Stowe's novel to the popular stage and once, according to the conventions of the day, Uncle Tom was portrayed by a white actor in blackface, melodrama was, in Eric Lott's words, "spliced to blackface performance" (Lott 1993, 211). Thus *Uncle Tom's Cabin*, the quintessential expression of abolitionist maternal sentiment, came abruptly into contact with minstrelsy, the quintessential expression of white male racist power and potency. How did they influence one another?

Figure 2.7   A minstrel show version of Uncle Tom pictured in an advertisement for *Stetson's Double Mammouth Uncle Tom* in which Tom is an ape-like "coon." (Harriet Beecher Stowe Center, Hartford, Conn.)

Figure 2.8 A sentimental Uncle Tom pictured in an advertisement for *Stetson's Double Mammouth Uncle Tom*, in which Tom is the domestic paterfamilias derived from Stowe's opening chapters. (Harriet Beecher Stowe Center, Hartford, Conn.)

Blackface minstrelsy began as individual songs and dances performed as brief burlesques in saloons and theaters in the 1830s. Legend has it that in 1831 T. D. Rice imitated, in blackface, a shuffle and song he had seen performed by a black boat worker in Pittsburgh. The dance, which Rice called "jumping Jim Crow"—because the dance imitated the movements of a lame crow hopping about—was, along with most blackface performance of the period, full of comic grotesqueries. By the 1840s these occasional songs and dances in saloons had grown into a complete evening's entertainment, divided into three parts and performed for white audiences by large groups of blackface minstrels. In the '30s and '40s, the appeal of minstrelsy was emphatically to working-class northern, often Irish immigrant, males. Later its appeal would broaden, its tone shift, and, like melodrama in the same period, it would become more respectable.

Early scholars have stressed the pro-slavery, Jacksonian affinities of these racial caricatures and their support of the "plantation myth" of happy slavery. Alexander Saxton, for example, quotes lyrics such as "Old Massa to us darkies am good" (Saxton 1990, 176). The white, northern, urban, often Irish, immigrants who put on blackface to perform popular "Ethiopian" and "Plantation Melodies" appropriated aspects of black culture, at least partially to escape a constraining Protestant ethic. Blackface was their bohemianism. Preposterously sexual, violent, or otherwise prohibited theatrical material that could never be brought on stage as "white" entertainment could be freely indulged in blackface.[19]

It is easy to condemn the unbridled racism of popular burlesque performances that manufactured a grotesque blackness for the primary purpose of indulging an orientalizing fascination, revulsion, and amusement on the part of white audiences. However, it is also important to recognize a number of crucial, if contested, observations about minstrel entertainment that have been raised recently by Eric Lott (1993) and Dale Cockrell (1997).[20] First, minstrelsy was America's first "native" music and first national cultural form to portray what might be called a cultural "mix." Lott quotes Putnam's *Monthly* from February 1854: "The only places of Amusement where the entertainments are indigenous are the African Opera Houses, where native American vocalists, with blackened faces, sing national songs, and utter none but native witticisms" (Lott 1993, 90). Second, though certainly a "theft" of black cultural materials for white dissemination and profit, minstrelsy was, before *Uncle Tom's Cabin*, the one place in American culture where racial feelings mattered to popular audiences; it was also the place where various "class fractions" came into contact and mediated their relations "over the bodies of black people" (Lott 1993, 3, 67).

Eric Lott persuasively argues that expressions of racial repulsion by white men in blackface easily slid into racial envy. The "theft" of black culture (however authentic or inauthentic that "culture" itself may be) by young Irish immigrants who shared the same bottom-of-the-barrel class niche as free blacks was as much a tribute—a form of "love"—as it was a form of theft (Lott 1993, 95). These Irish bohemians—the "white Negroes" and Elvis Presleys of their day—were at the beginning of what would become a long American tradition of white boys and men assuming their masculinity through an imitation of blackness. Lott's study presents a more nuanced picture of the forms of cultural contact achieved by blackface minstrelsy. It suggests that, if the Negro was a fetishized figure of fun often based on depictions of unbridled corporeality and sexuality, that "fun" did not always perfectly correspond with official ideology. In fact, minstrelsy's offensive humor could introduce "dangerous moments of pleasurable disorder that sometimes offended the racial regime of antebellum America" (Lott 1993, 142). An eruption of excessive corporeality, the Negro body was converted, through laughter, into a reassuring substitute for its more deeply disturbing aspects. White ridicule, love, and theft could thus be passed off as "naive" black comedy, although at some level both performers and audiences knew better.

Against Lott's insistence that ridicule became a form of celebration and thus, however inadvertently, created a "black" performance space in which to stand, Michael Rogin has more recently argued that the total effect of blackface was an "exclusion of actual African-Americans from their own representations" and an emphasis on the "grotesque, animalistic blackface mask" (Rogin 1996, 37). Rogin is right, I think, to insist on the overall harm of blackface in any kind of ultimate historical accounting. The greatness of his study is to imagine the alternative history that might have emerged had blacks represented themselves instead of being represented by Irish and then Jewish comedians. There can be no question of blackface representations being, in any sense, *for* blacks. Burnt cork drove free blacks from the stage and substituted for actual African (American) entertainers.[21]

But since blackface did exist, and was, in fact, formative of the identities of many a white entertainer in or out of burnt cork, one question is how to understand its influence and importance in the creation of white identities. A further question is how to understand its influence on black performers and black characters when African Americans begin to work in these popular mass-culture forms themselves. As Rogin insists (1996, 43): "Burnt cork contaminated every white American political perspective on race." However, if, as Rogin also notes, Ma Rainey, Ida Cox, and Bessie Smith all got their start in minstrelsy, there is no ignoring the importance of minstrelsy in the black as well as the white imagination.

Toni Morrison's (1990) introduction of the term "Africanist" into the debate about American culture's representations of blackness may help us remember that what is at issue here is in no sense the representation of "authentic" Africans or African Americans. Morrison defines Africanist as the denotative and connotative blackness that African peoples signify to a white population that has come to see itself as white through the contrast with blackness. Her study of American literature argues that Africanist characters are a form of blackface created by and for white Americans. But rather than dismiss these caricatures, Morrison, like Lott, believes their study helps reveal the meanings of whiteness. For our purposes in tracing the fundamentally white supremacist melodrama of black and white, the lesson seems to be that there is no pure and authentic representation of race free of the "contaminations" of either the ridiculing or the melodramatizing lenses of mass culture. Indeed, melodrama as a mode of sympathy is the flip side of farce, the mode of ridicule. Both forms elicit powerful bodily reactions in their viewers that are deemed excessive by more genteel arbiters of taste. Melodrama's sympathy could be described as the feeling of emotional connection to suffering victims, while farce's ridicule is an emotional distancing from a figure of fun. Uncle Tom on stage would always be a complex negotiation of both.

If it is necessary to disparage the expropriation of one culture by another, more dominant one, it is also important to recognize that it is also by stepping outside of their "skin" that members of different cultures and races sometimes find the power to resolve conflicts within the subject positions constructed by the "skin" that has been evaded. The tragedy for African Americans is that there has been so little maneuverability, so few options of performance beyond those of blackness or the "passing" escape of blackness, so little chance to play with identity on the mass-culture stage, while so many white men—and as we shall see, some women—have achieved both adulthood and a sense of national assimilation by playing at blackness. However, this tragedy should not blind us to how the white "theft" of black identity and black "theft" of white identity enable a look at the world through the eyes of another, or how such looks provide a protective cover to indirectly face conflicts within one's own, overly rigid, prescribed racial and gender roles.

Harriet Beecher Stowe's crossracial sympathies are certainly one form of blackface "love and theft." Speaking for the freedom of slaves, she says things she could not say in her own voice speaking for the freedom of women.[22] Just as the white, male, working-class minstrels used blackface to escape the constrictions of the Protestant ethic, so Stowe's empathic picture of the suffering black slave permitted her own escape from the impasse of an elite Protestant perfectionism into a more democratic vision of "life among the lowly." If Stowe's best-seller was written in the religious fervor of a new melodramatic gospel of the exalted suffering of the racially despised "lowly," its immediate generation of what we would today call product spinoffs—as minstrel show burlesques, stage melodramas proper, as sheet music and popular song, even as board games—immediately brought it into the new world of mass-produced commercial entertainment. Though hardly bohemian, her own blackface "love and theft" was not unlike that of her minstrel predecessors.

"Hulloa, Jim Crow!" says Mr. Shelby to the "quadroon" boy, Harry Harris, on page three of the novel, alluding, not as contemporary readers might think, to laws enforcing segregation, but to a generic name for a slave whose pleasure is presumed to be found in performing blackness for his masters. Immediately little Harry begins to dance and sing and to "walk like old Uncle Cudjoe, when he has the rheumatism" (3). Thus Stowe begins her novel within the familiar comic context of minstrelsy. Immediately, however, the sale of this little boy to a slave trader shifts the novel's emotional tone to melodrama. As long as minstrel mimicry was as upbeat as songs like "Jump Jim Crow," "Old Dan Tucker" (Emmett, 1843), or "De Camptown Races" (Foster, 1850), and as long as the affective relation to the Africanist figure was a mixture of repulsion and envy, caricature and desire, the affective relations of whites to blacks could be dismissed as comic derogation mixed with envy. But when laughter at the comic excuses of a lazy slave or the verbal acrobatics of a pretentious freedman turned to tears at the sufferings of virtuous victims, a deeper identification with Africanist feelings took place.

Consider, for example, the sad "home songs" that sang of parted lovers, lost children, and separated families sung in blackface in the second half of a typical minstrel show. Alexander Saxton has noted that such songs, sung in a "darky" vernacular that was not, in itself, considered comic, offered at least a limited means of entry for antislavery content into minstrelsy, making possible a white audience's identification with black sorrow. Though Alexander Saxton tends to downplay the antislavery possibilities of such sentiments and to assume the exclusively European, and non-African, derivation of their musical form (Saxton 1990, 177), the fact remains that once these sadder songs became part of the repertoire, the ridicule of the black body, per se, gave way to more complex identification and desire.

Eric Lott's appreciation of the contradictions of an upbeat happy minstrelsy that included sad "home songs" — plantation melodies with a decided emphasis on death, nostalgia, and doom — is here extremely useful. According to Lott, these later songs exposed the "gaping sore at the heart of all this cheer" (Lott 1993, 187).[23] The sad songs about parted lovers and lost homes were more "white" in structure than the upbeat songs based on riffs and shouts, but musically, thematically, and narratively they were already a hybrid. They spoke to restless migrants moving west, to recently transplanted rural folks in cities, and to rootless urban dwellers beginning to experience the anomie of modern city life (Lott 1993, 14–15). They did so, however, through the accents of "darkies" and the stories of parted slaves. Thus, long before its passing, the antebellum South began to be constructed through minstrelsy as a timeless, lost home, a safe imaginary childhood of innocence associated, however contradictorily, with the bondage of slaves. America's rural everyhome, the melodramatic "space of innocence," became fixed, through this music, as stereotypically southern and, for subsequent generations, as eternally antebellum.

Stephen Foster was the man who did the most to construct this musical myth, and, in our terms, to melodramatize minstrelsy. Foster was the one Irishman of the four most associated with minstrelsy (including T. D. Rice, Dan Emmett, and E. P. Christy) who did not also perform. His "Plantation Melodies" found their way into countless minstrel shows, and, as we shall soon see, into many a performance of *Uncle Tom's Cabin*. Foster wrote both "musematic"—upbeat songs composed of short units (like "Susanna") and balladic, sad "home" songs, both of which were central to the formation of American national identity. But the sad songs especially contributed to the literal *melo*dramatization of the slave narrative. Consider, for example, Foster's wildly popular "Old Folks at Home." Written in 1851, the same year Harriet Beecher Stowe was writing *Uncle Tom's Cabin*, the song would almost immediately find its way into the melos of the nation's most popular stage melodrama.

72

> Way down upon the Swanee ribber,
> Far, far a–way,
> Dere's wha my heart is turning ebber,
> Dere's wha de old folks stay.
> All up and down de whole crea-ation,
> Sad–ly I roam,
> Still longing for de old plan-ta-tion,
> And for de old folks at home.
>
> (Chorus)
> All de world am sad and dreary,
> Eb-ry where I roam,
> Oh! darkey how my heart grow weary,
> Far from de old folks at home.
>
> All round de little farm I wandered,
> When I was young,
> Den many happy days I squandered,
> Many de songs I sung.
> When I was playing wid my brudder
> Hap–py Was I.
> Oh! take me to my kind old mudder,
> Dere let me live and die.
> (Foster 1975, 59–61)

This song was performed in the latter, more sentimental, portions of countless minstrel shows, most famously by the Christy Minstrels.[24] It circulated along with Foster's more "respectable" nonracial songs like "Jeannie with the Light Brown Hair" (1854).

Stephen Foster was the first American professional songwriter to earn a living (however precariously) by publishing his music.[25] If Americans did not always know his name, since performers' names were more often attached to songs than writers', they were perpetually singing his music. The late forties saw a boom in the sale of sheet music, and it was through these sales that blackface minstrelsy entered the middle-class parlor and found its first female audience (Lott 1993, 171; Austin 1975, 25). Just as Stowe's novel broke the taboo against lady novelists writing in low dialect, so the publication of Foster's, and others', songs caused Negro dialect, if not actual blackface, to enter the bourgeois home.

Foster's earlier songs, like the spectacular upbeat hit "Susanna" (1847) or the contemporaneous "Ring de Banjo" (1851), had, like T. D. Rice's earlier, trendsetting "Jim Crow," established the "happy darky" mold. The sad home songs sung in the darky vernacular, however, struck an especially deep chord of responsiveness among white audiences, all the more, it would seem, for being channeled through the presumed experiences, dialects, and intonations of slaves. Both types of songs mimicked black sentiments, speech, and song. Here, however, was a new pathos unmistakably mixing familiar white nostalgia for a lost home with the weariness and sadness of a slave separated from his family. Before this song, music historian William Austin claims, listeners would not have thought slaves capable of sharing such sentiments. "Old Folks" not only rendered black people pathetic, it did so in a surprisingly refined and dignified way that was, according to Austin, instantly developed in the Christy Minstrel performances (Austin 1975, 247).

Middle-class families that would not be caught dead in 1852 at the melodramatic theater or at a minstrel show were nevertheless encountering the more seemly of the songs of minstrelsy on their home parlor pianos via the sheet music revolution of the era. If we consider that these same parlors were the frequent venues for family readings and amateur performances in which family members not only read aloud (as Stowe had done to her family while still writing) but performed the voices, accents (including slave), hymns, and songs embedded in the novel, then we can begin to grasp that even in the absence of the literal stage, both minstrel traditions and traditions of the melodramatic theater were encroaching on the American home.[26]

Here, then, were a wide range of melo/dramatizations of the story of bondage and escape converging in the early 1850s: the melos consisted of the songs of longing sung in blackface on the minstrel stage; the sometimes identical songs played on the piano in the parlor where middle-class white families would sing along in slave accents; and songs (again sometimes the same) that would become part of the dramatization of the novel sung in blackface on the stage over the next fifty years in the United States and abroad. Thus both melos and drama related to the stories of slaves were in various ways and to different degrees "blacked up" even before they coincided on the stage. The conventional melodrama's "space of innocence"—the often rural place of maternal goodness to which the fundamentally conservative form of melodrama always wishes to return—was thus associated almost permanently in the white American imagination with the "melos" of minstrelsy.

74   It is easy enough today to deplore the seemingly bogus sentimentalization of a Negro slave "longing for de old plantation," especially as it might compare to some of the more "authentic" musical expressions of slavery sung by the Hutchinson Family Singers or the later Negro Jubilee singers. However, there is no pure dividing line between authentic antislavery music and minstrelsy; any hope of "purity" is dashed by the fact that both the abolitionist Hutchinson Family Singers and the postwar Jubilee singers incorporated Foster tunes into their repertoire, especially the perennial favorite "Old Folks at Home." Songs like this, or the later "My Old Kentucky Home" (1852) or "Old Black Joe" (1860), would all eventually find their way into stage productions of *Uncle Tom's Cabin*. And once such songs became attached to the story of one particular slave "longing for the old plantation," the general sentiment of nostalgia and loss was harnessed to quite specific abuses. Consider, for example, the following scene from Act 5, Scene 3 of the Aiken-Howard *Uncle Tom's Cabin*, the most enduring of the many stage versions of the Tom story:

A Rude chamber. Tom is discovered in old clothes, seated on a stool. He holds in his hand a paper containing a curl of Eva's hair. The scene opens to the symphony of Old Folds [*sic*] at Home.

    Tom: I have come to de dark places; I's going through de vale of shadows. My heart sinks at times and feels just like a big lump of lead. Den it gits up in my throat and chokes me till de tears roll out of my eyes.... Dere's de bright silver dollar dat Mas'r George Shelby gave me the day I was sold away from old Kentuck, and I've kept it ever since. Mas'r George must have grown to be a man by this time. I wonder if I shall ever see him again.

(*Song "Old Folks at Home." Enter Legree, Emmeline, Sambo and Quimbo.*) (Gerould 1992)

    Though the lyrics of the song are not given in the text of the play, the song was undoubtedly sung, along with several others written by George C. Howard (Birdoff 1949, 49; Riis 1994, xv). Unlike the other songs performed for this version of the play, this one was not written specifically for it. Already a popular minstrel tune, it was simply appropriated to the needs of the play.[27]
    As *Uncle Tom's Cabin* grew in popularity, even more music attached to it, whether directly in performance or indirectly through association.[28] Soon other sentimental Foster "home songs" began to creep into the play. "My Old Kentucky Home," while not written for a specific production of the play, was written specifically for the character of Uncle Tom while the novel was

being serialized in the *National Era* in 1851. Though Foster ultimately deleted the references to the specific character (Austin 1975, 233), the song's lyrics speak to the situation of Tom, separated from the Kentucky plantation of his former master. The degree of its embeddedness in the "Tom" material can be gauged by the fact that the song's lyrics are given intertitles at both the beginning and end of a 1910 (Vitagraph) production of the film, quite possibly inviting the audience to sing along. By this time, Foster's music had been permanently attached to Uncle Tom for well over fifty years. Audiences would very likely have had little need to be reminded of the chorus, and the song's lugubrious end:

> A few more days, and the trouble all will end
> In the field where the sugar-canes grow.
> A few more days for to tote the weary load,
> No matter 'twill never be light,
> A few more days till we totter on the road,
> Then my old Kentucky home, good night!
> (Austin 1975, 233)

Like "Old Folks at Home," "My Old Kentucky Home" is also a ballad. However, it is worth noting some of the differences between the former (copyright 1851), originally written for minstrel performance, and the latter (copyright 1852), written under the more direct influence of Stowe's novel and not for immediate minstrel performance. One obvious difference is that "My Old Kentucky Home" has very little Negro dialect, suggesting at times that a white voice could be singing to Uncle Tom, imagining his sorrows rather than voicing them in his own accents.[29]

Thus, one direction of the song pulls toward the establishment of a sympathetic white voice. This voice appreciates the sorrows of a slave whose condition is distinctly different from his own and whose story was already, by 1852, well-known to the northern reading public. However, the published text still retains, in its last stanza, a trace of dialect—"for to tote the weary load." With these words the white onlooker's sympathy for the sorrowful slave bleeds over into the closely related emotion of empathy.[30] When Foster's song (briefly) takes on qualities of voice attributed to slaves, his original sympathy for a different person becomes empathy—imaginative identification—with the slave whose sorrows are like his own.[31] Divided between singing *about* the sorrows of slaves or singing *as* a sorrowful slave, the originally published lyrics of the song accordingly shift from the first line of the first stanza's "*the* old Kentucky home" to the final line's "*my* old Kentucky home." The home of the slave and the home of the white empathic witness to the slave's sorrows begin to merge. White identification with the virtuous suffering of black slaves is thus linked in a song that would become the anthem of the good American home.

76

Another difference between Foster's earlier and later songs is the shift
from a nostalgia for the "old plantation" in "Old Folks" to a more specific
nostalgia for the "little cabin" in "My Old Kentucky Home." The change
permits a distinction between the *house* of the larger plantation and what we
will see to figure most prominently throughout the American melodrama of
black and white: the *home* of the humble cabin. This distinction might seem
super subtle: A slave cabin is still on a plantation; the master owns both the
"big house" and the slave's home; Tom's cabin is precisely not his home as
long as slavery exists. Nevertheless, it makes a difference whether the white
listeners to the songs and viewers of the Tom plays saw themselves as identifying with home as represented by the big house of the plantation, or the
humble cabin of the slave. We will see in the next chapter, when the Tom
material undergoes a national shift from racial sympathy to racial antipathy
with Dixon and Griffith, how importantly the icon of the cabin figures in the
transfer of sympathy from slaves back to the former masters.

"Old Folks," written before the publication of *Uncle Tom's Cabin*, can
be seen to express an ambivalent identification, first with the plantation, then
later in the second stanza with the "little farm." In contrast, in Foster's directly
Tom-influenced "My Old Kentucky Home," home is quite specifically a slave
cabin where "the young folks roll on the little *cabin* floor,/ All merry, all happy
and bright." Foster's inspiration for this figure of the humble but happy cabin
home could easily have come from Stowe's description of Uncle Tom's cabin,
with its idyllic garden patch, flowers, and interracial sympathy cited above.
But as we are also seeing, Foster's songs, and minstrelsy's home songs in general, may well have influenced her, if not directly via the bawdy minstrel stage,
then in the more middle-class approved form of sheet music and parlor pianos.
It begins to be clear, then, how Stowe, a straitlaced New Englander who set
up house in Cincinnati, one of the frontier homes of minstrel performance,
and who employed a mulatta maid who fell victim to the Fugitive Slave Act,
could write a novel that was filled with both the melos and the drama of black
suffering under slavery without ever having traveled to the South.

Given the comic grotesqueries of minstrelsy and given the relative seriousness of Stowe's melodrama of slaves torn from their always-elusive
"homes," it is initially tempting to see antebellum minstrelsy and Stowe's
novel as diametrically opposed forces—one comic, the other sentimental. I
have been suggesting, however, that blackface minstrelsy provided much of
the ambivalent material substance for the sentimentalization of the American
Negro that Stowe developed in her novel. This is not to say that Stowe attended minstrel shows and directly borrowed blackface forms. It is to say,
however, that the popular "moving pictures" created in this novel and soon
to "leap" off its pages were already in the culture in a number of different
ways and perfectly accessible to a person like Stowe. It is true that Stowe's
novel worked against many of the comic stereotypes of minstrelsy in its senti-

mentalized Negroes. It is probably more accurate to say, however, that a sentimental strain of minstrelsy, already existing in the music of Foster and others,
and already circulating well beyond the minstrel stage in the middle-class
parlor, fed into a sentimentalized narrative of freedom and bondage also already in the culture, but now solidified for many general readers by Stowe's **77**
reversal of conventional narrative norms into female escape and male bondage. When all these traditions converged on the melodramatic stage, the effect
was something much greater than the oft-cited "watering down" of Stowe's
feminism and abolitionism. It was the birth of that highly impure entity, "the
Tom show," which we now must probe if we are to understand the roots of
America's multifaceted melodrama of race in its most popular manifestations.

Uncle Tom on Stage: The Antebellum "Leaping" Fish

Stowe's novel was phenomenally popular among the American (and international) reading public—no other nineteenth-century work of fiction came
close, and only the Bible outsold it. However, much of the American public
could not read, thus this public's entertainment came in the form of minstrelsy, variety acts, circuses, burlesque, comedy, opera, and melodrama.
Thomas Gossett (1985, 260) estimates that as many as fifty people eventually
saw the play of *Uncle Tom's Cabin* for every one person who read the novel.[32]
Because copyright law did not take effect in the United States until the mid-
1870s, playwrights were free to adapt any popular story to the stage without
much concern for the original. Within a year of the novel's publication, there
were four versions on the New York stage alone and eleven versions in England. (By the end of the century, five hundred Tom companies would be
touring the United States [Gerould 1992, 14]). To best understand the effect
the antebellum performances may have had on their publics, we do well to
describe the melodramatic stage prior to the arrival of *Uncle Tom's Cabin* on
its boards.

Stage melodrama was originally a French import. The nineteenth-
century American stage was dominated by British melodramas often derived
from French originals. British melodramas outnumbered American melodramas five to one (McConachie 1992, xiii). Though there were certainly many
native American melodramas—and native actors like Edwin Forest, who
made a career out of playing spontaneous American heroes—*Uncle Tom's
Cabin* is usually regarded as the work that put homegrown America melodrama on the map (Gerould 1992, 14). Bruce McConachie charts several
phases—or "formations"—in the American melodrama.[33] In the post-1845
period, McConachie identifies an emergent "moral reform melodrama" enjoyed primarily by more respectable men and Protestant families, including
women and the young (vii).

78

McConachie places *Uncle Tom's Cabin* in this later, moral reform tradition, using as his exemplary text Henry J. Conway's 1852 version of the work.[34] I would argue, however, that *Uncle Tom's Cabin* was never an ordinary melodrama of moral reform.[35] The presence of black(faced) bodies on a stage exhibiting the twin melodramatic ingredients of pathos and action would always mark this play as extraordinary, even in this, its politically least incendiary of happy-ending versions. What is missing in McConachie's account is the formative work of this play in shaping the new respectability of moral reform melodrama and the full variety of its permutations. To understand this, we need to grasp the general tenor of the many versions of Uncle Tom produced during the decade leading up to the Civil War.[36]

Before *Uncle Tom's Cabin* revolutionized the American melodramatic stage, a typical melodrama was a short play allowing for between-the-act performances of song, dance, and variety acts. Farcical "afterpieces" were also typical. There was no tradition of a single, serious play occupying a whole evening or afternoon's entertainment. Although melodramas often addressed controversial subjects, as in the popular anti-temperance melodrama, *The Drunkard* (1844), slavery in America had never been addressed as an issue. Certainly no black hero or heroine had ever occupied the central role in a serious play, though romanticized Native Americans had.[37]

The above helps explain why, despite the enormous popularity of Stowe's novel, it took several efforts to mount the play before a non-comic Tom would emerge. The first version of *Uncle Tom's Cabin* was actually a southern, "anti-Tom" play, full of comic minstrelsy, kindly masters, and loyal slaves, produced at the Baltimore Museum in January 1852, entitled *Uncle Tom's Cabin as It Is: The Southern Uncle Tom* (Lott 1993, 213). The first semi-serious attempt at adaptation followed on August 23, 1852, at the National Theater in New York City. This version, by Charles Western Taylor, was, like most melodramas of the time, only three acts long. Also like other melodramas, it shared the bill with the usual variety fare: a Herr Cline who executed three costume changes on a tightrope; a romantic Neapolitan dance performed by male and female partners; and, perhaps most interestingly, a *Burlesque of Otello* in which T. D. Rice (the legendary white inventor of blackface minstrelsy) played a comic Othello (Kesler 1968). The typicality of this burlesque minstrel mode for all forms of black representation suggests the reason for the happy-ending of the Taylor, and many other, versions: despite the popularity of Stowe's novel, there was no popular culture precedent for the pathetic and serious representation of a black character "in the flesh" on stage—except, of course, in the sad home songs of minstrelsy.

While not an "anti-Tom" defense of slavery, Taylor's version appears, from evidence in the playbill, to end with the "Return of Tom" to his cabin in what is described as a "Happy Denouement and Grand Finale" (Kesler 1968, 81). This version follows the initial story of Uncle Tom, though altering his fate, but it entirely eliminates the stories of Eva and Topsy—two of the most enduringly popular characters in all subsequent dramatic versions—and it gives new names to many of the principal characters. It is likely that this lack of similarity to the well-known novel is at least one reason for its relative lack of success (it ran only eleven nights). Yet significantly, it was not automatically evident to the work's first adaptors that an ending faithful to the novel would appeal to audiences. Indeed, many early stage versions of the novel, even those produced with a clear moral abhorrence of slavery, chose to rewrite Tom's fate as happy. To do so was automatically to soften the pain and suffering of slavery and to flirt with the plantation myth of happy slaves (Toll 1974, 28; Kesler 1968, 75; McConachie 1991).

Nevertheless, the mere fact of presenting even a portion of the story of Uncle Tom upon the stage, even in so happy a version, aroused the following criticism in the *New York Herald*: "The negro traders, with their long whips, cut and slash their poor slaves about the stage for mere pastime, and a gang of poor wretches, handcuffed to a chain which holds them all in marching order, two by two, are thrashed like cattle to quicken their pace" (Gossett 1985, 273). Another critic was clearly alarmed by what might be called the melodramatic power of this spectacle:

> But for the compromises on the slavery question, we have no constitution and no Union. . . . Here we have nightly represented at a popular theater, the most exaggerated enormities of Southern slavery, playing directly into the hands of the abolitionists. . . . What will our Southern friends think of our professions of respect for their delicate social institution of slavery, when they find that even our amusements are overdrawn caricatures exhibiting our hatred against it and against them? . . . We would, from all these considerations, advise all concerned to drop the play of Uncle Tom's Cabin at once and forever. The thing is in bad taste—is not according to the good faith of the constitution, and is calculated, if persisted in, to become a firebrand of the most dangerous character to the peace of the whole country. (Gossett 1985, 273)

Although this version of the play *was* dropped, the melodrama that was most certainly to "disturb the peace of the whole country" would be taken up again, in even more incendiary versions. Another happy-ending version was produced November 15, 1852, at the Boston Museum by H. J. Conway. This is the version McConachie takes as typical of moral reform melodrama in his study of the American nineteenth-century melodramatic stage. In this version, more explicitly critical of slavery than the other happy-ending Toms, the newly invented Yankee character, Penetrate Partyside, takes on the role of criticizing slavery and, as McConachie argues, is the source of the legal technicality (the crooked sale in Act 4) that permits master George Shelby, Jr., to achieve Tom's freedom.[38] In this "Compromise version," Tom lives and none of Stowe's important mothers—Mrs. Shelby, Mrs. Bird, Rachel Halliday—appear; Aunt Ophelia (called Aunty Vermont) is simply a comic old maid and Eliza has no heroic moment on the ice. Certainly this is "watered-down" abolitionism.

80

But if both Stowe's feminism and abolitionism are watered down by this version, there remains a general sentiment against the evils of black suffering at white hands. Legree's villainy, for example, is exaggerated and he dies in a Gothic scene that shows him haunted by his own demons. Good white male characters become the witnesses to the virtues of racially marked others (here exaggerated in the Partyside character's running, journalistic commentary on the excesses of slavery). It is significant, however, that these earliest versions of Uncle Tom to reach the melodramatic stage, while hardly to be accused of pro-slavery sympathies, found it impossible to render the beating death of the good uncle at the hands of white masters. As we shall see, even the version usually considered the most "faithful" did not, initially, represent this death.

Chronologically, the third Uncle Tom's Cabin to be performed on the stage—the so-called Aiken-Howard version—is usually considered the most important and, as melodramatic stage adaptations go, the most faithful. It was first performed in Troy, New York, in September 1852 at the same time that the Conway version premiered in Boston. Its most significant run, however, was in New York City, where it became the rival of Barnum's production of Conway's version, running for an unprecedented 325 performances (McConachie 1991, 5). This play has often been regarded as the only important stage version of Uncle Tom. More properly, it should be treated as the lone textual survivor, the one version still in print because its harsher view of slavery—including the beating death of Uncle Tom—corresponds most closely to the present view of that "peculiar institution." It was written by a twenty-two-year-old Boston playwright, George Aiken, who, in the tradition of heroic melodrama, had already written an antislavery play called Helos, the Helot, or the Revolt of Messene.

Consistent with the conventions of the day, Aiken's first version was in three acts, ending only with the death of little Eva and thus not resolving the fate of Uncle Tom. By omitting Tom's ordeal with Simon Legree, Aiken effectively avoided making the play vulnerable to the kind of North/South sectional divisiveness caused by the original New York version. But given Aiken's antislavery sympathies, I doubt that the real reason was a fear of sectional division. More fundamentally, there simply was no precedent on the stage for the sympathetic, pathetic, and serious representation of a black slave mistreated by whites. It would take the enormous popularity of this first part of the Tom story and that most compelling of financial incentives—the popular sequel—before Tom's beating death would finally be rendered on stage.

Basically a dramatization of the first volume of Stowe's novel, with Aiken himself as George Harris, this first Aiken-Howard version of Uncle Tom was a great success—primarily due to the popularity of four-year-old Cordelia Howard as Little Eva.[39] The sequel was a three-act dramatization of the second volume of the novel, entitled, significantly, *The Death of Uncle Tom, or Religion of the Lowly*, with many of the actors taking up the same roles (Kessler 1968, 127). Although this version did not have the popular presence of Cordelia Howard, it too was a success in Troy.

    81

What happened next made theater history. Howard and Aiken combined the two plays into a single "Grand Combination." The play that came to be known as the "complete" *Uncle Tom's Cabin* was advertised with the following announcement by Howard: "The desire of the entire community being to see the work from beginning to end, and the Manager wishing to gratify all patrons, is why this immense work is undertaken in one evening. Owing to the length of the drama, no other piece will be played. Change of Time; doors open 1/4 to 7, to commence at 1/4 to 8" (Kesler 1968, 128, quoted from *Troy Daily Times*, Nov. 15, 1852).

Given the fact that the earlier Boston Tom play had already run to six acts, I suspect that it was not length alone that constituted the immensity of the "Grand Combination." Performances of Victorian melodramas, including all their variety acts and afterpieces, could sometimes stretch to six or eight hours. The immensity of this work was not simply its length, but its singular focus on the sufferings of slaves. Originally six acts, eight tableaux, and thirty scenes, later expanded to seven acts and thirty-four scenes, *Uncle Tom's Cabin* broke the mold of previous melodrama. Its first three acts—depicting the flight of Eliza and the death of Little Eva—was paralleled in the second three by the more audacious suffering and death of Uncle Tom, unrelieved by a last-minute rescue by well-meaning whites, or by a minstrel burlesque of Othello, or by a daring "Herr Cline" on a tight rope.[40]

This version too contains many watered-down differences from the novel—the loss of the clever Tom and Andy who, by playing dumb, effect Eliza's escape; the loss of Mrs. Shelby; the loss of the Quaker Settlement; the addition of Aunt Ophelia and Topsy's comic adventures upon their return to New England; the addition of violent revenge on Legree enacted by white hands. However, compared to the Conway, or any of the previous stage versions of the novel, this was the most incendiary, abolitionist version. Its basic six-act structure retains the fundamental mirror relation between white racial suffering recognized by blacks and black racial suffering recognized by whites, with the first climax occurring at the end of Act 3 ("Death of Eva") and its revolutionary mirror occurring at the end of Act 6 ("Death of Tom"). Howard himself explained the significance of this "immense work": "Till the advent of 'Uncle Tom' in New York, no evening at the theater was thought complete without an after piece, or a little ballet dancing. When I told the manager 'Uncle Tom' must constitute the entire performance, he flouted the idea; said we would have to shut up in a week. But I carried my point, and we didn't shut up either. People came to the theatre by hundreds, who were never inside its doors before; we raised our prices, which no other theatre in New York could do" (Kesler 1968, 153).

First in Troy and then in New York City—at the same National Theater where an earlier happy-ending Uncle Tom had played—the play did, indeed, attract a new "class of audience." The National Theater was situated in a rough neighborhood where prostitutes solicited customers in the balcony, as was typical in many theaters in the pre-reform melodrama era. *Uncle Tom's Cabin*'s long run would earn this theater a new measure of respectability commensurate with the general trend in this era toward the solicitation of a new business-class clientele of mixed genders (McConachie 1992, 157–60, 178–84). Ultimately, the greatest measure of that respectability would occur the day in 1854 when Harriet Beecher Stowe herself would see a performance by the Howard Company in Boston, where she was reportedly much moved by Mrs. Howard's rendition of Topsy (Gossett 1985, 266; Birdoff 1949, 190). Purdy, the flamboyant manager of the National Theater, like P. T. Barnum in his rival production at the Barnum Museum, could thus advertise his the-ater as a "Temple of the Moral Drama," redecorating his lobby with scriptural texts, hanging in it a painting of himself with a Bible in one hand and *Uncle Tom's Cabin* in the other, and stressing the patronage of refined audiences composed of families,[41] ministers, and teachers (Drummond and Moody 1952, 318). During the run of the play Purdy also introduced the heretofore unprecedented feature of the matinee, catering to women and children (Gossett 1985, 270).

Church groups attended with their pastors. Upper tiers of more expensive seats had, according to one reporter, an unexpected "air of sanctity." Demure gentlemen who had never been to the theater before could be seen in boxes applying handkerchiefs to eyes "as the black apostle of liberty, Uncle Tom, was reading the Bible, or Little Cordelia Howard was suffering perhaps her hundredth martyrdom" (Gossett 1985, 270–71). But if this most serious ver-sion of the Tom material was responsible for making the theater newly legiti-mate in the exceptionally high class eyes of its audience, even more significant changes were taking place in a very different part of the theater: "The gallery was filled with a heroic class of people, many of them in red woolen shirts, with countenances as hardy and rugged as the implements of industry em-ployed by them in the pursuit of their vocation." This same reporter was puz-zled by the silence in the gallery when Eliza crossed the river. When he turned to look, he was astonished to discover that the entire audience, including the rough men in the gallery, were in tears (Gossett 1985, 270).

A gallery reduced to tears over the sufferings of slaves seems at least as important as the newfound respectable converts to melodrama in the upper tiers. As a reviewer in the antislavery *New York Tribune* noted, "No mob would have dared to disturb the Abolition party at the National Theater." Even though the audience for the play was composed predominantly of the sort of people who had previously composed the anti-abolition mobs that had burned down Freeman's Halls, destroyed printing presses, and assaulted public speakers, now, as the reporter put it, the "pro-slavery feeling had departed from among them" (Gossett 1985, 271).[42]

In addition to the transformed mob weeping in the pit and the more respectable newcomers in the gallery, there was yet a third element of this audience whose reactions are worth pondering, although they were not recorded by any newspapers. Purdy, the National Theater manager, admitted into a segregated but not badly placed section near the pit a number of free blacks.[43] This was not an anomaly. African Americans, both slave and free, attended theater in the North and South, usually sitting, as in this case, in segregated sections, though most often in the gallery (Dorman 1967). The oft-noted potential of the Tom material to foster racial divisions and even violence may have quite a bit to do with the simple existence of such an audience. The reality of a black audience witnessing the play's representation not only of black suffering at the hands of whites, but white recognition of that suffering, represented a major shift in racial feeling. For it was at least partly out of fear of the reactions of black audiences that *Uncle Tom's Cabin* was so vehemently banned (in all but pro-slavery anti-Tom versions) in the antebellum South and even long after the war. We thus do well to remember the always-incendiary potential of this material in either its pro- or anti-Tom versions and that the root of this potential is the spectacle of interracial violence. The original spectacle of white-on-black violence, as we shall see, always carried the seeds of reversal in black revolt and revenge.

These performances at the National Theater, much more than any private or parlor readings of the novel, and despite "watered-down" abolitionist politics, are evidence of a remarkable sea change in northern racial feeling. This first moment when white northern audiences (and an emerging black one) found it possible to weep over the fate of black(faced) bodies, to the accompaniment of sad plantation melodies, spectacularly displayed the power of racial melodrama to implicate audiences in racially marked pathos and action. Of course, at this time there were no real black bodies on stage in any of these performances.[44] In the case of Uncle Tom and Topsy, there were only white actors in blackface; in the case of Eliza, Cassie, and George Harris there was even less: white actors playing light-skinned mulattos escaping from slavery by passing for white. The white bodies performing blackness in Uncle Tom were thus inevitably marked by minstrelsy. Yet it may very well be that it was only through the marks of minstrelsy that the virtuous suffering of the black body could become visible in the first place to white audiences.

It is entirely likely that a black actor playing the role of Topsy or Tom without racial caricature would have been unrecognizable to white and black audiences alike.[45] For it was ultimately the familiarity occasioned by the grotesque parodies of minstrelsy that made possible the recognition of virtue so basic to melodrama. And in this recognition, musical forms and traditions borrowed, as we have seen, from minstrelsy indeed, were the emotional glue that made it all possible. To put on blackface was always to be susceptible to a minstrel caricature, but not to put on blackface was to preclude any popular reception (positive or negative) in the performance of race.[46]

By 1854 New York City alone had, in addition to the Aiken-Howard version of the play at the National Theater (billed as the only "correct version" of the novel), three other competing versions, all of which tended more toward outright minstrelsy than the Aiken version. The most important of these was P. T. Barnum's spectacular adaptation of Conway's happy-ending version from 1852. Barnum's mounting of the "Tom" show at his American Museum theater in New York tried to out-spectacle the Aiken-Howard competition even as it billed its version as the more realistic representation of slavery.[47] Instead of abolitionist fervor, Barnum offered more comedy and spectacle, including a grand panorama of the Mississippi by moonlight, painted by a popular scenarist, showing a steamer on the way to New Orleans with real rotating wheels, lights, and puffs of smoke emerging from its smokestack.

But it is not at all clear that Barnum's version could be construed as an outright defense of slavery, since even this version's happy ending sought denouement in the freeing of Uncle Tom, not, as in the southern "anti-Tom" plays, in the return to happy-go-lucky slavery on the plantation. But an out-and-out pro-slavery, "anti-Tom" version did occur in another New York production coincident with the Aiken-Howard version. In 1853, Christy and Wood's Minstrels performed a burlesque of the Aiken-Howard version in a one-act portion of their variety show entitled "Uncle Tom's Cabin, or Life among the Happy." The burlesque was so successful that in the spring of 1854 the company, as if parodying the grandiose length of the Aiken-Howard version, developed a full-length "opera" on the subject.[48]

By this time, performances of Uncle Tom's Cabin had become a crucial dimension of the public debate about slavery, carried out on the stage as a tug-of-war between melodramatic pathos and comic minstrelsy. Blackface, minstrel-inflected melodrama had put comic blackface minstrelsy on the defensive. Arguments about "the American dilemma" were not only carried out in the legislature and on the political stump. In every section but the South, where Uncle Tom was forbidden except in extreme burlesque form, the very fabric of American popular culture was infused with arguments about slavery enacted in the many long-running versions of Uncle Tom. Uncle Tom was becoming a permanent fixture of the culture with multiple versions sitting down for long stays in the big cities while touring companies "leaped" from one small town to another.[49]

Post–Civil War "Tommer Shows"

During and immediately after the Civil War the popularity of stage versions of Uncle Tom waned slightly, which is only to say that the play was just a bit less ubiquitous (Drummond and Moody 1952, 319). Even so, there were four productions in New York City, two in Philadelphia, and on the day Lincoln went to the theater to celebrate the end of the war, he could have seen a performance of *Uncle Tom's Cabin* had he chosen another theater and a matinee (Birdoff 1949, 203). In the late seventies, however, a new nostalgicizing energy poured into the productions of what came to be called "Tom," "Tommer Shows," or simply "Tomming." In 1879 the *New York Dramatic Mirror* listed routes of forty-nine Tommer Shows—acting companies given over entirely to productions of Uncle Tom. By the 1890s it was estimated that five hundred companies were offering such shows, crisscrossing the nation in tours that often resembled circuses. Many well-known performers of the twentieth century cut their teeth on Tom Shows. Even Mae West would play little Eva as a child (Pierpont 1996, 107). A 1902 reviewer estimated that in that year one in every thirty-five inhabitants of the United States would see a production of the play (Gossett 1985, 371). But what was it they would see?

It is nearly impossible to generalize about the nature of so many different productions, ranging from the smallest troupe in which one actor might take on two or three parts to the ever more spectacular, "mammoth," and "ideal" productions (with increasing numbers of dogs, horses, elephants, alligators), including, "real" Negro jubilee singers (freely mixing spirituals and minstrel songs) and the novelty "double mammoth" circus companies with two actors playing the same roles (see Fig. 2.7 and 2.8). It seems safe to say, however, that whether small or large, whether ostentatiously showing off the latest stage technology for a steamboat race between the *Natchez* and the *Robert E. Lee,* or whether reduced to an overage and overweight Eva, the moving pictures and the melos of a Tom show were felt differently now that slavery no longer existed.

Without the ability to spark the same level of intense sectional controversy, Uncle Tom appeared to have, in Henry James's words, "sat down . . . and made itself, so to speak, at home" during this postbellum period. As both the bondage and the escape elements of the drama began to be seen as part of an increasingly distant history, as slavery itself began to be regarded not as a divisive social and political question but as an almost quaint, "peculiar institution" never to be revived, but ritualistically to be indulged in the nostalgic glow of melodrama's "space of innocence," there was a tendency to imbue the work with even greater amounts of nostalgia for the lost "Kentucky" home while relaxing the representation of the suffering of slaves. No longer functioning to humanize the slave in white eyes through the hybridity of white and black musical forms, the stories, songs, and dances of Tom shows of this period may have more often served the purpose of humanizing whites in their own eyes by claiming fellow feeling with a nostalgicized way of life associated with slavery.

As the play gradually began to be performed in the South after 1870, the original antagonism between master and slave was downplayed, assuring more upbeat, minstrel versions in that region. As late as 1906, the Kentucky State Legislature passed a law making it illegal to present "any play that is based upon antagonism between master and slave, or that excites racial prejudice" (Gossett 1985, 375–76). In these more comic, less melodramatic versions, Topsy would sometimes also be aged up to an adolescent or adult.[50] In some performances her wild, comic wickedness could be transformed into sexual wickedness expressed in song and dance. Performances given after the Chicago Exposition of 1893 when Little Egypt made a sensation, for example, often made Topsy an exotic sex object. In other versions, however, racial violence between master and slave was actually exacerbated, offering white audiences sadistic pleasure in the beatings of Tom. It became traditional for Simon Legree to foam with rage and to beat Uncle Tom at length both with the whip and on the head with its handle. Tom would have a container of red fluid to smear over himself at such moments (Gossett 1985, 377).

Sometimes these beating scenes would turn into actual boxing matches. John L. Sullivan played the part of Legree in one touring company, whose featured attraction was the multiple knockouts of slaves. Audiences came to see how many slaves, including Uncle Tom, Sullivan could knock out. (This very same Sullivan would not deign to fight an actual black contender in the ring [Gossett 1985, 378]). It is interesting to consider how very psychosexually charged these ritualized moments of sadomasochistic white on black(face) stage violence could be. Indeed, Richard von Krafft-Ebing (1902, 144) reported in *Psychoathia Sexualis* that one of his patients found sexual pleasure in reading the scenes of beating in Stowe's novel meant to dramatize the horrors of slavery. The patient explained that he masturbated to the beating of Tom and identified while so doing with the beaten black man (Michaels 1987, 115–24). However, the reverse spectacle of a black man beating a white was not publicly tolerated. As late as 1912 a law preventing the interstate transportation of boxing films was enacted to prevent the showing of black boxer Jack Johnson's earlier victory over the white Jim Jeffries (Staiger 1992, 143; Grieveson 1998).

There were also important changes in the narrative in the postbellum period that were affected by the end of slavery. In addition to the standard ending showing some variation of Tom's ascent to or arrival in heaven where Eva is already gloriously ensconced, in the 1890s new tableaux were created.

These showed Union armies triumphing over those of the Confederacy. In place of the story's original salvation in the Christlike suffering of first Eva and then Tom, history itself becomes a force of salvation capable of redeeming Tom, Eliza, George, Emmeline, and Cassy from the horrors of slavery. In some versions an end tableau showed Lincoln signing the Emancipation Proclamation or portrayed the Union army singing a patriotic song. During the Spanish-American War, American troops were shown united in triumph over Spain instead of killing one another in fratricidal war (Gossett 1985, 383).[51] Thus postbellum history could be deployed to provide historically reassuring, relatively happy endings to the antebellum Tom Story, if not always for Tom himself, then for his fellow slaves.

Early Film Versions of Uncle Tom

It is in the earliest extant film version of the play that we can perhaps come the closest to a concrete glimpse (though without the all-important melos) of how the "moving pictures" of at least one Tom show might have been arranged at the turn of the century. It is also in these early film versions of Uncle Tom that we can glimpse the beginnings of the transformation of stage melodrama into film. Edwin S. Porter's 1903 *Uncle Toms* [sic] *Cabin or Slavery Days*, produced by the Edison Manufacturing Company, is a twenty-minute, two-reel film organized into fourteen scenes performed by members of a traveling Tom show (Musser 1990, 242). The Tom in this production is a tall, aged, slightly pot-bellied white man in blackface with a fringe of white hair on a balding head. For reasons that may have quite a bit to do with the fact that his role called for the frequent handling of Little Eva, stage Toms tended to be white-haired rather than the vigorous, broad-shouldered middle-aged man of Stowe's novel, or of the book illustrations by Hammatt Billings (and later by E. W. Kemble). According to most reports, the stage Tom was more like the doddering elderly figure we encounter in these early film versions. It would seem that it was one thing for verbal pictures and insubstantial drawings to depict the work's cross-gender interracial amity and quite another to actually see real human bodies interact (even with the artifice of blackface).

What is perhaps most striking about the film to contemporary audiences is its lack of continuous narrative. Each scene is preceded by an introductory title that "gives away" in advance its action, giving the impression, as Ben Brewster and Lea Jacobs (1997, 54) have noted, that the film has simply excerpted the scenes most consecrated within the play's performance tradition. The first scene, for example, entitled "Eliza Pleads with Tom to Run Away," makes no attempt to explain why Eliza wishes Tom to run away, opting instead to show the melodramatic highlight of her pleading and Tom's steadfast refusal. The second scene, "The Escape of Eliza," shows Eliza on the ice pursued by the dogs that, although they were not mentioned in the novel and were not seen in the early novel illustrations, had become axiomatic to most stage productions of the postbellum period. Again, however, we need to know the story to understand why Eliza is so pursued. In this scene the background shows a painted backdrop of the far bank of the river. In the foreground is the near bank. In the middle ground are some moving ice floes that look distinctly like papier-mâché (this touring company does not appear to have performed one of the more opulent versions). Eliza climbs on an ice floe that conveys her across the river while her pursuers shake their fists in anger. A comic bit of business shows the lawyer Marks falling in the water and repeatedly failing to pull himself out with the use of his umbrella.

Another feature of the film is that, despite the intensity of the condensed pathos and action, many scenes begin with slaves gaily dancing. These dancers, unlike the principal black characters, are portrayed by actual black people. "Tom and Eva in the Garden," for example, opens with a group of elegantly attired blacks on the St. Clare plantation doing an elaborate cakewalk before Eva and Tom enter to have their vision of paradise in the garden.[52] Dancing also opens the scene "Auction Sale of St. Clare's Slaves." Here slaves in rags dance while others gamble, incongruously setting a happy context for the auction of Emmeline and Tom that follows. The ninth scene, "The Death of Eva," shows Eva on her deathbed with Tom, St. Clare, Aunt Ophelia, and Topsy weeping beside her. In a rare moment of cinematic (as opposed to stage) effect, we see the superimposition of an angel, who descends to Eva and takes her equally superimposed image up to heaven.

Clearly, this first film version has opted to display dramatic and musical highlights instead of the causal links between scenes—although the two-reel film is quite long for films of this period. Featured prominently in these highlights are various "tableaux" inherited from the melodramatic stage. Tableaux are dramatic moments of a play in which the actors freeze their positions in order to heighten and prolong emotional or pictorial effects. Brewster and Jacobs (1997, 54–57) note that stage tableaux generally served to introduce abstract interpretive frameworks that put the audience at one remove from the immediate plot. A tableau might summarize a plot point (as when in the play Eliza prays on one bank of the river and Haley curses on the other), offer an allegorical comment on the action (as when Eva is seen in heaven on the back of a snow-white dove), or portray a moment of dramatic impasse (as when Cassy and Legree stand opposed to one another over the fate of Uncle Tom).[53]

Much has been made of the narrative incoherence of this, and other early films, by historians of early cinema. Noel Burch (1990, 186–93), for example, has suggested that audiences of pre-1909 cinema had a quite different sense of temporality and causality than did those of later years and were more interested in spectacle and movement than with the continuous unfolding of linear narrative. Tom Gunning (1986, 1989) has elaborated a notion of an early "cinema of attractions" to define these pleasures. More recently, Janet Staiger has argued with respect to this particular film that audience familiarity with novel and stage versions of this best-known story of the second half of the nineteenth century made the telling of a chronologically sequential story by Porter unnecessary. Staiger goes on to argue that after 1909 films began to provide, within the film itself, causality and motivations that had earlier been supplied by the audience or a lecturer accompanying the film. Audiences who saw the various tableaux of this film, Staiger contends, could, unlike contemporary audiences, call up a whole "causal chain of events, fully motivated in the psychologies of characters, and complexly ordered into a story that involved a simultaneity of events as well as sequentiality" (Staiger 1992, 118).

89

Staiger's point that film scholars have often sought a romantic "otherness" in the early film viewer's ability to enjoy unnarrated spectacle is well taken. Given the remarkable familiarity of the Tom material—indeed its exceptional familiarity as the best-known story of the era—it seems obvious that film viewers did not need Eliza's motives for escape explained to enjoy the show. Yet an "otherness" does persist, if not in the formal features of a narrative that was fully understood by audiences who knew the basic outlines of the story, then in the wildly fluctuating, often contradictory, racial feelings elicited by the material. For as we have seen, the very motive and causality of the story of Uncle Tom was in radical flux. Tom died in some versions, survived in others; Topsy could be a mischievous imp in one version, a lascivious Little Egypt in another. Eliza might escape to Canada in one version, be recaptured by Legree in another, be totally forgotten by another. Nor were these narrative and performative differences merely formal ambivalences: they could say a lot about the formation of racial attitudes in one period compared to another.

By 1903, the evidence of Porter's film version of Uncle Tom suggests that white Americans had highly contradictory feelings about "Slavery Days." On the one hand, these days were fondly remembered as a period of innocent childhood, of happy, well-dressed real Negroes doing cakewalks on the plantation, of intergenerational communion between an extremely elderly blackface Tom and a terminally innocent Eva. On the other hand, they showed the cruel separation of families, the flight of the innocent, and the flogging death of Tom carried out directly by Legree. "Slavery Days," in other words, was both a nostalgic heaven of interracial amity—melodrama's always problematic space of innocence—and a cruel hell of interracial violence.

Consider, for example, the succession of historical tableaux that follow the death of Tom in Porter's film. We see Tom die, as he does in both the novel and the Aiken-Howard play, in the arms of George Shelby, Jr. (Audiences familiar with both novel and Aiken play might remember the lines "Oh Mas'r George, you're too late. The Lord has bought me, and is going to take me home," from Act 6, Scene 6.) But in addition to the early theatrical versions' convention of the appearance of Eva in heaven amidst "gorgeous clouds" or "Eva robed in white on the back of a milk-white dove," we also see in a "balloon" or circular vignette, on the right side of the screen opposite where Tom lies, the following succession of superimposed still images:

> a) a version of the famous painting of the legendary martyr John Brown, who led a slave revolt at Harper's Ferry Federal Arsenal in 1859. Entitled "John Brown Going to His Execution," it shows Brown pausing on the way to his execution to kiss a black woman's child.
>
> b) an American flag in the battlefield of the Civil War.
>
> c) Lincoln standing with a slave crouching at his feet with broken manacles (a paternalistic allusion to the Emancipation Proclamation).
>
> d) Confederate and Union soldiers shaking hands with a winged figure standing between them (the reunion of North and South).

The ending of the film thus alludes, in highly condensed fashion, to the history that divides the novel's "slavery days" from the film's present: John Brown's revolt, the Civil War, emancipation, the reunion of North and South. As in many of the late stage versions, history becomes the melodramatic *deus ex machina* whose subsequent events serve to soften the blow from Legree's whip. Tom and Eva die, but not, the film seems to say, in vain since John Brown's martyrdom, the conflagration of war, emancipation, and reunification follow soon after. A historical happy ending is thus literally superimposed on the now somewhat truncated, sad ending of Tom's death and glory, permitting audiences to feel good about the now corrected horrors of slavery. Black and white suffering that had once been deeply disturbing to the very idea of national union becomes here a source of reassurance. Even a Tom story in which Tom dies could now be told to make whites ease their consciences about the past sins of slavery.

The early film versions of *Uncle Tom's Cabin*, like the story of early cinema itself, is a tale of the gradual elimination of theatrical stage effects and the adoption of more "cinematic" editing of shots taken from more naturalistic settings. Ben Brewster and Lea Jacobs (1997, 58–61) have meticulously traced the gradual "decomposition" of the static theatrical tableaux in subsequent early film versions of *Uncle Tom's Cabin*, as editing within scenes became the dominant cinematic form. They show, for example, how the next film version of Uncle Tom, a Vitagraph three-reeler from 1910, began to mix painted backdrops with, for example, real water in the Ohio River, and how the punctuation of tableaux effects began to be dispersed across a number of shots while still preserving the emotional integrity of most of the canonical stage tableaux. Instead of freezing the action, the elements of the tableaux are dissolved into more fluidly edited sequences. Thus Brewster and Jacobs argue for a certain autonomy of film melodrama, rather than for the simple prolongation of old-fashioned theatrical effects in cinema. This argument is important if we are not to fall into the trap of considering melodrama inherently theatrical, attached to a single medium.

91

Nevertheless, while these early film versions of Uncle Tom are full of the excitement of the melodramatization of a new medium, it was not the Tom story that drove the development and legitimacy of the new medium of film as it had driven the development and legitimacy of the melodramatic stage. Reviewers were respectful of the now hallowed material, often noting that the work held their interest despite expectations that it had outlived its power. *Moving Picture World* (August 6, 1910) wrote of the 1910 film version, "While the story has lost most of its power with the removal of the reason for its existence, it still has a fascination which few are able to resist." A September 5, 1913, *Variety* review of yet another version, describing the film's appeal at a matinee for adults and children, is also somewhat surprised at the work's power, noting that the audience followed the action "with the expectancy that properly belongs to melodrama."[54] However, this reviewer confesses an ignorance that would have been unthinkable in the heyday of Uncle Tommitudes: "I had never read 'Uncle Tom' or seen it played, and had no traditions to bother my review." Despite mild criticism of a title character who was too robust in physique for his woolly white wig, the reviewer asserts that "Mrs Stowe's drama is as vital today in the movies as it was in the good old days of its stage acclaim."

Claims to vitality notwithstanding, reviewers were increasingly given to praising the authentic-looking locales of the post-Porter films more than the excitement and feeling of the familiar story. A 1914 version of the work, produced by World Producing Corporation and directed by Robert Daly, is indeed striking in the authenticity of its river boats, ice floes, and even its depiction of the harsh life of slaves on Legree's plantation. This film is also memorable for another, more innovative, piece of authenticity—the use of a black actor in the role of Uncle Tom. The seventy-two-year-old actor Sam Lucas, who had long played Tom on the stage, here offers a feeling, if also doddering, interpretation (Fig. 2.5).[55] Remembered today as the first white-produced film to feature a black actor, Daly's film is perhaps more memorable for its staging of an unprecedented moment of black-on-white violence. The film follows the conventions of the Aiken-Howard version with two important differences. Making Legree's sexual intentions on Emmeline (the slave girl purchased along with Uncle Tom) explicit, the film then has Cassy steal Legree's gun with the aim of preventing his rape of the young girl. Cassy holds the gun to the sleeping Legree's head but cannot shoot (Fig. 2.9). Instead, she makes preparations to escape with Emmeline. Later, however, when the beaten Tom is near death, a young male slave whom Tom had earlier refused

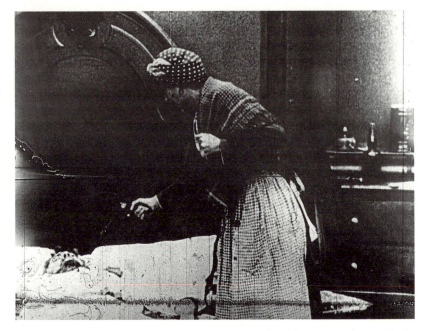

Figure 2.9 Cassy holds a gun to Simon Legree's head but cannot shoot. (*Uncle Tom's Cabin*, World Producing Corporation, Robert Daly, 1914)

to whip—and played, like Tom, by a black actor—picks up the gun Cassy had abandoned and stalks Legree (Fig. 2.10).

These two moments in which black hands hold guns to white human targets are unprecedented in the Tom tradition, and perhaps in all previous American film. Until this moment, interracial violence had been pictured exclusively as that of white masters abusing black slaves. This second instance, which culminates in the male slave actually shooting Legree, is especially striking. In a subjective, slave's-eye view, we see in the foreground the black hand of the male slave holding the revolver (Fig. 2.11). The trigger pulls and in the distant background Legree falls.

Nowhere else in any of the Tom material I have seen (including a 1927 version we will consider in the next chapter) is there a similar moment of black-on-white violence and revenge. Stowe's novel had considered Legree's guilty conscience and "haunting" by Cassy and Emmeline revenge enough. Most stage versions did avenge Tom with the death of Legree but only at the hands of the white George Shelby, Jr. Even heroic George Harris—who engages in a shootout with slave catchers in the Aiken-Howard version—is only violent in defense of his family, not in revenge. The stunning surprise of this scene, unleashing a possibility of wronged slaves not simply foiling their masters by escape but avenging the violence committed upon them, goes against

Figure 2.10   A slave befriended by Tom stalks Legree. (*Uncle Tom's Cabin*, World Producing Corporation, Robert Daly, 1914)

Figure 2.11   The sight down the barrel of the gun as the black slave shoots Legree. (*Uncle Tom's Cabin*, World Producing Corporation, Robert Daly 1914)

94   the Christian ethos of Stowe's original melodrama and, indeed, against the ethos of all subsequent stage and screen versions of Uncle Tom. Nevertheless, this brief eruption of the reversal of interracial violence exploding into the Tom tradition may help to explain what we shall see to be at the heart of the dialectical reaction to the "Tom" and "anti-Tom" tradition: white terror at the potential revenge of slaves, and tacit white recognition that the terror and sexual violence practiced by masters on slaves could be reversed. We need look no further than this 1914 film to begin to see that interracial violence is at the core of the American melodrama of black and white. The logic of a work that begins in the pathos of the beating of the black man by the white is the action of black revenge. But the spectacle of righteous black revenge is deeply incendiary—so incendiary, in fact, that some prints of Daly's film omit the scene.[56]

The fact that black violence had even become representable within the confines of a work that had come to be known, as Thomas Cripps (1993a, 157) puts it, as the "perfect vehicle for interracial amity," is of great interest, however. It shows us the logic, within an evolving tradition of action-centered film melodrama, of putting black actors (in all senses of the word) in charge of their fate. If Daly's film had been as powerful in its action sequences as it was in its authentic locales and in this one shocking image of black-on-white revenge, it might have lent a new lease on life to the Tom material, spurring it to develop these deep-seated issues of interracial violence with black actors at their center. It might even have represented a counterforce to the violent, negrophobic, "anti-Tom" tradition that emerged the very next year in Dixon and Griffith's *The Birth of a Nation* and to which we will turn in the next chapter. In all other ways, however, this version of Uncle Tom is singularly ungripping, especially if held up against the following year's film. Its action is never cross-cut, suspense never builds, and there is none of the rhythm of "too late" and "in the nick of time" of the classic cinematic melodrama emerging so powerfully in Griffith and others at this point in film history (as described in the first chapter). As we expect, Eliza escapes and Tom is martyred, but in unexciting, predictable ways even though the authenticity—of moss on trees, of Legree's decrepit plantation on the Red River, and real black actors—is otherwise unprecedented.

It is not that *Uncle Tom's Cabin* would remain exclusively wedded to the melodramatic stage; there would be subsequent film versions that would infuse the work with more modern forms of melodrama. But if it was a work that could "leap" from one medium to another, "Mrs. Stowe's picture" had found its securest, most popular home on the stage in the second half of the nineteenth century. As we have seen, it was many things to many people during this period. Now, however, the story that had once excitingly reversed the conventional gender and racial expectations of melodrama with a feminized black male martyr and a masculinized black woman escapee was shopworn. It could not simply be made new by the simple infusion of authentic locales and real black actors. What would occur, instead, was a new melodramatization, an appropriation of the newer realist possibilities of cinema to renewed melodramatic purpose. As the "world's greatest hit," Uncle Tom would certainly carry on, on stage and in film, throughout the first half of the twentieth century until the civil rights movement would finally and thoroughly discredit the value of a Tom-like martyrdom. But as we shall see, an inverted version of Uncle Tom would derive energy from a new set of racial conventions arising out of a conscious southern opposition to Tom in the work of Thomas Dixon and D. W. Griffith. So while the Tom tradition is by no means over in 1914 with this film, it will not be possible to understand its further development without exploring the negrophobic anti-Tom tradition that counters it in the rise of the medium of film.

3 Anti-Tom and *The Birth of a Nation*

The white women of the South are in a state of siege. . . . Some lurking demon who has watched for the opportunity seizes her; she is choked or beaten into insensibility and ravished, her body prostituted, her purity destroyed, her chastity taken from her. . . . Shall men . . . demand for [the demon] the right to have a fair trial and be punished in the regular course of justice? So far as I am concerned he has put himself outside the pale of the law, human and divine. . . . Civilization peels off us . . . and we revert to the impulse . . . to "kill! kill! kill!"

—South Carolina senator Ben Tillman, 1907

Some people were crying. You could hear people saying God. . . . You had the worse feeling in the world. You just felt like you were not counted. You were out of existence. I just felt like . . . I wished somebody could not see me so I could kill them. I just felt like killing all the white people in the world.

—William Walker (on recalling viewing *The Birth of a Nation*)

In July 1914, carpenters working on a large vacant lot between Sunset and Hollywood Boulevards began to construct the main street of Piedmont, South Carolina, for the primary set of D. W. Griffith's new film, then titled *The Clansman*. According to Karl Brown, Griffith's assistant camera operator, force of habit instilled by years of backstage training caused the carpenters building the street to include hinges on scenery so it could be easily "folded up and shipped to any op'ry house in the country" (Brown 1973, 64). These unnecessary hinges on stationary film sets for an antebellum southern town are a dramatic reminder of the importance of the melodramatic stage

Figure 3.1   Main Street, Piedmont, South Carolina, the primary set for *The Birth of a Nation*.

tradition to the developing medium of film and of the crucial architecture of *Uncle Tom's Cabin* within this tradition (Fig. 3.1). Brown explains in his memoirs:

> There was no question as to what the town should look like or how it should be dressed. I doubt if there was a man on that work crew who hadn't been out with a "Tom" show, as the *Uncle Tom's Cabin* shows were called. There were Tom shows scattered all over the country by tens and dozens. It was not so much a show as an institution, a part of the American scene for the past sixty-odd years. . . . Stage crews had been constructing Tom shows for so long that there wasn't a detail of the Civil War period, inside or out, that they hadn't built, up to and including wobbly ice for Eliza to flee across, one jump ahead of the bloodhounds, which were usually Great Danes. (Brown 1973, 63)

Brown's anecdote encapsulates the strange confluence of the most popular and influential play of the nineteenth century with the most popular and influential film of the early twentieth century. To evoke an antebellum southern town (which for Brown condenses, in the wake of the influence of the very film he had photographed, into a more general "Civil War period") was automatically to conjure up the conventional architecture of *Uncle Tom's Cabin*. These two works, premiering in theaters over a half-century apart, were the unparalleled hits of their respective centuries and the pioneers of their respective media. Indeed, the multiple theatrical versions of *Uncle Tom's Cabin* seem to have occupied something of the same position in the history of the melodramatic theater that the first run of Griffith's film occupies in the history of motion pictures. Both were heralded as the first native-born triumphs of their respective media, the first immensely popular works to treat distinctly American themes and problems.[1] Both brought an unprecedented length and legitimacy to their respective media and both generated racial controversies that altered the way white Americans felt about blacks, and how they felt about being white. To be a white American who saw a Tom show in the 1850s, or who saw *The Birth of a Nation* on its first release in 1915, was to be converted both to the power of a previously slighted medium and, through that power, to new kinds of racial feeling.

Woodrow Wilson's famous, though apparently apocryphal, statement—"It is like writing history with lightning"—has been the best remembered description of the film, conveying the thunderstruck impression of most audiences who became immediately convinced of its historical "truth."[2] What is often not recognized in this remark is the fact that the "truth" recognized here—the "southern view of slavery and Reconstruction"—had been previously disparaged. What *The Birth of a Nation* did, as a film, was to convert the nation to southern sympathy. More specifically, it converted an Uncle Tom–style sympathy for the sufferings of a black man to an anti-Tom antipathy for the black male sexual threat to white women. A somewhat less exalted critic than Woodrow Wilson, the gossip columnist Dorothy Dix, conveys the sense of how linked this conversion to a new racial sympathy and new historical "truth" was to the discovery of the new emotional power of the movies themselves: "I had considered the moving picture interesting, instructive, amusing, diverting, beautiful, spectacular, but I had believed that the silent drama never could touch the emotions very deeply. I had thought that to grip an audience, to melt it to tears with pathos, to thrill it with high heroic sentiment, required the spoken word and the magic of the human voice." But Dix finds *The Birth of a Nation* an "apotheosis of the moving picture" which can work up an audience to "a perfect frenzy" (Schickel 1984, 278–79).

Another critic of the time, Ward Greene, writing for the *Atlanta Journal*, comes closest to saying what was so unprecedented in the frenzies of feeling generated by the film: "Not as a motion picture, nor a play, nor a book does it come to you; but as the soul and spirit and flesh of the heart of your country's history, ripped from the past and brought quivering with all human emotions before your eyes" (Lang 1993, 179). A new sense of national historical truth; a new emotional power wedded to that "truth"—such were the feelings aroused by Griffith's deployment of the new medium. And these new feelings were inextricably wedded to specific racial vilifications and victimizations. Greene's description of the emotional power of the film's climax offers an unguardedly precise identification of what the new medium had to offer:

> In the little town of Piedmont the blacks are celebrating, far away **99** across the hills the Klan assembles. Back and forth the scene changes—one moment a street in Piedmont swirling with mad Negroes, the next a bugle blast from the orchestra and out of the distance riders of the Klan sweeping on and on. Back to the street and a house where a white girl trembles in fear before the black horde without, back with the bugle blast to the onrush of the Klan. They are coming, they are coming! . . . You know it and your spine prickles and in the gallery the yells cut loose with every bugle note. The Negro mob grows wilder and wilder, the white-shrouded riders are tearing nearer and nearer. Then, with a last mighty blast from the bugle, they sweep into the town and with a shattering volley hammer into the crowd. They fire back, they break, they flee. The Klan beats on them and over them . . . to rescue and retribution and final triumph. . . . And after it is all over, you are not raging nor shot with hatred, but mellowed into a deeper and purer understanding of the fires through which your forefathers battled to make this South of yours a nation reborn! (Lang 1989, 179, 181)

Here is a melodrama of pathos and action brought to new heights of "spine prickling" immediacy as moving pictures become literal movements of photographic pictures on the giant screen and as a full symphony orchestra pounds out the melos (indicated here in the blasts of the bugle). Though it is tempting to interpret Greene's enthusiasm as mere southern partisanship, I believe it is an accurate description of how the moving pictures of this film helped forge a new sense of national solidarity and identity—"a nation reborn!"—out of the sexual threats of black villains toward defenseless white women.

Uncle Tom's Cabin had deployed melos, pathos, and action to draw northerners who had previously been uninvolved in the debate over slavery into its orbit, making the "good nigger" into a familiar and friendly icon, for whom whites had sympathy. Now, sixty years later, on the fiftieth anniversary of the end of the Civil War, *The Birth of a Nation* solidified North and South into a new national feeling of racial antipathy, making the black man into an object of white fear and loathing. We can see, then, that each work in its time succeeded in moving unprecedentedly large numbers of the American public to feel implicated in the trials and tribulations of groups whose virtue forged through suffering had not previously been recognized by the mass audience: African-American slaves in *Uncle Tom's Cabin* and white women in *The Birth of a Nation*.

To the degree that critics have recognized the tradition that I am calling black and white racial melodrama, they have tended to emphasize its epic dimensions. Leslie Fiedler, for example, identifies a tradition of "inadvertent epic," extending from *Uncle Tom's Cabin* through *The Birth of a Nation*, *Gone With the Wind*, and *Roots*, whose essence is a "subliterary" repository of the "most wild paranoid delusions" and "most utopian hopes" about the "relations of races, sexes and generations" (Fiedler 1979). To Michael Rogin, writing about *The Birth of a Nation*, epic is also the key: "American movies were born . . . in a racist epic" (Rogin 1984, 191). James Chandler (1990) has also argued for the epic influence on Griffith by opposing a traditional melodramatic lineage extending from Dickens, first argued in Eisenstein's influential essay, to a countertradition extending from Sir Walter Scott.[3] What these different claims share is an appreciation of the greater role of historical background in narratives that seem to shape the "imaginary community" of national self-consciousness.

While the term epic allows us to identify aspects of the Dixon-Griffith tradition that are new to the sequence of American melodramas of black and white I have been tracing—most significantly a new insistence on the texture of history itself—the appreciation of this texture should not keep us from perceiving the *melodramatic* "state of vision, of feeling and of consciousness" (James 1913, 168) most basic to these "moving pictures." To call *The Birth of a Nation* epic is to acknowledge its sheer size and historical appeal, but it is to miss the modernity of its melodrama and the uniquely American yoking of melodramatic form to a dialectic of racial pathos and antipathy. What is new about *The Birth of a Nation* is that it links new feelings about race to equally new feelings of national identity, based on an overt celebration of white supremacy developed as an answer to Tom sympathy. These Manichaean polarities of good and bad, black and white, need to be viewed as melodrama as well as epic. When Michael Rogin writes that American movies are born in a racist epic, he means, I think, that race has been a central and determining factor in the narratives of good and evil that white Americans have told themselves at the movies, and that with *The Birth of a Nation* movies became capable of forging a myth of national origin grounded in race to spectacular effect. However, we should not let the epic dimension of the big screen blind us to the fact that what this film does is what melodrama does: it stages a recognition of virtue through the visible suffering of the endangered white woman. My goal in this chapter will thus be to examine what is melodramatically familiar in Griffith and Dixon's film even as it inverts the racial values and feelings of *Uncle Tom's Cabin*.

I should add that I am fully aware that the danger in this project is that it could fall victim to its own melodramatization by casting Stowe's novel in the role of virtuous, suffering maternal victim, and Griffith's film in the role of evil, patriarchal villain. In this case, Stowe's maternal vision of the virtuous humanity of slaves can be seen to do battle with the paternal "dark" view of their bestiality once freed.[4] Certainly this melodramatic conflict between "good" feminine and "bad" masculine racial melodrama animates some of the drama of the opposition. However, it is the further insight that these two traditions are ultimately two sides of the same coin that I hope will temper **101** the melodramatic tendency of my own study. For what is fascinating in this tradition is not that the starkly contrasted "good" or "bad"—maternal or paternal, black or white—melodrama wins out in the end, but how imbricated each side of the opposition is in the other. There is no anti-Tom, to use Fiedler's useful term, without Tom. Let us begin, then, by trying to understand how Stowe's Tom story of racial sympathy became Griffith's anti-Tom story of racial hatred.

Thomas Dixon's Anti-Tom Novels

Harriet Beecher Stowe's novel, and the plays it spawned, generated an immediate cottage industry of literary and theatrical response in the South. We have already examined some of the stage versions of the anti-Tom response. Though inimical in racial feeling, these plays were deeply indebted to the Tom material for characters and situations. Twenty-seven plantation novels were written between 1852 and 1861. Many of these novels—written as apologies for slavery and featuring kind masters and happy slaves—frankly set out to "answer" the Tom story, and most of the rest directly attacked it in some form.[5] Like Stowe's novel, the anti-Tom literature is full of long polemical speeches addressed to the reader—speeches defending slavery through close readings of the Bible and the Constitution. Though both northerners and southerners produced this literature, the southern versions were more vehement defenses of the whole southern way of life. The heroes of these novels are kindly plantation masters who, unlike George Shelby, hold on to their slaves despite debts; the slaves are faithful and happy or sometimes misguided rebels; whippings occur only rarely and for the slaves' own good; escaped slaves find unhappiness in the North and pine for the paternalistic care of their former masters (Gossett 1985, 212–38).

When Thomas Dixon, Jr., gave up his popular ministry to write a series of novels about the Reconstruction period, he revised this familiar antebellum, anti-Tom, novelistic tradition. His inspiration to write came in 1901 at a performance of a Tom play. Infuriated by what he saw as the injustice of the play's attitude toward the South, he vowed to tell what he considered to be its true story. The result of his first attempt, published the next year, was a sprawling 469-page historical novel entitled *The Leopard's Spots: A Romance of the White Man's Burden 1865–1900*. It would be followed in 1905 by the more tightly focused *The Clansman: An Historical Romance of the Ku Klux Klan*.

Both of these novels would then be combined into Dixon's 1905 play, *The Clansman*, which in turn became the basis of Griffith's 1915 film.

Dixon's work is distinguished from the earlier anti-Tom tradition in its focus on the postbellum period and in its revisionist concession that slavery had been a mistake. However, the primary impetus of his work originates, like the earlier anti-Tom novels and plays, in a passionate refutation of the main line of romantic racialist feeling generated by Stowe.[6] In *The Leopard's Spots* an "unreconstructed" southerner gives Harriet Beecher Stowe every bit as much credit for causing the Civil War as Lincoln once did: "A little Yankee woman wrote a crude book. The single act of that woman's will caused the war, killed a million men, desolated and ruined the South and changed the history of the world" (Dixon 1903, 264).

In 1852 Stowe was writing against the injustices of the present. In 1903, Dixon was writing against the injustices of the past (specifically attempts to give the vote to African Americans during Reconstruction). As James Chandler (1990, 230–31) has noted, this focus on the past lends his work its distinctive quality of historical romance. Yet by the time Dixon was writing against Stowe, her novel and the entire Tom tradition had itself passed into history, with Tom, Eliza, Topsy, and Simon Legree perceived as the very icons of the antebellum and Civil War era.[7] We can see, then, that part of the appeal of the historical form he adopts is that it offered his best possible response to what was by then seen as Stowe's own historical tradition. It is not surprising, then, that Dixon's strategy, in his first anti-Tom novel, was to write a kind of historical sequel to the adventures of some of her main characters.[8]

The Leopard's Spots begins at the end of the Civil War, with ragged Confederate soldiers returning to face a new struggle against a black enemy at home. The characters derived from Stowe's novel do not occupy central stage; they are brought on to score ironic points against the general ethos of interracial amity of the Tom material. Recognizing that Simon Legree had become the very type of the melodramatic villain, Dixon makes no effort, as earlier anti-Tom literature did, to rehabilitate him as a kindly master. Rather, he attempts to one-up Stowe historically by using him as the ideal representative villain for each of the later historical periods portrayed. Thus Legree becomes a cowardly draft dodger disguised as a woman during the Civil War, a carpetbagger politician stirring black men to agitate for the right to marry white women during Reconstruction, and a rapacious Yankee industrialist during the latter part of the century.[9] This final incarnation allows Dixon to bring Legree into conflict with yet another of Stowe's characters, "George ([*sic*]) Harris," the mulatto son of George and Eliza, named Harry in Stowe's version.[10]

Dixon has George Harris sent to Harvard to become the protégé of the Honorable Everett Lowell of Massachusetts. Encouraged to improve himself by Lowell, George eventually aspires to do so by marrying Lowell's daughter.

When he is rudely rejected by Lowell, George wanders the nation in search of work. Aided by a labor leader and Quaker preacher who is another descendent of a Stowe character, George is turned away everywhere, eventually even at one of Simon Legree's mills. Throughout this sequel Dixon drives home his ironic anti-Tom moral: the Harvard-educated son of George and Eliza Harris begs in vain for the privilege of serving as Legree's wage slave.[11] Despairing of work in a world run by Simon Legree, George turns to crime and uses his proceeds to place wreaths on the ash-heaps of lynched Negroes, feeling constantly "the grip of Simon Legree's hand on his throat" (Dixon 1903, 407).

Without actually idealizing the "good old days" of slavery—which he has several staunch southern characters admit were an economic and social mistake—Dixon nevertheless wants his readers to long for a time when blacks knew their place and did not need to suffer the agonies of lynching, for political and social equality inevitably leads in Dixon's novels to the black male claim to the white woman as a mate. As one character puts it, "The beginning of Negro equality . . . is the beginning of the end of this nation's life" (244). "Mongrelization" of the races is Dixon's greatest fear. The burning question of the novel is posed repeatedly and italicized for emphasis: "*Can you hold in a Democracy, a nation inside a nation of two hostile races?* We must do this or become mulatto, and that is death" (Dixon 1903, 244).[12]

Such, then, are the explicitly racial, explicitly anti-Tom politics of Dixon's first novel, as it directly attempts to refute Stowe's romantic racialism with a new twentieth-century demonic racism. Dixon attempts to dismantle this structure by turning the "good nigger" bad by sexualizing his relations with white womanhood and by having him assault the "holy of holies"—the white female virgin. The effect, in terms of its affront to the Tom tradition, is as if Tom were shown to lust after Little Eva. Thus Stowe's antebellum, feminized "good Negro" is sexualized and demonized into the postbellum, hyper-masculine rapist who can only be stopped by lynching. Stowe describes Uncle Tom in the novel as "a large, broad-chested, powerfully-made man, of a full glossy black, and a face whose truly African features were characterized by an expression of grave and steady good sense, united with much kindliness and benevolence" (1983, 18). Stowe's Tom is certainly not feminine in his physical features—"large, broad-chested," "glossy black"—but his masculine physicality leaves the details of his "truly African features" quite vague, tempered by feminine qualities of soul—kindliness, benevolence, dignity, humility, and so on.[13]

Compare Dixon's description from his second novel, *The Clansman*, of another uncle, Uncle Alec:

> His head was small and seemed mashed on the sides until it bulged into a double lobe behind. Even his ears, which he had pierced and hung with red earbobs, seemed to have been crushed flat to the side of his head. His kinked hair was wrapped in little hard rolls close to

the skull and bound tightly with dirty thread. His receding forehead was high and indicated cunning intelligence. His nose was broad and crushed flat against his face. His jaws were strong and angular, mouth wide, and lips thick, curling back from rows of solid teeth set obliquely in their blue gums. . . . His thin spindle-shanks supported an oblong, protruding stomach, resembling an elderly monkey's, which seemed so heavy it swayed his back to carry it. (Dixon 1905a, 249)

In contrast to Stowe's generality, Dixon offers specifics, assuming that villainous qualities of soul emanate from "angular jaw," "thick lips," "cunning forehead," and "spindle shanks." To Stowe the feminine soul transcends the masculine body. To Dixon there is no spiritual transcendence for the Negro who is all animal, even when, like Uncle Alec, he *isn't* lusting after white women. Thus it is not simply that Stowe feminizes the black man, while Dixon hypermasculinizes him; it is also that Stowe deemphasizes the corporeal for the spiritual, while Dixon sees blackness as an excess of the corporeal that harks back to the jungle and retards civilization.

Where the antebellum, anti-Tom literature had shared minstrelsy's fascination with a highly visible, commodified black body, viewed as comically different, Dixon counters these familiar comic stereotypes with a rabid horror of all things black. In effect, he challenges both Stowe's depiction of black spirituality and minstrelsy's depiction of comic sexuality. In *The Clansman*, for example, the traditional northern distaste for the physical features of blacks — criticized by Stowe in Aunt Ophelia's first reactions to Topsy — is vindicated. Elsie Stoneman, daughter of the Radical Reconstructionist Austin Stoneman (modeled on the Radical Reconstruction leader Thaddeus Stevens), recoils at the touch and smell of Negroes and fires her black cook for feeding her children in the kitchen.

Insistently, Dixon counters the myth of the gentle, familiar, melodic, and rhythmical "good nigger" with a new myth of the rapacious "bad nigger." Citizenship had transformed the black man from a piece of property into the potential owner of property, including the property of women. As Robyn Wiegman explains, the black man's threat to white masculine power thus "arises not simply from a perceived racial difference, but from the potential for masculine sameness" (1995, 90). It was this possibility of sameness that the rape myth disavowed. Its peculiar logic was to exaggerate the very quality of masculinity that granted black men the vote. Excessive, hypermasculine corporeality disqualified him from manhood, reducing him to the status of beast. Dixon's predatory beast is forever baring his fangs and claws.

This new dangerous corporeality of the black male also operated to mask the white male's own previous participation in miscegenational sexual activities. Projecting his own sexual unruliness onto the villainous beast, the white male placed on southern women the burden of preserving an integrity of racial distinctions that many white masters, like Simon Legree, had often violated. The myth of the bestial black rapist transferred the focus of sexuality from the white man's quasi-sanctioned (because economically productive) sexual activities with black women to the spectacularized bodies of black men (Wiegman 1995, 84). Thus, instead of Stowe's discrete portrayal of a historically more accurate white male / black female interracial sexual violence, Dixon offers a historically exceptional example of black male / white female sexual violence.

105

The painfully obvious double standard could only mean that white women were meant to be the sole property of white men, while black women could be the property of all. The myth of the black rapist reached its most pathological proportions at the turn of the century (the time of Dixon's writing), due partly to its congruence with the exaggerated sexual tensions of a dying Victorianism. According to Jacquelyn Dowd Hall, it may have been no accident that the vision of the hypermasculine Negro flourished during a time that was also the first organized phase of the women's rights movement in the South (Hall 1993, 148, 153). The New Woman, for example, hovers over Dixon's novels as a potential threat to white patriarchy much more forcefully than she does over Griffith's film.[14]

The Clansman: An Historical Romance of the Ku Klux Klan (1905) abandons the vast historical panorama of *The Leopard's Spots* to concentrate on the immediate period of Reconstruction and the rise of the Clan. Dixon here makes his main character, Ben Cameron, a Clan leader and makes the novel's climax a dramatic rescue. The result is a more effective melodrama, alternating political drama in Washington with the story of the aristocratic Cameron family of Piedmont, South Carolina, and the northern Stoneman family. Thus, while the Radical Republicans maneuver to impeach Andrew Johnson, the Camerons pick up their lives after the war and become romantically entangled with the Stonemans.

In this novel, Dixon stages the pathos of the white women endangered by black men in a key scene showing the brutal rape of Marion Lenoir, by the former slave Gus. Gus's punishment by lynching can be read in gendered terms as a castration that returns the hypermasculine body to its prior feminized state.[15] Dixon, however, gives very little physical detail, either of Gus's attack or of the Clan's lynching of Gus. He concentrates, instead, on an almost obsessive deployment of evidence of the crime. In a first instance, he has Dr. Cameron examine the dead eyes of the mother who witnessed the crime.

> "I believe that a microscope of sufficient power will reveal on the retina of these dead eyes the image of this devil as if etched there by fire. The experiment has been made successfully in France. . . .

> Impressions remain in the brain like words written on paper in invisible ink. So I believe of images in the eye if we can trace them early enough. If no impression were made subsequently on the mother's eye by the light of day, I believe the fire-etched record of this crime can yet be traced." (Dixon 1905a, 312–13)

Though Dr. Cameron does indeed find "evidence" of the crime etched in the woman's retina, he resorts to yet another form of indexical registration of the body of the black rapist in measurements of his bare footprint: "The white man was never born who could make that track. The enormous heel projected backward, and in the hollow of the instep where the dirt would scarcely be touched by an Aryan was the deep wide mark of the African's flat foot" (Dixon 1905a, 310). These putative racial characteristics of the foot are then presented as evidence at the Clan's "trial" in a cave. The primitive cave location suggests Dixon's at least unconscious awareness that he is dangerously flirting with the white man's own regression to primitive, beastlike status.

The crowning piece of evidence, and high point of the melodrama in the chapter entitled "The Fiery Cross," is the moment the ever-scientific doctor hypnotizes Gus to induce him to reenact the crime by the torchlight of the cave with hooded Clansmen as jury.

> Gus rose to his feet and started across the cave as if to spring on the shivering figure of the girl, the clansmen with muttered groans, sobs and curses falling back as he advanced. He still wore his full Captain's uniform, its heavy epaulets flashing their gold in the unearthly light, his beastly jaws half covering the gold braid on the collar. His thick lips were drawn in an ugly leer and his sinister bead-eyes gleamed like a gorilla's. A single fierce leap and the black claws clutched the air slowly as if sinking into the soft white throat. (Dixon 1905a, 323)

These various strategies of evidence all boil down to detailed descriptions of the black male body—of Gus's jaw and lips as imprinted on the mother's retina, the indexical imprint of his oversized foot, and his whole racialized and sexualized body as he physically reenacts the crime. In each case, the very absence of hard evidence of the act itself becomes the occasion for a ritualized enumeration of the features of the black body that are themselves considered incriminating. These features come to stand in for the unmentionable details of the crime itself.[16]

The other side of this obsession with the unmentionable act of sexual violation was, of course, the often equally sexualized punishment of lynching.[17] The term lynching originated during the Revolutionary War when Charles Lynch of Virginia formed a vigilante association to rid the area of plundering Tories. After the war, Lynch's illegal violence was exonerated by the legislature, and the verb form of his name came to mean a half-accepted form of vigilante justice, often carried out by elite landowners but rarely involving murder. After the Civil War, however, lynching came to take on new meaning: as systematic terror against blacks, actually reaching its height not during Reconstruction and the reign of the KKK but in the 1880s and 1890s.[18] In this period "lynching" could include torture, hanging, burning, mutilation, and castration.

In *The Clansman*, Dixon's description of Gus's punishment is remarkably reticent. After the "trial," when the hysterical Clansmen are ready to rip Gus to pieces, Dr. Cameron is seized instead by "a sudden inspiration." Taking a silver cup, he mixes the blood of the raped virgin with river water and ties together two sticks in the form of a cross. Back inside the cave he adapts "the old Scottish rite of the Fiery Cross" to a new form of worship, proclaiming that the liquid "red stain of the life of a Southern woman" represents a "priceless sacrifice on the altar of outraged civilization." At this point Ben Cameron removes his hood and pronounces Gus's sentence of execution. How he dies, we do not learn. Thus, in Dixon's novel, the animal passion of the Clansmen is sublimated into the ritual celebration of the southern woman's "priceless sacrifice."

Dixon builds white male solidarity around the ritual celebration of the white woman's bloody "sacrifice," rather than around the bloody sacrifice of the black male scapegoat. As Jacquelyn Dowd Hall notes, the constant threat of rape was not simply a rationalization used to obscure the real function of keeping black men in their place, it was also a way to keep white women in their place. The "fear of rape, like the threat of lynching, served to keep a subordinate group in a state of anxiety and fear" (Hall 1993, 153). Thus, it is in a very real sense that the white woman is sacrificed "on the altar of outraged civilization." White men need her to be sacrificed to keep both blacks *and* women in their place. This sacrifice, ultimately, was Dixon's most successful revenge on Mrs. Stowe.

Aside from the radical shift from Stowe's negrophilia to Dixon's negrophobia, the biggest structural difference in these novels is the displacement of Stowe's narrative of bondage and escape into the familiar model of heterosexual romance.[19] In his 1905 play *The Clansman*, a theatrical condensation of key elements of his two novels, Dixon would find a more powerful anti-Tom formula by forgoing his attempt to respond to Stowe explicitly.[20] Abandoning the Legree villain altogether, Dixon replaced him partly with the Radical Republican senator Austin Stoneman, and partly with the ironically named Silas Lynch, his mulatto protégé. Where the George Harris figure in *The Leopard's Spots* had been a figure of pathos, wandering the country from ash heap to ash heap of lynched Negroes, Silas Lynch—whose very name, as Michael Rogin (1984, 208) notes, turns black victims of lynching into aggressors—combines the pathos of the tragic mulatto (doomed to be accepted by neither race) with cunning villainy.[21]

When, in his play, Dixon decided to make Silas Lynch a primary villain, not merely offending Elsie with his corporeal presence, but sexually forcing that presence upon her, he finally found the perfect replacement for Simon Legree. The echo of their initials suggests that Dixon was aware of their similar functions. Where Simon Legree is a white man in sexual possession of mulatta concubines, Silas Lynch is a mulatto seeking possession of a white woman. Turning the mulatta victim into a mulatto villain, Dixon neatly reverses the racial markers of villains and victims. "Blame the mulatto" would seem to be one part of his racial melodrama. "Blame the mulatta" is its other part.

In the novel Austin Stoneman's mulatta "housekeeper," Lydia Brown, rules his household in Washington. Dixon hints that she is the real power behind the throne of radical reconstruction. He attributes Stoneman's desire to crush the South with Negro misrule to his perverse desire for this woman of "extraordinary animal beauty" (1905a, 57), who lords it over his hypocritical Radical Republican cronies.[22] As Michael Rogin 1984, 208–09 has persuasively argued, the Stoneman/Brown sexual relation in Griffith effects a double reversal that shifts blame for forced white male/black female interracial sexual relations from the South to the North and from the white man to the colored woman. Thus in the novel Lydia Brown becomes the racialized locus of evil female sexuality and Silas Lynch becomes that of the male.[23]

Dixon's two novels were instant popular successes.[24] They invited extravagant praise and condemnation along predictable sectional lines (Cook 1968, 73). The same thing was not true, however, of their theatrical combination. Produced by the aptly titled "Southern Amusement Company," the play swept triumphantly through the South, garnering enthusiastic reviews and sometimes generating controversy among those southerners who subscribed to more liberal racial views.[25] Dixon exacerbated the controversy by giving curtain speeches to make sure audiences got his point.[26] The play's tour continued to sell out throughout the Midwest and the West, where it was more controversial but still successful. On the strength of these successes, a second company was put together for New York City that premiered January 8, 1906, at the Liberty Theatre—where *The Birth of a Nation* would receive its New York premiere nine years later. Here was Dixon's chance to "teach the North" its lesson about white southern suffering. To the surprise of many, it sold out there as well (Cook 1968, 145–46).[27]

Thus Dixon capitalized on the notoriety of his play to preach the anti-Tom message that had impelled him to write fiction and drama in the first place.[28] Five years after he had seen the Tom show whose love for the antebellum Negro had changed the racial sentiments of the North, Dixon had made a significant assault on those sentiments. However, his radical racial views excoriating Negroes still represented the extreme fringe of southern politics. Though the tour of his play beyond the South represented a measure of success, conservative racial views, which simply wanted to maintain the Negro's inferior position, were still much more dominant in the South. Liberals supporting uplift represented another minority. As melodrama, however, Dixon's ideas had an emotional viability and power that his speeches and sermons did not. The ultimate proof of that viability would, of course, be the reconfiguration of its major sentiments by Griffith into a film that would finally do in the Progressive Era what *Uncle Tom's Cabin* had done sixty years before and what the minor success of Dixon's novels and plays had not done: alter *national* sentiments about race.

109

The Birth of a Nation

Legend has it that when D. W. Griffith's film *The Clansman* was given a preliminary screening at New York's Liberty Theater, Thomas Dixon called out to Griffith across the auditorium that its title was too tame for such a mighty work and that it should be called *The Birth of a Nation* (Williamson 1984, 175; Cook 1968, 168). Richard Schickel (1984, 246, 268) doubts the authenticity of this story, since there is evidence that the name had already appeared as a subtitle in early advertising of the film. It seems likely that Dixon's renaming was more a confirmation of a title that had already been floated by publicists. Either way, however, the idea of a spirit of national rebirth forged through the expulsion of racial scapegoats is deeply embedded in Dixon's work.[29]

One effect of this renaming, over time, has been to distance Griffith's film from its sources in Dixon. Though Dixon's contribution would often be acknowledged, it would more frequently be viewed as a source that had been transcended. Poet Vachel Lindsay's *The Art of the Moving Picture*, published in 1915, set the trend. Lindsay claims that whenever Griffith follows *The Clansman* his film is bad, but whenever "it is unadulterated Griffith, which is half the time, it is good" (Lindsay 1915, 75–76). As we saw at the beginning of this chapter, *The Birth of a Nation* came to be regarded as the film in which the movies themselves were born and D. W. Griffith became known as the first "father" of film. By 1939 Lewis Jacobs would claim that *The Birth of a Nation* "foreshadowed the best that was to come in cinema technique," and that it "earned for the screen its right to the status of art" (Jacobs 1939, 171). In 1958, southerner James Agee went beyond all previous claims with this much-quoted pronouncement: "He achieved what no other known man has ever achieved. To watch his work is like being witness to the beginning of melody, or the first conscious use of the lever or the wheel; the emergence, coordination, and first eloquence of language; the birth of an art: and to realize that this is all the work of one man" (313). More recently, in a 1981 history of world cinema, David Cook writes:

110

> The achievement of David Wark Griffith (1875–1948) is unprece-
> dented in the history of Western art, much less Western film. In the
> brief span of six years, between directing his first one reeler in 1908
> and *The Birth of a Nation* in 1914, Griffith established the narrative
> language of the cinema as we know it today, and turned an aestheti-
> cally inconsequential medium of entertainment into a fully articu-
> lated art form. He has been called, variously, and for the most part,
> accurately, "the father of film technique," "the man who invented
> Hollywood," "the cinema's first great auteur," and "the Shakespeare
> of the screen." (Cook 1981, 59)

In most of these claims there is a persistent tendency to attribute what is
great and wonderful in Griffith to his position as godlike, autonomous origina-
tor positioned outside of time and history, and to attribute what is embarrassing and racist in him to his local, time-bound influences. This is how
historian David Cook continues his assessment: "He was unquestionably the
seminal genius of the narrative cinema and its first great visionary artist, but"—
and with Griffith there is always this "but"—"he was also a provincial Southern romantic with pretensions to high literary culture and a penchant for
sentimentality and melodrama that would have embarrassed Dickens." Moreover, he was "a muddleheaded racial bigot, incapable of abstract thought,
who quite literally saw all of human history in the black-and-white terms of
nineteenth-century melodrama." The following is how James Agee puts his
"but": "Even in Griffith's best work [there is much] that is poor, or foolish, or
old-fashioned." Agee then goes on to note how limited Griffith was, with no
"power of intellect," no "subtlety," little "taste," no capacity for growth, and
saturated by the "mannerisms . . . assumptions and attitudes of the 19th century provincial theater" (Agee 1958, 315, 317).

What is striking in these reservations is not only how harsh they are following such high praise, but the dichotomy created between a "good"—aesthetic and universal—Griffith, speaking to all mankind, and the "bad"—nineteenth-century, melodramatic southern racist—Griffith, speaking only of the
past and to whites. With respect to *The Birth of a Nation*, these dichotomies
often boil down to the "good" first half of the film, showing the quaint ways
of the antebellum South culminating in the Civil War, and the "bad" second
half, showing the horrors of black rule corrected by the Ku Klux Klan. The
"good" first half was seen as more Griffith's invention and the "bad" second
half was blamed on Dixon.

A more recent tradition of scholarship on *The Birth of a Nation* has put
the issue of race first and tackled head-on the evasions of past criticism. Michael Rogin (1984, 191), as we have already seen, begins his groundbreaking
essay with the proclamation that American film is born "in a racist epic."
And Clyde Taylor (1991, 13) rightly accuses the entire field of film studies of

celebrating the aesthetics of Griffith's film at the expense of investigating the meaning of an allegory of national identity founded on the exclusion of blacks as a co-defining anti-type.[30] Both critics have brilliantly argued that there is no separating the film's celebrated rhetorical and narrative achievements from its defamation of African Americans. Both works have also moved from blaming Dixon for the white supremacist ideology in the film to finding Griffith's adaptation even more hateful.[31]

My consideration of Griffith's film follows the lead of these important reassessments of the deeply embedded racism of this most influential of American films. However, because I am interested in the larger tradition of black and white racial melodrama, I argue that by the time Griffith's film swept the nation, it swayed national sentiment toward white southerners as victims of black "misrule," not because it was more vehement than Dixon, but because it drew more effectively on the pathos, action, and melos of what the Tom story had become in the postbellum period: a nostalgic look at the old South that included kindly affection for the black bodies that Dixon's radical credo so abhorred. Indeed, if there is a sense in which we can say that mainstream American film was "born" in a racist epic, then we need to see that this birth was not virgin; it was from the beginning already cross-fertilized by the romantic racialism of the Tom tradition. Thus it is not quite accurate to claim, as Rogin and Taylor do, that *The Birth of a Nation* represents the dramatic moment in American popular culture when sympathy for blacks converted to outright national race hatred, typified by the new sympathy for energetic white heroes rescuing white maidens in distress. Rather, as with its folded sets whose hinges and architecture were borrowed from Tom shows, our deepest understanding of this film will come through an appreciation of its place in a developing melodrama of black and white.[32]

We saw in the last chapter that when *Uncle Tom's Cabin* was first brought to the stage, numerous versions were realized before any dared to show the beating death of Uncle Tom. But once this hurdle was passed, any performance of the play in the antebellum period that depicted Tom's martyrdom became a potential threat to the Union. The more Tom suffered, the more sectional divisions were exacerbated, and the more incendiary the work.[33] We have also seen how postbellum theatrical and film versions attempted to paper over these divisions with icons of reunification, usually of Union and Confederate troops shaking hands on the battlefield. But no matter how much these latter versions tried, the old Tom story, whose most convulsive moments had come to stand for sectional division, could not be used to generate warm feelings of national reunion. Thomas Dixon had understood that the answer to Stowe could be found in the exaggerated suffering of the white woman at the hands of the hypersexual black man: the more the white woman suffered, the more sympathy would flow to the South. But like the novel and the stage versions of Uncle Tom, his version of the anti-Tom story did not bring about national union either. It would take a new kind of Tom story—Dixon's rabid anti-Tom diatribe in solution with the more racially amical elements of Stowe's Tom story—to cover over these sectional divisions and to effect a "rebirth" of (a white supremacist) nation. *The Birth of a Nation* became an agent of national reunion because it offered to many whites in the North and South what felt like a fitting conclusion and answer to the sectional disunion of the Tom story. Thus, while later Tom shows and films attempted briefly to narrate the history of North and South in the aftermath of conflicts that its very story had helped to generate, Griffith's film, despite its radical shift from negrophilia to negrophobia, came to seem the logical continuation of the story of slavery. One reason was that, unlike Dixon but like Stowe, it told this story from the beginning.

The film begins with a prologue that treats the origins of slavery in the United States. An intertitle blames disunion on the presence of black bodies: "The bringing of the African to America planted the first seed of disunion." We see a minister praying over manacled slaves to be auctioned in a town square. The next intertitle notes: "The Abolitionists of the Nineteenth Century demanding the freeing of the slaves." We see a crowded church or meeting house in which a speaker gestures toward a slave while a black child is led up the aisle. Jane Gaines and Neil Lerner (2000) have shown that Joseph Carl Breil's original score introduced a theme labeled "The Motif of Barbarism" to accompany these early, and all subsequent, appearances of the threatening and ominous "black seed."[34] According to Breil, Griffith had hummed and chanted "some of the old croons of [the] mammies and [the] loose jointed young plantation negroes" to help Breil compose "the theme which opens the film . . . and which is thereafter ever applied to the description of the primitive instincts of the blacks" (Marks 1997, 186).

This "Motif of Barbarism" is of special interest to the study of black and white melodrama because it represents the first moment in this tradition in which the syncopated folk melos associated with Africans was appropriated to ominous, rather than nostalgic, or happy, purposes. In its first appearance here the "Motif of Barbarism" is immediately associated with a "tom-tom rhythm beating underneath a mildly syncopated melody" (Gaines and Lerner 2000, 5). Syncopation attached to connotations of "the primitive" was already well known in American popular music. It had become primarily known in the guise of portraying "happy-go-lucky darkies"—Breil himself uses variations on "Turkey in the Straw" to portray the slaves dancing near their cabins on the Cameron plantation several scenes later. However, syncopation attached to predatory sexual instincts was new. As we have seen, Thomas Dixon had regularly excoriated the "jungle rhythms" of African music. But he never succeeded in making his readers feel the evil of this music.[35] It would seem that Breil's score succeeded at vilifying some aspects of popular African-inflected folk music by replacing Dixon's diatribes against the music with a felt sense of its evil, even as it maintained the Stephen Foster tradition of associating virtue with the African "home." For Griffith also did not hesitate to have Breil, like the stage adaptations of Stowe, portray the "quaintly way" of the "Southland" via an adaptation of Stephen Foster's "Old Folks at Home."

Dixon had refused to tell "the story of slavery," not wanting to become an apologist for the very institution that brought the villainous "black seed" to American shores. Griffith seems to follow Dixon's sentiment toward slavery, blaming it on the slave traders.[36] But his willingness to take on a version of the story of slavery in this brief etiology, and to play out a more traditional antebellum anti-Tom plantation myth of the well-treated, childlike slaves in the rest of this first part of the film, gives him the ability to tell the story of slavery in a way that seemed a natural extension of Stowe. Not by telling the sequel of Stowe's characters, but by adapting and *detourning* her familiar story of slavery, Griffith becomes something more powerful than Stowe's anti-Tom opponent. He becomes her inheritor.

Dixon's novels and plays are full of speeches about sectional reunion. His ride of the Clan to save northerner Phil Stoneman at the end of his Clansman novel and Elsie Stoneman at the end of his play enacts a common purpose between North and South. Nevertheless, it was Griffith's film, and not Dixon's novel and play, that achieved the "moving picture" felt by many whites to heal national divisions. For it was not until Griffith's much grander ride "to save a nation" managed a much more effective form of racial exclusion than Dixon's lurid race hatred that audiences most deeply felt a sense of national rebirth in the empowering of the film's white hero.

Griffith's own explanation for the film's effect—that his "ride to the rescue" transcended that of ordinary melodramatic rescues—points to the important phenomenon of "multiple rescue operations" discussed by Michael Rogin. Rogin quotes Griffith's statement in his autobiography that upon reading Dixon's novel he skipped quickly through the book until he got to the Clan's ride: "We had all sorts of runs-to-the-rescue in pictures and horse operas. . . . Now I could see a chance to do this ride-to-the-rescue on a grand scale. Instead of saving one little Nell of the Plains, this ride would be to save a nation" (Rogin 1984, 191; Hart 1972, 88–89). The power of the grand climax of the film, to which many critics of the time refer, has been understood by Rogin as the effect of a new spatial-temporal organization made possible by the dynamization of cinematic editing.[37]

Most importantly, Rogin argues that the multiple rescues enacted by the ride of the Clan reenacted and reversed the Civil War battles that Griffith added to the first half of his film. Where blue and grey intermingle and become almost indistinguishable in the Civil War charges in the first half, the white robes of the Clan stand out against black masses in the second. Clansmen on horseback tower over black men on foot. "Civil War close-ups show suffering; Clan close-ups show movement and power" (Rogin 1984, 222). Thus, the extreme pathos of the defeat of the South, which Dixon did not represent, resonates powerfully against the extreme action of the climax in which the Clan rescues everyone in sight. The extremes of pathos, typified by sufferings on the battlefield and in the famous painfully slow homecoming in which Ben Cameron registers the full measure of southern defeat in the soot-daubed cotton ("southern ermine") of his little sister's dress, are balanced by the extreme action of the Clan's vengeance on Gus and rescues that exceed Dixon's rescue of Phil (in the novel) or Elsie (in the play).

In these exciting climaxes Griffith, unlike Dixon, sets up two endangered groups, both in need of rescue. Northerner Elsie Stoneman is caught in the clutches of Silas Lynch in his house in town while a mixed northern and southern group composed of Dr. Cameron, his wife, daughter, the Cameron family's two former slaves, and Phil Stoneman are trapped in a rural cabin with two Union veterans. This cabin is surrounded by attacking black troops. Since this second endangered group differs considerably from its source in Dixon, it is worth examining.

As Negro "misrule" grows, Dr. Cameron is arrested for possession of a Clan costume—for which the penalty is death. After arrest he is taunted and humiliated in the slave quarters (a title reads, "The master paraded before his former slaves"). Two of his former slaves, Mammy and Jake, sympathetic "good" slaves borrowed from the Tom tradition and eschewed by Dixon, pretend to join the black mockers in order to position themselves to rescue the doctor. Jake jokes with the white captain, asking him "Is I yo equal cap'n—jes like any white man?" just before knocking him out.[38] Mammy, at the same time, pretends friendliness to two black soldiers, putting her ample arms around them and then crushing them to the ground with the weight of her body. Thus Griffith, unlike Dixon, comically heroicized his "faithful souls"— by which he means the types of Negroes who, like Uncle Tom, remained faithful and selfless in the service of kind masters[39]—by involving them in the rescue. The comic vein of these heroics, however, employing the obese (blackface) Mammy's body weight and an outlandish claim to equality, undercuts their seriousness. Nor are they very effective, since this preliminary rescue party led by "faithful souls" fails when a wheel falls off their wagon, causing all to seek refuge in a nearby Union Veterans' cabin. This failed rescue thus permits Griffith to maneuver this interracial group of whites and blacks, northerners and southerners, into a rural cabin where they will eventually be rescued by the Clan. Thereafter, the film cuts rapidly between Lynch's sexual threat to Elsie, the discovery of that threat by "white spies" disguised as blacks, the endangered extended "family" fighting off the black troops, and the Clan riding first to the rescue of Elsie, then to the family in the cabin.

The Cabin

Michael Rogin brilliantly argues that this rescue of the family from the cabin is not just from any cabin but a "Lincoln log cabin" whose refuge ironically democratizes and merges, as the famous intertitle puts it, "former enemies of North and South . . . reunited again in common defense of their Aryan birthright." Rogin thus shows us the national unity that Griffith's rescue accomplishes and that Dixon's didn't (Fig. 3.2). For if Dixon had radically shifted Stowe's sectionally divisive narrative of escape and bondage to romance and rescue, Griffith's innovative rescue of the cabin by the Clan radically shifts the meaning of what is rescued. The cabin wraps the former slave owners in the mantle of humble beginnings and reconciles former enemies (in the first part of the scene "Auld Lang Syne" is played). For while it is "former master" Dr. Cameron who is actually rescued, his location in the rural cabin—and his association with the humble Union Veterans frying bacon over their hearth—dissociates him from the once grand Cameron Hall and the institution of slavery. Griffith could easily have had the doctor take refuge in his own home and had the black troops surround it. During the first half of the film he had done just that when he showed the Cameron parents and daughters besieged in the house, while "black guerrilla" troops raided the town. However, this later variation of rescue replaces the iconography of the grand plantation with the humble home of the cabin, which the reenergized doctor defends vigorously with his North and South, rich and poor, black and white comrades. Griffith, unlike Dixon, thus makes his audience feel Stowe-like emotions of democratic inclusion even while rooting for the "common" defense of an exclusive "Aryan birthright."

But perhaps the real reason Griffith can get away with such contradictory gestures of white supremacy and democracy is that the association of this cabin is not limited to Abraham Lincoln. Its emotional and iconographic resonance extends further back than Lincoln, whom we have seen appear as an icon at the end of the post-war Tom shows, to the iconographically prior cabin of Tom himself.[40] We have seen how nostalgia for a democratic and humble "space of innocence" so central to all melodrama was located in the icon of Tom's cabin—the integrated place where Master George Shelby, Jr., once taught Tom how to read, where Mrs. Shelby came to weep with Tom and Chloe, and of which the songs "Old Folks at Home" and "My Old Kentucky Home" sang nostalgically. This cabin, which seems to function out of all proportion to its actual importance as a locale in the novel, hovers, as we have seen, over all Tom's longing, in speech and song, for the impossibly good, lost Kentucky home.[41]

The cabin, which we have seen on the cover of volume one of the novel's first edition (showing the doorway, several children, Aunt Chloe, and Tom;

Figure 3.2 The "Lincoln" and "Tom" cabin besieged by blacks. (*The Birth of a Nation*)

see Fig. 2.1), also figured in the first act of most stage productions of the play. After the Civil War, traveling Tom shows would frequently include a mobile cabin as part of their parade through the streets of each new town. As the American *locus classicus* of honest and humble beginnings, the cabin has now become in Griffith's film as important a mantle of virtue for the former masters as it once had been for the former slaves. Symbolizing variously the elusive lost home of slaves, the poor but honest home of the free white man, it now attempts to spread its mantle of homey virtue over the sins of the former masters.

By "integrating" the cabin with the "Tom" figures of Mammy and Jake, with the humble Union veterans and Phil Stoneman, son of the Radical Republican, as well as with the former members of the slavocracy, the Cameron family, Griffith refunctions melodrama's all-important "space of innocence." The melodrama that once pictured Tom and Chloe as victims of an economic system that reduced humans to objects of exchange now makes the equivalent figures of Tom and Chloe "faithful souls" who participate as good guys in the melodrama of white victimization. Inside the cabin, Mammy fiercely and heroically fights off the black marauders, clubbing each intruding black head after the besieged group is out of ammunition; but, like her comic flattening of two black soldiers, her actions lack the heroic status of Eliza's desperate protection of her child or Tom's heroic martyrdom. She has become the proto-type of countless stage and screen Mammies to come, sharing in the pathos and action of white main characters. For her story only matters so long as the former masters and their new allies are themselves racially endangered.[42]

Stowe paints Tom's integrated cabin as an exceptional Eden in a state **117** with the "mildest form of slavery," and then shows how "hard times come a' knocking at the door" in the form of sale downriver. The problem the Tom material faced was how to make the happy ending of the reunion of George and Eliza and Cassy feel as if it had regained something of this initial space of innocence when it could not physically locate that space in Kentucky—or indeed any place in the nation.[43] As we have seen, Stowe's projected reunion of the African family in Liberia lacks emotional conviction. Africa cannot resonate as home the same way as "Kintuck"—at least until Alex Haley rewrites Tom and anti-Tom to generate a new nostalgia for a lost African home.

Griffith, too, faced the problem of establishing a melodramatic space of innocence. He solved it by adapting Dixon's Reconstruction drama to a glowing portrait of antebellum culture much in the fashion of the earlier, anti-Tom, plantation novels. But Griffith could get away with such a regressive move because, unlike Dixon and the earlier plantation novels, he also told the story of the Civil War and Reconstruction. The representation of these more recent events made any idea of return to the good old days of the plantation impossible. Indeed, there is even a sense in which Griffith's por-trayal of antebellum life pretends to the prelapsarian innocence of small-town rural America that is deeply indebted to the iconography of the postbellum Tom show.

Consider, once again, the architecture of the main street (Fig. 3.1), which Karl Brown informs us was built with unnecessary hinges that paid homage to the tradition of the traveling, postbellum Tom show. The set reveals that Griffith clearly understood that the locus of virtue does not reside in the big house of the plantation but in the humble rural home. Architecturally his street set is, in its own humble way, as revealing of the informing contradic-tions of his ideology as is the grand set of Babylon in his next film, *Intolerance* (1916).[44] The shot depicting Piedmont's main street is the first to introduce Griffith's "Southland," where, as an intertitle puts it, "life runs in a quaintly way that is to be no more." It is pictured as a street and sidewalk in a sleepy southern town where white folks lounge on their front porches and stroll on the sidewalk, and a crowded cart with a group of Negroes passes by. In this frame enlargement, we see the cart as it passes before the modest picket fence of the Cameron abode. Inside the fence Jake stands facing the street and Mammy stands serving tea. The doctor and Mrs. Cameron sit near the classi-cal columns of their porch. Soon, as the wagon in the foreground pulls down

Figure 3.3 The Clan rides through the main street of Piedmont and past the humble site of the Cameron home. (*The Birth of a Nation*)

the street, two black children comically fall off it; a black man picks them up and carries one of them off. The Cameron family looks on in amusement.

At this point in the film the residence that is elsewhere in the film called Cameron Hall seems to be a modest house in town. Except for the four white classical columns, making it the most imposing house on the street, it nevertheless blends in with the other houses as one of several arrayed in a row. At the end of the street is a building that seems to be a modest church. Much of the action of the film will transpire on this main set, as for example when the Clan rides through town (Fig. 3.3). Clearly, what the Clan defends is meant to be seen as the values of such a modest white-picket-fence town.

At other points in the film, however, and especially when we see its interior, Cameron Hall earns its name as a grand manor. When the officers of what seems to be the entire Confederate army dance at its farewell ball we see a whole different world of size, scale, and elegance that is incommensurate with the modest front porch on the sleepy main street depicted earlier. At these points Cameron Hall becomes a grand plantation with cotton fields, slaves, and slave cabins. "Out back," the younger Camerons and Stonemans are seen to stroll, as an intertitle puts it, "Over the plantation to the cotton

Figure 3.4 Cameron Hall as plantation. "Over the plantation to the cotton fields." (*The Birth of a Nation*)

fields" where happy slaves pick cotton in the background (Fig. 3.4) to the accompaniment of Breil's adaption of Stephen Foster's "Old Folks at Home." Later, these same slaves dance to the tune of "Turkey in the Straw," during what the intertitles tell us is "the two hour interval given for dinner, out of their working day from six until six." After this familiar dance, so typical of the early portions of a postbellum "Tom show," a kindly Ben Cameron shakes hands with his slaves.

Griffith here deals with the same structural problem as Stowe: how to establish a melodramatic space of innocence within the culture of slavery. Both Stowe and Griffith needed a "home" whose virtue the happy ending could regain. To provide the felt sense of that home, Griffith paints both a traditionally romanticized picture of grand plantation life *and* a picture of a modest rural home iconographically borrowed from the postbellum Tom show. He thus constructs nostalgia for kindly masters and happy childlike slaves that Dixon, who abhorred the "black beast," did not share. The architectural contradiction that conceives of Cameron Hall as an ordinary house on Main Street—eventually to be converted into a humble boarding house—at the same time as a grand plantation is something more than a convenient condensation of locales necessary to the film's action. It is a condensation that makes slavery itself morally legible to a Progressive Era audience impressed by the grandeur of the old South but democratically offended by the feudal conditions of bondage.

Thomas Dixon's anti-Tom strategy had been to avoid all romanticized depictions of the antebellum era, believing, as he did, that slavery had been a mistake in its importation of "black blood." Thus Dixon was at least consistent in his exclusion of blacks—even the "faithful" ones—from any nostalgic image of the past or any happy ending pointing to the future. Griffith, on the other hand, was democratically inclusive. He freely borrowed the nostalgicized musical associations with black culture that Dixon had so vehemently eschewed when he had Elsie give up the banjo and when he used "vulgar" Negro tunes to underscore the deaths of his raped white women.[45] He freely included Mammy and Jake as the good folks in need of rescue, granting them comic heroic status. Yet by virtue of including "faithful" blacks in the emotional sense of what the Clan was rescuing, he was later able to exclude them all the more effectively from any real presence in the "newly born" nation.

Griffith's exclusion of blacks is never represented as a calculated policy of Jim Crow politics but as a natural result of the rescue of the white woman from the black rapist. In each of the multiple rescues carried out in the last third of the film, black men are quite literally wiped from the screen by what poet Vachel Lindsay once called the "white Anglo Saxon Niagara" of the Clan.[46] Indeed, the ride of the Clan is repeatedly figured as a flushing of blackness from the screen. Chaos and disorder represented as dark bodies in riot (Fig. 3.5) are swept aside by the Clan (Fig. 3.6). This pattern is repeated with each new rescue, in which nearly all-black frames are suddenly flooded with white. When Elsie is rescued the shot begins with the white-robed Elsie, partly hidden behind her dark-clad father, surrounded by the black-clad Lynch and his dark-clothed black henchmen. When the white-robed Clansmen enter, they push the dark-clad Lynch and Stoneman to the side. Lynch cowers to the left and Stoneman is now mostly hidden behind Elsie's white gown (Fig. 3.7).

A most striking moment of black exclusion also occurs in a scene that an intertitle calls "Disarming the blacks." Griffith shows a group of black soldiers on foot in their dark Union uniforms surrounded on both sides by white-robed Clansmen on foot and horseback. The dark soldiers drop their guns and rapidly exit both front and rear of the frame, leaving an empty white middle that now blends with the white Clansmen on both sides. The culminating shot effectively "parades" the racial cleansing that the multiple rescues have accomplished in what an intertitle of some prints calls the "Parade of the Clansmen." Elsie and the group rescued from the cabin are surrounded on both sides by the white-robed and -hooded Clansmen. Since Elsie is still in her white gown and the rescued men are mostly without jackets, the effect is again of a flood of white almost completely filling the screen (Fig. 3.8). Not

Figure 3.5   The chaos and disorder of rioting black bodies. (*The Birth of a Nation*)

Figure 3.6   Dark chaos swept aside by the "white Niagara" of the Clan. (*The Birth of a Nation*)

Figure 3.7   Elsie rescued by the Clan. Evil black is pushed to the sides and background of the frame. (*The Birth of a Nation*)

surprisingly, neither Mammy nor Jake—nor any other "faithful souls"—are anywhere to be seen. The following shot shows a group of blacks watching the parade in fear, turning and almost tiptoeing away, again leaving the frame white. Repeatedly and variously, then, white images displace black. It would seem that Griffith's greater ability to borrow elements of Stowe's interracial amity in the picture of kind masters and "faithful souls" ultimately aids him in accomplishing a total whitewash of the screen.

Griffith's "good Negro" appears to have made it possible for his activation of greater race hatred as well—both in the sexual attacks on white women and in the Clan's punishment of Gus. For even though in Dixon's novel Gus actually rapes the Cameron family friend, Marion Lenoir, we have seen that Dixon substituted detailed descriptions of the horror of the lascivious black male body for descriptions of the horror of the act of rape. In his stage version, however, he was less willing to show the black beast in physical contact with the white woman and so changed the crime to Gus's pursuit of Flora Cameron (no longer Marion), culminating in her jump off a cliff to save herself from the proverbial "fate worse than death." In both the case of rape (in the novel) and attempted rape (in the play), he has Gus narrate the scenes while in a hypnotic state and thus avoids any direct depiction.

Figure 3.8   The parade of the Clan and the predominance of white filling the entire screen. (*The Birth of a Nation*)

Griffith, of course, directly depicts the Gus/Flora episode in the form of a prolonged chase, with Ben Cameron arriving too late for the rescue. However, his adaptation does not include any instances of actual black/white sexual aggression. To modern audiences used to all kinds of sexual attack, the sequence seems tame and Flora's jump a trifle premature.[47] But Griffith's other scene of sexual attack in the Elsie/Lynch episode is without parallel in Dixon, or in the history of film, for its depiction of black lust.[48] Indeed, Dixon's novel has no scene depicting Lynch's sexual assault—Lynch does not even ask for Elsie's hand. Although his play includes a scene in which Lynch asks both Elsie and then her father for her hand, it does not depict Lynch forcing his attentions upon her. In Griffith's film, however, Lynch begins the scene already, as an intertitle puts it, "drunk with wine and power." His strikingly lascivious sexual overtures to Elsie are drawn out over a long scene frequently intercut with the assembling of the Clans. In the first instance, after his initial proposal has been rudely repulsed, Lynch (played by the large and, here, swarthy George Siegman) kneels beside the seated Elsie and presses the hem of her white blouse to his lips. Elsie withdraws in horror to the door, which she finds locked. In the second instance Lynch, now seated in a chair and smiling at her, thrusts his hips forward and rubs his thighs insinuatingly (Fig. 3.9). If there was any doubt as to the sexual nature of his gesture, Elsie's widening eyes and scream of horror make it clear (Fig. 3.10). It is at this point that Griffith first cuts to two Clansmen on horseback. The ride of the Clan thus appears entirely activated by this assault on a white woman. The scene continues, punctuated by frequent, brief crosscutting with the gathering of the Clans, Lynch grabbing Elsie and pushing her to the center of the room. He shakes a fist and pounds his chest, explaining the forced marriage; then he chases her further around the room until she finally faints into his arms and is held close to his body (Fig. 3.11) before being restrained in a chair.

The last twenty minutes of the film builds sexual threat upon sexual threat. The besieged "family" in the cabin is depicted in a melodramatic tableau showing Margaret Cameron kneeling at her father's feet as he holds the butt of a rifle over her head. In a parallel shot the young daughter of the Union Veteran embraces Mrs. Cameron. Over her head her father holds a rifle as well. In the next room of the cabin, already invaded by the black troops, a soldier leers over a white handkerchief left by one of the women. The melodramatic tableaux of two white fathers holding empty guns poised to bludgeon their daughters before permitting them to fall to the encroaching hordes, are reminiscent of Elsie's imminent danger of forced marriage to Lynch and Flora's solution of preferring death to the touch of the black man. Griffith thus multiplies the sexual threat to white women and with it the need for white counterviolence.

We saw in Dixon's treatment of the Clan's "trial" and punishment of Gus that Dixon seemed to be aware of the danger that white punishment of the black man for his sexual threat to white women might betray the white man's tenuous claim to be the guardian of civilization. When the Clansmen hear Gus's hypnotized reenactment of the crime, they prepare to rip Gus to pieces. However, Dixon had Dr. Cameron sublimate these emotions of naked race hatred into the solemn ritual of quenching a fiery cross in the blood of the white female victim. This ritual dignified white supremacist solidarity without indulging in the kind of naked brutality indicated in South Carolina senator Ben Tillman's 1907 speech quoted at the beginning of this chapter—the blood-hungry brutality of "kill! kill! kill!" Eschewing the black demon's right to a fair trial and advocating "lynch law," Tillman declaims: "Civilization peels off us . . . and we revert to the impulse . . . to 'kill! kill! kill!' " As Robyn Wiegman (1995, 96–97) points out, at such moments the racialized opposition between civilization and primitivity upon which white supremacy depends breaks down as the white man loses his own civilized veneer; civilization, like skin, " 'peels off' leaving only an aggressive impulse to kill."

Where Dixon seems wary of the danger of becoming like the black beast, and maintains a thin veneer of civilization by focusing on the ritual in place

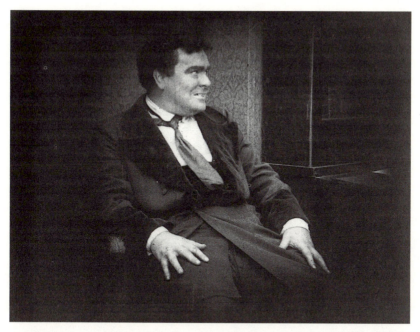

Figure 3.9 Lynch rubs his thighs insinuatingly. (*The Birth of a Nation*)

Figure 3.10 Elsie responds with horror to Lynch's insinuations. (*The Birth of a Nation*)

Figure 3.11   Elsie faints in Lynch's arms. (*The Birth of a Nation*)

of the blood lust for Gus, it remains to be determined whether Griffith was equally wary. We cannot tell if his depiction of Gus's punishment is an example of civilization "peeling off," since no copy of the film contains a scene of punishment. The "missing scene"—as remembered in some detail from a 1933 screening of a supposedly more complete print by Seymour Stern—*could* constitute a clear example of civilization peeling off the white avenger, if we can trust Stern's memory. As Michael Rogin's essay on Griffith has argued (following Stern), today's prints of the film show Gus alive at the start of the trial, prostrate before the Clan jury, and then suddenly dead after a title pronounces the verdict: "Guilty." His body is then dumped on the porch of Silas Lynch's headquarters. Later in the film, as the Clans begin to gather, Ben Cameron performs the ceremony that Dr. Cameron performs in the play and novel, quenching the fire of the cross in the blood of the martyred woman.

Rogin thus accepts Stern's account of the missing footage, which runs as follows:

> Upon the pronouncement, "Guilty," a Clansman steps one pace forward and towers over *Gus*'s huddled figure on the ground. . . . Then, as *The little Colonel* performs a mystic ceremony . . . the first Clansman, now to camera-left, back to camera, swiftly raises his arm, draped in white, and holds it aloft for one restraining second. The upraised

hand clutches what appears to be a carving-knife or small sword. . . . Beethoven's music [the "Storm and Tempest" section of the Pastoral Symphony] now *cuts on the movement* of the Clansman stepping forward, which instantly follows the "guilty" *subtitle* [sic]. . . . It is upon the split-second *cut* of the first Beethoven outcrash that the Klansman's hand plunges the first time—and comes quickly up. . . . As the white-sleeved arm again poises for a split-second, the second crash of Beethoven's thunder is heard, and the avenging hand again swiftly plunges—and as swiftly pulls up in the same ritualistic and totemic gesture. . . . There is an instantaneous *cut* on the sound of the string instruments to the face of *Gus*, in close-up, the mouth flowing blood, the eyes rolling white in agony, the head falling back. The strings suddenly are dimmed by a third, terrifying, unexpected outcrash . . . roaring, like a final judgement over the dying Negro's face. In flash-cuts, the Klansman's hand now plunges and rises, plunges and rises, again, again, and still again, on each down-beat of the timpani, all within a few frames of film. On the final thunder-crash of the series, there is a final flash of the castrated Negro's pain-racked face and body. *Gus* is dead. (Stern 1965, 123–24).

Although Stern himself tries to argue that the sequence elicited "sorrow and pity" for Gus, his account of Beethoven's music, in concert with the rhythms of the plunging knife, suggests the visceral, irrational power of a sequence whose "emotional devastation" was "incalculable" (Stern 1965, 124). What is incalculable about his description of the devastation is, of course, the extreme aestheticization of the brutal gestures of the knife matched to the musical rhythms of the "Storm and Tempest" passage, and to the stacatto rhythm of the cutting. If Stern's description of the sequence is accurate (and I think we need further corroboration from someone else at this 1933 private screening, since the print has never again surfaced and only Stern attests to it), it would represent an aestheticized moment of cinematic montage whose (implied) violence is on par with Alfred Hitchcock's no less sexualized attack on the body of Marion Crane in the shower sequence in *Psycho*.[49] That a montage with such "flash cuts"—even if cutting only to the suffering *face* of the black victim—would have anticipated by a full decade a style of cutting not known until the twenties is reason enough to doubt Stern's account. The absurd idea that it would have elicited "sorrow and pity" for Gus is even more reason to doubt. Rogin is right, however, to point to a gap in the narrative that was most likely filled by some form of violence performed on Gus. Whether that punishment was depicted as castration remains in doubt. So too does Michael Rogin's statement that "the nation was born in Gus's castration, from the wound that signified the white man's power to stop the black seed" (Rogin 1984, 219). It seems unwise to ground such a statement on a segment of film recalled by an otherwise not very reliable witness. However, Rogin's more general point that the suppression of blacks was a form of castration consistent with the Jim Crow politics and widespread lynching of the Progressive Era is well taken. To a certain extent, Griffith's veneer of "civilization peels off," as he uses the full power of his art to give white audiences the thrill of watching the suppression of blackness. I think that the much more insidious suppression accomplished by the film is not a missing scene of castration but the systematic and much more "natural"-seeming disappearance of blacks over the course of the film.

Griffith's film achieves its power to the extent that it does not appear to be an exhortation to race hatred, but a natural process of heroic rescue that, in the process, just "happens" to wash the screen "clean." Even without the depiction of Gus's castration, members of the black audience understood what the film was saying and returned the sentiment. William Walker, a black man who saw the film in a black theater in 1916, recalls as quoted in the epigraph, "Some people were crying. You could hear people saying God . . . You had the worse feeling in the world. You just felt like you were not counted. You were out of existence." Walker does not explain how the film accomplished his sense of eradication, of being "out of existence," but I would submit that it had more to do with the visceral experience of the logic of black disappearance than specific instances of white-on-black violence or even of more explicit depictions of black men attacking white women. Walker seems to have recognized that what he had seen spelled the end of his very representation in any but the most servile or villainous roles in the new medium being born. Indeed, his further reaction extends the logic of his having been made invisible: "I just felt like . . . I wished somebody could not see me so I could kill them. I just felt like killing all the white people in the world."[50]

Griffith's film, which would be used as a recruiting tool by the Clan later in the decade, sparked a vigorous campaign by the NAACP to have it banned. Though the campaign ultimately did not succeed, the film was in fact banned in eighteen states and numerous cities and the campaign did bring about some cuts. However, for every mayor who banned the film out of respect for blacks or a desire to keep the peace, there were, as Jane Gaines tells us, others who did so for its depiction of interracial sex (Gaines 2000). One thing is clear, however: Griffith's film was more incendiary, more racially hateful in its consequences, more likely to produce the phenomenon of race riot (which more often than not meant white's attacking blacks) than Dixon's novels and play. But the reason may not only lie in the greater lust of his Lynch or the greater violence of missing sequences. At a deeper level its effectiveness as race hatred, its ability to make William Walker impotently despair of ever being counted and to resolve that the only possibly effective reaction would be, like Tillman, to "kill! kill! kill!" in turn lies in Griffith's greater willingness to deploy the familiar features of the Tom material. For it was Griffith, not Dixon, who ultimately created the most effective counter to the Tom story. He did so, not by writing the sequel to the stories of Simon Legree and George (Harry) Harris, but by refunctioning the enormous emotional appeal of the antebellum story of the old South into a new kind of racial melodrama. As we have seen, this refunctioning occurs in many ways: in the redeployment of the icon of the cabin and the architecture of the good home; in the rewriting of Tom and Chloe into the much more subsidiary "faithful souls" of Mammy and Jake, whose own stories only matter insofar as they aid the white former masters; and in the displacement of evil sexual violence from Simon Legree onto the mulatto Silas Lynch. This last refunctioning, however, brings up a further twist involving the Gothic dimensions of both Tom and anti-Tom.

Ghosts in White Sheets

In Stowe's novel Simon Legree's mulatta concubines escape bondage by hiding in the garret of Legree's house. Legree fears the garret because he believes it is haunted by the ghost of a woman slave he once murdered there. Cassy and Emmeline exploit his superstitions by emitting strange, ghostlike noises and walking about under white sheets. Haunting in Stowe's novel is the ingenious means by which Cassy saves Emmeline from rape by Legree while also avenging Legree's murder of Tom.[51] While Eliza's sensational escape across the ice, occupying one paragraph in the novel, was included in most Tom shows—and considerably augmented with pursuing "bloodhounds" and added comic business (Marks and his umbrella)—Cassy and Emmeline's lengthily narrated escape-by-haunting was much less frequently depicted. It turns up, however, in the 1910 Vitagraph version of the film in which Cassy puts a sheet on Emmeline and Legree cowers in fear (Fig. 3.12).

Griffith refunctions Stowe's haunting to fit patriarchal, rather than maternal, goals in a scene that depicts the inspiration for the birth of the Clan. After the film has related a series of "outrages," including shoeless Negroes drinking and eating in the South Carolina State House, the passing of bills providing for the intermarriage of blacks and whites, and black representatives leering at white women in the gallery, Ben is pictured high on the bank of a river "in agony of soul over the degradation and ruin of his people." At that moment he spies two white children hiding themselves from their black playmates under a white sheet. When the laughing black children suddenly see movement under the sheet they run away in fear. A title reads, "The inspiration," and Ben rises with an "aha!" look in his eyes.

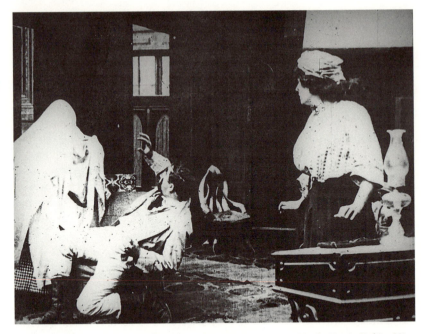

Figure 3.12 The haunting of the superstitious Legree. (*Uncle Tom's Cabin*, Vitagraph, 1910)

This seemingly innocent scene replaces the more elaborate invention of transposed Scottish Rites in Dixon with a simple "recognition" of the superstitious simplicity of childlike blacks (played, moreover, by "cute" black children). Out of a Stowe-like scene of apparent interracial amity, Griffith naturalizes the birth of the Clan, and by extension the "birth of the nation." By downplaying the superstitious, semi-pagan, totemic Christian ritual of Dixon's novels and play, he makes the Clan seem a very spontaneous, red-blooded American institution, motivated by the natural superstition of Negroes. Subsequent scenes of Clan members who need only show themselves to quaking Negroes to make them disappear reveal the apparent naturalness of white supremacy.

Stowe's white-sheeted haunting of Legree activated the power of the black female haunter against the white male haunted. Her female slaves deployed white guilt to make the slave owner cower. Griffith's refunctioning of the white sheet reverses the races of haunter and haunted. Vulnerability to superstition is now attributed to blacks and with it comes the notion of their proper childlike servility. Stowe, it seems, would forgive Legree his sins as long as he trembled before this specter of feminine (and black) Christian power.[52] Griffith, it seems, would forgive the former slaves—as Dixon would not—as long as they too cowered before the newly configured specter of white male rule. Cower, cringe, and disappear is what they would continue to do in the subsequent history of mainstream cinema until long after the civil rights movement took up the struggle for more equitable representations.

131

Escape and Rescue

The contrast between Stowe's use of ghosts in white sheets to achieve her female characters' escape from bondage and Griffith's use of those same ghosts in white sheets to wreak revenge and effect rescue points to a crucial structural difference between the two racial melodramas. The Tom story combines the pathos of black bondage and the action of black escape. The anti-Tom story, in contrast, combines the pathos of white female "bondage" to the black man and the action of white rescue. The failed rescue of Flora by Ben prepares the multiple rescues of white women from black men that follow. We have seen how Stowe importantly reversed the usual gender conventions of the slave narrative, feminizing the freedom narrative and masculinizing the bondage narrative, reenergizing what had already become, by 1852, stale melodramatic conventions. Escape offers exciting action and the Tom story's popular appeal on the stage had much to do with its initial exciting escape of Eliza, and the later escape of her entire family from slave catchers. Escape, however, is an action involving only two elements—pursuer and pursued.

Rescue, on the other hand, offers a potential three-way alternation between the endangered person, the entrapper (or pursuer), and the rescuer. When depicted in the alternating back-and-forth rhythms of an edited film, the dual elements of escape prove less dynamic and exciting than the triple elements of rescue. The possibilities for suspenseful prolongation of the action, as Griffith had developed in his years at Biograph, and then most memorably in *The Birth of a Nation*,[53] were inherently more melodramatic in the case of rescue because they offered not only escape's action of getting out of a bad place but rescue's possibility, as demonstrated in the "homecoming" "Parade of the Clan," of returning to the good place. For African slaves, especially, escape has posed the perpetual problem of what to escape *to*. Some of the variant stage versions of *Uncle Tom's Cabin* seem to have acknowledged this when they had Eliza recaptured soon after her escape, sold back into slavery along with Tom to Legree, so that she may be rescued at the end by the good master George Shelby, Jr., and taken "home."[54] We have also seen the problem this lack of home posed to George Harris in the novel as he tried to propose a "mother" African homeland in a place he had never known. The fallback position for many a Tom show was, as we have seen, for Kentucky to continue to function as that good home. Escape, then, does not as easily further the inherent melodramatic need to get back, literally or in some felt way, to the original "space of innocence" as rescue does, since escape is not intrinsically a nostalgic movement of return but a movement away from a known evil to a hoped for, but not necessarily known, better place.

Coda: A Post-Griffith Tom Show

Rescue wins out as the more exciting action in black and white racial melodrama because it provides more suspense and because it is more secure about the moral legibility of its home "space of innocence." Given the dominance of the form and content of this new racial melodrama, feeding as it did upon the preexisting appeal and dominance of the "wonderful 'leaping' fish" that was Uncle Tom, it is interesting to consider what happens to the "Tom show" of bondage and escape when it is revived in the twenties, now under the influence of Griffith's famous "multiple rescue operations." In what must be considered the last of the truly important film versions of *Uncle Tom's Cabin*—a two-million-dollar 1927 Universal silent film (Fig. 3.13)—we have an opportunity to observe the influence of Griffith's anti-Tom film on the Tom material "itself."

Director Harry Pollard originally hired Charles Gilpin, a black actor of some repute who had played the lead in *The Emperor Jones* on Broadway, for the role of Tom. According to most reports, Pollard, who had once played Tom in blackface himself, reportedly ordered Gilpin to be meek and submissive in his interpretation.[55] Gilpin was apparently disgusted by the order and finally refused the part (Gossett 1985, 384). Despite these difficulties, the black actor James B. Lowe, who was both younger and stronger than any previous stage or film Tom, offered a very dignified and moving interpretation in a film that was the sixth most popular film at the box office in 1927 (Koszarski 1990, 33). Lowe was the first black actor to actually be promoted by a Hollywood studio in a noncomic starring role, and his presence in the film was highly significant to the black community, taken as a counter to the dominant negrophobia established by Griffith and Dixon.

However, neither the undeniable popularity of a film that was relatively faithful to the Aiken-Howard version of its Tom story, nor the innovative vigor of its black—rather than blackface—Tom, could counter the deeper sense in which, for all its negrophilia, this Tom story was now taking its lessons in melodramatic pathos and action as much from Stowe as from Griffith. A long beginning section idealizes the Shelby plantation in an elaborate marriage ceremony of George and Eliza that is every bit as romanticized and prolonged as Griffith's leisurely depiction of the "quaintly" ways of the South. The sequence establishes the goodness and innocence of these light-skinned slave protagonists (and by extension, how "almost" like white folks they are, as one

Figure 3.13   Poster for the 1958 reissue of the original 1927 film,
Uncle Tom's Cabin, directed by Harry Pollard. (Courtesy Harriet Beecher Stowe
Foundation, Hartford, Conn.)

woman slave observes in the film). Soon, however, George Shelby sells Eliza's son Harry, forcing Eliza to make her escape. But here, the traditional iconography of the self-propelled flight of the bondswoman with the hounds nipping at her heels is inflected by the now much more influential rescue of the maiden in distress rendered so exciting, not only in Griffith's *The Birth of a Nation* but in the rescue-from-the-ice of *Way Down East* (1920) (Fig. 1.3). Instead of making her own way to freedom with Phineas Fletcher watching from the far shore, as in Stowe and Aiken-Howard, Eliza here acts more like the helpless Anna of *Way Down East*. Trapped on an ice floe in the midst of a Niagara-like torrent, about to be swept over the waterfall, this 1927 Eliza is rescued in the nick of time by the kindly Quaker Phineas Fletcher, who hangs like a trapeze artist upside down from a tree branch extending over the precipice. *Way Down East*, which had borrowed the melodramatic topos of the heroine on the ice from *Uncle Tom's Cabin* in the first place, here gives back the lesson under Griffith's influence. Stowe's slave woman who saved herself has now become a Gish-like heroine in need of masculine rescue. In yet another debt to Griffith, Pollard's film has Simon Legree played by George Siegman, the same actor who had played Silas Lynch (with only slightly swarthier skin) in *The Birth of a Nation*.

Pollard's film has learned its lesson from Griffith so well that it even has Eliza promptly recaptured so that she might be rescued a second time. According to the logic of its narrative, this second rescue should be accomplished by the efforts of another heroic male. Indeed, the film appears to set up just such a rescue by Eliza's husband, George. Improbably acting as a sort of camp follower of the Union army as it cuts its way through the South, George and little son Harry are searching for Eliza when they and the army happen upon Legree's plantation. Hearing Eliza scream when caught in the clutches of Legree, George begins to go to her rescue. But lest he enact the same kind of black-on-white violence we saw at the end of the 1914 film version of Uncle Tom discussed at the end of the last chapter, Pollard's film redeploys the motif of ghosts in an entirely new way. This time Uncle Tom's ghost diverts Legree from a struggle with Cassy and Eliza and lures him to his doom. In yet another twist on Stowe's motif of haunting, a superimposed shirtless apparition of Tom appears to a guilty and terrified Legree, preventing him from carrying out his sexual designs on Eliza and from killing Cassy. Pursuing the disembodied image, Legree plunges out a window to his death just as the army and George, who now does not need to carry out his own Clan-like rescue, arrive.

Pollard's version of Uncle Tom thus appears stranded halfway between the Tom story of escape and the Griffith story of rescue. Neither granting the power of heroic rescue to George, nor the power of escape to Cassy and Eliza, it nevertheless grants the ghost of the martyred Tom the power to haunt the guilty white villain. Instead of the ghostly white-sheeted Clan, the literal ghost of Tom saves Eliza from an encounter with "a fate worse than death." In the 1958 sound reissue of the same film, a prologue and voice-over sound track were added. Raymond Massey, the craggy-faced actor who had famously played Lincoln in the 1939 *Abe Lincoln in Illinois*, appears as himself in a prologue that, somewhat condescendingly, introduces the "classic" story. His voice then narrates and interprets it rather than letting the silent images speak for themselves. The effect is to replace what was left of Stowe's maternal voice with the paternal voice of the man she called "Father Abraham."[56] It is as if Abe Lincoln were narrating the novel from the perspective of post–Emancipation Proclamation moral certainty. What was once a maternal melodrama of female escape and male bondage fighting slavery has, by the time of this late reissue, and under the very influence of *The Birth of a Nation*, become a paternal melodrama of female bondage and rescue. However, what rescues Eliza is not the action of her heroic slave husband but a combination of the event of the Civil War and the moral ghost of Uncle Tom, both of which reassure viewers of slavery's historical happy end.

In 1927 the Tom show was not altogether dead as a force in American culture. It was still capable of generating sympathy for suffering blacks and, as we shall see in the next chapter, its romantic racialism would in that same year be put to new uses in the appropriation of black virtue by white performers in blackface. But now that cinema had become the dynamic, exciting medium where the moral legibility of race was played out, the Tom show adapted to the exigencies of the new medium. There is no greater example of the power of Griffith's refunctioning than this post-Griffith cinematic "Tom show." In the confluence of traditions this chapter has been tracing, the negrophilia of the Tom melodrama was overturned by the negrophobia of anti-Tom. White women became the victim-heroes of black lust and white men were empowered to accomplish their rescue. We have seen, however, that these two traditions, so antithetical in their racial sympathies, are deeply implicated in one another. Just as the architecture of Griffith's film was based on the theatrical traditions of the Tom show, so any new cinematic attempt to present the Tom tradition after Griffith had to build on the architecture of the good southern home and the excitement of a last-minute rescue.

4 Posing as Black, Passing as White: The Melos of Black and White Melodrama in the Jazz Age

We have seen that the "melos" of melodrama is crucial to black and white racial melodrama. What is Uncle Tom's suffering without the emotional strains of "Old Folks at Home?" Where is the virtue of the old South in *The Birth of a Nation* without this same song, along with the accompanying strains of "Dixie"? In the Jazz Age, however, music did not just accompany the melodramatic construction of racial virtue; it became, in two key works that forever altered their media, a primary vehicle of melodramatic racial feeling. In 1927 two related forms of "the musical" were born. *The Jazz Singer* was born in film, simultaneous with the birth of the "talking" picture. *Show Boat* was born on Broadway, simultaneous with the birth of "serious" musical theater. Both deployed forms of blackface; both mixed narratives of racial pathos and suffering with narratives of assimilation and success for whites in backstage narratives; both flirted with the specter of miscegenation; and both did so in newly "integrated" forms of music and narrative.

Music in slave culture had a special power to speak the sorrows that otherwise could not be spoken. As the "grudging gift that supposedly compensated slaves not only for their exile from the ambiguous legacies of practical reason but for their complete exclusion from modern political society," music has been viewed as an enhanced mode of communication, "beyond the power of words" (Gilroy 1993, 74–76). When the African American Fiske Jubilee Singers went on tour in the early 1870s, they could not be seen or heard apart from the context of their minstrel precursors for which many audiences mistook them. Even though they soon set new standards of authenticity for black musical expression, the very legitimacy of this new folk musical form needed to be established through its difference from minstrelsy (Gilroy 1993, 90). Paul Gilroy's lesson from the Du Boisian "double consciousness" of this music is that there is no pure "authentic folk" black particularity. Rather, there is a complex history of borrowing, displacement, transformation, and continual reinscription in the flow of music from one culture to another. We thus cannot continue to think of diaspora as a one-way flow of African authenticity from east to west (Gilroy 1993, 80, 96).

137

The question I would like to pose in the following chapter on *The Jazz Singer* and *Show Boat*—two musicals filled with their own sort of borrowings, displacements, transformations, and reinscriptions of "black" folk musical forms—is how they too demonstrate a double consciousness. We shall look closely at the melos of these melodramas in order to ask how it is that, in these two groundbreaking works that forever altered the medium in which they appeared, white characters acquire virtue by musically expressing a suffering that is recognizable as "black." Al Jolson's blackface "jazz singer" has been much commented upon in recent scholarship focused on the scandal of blackface and the arrival of sound film.[1] But this scandal has been discussed in more visual than musical terms. *Show Boat*'s uses of both literal and metaphorical blackface, and its borrowings from spirituals and blues, has been less discussed, though it is equally important and perhaps even more typical of the era.[2] Both works represent that moment in American popular culture when the protean "leaping fish" of American racial melodrama dramatically forged a new musical form in which "singing black, feeling black" became a testament of white virtue. Once again we must ask why and how the pathos of racial suffering came to animate new forms of media.

Uncle Tom's cabin and old Kentucky home had functioned as a melodramatic icon for the "space of innocence" in the "Tom" melodrama, whether in the novel, on stage, or on screen. In these two pioneering racial melodramas of the Jazz Age, both of which made their biggest impact in 1927, a melodramatic melos associated with the sufferings of African Americans links the virtue of a lost rural America with music that continues to be associated with the sorrows of former slaves. For a whole new generation of Americans, slavery, the Civil War, and Reconstruction were no longer pressing memories of national self-definition. Yet a black-inflected musical sympathy still connected to the lost home of the antebellum rural south, and still longing for "de old folks at home," continued to define what it meant to be American. Amidst the modernity of urban life, the ideal "folk" of this nostalgic longing became fixed in the white imagination as black.

The nostalgia for the good rural southern home of the white imagination is most certainly racist and imperialist. It seeks a more primitive folk authenticity such as that caricatured by minstrelsy, and it takes the form of a desire to become (at least temporarily) the primitive "Other" depicted in the caricature. The term "imperialist nostalgia"[3] can help to explain the peculiar mixture of brutal domination and sorrowing lament in white appropriations and imitations of putative African culture. As we have seen in previous chapters, the "space of innocence" of racial melodrama is poisoned by forms of entwined racial and sexual domination. But the power to generate raced and gendered sympathy and antipathy has rarely been analyzed as a living, enduring, vital cultural force.[4] In the Jazz Age, the melodramatic "space of innocence" swung away from the anti-Tom negrophobia that had dominated the Progressive Era and returned toward the crossracial identification of the Tom story. But even more than in the stage versions of that story, music became a crucial vehicle of the expression of racial virtue. While I am aware that this nostalgia for the oral, the originary, and the primordial can never be anything but a kind of "minstrel-speak" (Gubar 1997, 139), my conviction that this minstrel-speak became the lingua franca of popular modernism compels me to investigate its power to change the way American audiences came to feel racialized forms of virtue through the melos and the drama of these two groundbreaking works.

On October 6, 1927, the Warner Brothers adaptation of Samson Raphaelson's short story and Broadway play *The Jazz Singer* to the singing talents of Al Jolson made movie history as the first "talking"—and singing—featurelength motion picture. The story concerns the conflict between two musical forms: Jakie Rabinowitz's desire to sing what the film calls "jazz" on the stage and his father's desire that he sing sacred music in the synagogue. The film's unemphatic "love story"—between the ambitious and conflicted Jew and the non-Jewish dancer Mary Dale—takes a back seat to family melodrama about intergenerational father-son conflict and to effusive expressions of mother-son love.

On December 27, 1927, some two months after the premiere of *The Jazz Singer*, Edna Ferber's sprawling novel *Show Boat*, covering fifty years and three generations of the history of an American family, was transformed into a musical by Jerome Kern and Oscar Hammerstein II and premiered at the Ziegfeld Theater. Here, too, was a new kind of indigenous, family melodrama formulated as backstage "show" musical. And here too the melodrama was played out against a background of "black" musical idioms authored by a Jewish writer and turned into a musical by Jewish songwriters. Only in this case, the "show" world represented is not only the contemporary world of "jazz" music but a nostalgic panorama of the entire history of American popular song and culture. This history begins with gas-lit melodramas performed on the eponymous show boat and extends through vaudeville, Broadway musical review, and folk revival to end with the contemporaneous "jazz age" present.

The unprecedented popularity of *The Jazz Singer*—followed closely by a second Jolson blackface hit, *The Singing Fool* (1928)—is most often attributed to the novelty of the film's sound sequences and the infectious, enthusiastic performance of Al Jolson, who had been the model for Raphaelson's jazz singer (story and play) from the start. What is less often appreciated is that *The Jazz Singer* did for the instantly born movie musical what *Show Boat* did that same year for the newly formulated Broadway musical. Both works deployed a "backstage" story about show people as a "realistic" means to integrate musical forms of nostalgia and pathos into their narratives. Both works linked this pathos through forms of crossracial performance and other thematizations of a racialized "space of innocence" to the now-familiar sufferings of African Americans popularized by *Uncle Tom's Cabin*. And in the process both forged a new, intensely pathetic form of musical family melodrama.

The narrative device of showcasing music within the context of a "backstage" or "show musical" plot was a natural for movies, permitting a maximum of singing with a minimum of narrative justification (Altman 1987, 210). It was also a natural for the stage, though in fact it did not develop there before 1927. The show musical afforded an easy integration of song and dance into narrative, permitting an intensified mediation between the real world of the performers and the ideal world of the shows they create. Rick Altman demonstrates that in later movie musicals this opposition would fall into a familiar semantics in which the success of a show's musical performances would come to resolve the conventional romance plot: success of the show would signal success in love. In these later, romantic film musicals, musical performance would become the material vehicle of the love story's happy end.

In the earlier show movie musicals, however, the presence of music offered no assurance of a happy ending (Altman 1987, 209–11).[5] Rather, music was the vehicle of primal emotions, including, but also ranging beyond, familiar love songs. It often expressed what we have seen to be the "primary psychic roles" of melodrama (Brooks 1995, 4): powerful, familial forms of love and loss. Musical theater had, of course, long existed on the Broadway stage, but before *Show Boat* standard American musical theater had either consisted of extravaganzas, comedies, and reviews or, on the more "serious" side, European-derived operettas set in fairy-tale worlds.[6] Not until the arrival of *Show Boat* on stage and of *The Jazz Singer* on film did distinctively American songs grow naturally out of stories set in distinctively American, albeit "show business," contexts.

What was most distinctive about the "American context" of these two musical works is precisely their different forms of crossracial impersonation. The most ostentatious of these forms of adulatory mimicry is Jolson's famous blackface performance of "My Mammy" at the end of *The Jazz Singer*, to be examined closely below. No less a form of white posing as black, though without the blackface, was Magnolia Hawks-Ravenal's singing of "Can't Help Lovin' Dat Man" in *Show Boat*. Magnolia sings with a depth of feeling that is shown to derive from her childhood spent in proximity with singing Negroes. In these two examples of crossracial impersonation, with and without blackface, white characters achieve virtue by posing as—and singing like—blacks. While white men alone had participated in the mimicry and mockery of the nineteenth-century minstrel stage, now white women too were beginning to participate in both literal and metaphorical blackface.

My goal in the discussion that follows is to understand the process by which racial melodrama elicits sympathy for the racialized Other even as it deprives this Other of its Otherness. There can be no genuine, uncontaminated white or black cultural identity and autonomy in a culture so permeated by crossracial posing.[7] For blacks to adopt the heritage of minstrelsy is to collude in their own fetishization. But not to adopt (and adapt) this heritage is to lose the very means with which to engage with an important part of the cultural past. Similarly, for whites to so vilify the imperialism of their nostalgia for the racial Other as to reject it entirely is to fail to recognize the way whites have relied on Africanist figures to provide them with some of their more "authentic" feelings.

Posing as Black: The Career of Al Jolson

Let us begin by considering the phenomenon of *posing as black* in the career of Al Jolson. Jolson first donned blackface in 1904, in a skit set in a sanitarium. Having previously only played a straight man, Jolson was at first uneasy in a comic role. He was advised by James Francis Dooley, an Irish blackface monologist, that burnt cork could function as a mask that would make him feel comfortable on stage (Goldman 1988, 35–36). The blackface mask promised to hide the discomfort of the embarrassed Jew.[8]

In *The Jazz Singer*'s promotional souvenir program, the moment in which Jolson first donned blackface is recounted in a slightly more mythologized form. In this version, Jolson, who is described not simply as a comedian seeking laughs but as a benevolent white man with a "sympathetic interest in negro life," has a chance conversation with a loyal "old darky" dresser. Hearing of Jolson's problem getting laughs, the dresser advises: "Boss, if yo' skin am black they always laugh" (Kreuger 1977b, 6–7). In this "screen memory"—strongly reminiscent of the mythological moment in which T. D. Rice was supposedly given the gift of blackface by an African porter whose clothes he borrowed (Lott 1993, 18–19)—what is conveniently screened out from the original event is the Jewish and the Irish contexts of minstrelsy, replaced by a simple black/white binary. Black/white sympathy replaces the more complex relations of Jewishness and Irishness to whiteness, mediated by the mask of blackface. This screen memory would seem to want to forget the degree to which blackface permits the Jew posing as black to eradicate signs of Jewishness.

Michael Rogin (1996) argues that blackface became a means of whitewashing the assimilating Jew. Jewishness disappeared, Rogin argues, behind the mask of blackface. Posing as black is ultimately a way to pass as white. This is certainly the case in the screen memory of the "darky's" gift of laughter, and it may as well be true, as Rogin argues, of the gradual eradication of Jewish particularism in the "Hollywood melting pot." However, it may not be entirely true of the history of Jolson's stage career in the teens and twenties, which often tells of a quite explicit performance of Jewishness against a foil of blackness mediated by Irishness. Nor is it entirely true, as we shall see below, of *The Jazz Singer* itself.

Throughout the teens and well into the twenties, in the heyday of his popularity as a Broadway entertainer, Al Jolson made his mark in musical comedies that were often not far removed from the racial humor of his comic beginnings. To audiences only familiar with Jolson through his recordings or films (or the two biopics starring Larry Parks) it may come as a surprise that the original stage persona upon which his fame grew was that of a blackface comic trickster, essentially a Jewish adaptation of the comic slave characters of Roman comedy: the cowardly, lying, but lovable sidekick to the bland hero. As Jolson's popularity grew, these sidekick roles became the real show. He was Friday in the musical *Robinson Crusoe Jr.*; he was Inbad the black porter in *Sinbad*; and he was Bombo, Christopher Columbus's black navigator, in *Bombo*. While none of the names of these comedy reviews have survived as important milestones of American musical theater, their songs, many of which were recycled into the musically and narratively integrated *Jazz Singer*, have. It is to that film and those songs that we must now turn to grasp the melos of black and white melodrama in the Jazz Age.

The Jazz Singer

When Samson Raphaelson remembered Al Jolson singing in the musical *Robinson Crusoe Jr.*, he did not remember the persona of the comic trickster. Instead, he remembered a "grotesque figure in blackface, kneeling at the end of a runway which projected him into the heart of his audience, flinging out his white-gloved hands" and "embracing that audience with a prayer—an evangelical moan" (Kreuger 1977b, 14). Raphaelson's insight—"My God, this isn't a jazz singer. This is a cantor!"—became the basis for a short story, "The Day of Atonement," published in 1922 and then later for his 1925 Broadway play, *The Jazz Singer*, and finally for the Warner Brothers's film, directed by Alan Crossland. This theatrical version starred the vaudevillian George Jessel in the role inspired by Jolson. In the play's preface Raphaelson explains why his work is based on a Jewish performer:

> The Jews are determining the nature and scope of jazz more than any other race—more than the negroes from whom they have stolen jazz and given it a new color and meaning. Jazz is Irving Berlin, Al Jolson, George Gershwin, Sophie Tucker. These are Jews with their roots in the synagogue. And these are expressing in evangelical terms the nature of our chaos today. . . . you find the meaning of the songs in the souls of the minstrels who create and interpret them. In "The Jazz Singer" I have attempted an exploration of the soul of one of these minstrels. (1925, 10).

Whatever we may think of Raphaelson's remarkably Jewish definition of jazz (and his pointed exclusion of the names of the "negroes" from whom it was stolen), his inspiration for the story clearly derives from the perception that jazz was a potent amalgamation, and that one could hear an explicitly Jewish religious fervor—a kind of prayer—in the music. His short story and play are based loosely on the life of Jolson, who was himself the son of a cantor. They revolve around the divided soul of a blackface mammy singer deeply torn between an assimilative desire to be part of America and a more melancholy pull toward the traditional song and religion of his fathers. When his father dies the night his big show opens, Jakie Rabinowitz, now "passing" as Jack Robin, gives up his big chance on Broadway to sing the "Kol Nidre" in the synagogue in place of his father. Although Raphaelson's play climaxes around two climactic musical numbers—one "jazzy" and secular, the other sacred—the work is not a "musical." The two musical climaxes are performed offstage, foregrounding on stage characters' dramatic reactions to the music rather than the musical performances themselves.

In the play's first number Jack's mother listens in his dressing room as Jack begins the dress rehearsal of "Dixie Mammy," the performance of which is described in stage directions as wallowing in "plaintiveness" with moments of "staggering dramatic intensity" that tell us "we are listening to a Cantor in black face" (Raphaelson 1925, 115). In the second number Jack gives up the opening of his show to sing the Kol Nidre—a prayer for the Day of Atonement—for his already-dead father. His impassioned performance gives evidence that he is still a "blackface comedian" but one now heard "singing to his God" (152). Thus on Broadway we hear the cantor's prayer; in the synagogue we hear the Mammy singer.

Samson Raphaelson's insight about the prayer lodged in Jolson's Mammy singing and the Broadway lodged in his Kol Nidre was expressed in his play through the contrast between these two musical forms. To Raphaelson the addition of other songs—the transformation of his play into an actual musical—was extraneous to this insight.[9] It was the film's reformulation as a fully "integrated" musical, overwhelmed by the performing charisma of Jolson, to which Raphaelson objected.[10] Yet it is precisely this quality of maudlin musical melodrama governed by the pathos of "too late!" and the action of "in the nick of time" that needs careful scrutiny if the new melos of black and white racial melodrama in the Jazz Age is to be fathomed.

The most obvious change from play to film was the addition of five more songs, all well-known Jolson hits. These songs are performed in contrasting pairs, either as two different songs or as two different versions of the same song. This pairing structure exists neither in Raphaelson's play nor in the published script. It permits Jolson, a performer who desperately needed audience approval, and who would often keep singing as long as audiences continued to applaud, to make the performance of the second song of each set a response to audience enthusiasm for the first.[11]

The dual song structure also permitted a bridge of impromptu dialogue between songs as well as a dramatic contrast between types of songs. For example, the young Jakie (Bobby Gordon) sings a pair of songs in Muller's Bar at the beginning of the film, introducing a pattern of a slow, traditional song followed by a more up-tempo, modern one. In every case the more modern, second song introduces unmistakable African musical influences that contrast with the lack of syncopation in the first song. In this case the first song is the slow, sentimental Irish ballad, "My Gal Sal" (Dresser). It is sung hat in hand, in Jakie's little-boy tenor, in a fixed, upright position until coming down on one knee at the end—an anticipation of Jolson's later Mammy singing gesture. Hearing the song, Yudelson, the cantor's friend, runs to inform the cantor that his son is singing "raggy time" songs in a bar. In fact, Yudelson is anticipating. It is Jakie's second song, "Waiting for the Robert E. Lee" (Lewis F. Muir and L. Wolfe Gilbert)—which had been attached to Jolson since his performances at the Winter Garden Theater in the early teens—that fits the description of ragtime.[12] In this song, Jakie's body becomes all undulating movement as he gives a ragtime rhythm to a minstrel style tune (Fig. 4.1).

Ragtime was a late-nineteenth-century musical innovation that began as accompaniment to a range of Negro dances. Preceding the wide popularity of both blues and jazz, it introduced complex rhythms and repetitions unknown to European music and in strong contrast to that music's more linear, forward development. On the piano a rhythmically inventive right-hand treble plays against a steady 2/4 march rhythm in the left-hand bass. As Ann Douglas (1995, 367) has noted, the rhythm was African-derived, the march European. Though "Waiting for the Robert E. Lee" is not a pure example of ragtime in the manner of Scott Joplin's great piano compositions, it is a minstrel-style song given a "ragged" time—that is, a percussive rhythm that falls on the "off" beat. The lyrics celebrate the dances of Negroes waiting on a levee for the

Figure 4.1   Jakie sings "Waiting for the Robert E. Lee" with undulating syncopation (*The Jazz Singer*, Alan Crosland, 1927).

arrival of a steamboat: "Watch them shuffle along/See them shuffle along. . . ."[13] Jakie's syncopations are just building up steam when his father, the perpetually prohibiting cantor, pulls him off the stage by the ear.

The second pair of songs repeats this pattern. Now grown, Jakie again sings in a bar, without the trademark Jolson blackface.[14] His first number is again a slow ballad. This sentimental song of parental love for a young son, "Dirty Hands, Dirty Face,"[15] contains passages that are spoken rather than sung, in Jolson's trademark oratory, often used to heighten the pathos: "Dirty hands, dirty face, leads the neighbors a chase/ But to me he's an angel of joy." When the audience applauds, Jakie launches into a second song. As before, it is an up-tempo, imitation "ragtime," the 1922 Jolson hit, "Toot, Toot, Tootsie Goodbye" (Kahn, Erdman, Russo), riffing on the staccato rhythms of its first three words.[16] Like Stephen Foster's "Oh Susannah!" of which it is a breezy Jazz Age counterpart, it is an upbeat song of parted lovers that overlays pathos with gay bravado.

As with the beginning pair of songs, audience approval leads to a more enthusiastic "jazzed up" second song. In this second pairing, however, enthusiastic applause for the first song triggers, not the father's wrath, but the film's first movement to speech in the trademark Jolson line—"Wait a minute! Wait a minute! You ain't heard nothin' yet!"—before he launches into the second song.[17] In this first and most memorable moment of speech in a feature-length "talking" film, speech seems to flow naturally out of song and leads, just as naturally, back into it.

Ann Douglas has argued that "Negro dialect" was a form of exaggerated slang that was often used by white and black artists alike in the nineteenth and early twentieth centuries to represent a stereotype of the perceived "incorrectness" of black speech. Douglas argues that "Negro dialect" as represented in literature and song was never an accurate transcription of black speech but always a defiance of the conventional inhibitions of white middle-class speech (Douglas 1995, 369). I would argue, however, that in this brief bridge of speech between two distinct types of popular song—traditional (white ethnic) Irish ballad and syncopated (black-inflected) ragtime—we also hear the accents of Jakie's Jewish immigrant origins. For "ain't" and "nothin'" are not only white imitations of Negro dialect; they also contain accents of a lower class, Lower East Side Yiddish. Both Jakie and his mother say "ain't" in Raphaelson's play and in the written intertitles in the film. Jewishness is heard in the confident self-advertisement of the brash, assimilating, young Jewish entertainer who knows instinctively that the most modern expression of Americanness do not derive from any proper emulation of Standard English but in the mixed and melded accents of an American vernacular. He also knows that popular success is often not a planned occurrence but the spontaneous interruption of planned events, as in "Wait a minute! Wait a minute! You ain't heard nothin' yet!"

The third "pair" of songs structuring this backstage musical is actually one song performed in two sections, once again with spoken dialogue in between. It is Irving Berlin's "Blue Skies," written especially for the film.[18] The up-and-coming "jazz singer" about to open on Broadway returns home to visit his adored mother and to try to make peace with his still-disapproving father. He sings "Blue Skies" to his mother, accompanying himself on the parlor piano. After the first run-through, and once again meeting with audience approval—this time by an adoring maternal audience of one—Jakie launches into a second outburst of spontaneous speech—a supposed "dialogue" between mother and son in which the son actually does all the talking. Flirting outrageously with his mother, Jakie effusively makes plans for her more upscale life after he is a success in the show. He imagines a trip to Coney Island where he will kiss her in the tunnel of love, a new black silk dress, a pink dress, and even a new home in the Bronx "near the Ginzbergs, the Guttenbergs, the Goldbergs and a whole lotta bergs, I don't know 'em all." Once again, spontaneous speech seems to grow naturally out of the performance success of the first song and to lead into a more sexually provocative, "jazzed up" second performance. Once again that speech takes the form of a specific dialect and intonation that flies in the face of Standard English: "Mama darlin', if I'm a success in this show, well, we're gonna move from here. Oh yes, we're gonna move up in the Bronx." Colloquialisms and dropped final g's

Figure 4.2 Jakie's song for his mother is interrupted by his father's single spoken word: "Stop!" (*The Jazz Singer*, Alan Crosland, 1927).

mixed with Jewish names and places enable a quite specific hearing of the accents of Jewishness. We thus hear, at least at this point, what Michael Rogin (1996) argues has been "whitewashed" out of the film.[19]

After this extended interlude of spoken ethnicity, Jakie returns to "Blue Skies," telling his mother that he will now sing it "like I would when I go on the stage.... you know, jazzy." This version of the song is even more flamboyantly up-tempo and vamped than the first, with exaggerated "slappings" of the piano keys.[20] Once again internal audience approval encourages the emergence of a more aggressively contemporary and sexually exuberant "black" musical idiom. And once again, as in the first pair of songs sung by Jakie as a child, this sexier, "jazzier" version is terminated in mid-phrase by the wrath of the father, speaking his only word of dialogue in the film: "Stop!" (Fig. 4.2). Paternal prohibition stops the music at precisely the moment an intensified syncopation imitates "black rhythm."

The father's prohibition plunges the film back into an intensely embarrassing silence. For a stunningly prolonged moment, it is as if the film does not know what to do. Eventually, of course, it falls back into conventionalized pantomime with recorded background music and picks up the plot as, for the second time, a crestfallen Jakie leaves his father's house, his "jazz" viewed as a profane (and perhaps even an incestuous) threat to the father's power. The suspense of the moment of silence is all the more striking, however, because it interrupts not only Jakie's song but the first extended instance of speech and song in the history of film. Indeed, music and speech flow into one another and his monologue echos the song; just as the song is about clearing skies and a bright sunny future, so his speech looks forward to the happy days that will follow success in the Broadway show.

Thus far, *The Jazz Singer* has offered patterns of paired songs sandwiching brief but memorable moments of speech. The second, black-influenced, "jazzy" songs are either applauded (by a loving audience or mother) or interrupted (by a stern Jewish father). The film's resolution will be to merge the love of audience with the love of mother while conveniently getting rid of the disapproving father. While the syncopated irruptions of "jazz" consistently oppose more traditional musical forms, "jazz" is not the music that prevails in the end. Instead, the two decidedly non-jazzy blackface "mammy songs" that conclude the film triumphantly resolve tensions between the musically new and the musically old, between the sexual liberty of syncopation and the familial constancy of Jewish sacred music.

A "mammy song" is a sentimental ballad, sung in blackface about mother or home. In some instances it explicitly evokes the "good old plantation" of the minstrel tradition; in other instances the mere presence of blackface accomplishes this evocation. The actual song "My Mammy" was first sung by Jolson when it was interpolated into a 1920 revamped production of *Sinbad*.[21] Although the term "mammy singer" dates from the showstopping performances of that musical's tour,—a number of earlier songs with allusions to "mammies" had already forged Jolson's reputation as a mammy singer *avant-la-lettre*. Most famously, "Rock-A-Bye Your Baby with a Dixie Melody" (Jean Schwartz, Joe Young, Sam Lewis)[22] set the mold for new jazz age versions of the sentimental "home song" ballads of the minstrel tradition (see Chapter 2). In this case the home song takes the form of a reverse lullaby sung by an adoring son to a black Mammy.[23]

Jolson's mammy songs, sung with a fervor that Samson Raphaelson considered religious, were obvious throwbacks to an older minstrel tradition, often explicitly alluding, as does "Rock-a-bye Your Baby," to Stephen Foster's black home songs. Jolson's homages to minstrelsy introduced a showstopping pathos into otherwise comic shenanigans of the reviews in which he starred. When "My Mammy" was written in 1920, it simply gave a new musical association to the already well-established melos of black suffering. In a ghostwritten article Jolson explained his associations with the song: "I always have a picture in my mind of a black boy and his life story when I sing that song. A southern Negro boy who has found life a bitter and terrible tragedy. . . . He can't think of one human being in all the world who has treated *him* like a human being . . . and he is just about ready to give up the battle of life in despair, broken hearted over cruel fate, when he thinks of his 'Mammy' and the soul in him cries out for her" (Goldman 1988, 115).

We have seen that *Uncle Tom's Cabin* represented the moment in American history when white readers and audiences found African (Americans) to be novel objects of sympathy. We saw also that this once-novel empathy—based on the virtue of racially victimized blacks—was not forged through the simple identification of white audiences with African suffering. Rather, it was created through the equation of black suffering with the more conventionalized and familiar suffering of innocent (white) children that was already a cliché of Victorian sentimental fiction and melodrama. Harriet Beecher Stowe's achievement was to have taken a racial group familiar as objects of fun and, by linking their suffering with that of the more familiar and conventional sufferings of loving (white) mothers and dying (white) children, to create two historically new figures of melodrama: the martyred Tom, the fleeing Eliza. *The Jazz Singer's* achievement was to take another group unfamiliar to dominant mass culture as objects of sympathy—recently emigrated, rapidly assimilating Jews—and to ennoble their travails of assimilation through association with the by now thoroughly conventionalized afflictions of slaves.

As Lauren Berlant has convincingly argued, we live in a modernity that appropriates the "mythified archaic authenticity of slave affliction." However, the historical specifics of that affliction have been represented primarily through "a genealogy of entertainments whose place in collective memory makes up a nation that takes on the shimmery, intimate, and distant quality of the commodity form" (1996, 400–401). The backstage musical as it was formulated in theater and film in the Jazz Age and beyond became one such important commodity form synthesizing the collective memory of the nation. Slavery remains important to that collective memory but only, as Berlant has it, as a "mythified archaic authenticity" commodified here as part of a Broadway show. When Jakie learns that he has been plucked out of a vaudeville review touring the country to join a Broadway show, an intertitle lists his three-word response in increasingly large letters: "Broadway—Home—MOTHER." This association of home and mother with the pleasure machine of popular culture is accomplished through the merger of the suffering of Jews with the now-"archaic" sufferings of African Americans. The two blackface "mammy songs" clustered at the end of the film represent the apotheosis of the popular culture connection between these two sufferings.

The prolonged climax of *The Jazz Singer* vindicates a new popular culture form whose very power to "speak" to audiences was connected to its power to speak of racial affliction through music. The critic for *Variety* was clear on this point: Without Jolson's songs, it would be "doubtful if the general public will take to the Jewish boy's problem of becoming a cantor or a stage luminary." "Minus the voice feature" the film would only "be a contender for Jewish neighborhoods." With Jolson's voice, however, the combination of the "religious heart interest" of Kol Nidre and the two "mammy songs" "resulted in a tumultuous ovation. Jolson, personally, has never been more warmly greeted than at this premiere" (October 12, 1927). It is worth asking, then, how these songs and blackface came together to compel the sense of revelation about the new cultural power of sound film.

The first "mammy" song occurs at the end of an extended backstage scene that begins with Jakie applying blackface and wool wig in preparation for the dress rehearsal. There is a ritualistic quality to this donning of blackface that would be repeated the following year in *The Singing Fool*. In his stage performances, Jolson had simply appeared in blackface. But in his early talkies, the donning of blackface occurs at acute moments of indecision and suffering in which themes of race and family are in conflict with career. The reviewer for the *New York Times* singled out the scene:

> One of the most interesting sequences of the picture itself is where Mr. Jolson as Jack Robin (formerly Jakie Rabbinowitz [*sic*]) is perceived talking to Mary Dale (May McAvoy) as he smears his face with black. It is done gradually and yet the dexterity with which Mr. Jolson outlines his mouth is readily appreciated. You see Jack Robin, the young man who at last has his big opportunity with a couple of smudges of black on his features, and then his cheeks, his nose, his forehead and the back of his neck are blackened. It is an engaging scene where Jack's mother comes to the Winter Garden and sees him for the first time as a black-face entertainer (*New York Times*, October 7, 1927).

One reason this entirely silent sequence of blacking up may have been so compelling is that it triggered the first explicit articulation of Jakie's Jewishness to Mary, his gentile girlfriend. This articulation makes us recognize the extent to which Jakie has been previously passing, not simply by virtue of his stage name, but also by not mentioning anything about his origins to his colleagues.[24]

Now, however, caught in an agony of indecision between performing in the show's premiere that night and singing Kol Nidre in the synagogue for his dying father, Jakie sits before a mirror and applies burnt cork. As he looks at his face in the mirror, its blackness dissolves into an image of his father in white robes and yarmulke singing in the synagogue. Thus one conventionally racialized picture of "blackness" blends into another racialized picture of Jewishness. Jakie then explains to Mary in an intertitle: "The Day of Atonement is the most solemn of our holy days—and the songs of Israel are tearing at my heart." With tears in his eyes and the exaggerated, forced smile of the blackface minstrel on his lips, he is transformed into a black Pagliaccio (Fig. 4.3).[25] He tells Mary "there is something, after all, in my heart. Maybe it's the call of the ages—the cry of my race." The word "race"—here

Figure 4.3 Jakie is transformed into a black Pagliaccio. (*The Jazz Singer*, Alan Crosland, 1927).

designating Jew—resonates with the sight of Jakie becoming black to take on a double meaning. It is both the Jewish "race" of which he literally speaks— the race that pulls him away from Mary and Broadway—and the visible African race—the race whose mask will ultimately enable him to have it all. The blackface that once provided the mask behind which Jolson could hide his embarrassment and make audiences laugh now offers a mask through which it becomes possible to make audiences cry.[26]

Jakie remains in an agonized state of indecision when his mother arrives to plead with him to sing Kol Nidre for his father that night. Torn away from her by a call to dress rehearsal, he goes on stage. The song he sings, however, is not the much-anticipated "My Mammy" but a sentimental Irish ballad, "Mother of Mine" (Jolson-Silvers).[27] The lyrics of the verse apply directly to his narrative situation with his own mother: "Mother I'm sorry I wandered away/Breaking your heart as I did./Now that I'm grown up I've come back to say/Things that I felt as a kid." The rest of the song is a pathos-filled, crescendo-building ballad in praise of the constancy of mother love (Fig. 4.4). Though its lyrics sing of a reassuring faith in mother love, its performative tone—in keeping with the agony of indecision that wracks Jakie at this moment—is anxious and despairing, building to a half-spoken, half-sung ascending climax:

Figure 4.4   Jakie sings "Mother of Mine." (*The Jazz Singer*, Alan Crosland, 1927).

"Gee ain't it funny/When skies are sunny/That's when my pals all haunt me./ When things go wrong and they don't want me/Mother I still have you!"

It is precisely this fervent wish for maternal constancy—dually constructed as the pathos of the Jewish and the "black" son in the form of an Irish ballad—that the film's narrative threatens with loss. Listening to her son sing in blackface, Sara Rabinowitz recognizes what she did not hear when Jakie sang "jazz" to her in the apartment without blackface: that the melodramatic virtue of his Broadway singing is a product of race: "Just like his father, with the cry in his voice." Sara leaves the theater in mid-song, recognizing that the secular cry of the son in blackface is an echo of the sacred "cry" of the father in white robes and prayer shawl. It is as if, having glimpsed the way in which the pathos of blackface minstrelsy and the pathos of the father's singing resemble one another, she can relinquish possession of the specific Jewish boy and forgive his assimilation: "He's not my boy anymore," she says as she leaves the theater; "he belongs to the whole world now!" Jakie, however, is forlorn. Rushing backstage to find the mother whose constancy he has just extolled in song gone, he collapses in tears (Fig. 4.5).

Anxiety about the loss of mother love—more important than the narrative's ostensible drama of paternal approval—animates this entirely maudlin yet (melo)dramatically effective song.[28] Racial suffering has here become a

Figure 4.5 Jakie collapses in tears when he finds his mother gone. (*The Jazz Singer*, Alan Crosland, 1927).

more diffuse pain—a generalized longing for a lost home. Blackface is a symbol of the triumph of assimilation as well as of its attendant loss. Uncoupled from the specific historical persecution of blacks and the specific persecution of Jews, it is a suffering that becomes embodied in the melodramatic performing persona of Al Jolson, the Jewish, blackface mammy singer.[29] But these excessive expressions of mother love also divert attention from the miscegenation inherent in the muted love story between Mary and Jakie.[30] Although Mary occupies the position of the film's "love interest," Jakie's sexual interest in her is underplayed. Indeed, in the same conversation in the dressing room in which he puts on blackface, Jack confesses to Mary that his love for the stage is greater than his love for her. Since his very next act is to sacrifice his career on the stage out of love for his mother, it is clear where his true love interest lies. The only true love scene, as Rogin notes, is that played out between Jakie and his mother at the piano (Rogin 1996, 83). However, this obsession with mother love verging on incestuous desire might well be a means of drawing attention away from the miscegenational relations that would have to be confronted were Jakie not pulled back into the orbit of melodrama's more "primary psychic" relations. "Mother of Mine" and the finale, "My Mammy," may well bear the burden of avoiding this deeper problem.[31]

Though there had been hundreds of love songs in hundreds of European-influenced operettas, and hundreds of sad-home songs and mammy-style songs in hundreds of minstrel shows, on the vaudeville stage, and in musical reviews (including those in which Jolson himself had starred), there had never been a song in a film or on stage that expressed so much primal emotion so directly linked to narrative conflict. This, I argue, is the real power of the film's technological innovation of sound—not the much-touted breezy spontaneity of the Jolson persona, but the melodramatic poignancy of an "integrated" song about mother love in a narrative threatened with its loss. The lyrics of "Mother I Still Have You!" express the fullness of maternal presence, but there is a despairing fear of loss that underlies the song's performance as the "grotesque" pleading son in blackface clasps his hands and half sings, half wails his need for maternal constancy. Here is the melodrama of "too late!" and "in the nick of time" transposed into musical terms. Just as the last-minute rescues of action melodramas prolong the suspense of whether the rescue will occur in the nick of time, so this new form of musical melodrama prolongs suspense by singing about what the narrative most fears will be lost. It will thus only be through musical performance that Jakie will rescue his connection to his mother by singing for his father in a manner that is both "too late" *and* "in the nick of time."[32]

Jakie rushes home and agrees to sing Kol Nidre in his father's place, thus forfeiting his opening night. Sandwiched between two blackface Mammy songs sung to the mother, Kol Nidre is, both theologically and narratively, a song addressed to the father.[33] Hearing Jakie sing through an open window, the cantor dies happy, saying, "Mamma, we have our son again." Jolson sings the prayer with a fervency that echoes the emotionality of the "mammy" singer, clasping hands together, swaying from side to side, delivering Raphaelson's insight that the two cultural forms—cantor and mammy singer—resemble one another (Fig. 4.6).

Having sung just "in time" to make his father die happy but "too late" to save him from death, the film's final number shows Jakie some time later on stage in the Winter Garden Theater, performing before an adoring audience that includes Yudelson and his mother in the front row and an adoring Mary watching from the wings (what this means for their future relationship, however, is left unspecified). Finally Jakie performs Jolson's signature song, "My Mammy" (Louis-Young-Donaldson). Like "Mother of Mine," it mixes confidence in the constancy of mother love and hysterical fear of its loss. It begins confidently and jauntily:

> Mammy, Mammy,
> The sun shines east
> The sun shines west,
> I know where the sun shines best

Mammy, my little Mammy
My heart strings are tangled around Alabamy.

The song's release, however, introduces a note of urgency. Going down on one knee on the ramp in the Winter Garden Theater to lean toward his mother, Jakie grows anxious and cries, rather than sings (Fig. 4.7):

Mammy I'm a comin', I hope I didn't make you wait!
Mammy I'm a comin', Oh God I hope I'm not late!
Mammy, look at me! Don't you know me? I'm your little baby!

The song asserts the strength of filial devotion—"I'd walk a million miles for one of your smiles, my Ma-ammy!" Its filial plea for recognition is fulfilled in the narrative—Jack's mother *is* there in the audience to recognize her "little baby"—and the song ends on a triumphant note. Nevertheless, the hysteria performed in relation to these possible moments of nonrecognition is not fully resolved by this musical finale, which recalls the previous scene of his father's death-bed. Residues of pathos are heard in the wailing call of a son who has wandered too far, and seen in the imploring, bended-knee despair of the blackface Pagliaccio.

The Jew who puts himself in the place of the stigmatized black Other thus takes on the mantle of the Other's suffering. In the process, however, as Michael Rogin (1997) and Susan Gubar (1997) have both argued, he eradicates the particularism of his and the black's history. While claiming an affinity and likeness, the blackface Jew simultaneously asserts that blacks themselves need not exist. Rogin, for example, argues that the blackface musical performance that occurs at the end of the film will permit the Jewish entertainer to have it all: assimilation to a whiteness that includes access to the gentile woman and the continued adulation of the Jewish mother after the father's death. His critique of the film is ultimately a critique of the reduction of Jewish-American history to a family melodrama in which problems are between fathers and sons rather than between whites and Jews, and in which the generalized woe of slaves speaks for the woe of Jews (Rogin 1996, 87). For Rogin, then, anti-Semitism is the film's structuring absence, while blackface performance, reaching back to the origins of American mass entertainment in minstrelsy, disguises this absence through the substitute pathos of mammy songs.[34]

Rogin's argument about *The Jazz Singer* is ultimately an argument about the way blackface has been used to obliterate two histories and cultures: those of Jews *and* those of African Americans. Blackface performance is to him an obliteration of "real" African-American jazz that it might otherwise have been possible to hear. Rogin's term for this obliterating music is "white noise": "In the silenced, racial, blackstory, Jolson's white noise obliterates

Figure 4.6 Jakie sings "Kol Nidre" with a fervency that echoes the emotionality of the "mammy singer."

Figure 4.7 Jakie sings "My Mammy" to his mother in the audience. (*The Jazz Singer*, Alan Crosland, 1927, Museum of Modern Art Film Stills Archive).

jazz" (Rogin 1996, 115). The watered down, commercial commodity that was sold in this and other Jolson films in the name and in the place of the music of the cosmopolitan New Negro is, to Rogin, a cacophonous, impure, and bogus entity.

"White noise" is a conceptually brilliant response to the visual stereotype of blackface. However, it has the unfortunate consequence of equating the visual register of film image with the aural register of film sound at precisely the moment in film history when it becomes imperative to listen to movies. It assumes that just as blackface visually seeks to cover up the look of Jewish ethnicity, so the songs emanating from the blackface "mammy singer's" carica-tured lips obliterate what we might otherwise be hearing: authentic black jazz. It is as if the "look" of burnt cork, and the knowledge of the erasure of more authentic black visual expressiveness that this blackface represented, prevents Rogin from any further desire to hear the ways a caricature of blackness and a caricature of Jewishness (and even a measure of Irishness) blend together in both music and speech. However, if we are to understand the black and white racial melodrama of this film, we must consider the popular songs that constitute the melos of this so-called "white noise." Contaminated and impure as they are, these hybrid tunes expressing an assimilating, "mongrelized"[35] identity become, at this point in American history, new transfer points of melo-dramatic virtue. Operating in the further commodified and dehistoricized Uncle Tom mode of sympathy for the racialized Other, they replace the home songs of minstrelsy with an even more abject longing for a racially marked good home. The genius of much American popular song of this period was to tap into the poignancy of the suffering of those persons—Jews and blacks—victimized by racial prejudice and inequity and to appropriate that suffering as the very energy and meaning of the nation.

If it is true that there is no "authentic" jazz in The Jazz Singer, there is a popular music that is distinctively American, there is a music that is distinc-tively of the Jazz Age era, and there is a music that is associated with both African Americans and Jews.[36] One may rightly scoff at the audacity of associat-ing Al Jolson with jazz, just as one may scoff at the coronation of the aptly named Paul Whiteman as the "King of Jazz."[37] However, as music scholar Henry Pleasants has argued, a singer like Jolson was at once a product and a representative of that "process of imitation and counter-imitation—black imitating white, and white imitating black imitating white—through which, beginning with ragtime and even earlier, African musicality was entering the mainstream of Western music in America" (Pleasants 1974, 56–57). It is that mainstream vernacular, and not just the "pure" New Orleans–descended jazz, that permeates American popular culture.

Al Jolson was a singer who found traditional European ballad structures restrictive. To the extent that he added vocal or whistling embellishments, oratorically spoke rather than sang, and improvised on tunes, he can indeed be considered a jazz singer, though certainly one whose influences have been significantly diluted by popular show business commercialism. If Jolson's departures from regular rhythms and fixed melody were not very adventurous or imaginative by the standards of earlier ragtime, of contemporaneous blues, or of the later developments of jazz, these departures nevertheless enabled his singing to show a new vitality and depth of feeling that was popularly perceived as derived from African roots. My point is not to argue about the ultimate meaning of jazz, or the quality of Jolson's jazz, but to recognize that Jolson's importance as an American singer can only be assessed through some kind of African-American frame of reference. I have tried to suggest that the frame of reference operating in this particular film is best understood in the context of the melos of black and white racial melodrama as it came into contact with the more urban and contemporary forms of "jazz."[38]

The emotional excess of the "mammy songs" surrounding Kol Nidre at the end of the film have another important function in relation to the more syncopated, jazzier music opposed by the father in the earlier parts of the film. We have seen how the pattern of pairing traditional songs with syncopated jazz consistently contrived to have the father interrupt the more modern, jazz versions—"Waiting for the Robert E. Lee" and the up-tempo versions of "Blue Skies." In contrast to these songs, the blackface "Mammy songs" have a veneer of folk authenticity, and a marked lack of syncopation, that allies them with Kol Nidre. Thus the film's opposition between traditional (white) popular music and syncopated (black) "jazz," of which neither father nor mother approve, gives way at the film's climax to a conciliatory similarity between the folk accents of blackface "Mammy song" and Jewish sacred music.

This musical racial legibility is recognized by the mother and then by the "whole world" in both the "mammy singing" and the sacred singing of Al Jolson. The Aramaic foreignness of Kol Nidre surrounded by the blackface of two "Mammy songs" offers a "folk" reconciliation of two divergent expressions of racial virtue. There *is* jazz in *The Jazz Singer* if we take jazz to be popular, syncopated, black-inflected music melded with other musical idioms, but this jazz is performed in the nonblackface songs like "Toot, Toot, Tootsie, Goodbye" and "Blue Skies." These songs, however, are dramatically superseded in the film's climax by the plaintive wail of a "folk" music that forges an amalgam of deracinated black and Jewish suffering.

Jakie's overt choice is solidarity with his "people."[39] He misses opening night in order to sing in his father's place, ostensibly sacrificing career (and assimilation) for religion, race, and mother. However, with Jolson in the role it was impossible to end the film, as Raphaelson had ended his play, with the performance in the synagogue. As the triumphant Broadway mammy singer incarnate, Jakie had to be resurrected on Broadway and a "happy end" of show business success—figured as a form of folk authenticity—had to be superimposed on the plaintive wail of Kol Nidre. But, as we have seen, this happy end is deeply ambivalent. Embedded within it, within the very form of the blackface mammy song, is a sense of hurt and longing that exceeds its apparent triumph. The pathetic figure in blackface, now an empty icon of African-American suffering invested with Jewish dilemmas of integration and miscegenation never imagined by Stowe, presides incongruously and precariously over a new musical form of racial melodrama in the Jazz Age.

Passing as White: *Show Boat*

On December 27, 1927, two months after the premiere of *The Jazz Singer* forever altered the course of American movies, Florenz Ziegfeld's production of Jerome Kern and Oscar Hammerstein II's *Show Boat* did the same for musical theater. Like *The Jazz Singer*, it used music in a backstage format to present the story of an upwardly mobile, successfully assimilating white character, in this case a woman abandoned by her gambler husband. Magnolia Ravenal achieves success on stage as a "coon singer" performing the Negro songs of her show boat childhood accompanied on a banjo.

Show Boat achieves its recognition of racialized virtue in a veritable parade of adapted and imitated popular musical forms ranging from "coon songs," folk songs, spirituals, ragtime, blues, operetta, and Tin Pan Alley pop performed against a panoramic history of American entertainment whose most vital mode is melodrama. Edna Ferber's novel tells the story of Magnolia Hawks, daughter of a show boat captain, raised on the river where melodramas like *East Lynne, Lady Audley's Secret,* and the perennial *Uncle Tom's Cabin* are performed to naive, backwoods audiences in river ports up and down the Mississippi. An early passage describing the effect of the "electric current" of these crude performances on the young Magnolia is a veritable paean to the American stage melodrama:

> But she did thrive on the warm electric current that flowed from those river audiences made up of miners, farmers, Negroes, housewives, harvesters, backwoodsmen, villagers, over the footlights, to her. A naive people, they accepted their theater without question, like children. That which they saw they believed. They hissed the villain, applauded the heroine, wept over the plight of the wronged. The plays were as naive as the audience. In them, onrushing engines were cheated of their victims; mill wheels were stopped in the nick of time; heroes, bound hand and foot and left to be crushed under iron wheels, were

rescued by the switchman's ubiquitous daughter. Sheriffs popped up unexpectedly in hidden caves. The sound of horses' hoofs could always be heard when virtue was about to be ravished. They were the minstrels of the rivers, these players, telling in terms of blood, love, and adventure the crude saga of a new country. (Ferber 1994, 129)

Just as *The Jazz Singer* becomes a self-conscious celebration of the quasi-archaic form of blackface, updating minstrelsy for the Jazz Age, so Ferber self-consciously updates melodrama. When a local sheriff arrives to arrest the show boat couple suspected of committing miscegenation, he is described as "the sheriff of melodrama . . . black moustaches, wide-brimmed black hat, flowing tie, high boots, and all" (109). In this novel, characters both earnestly play out the clichés of racial melodrama and know when they are caught up in it: "They had not played melodrama for years without being able to sense it when they saw it" (108). In the *coup de théâtre* that follows—one that Kern and Hammerstein will hardly alter at all—melodrama is self-consciously recognized and played for all it is worth. When the interracial couple, Julie and Steve, are exposed and expelled from the boat, Magnolia, the captain's daughter, becomes the show boat's new star, playing opposite the dashing Gaylord Ravenal and then eloping with him. But in one of those realistic and feminist twists that has always served to modernize melodrama, the dashing young hero proves an inconstant gambler who abandons his wife and child in Chicago after an extended losing streak. It is then that Magnolia draws upon her show boat childhood to sing "coon songs" on the variety stage. Ferber's novel stresses throughout that it is Magnolia's ability to connect with the authenticity of both these musical and melodramatic roots that makes her a star.

When Jerome Kern read Edna Ferber's novel in the fall of 1926 he immediately asked her to allow him to make a musical (Bordman 1978, 275; Kreuger 1977a, 18). Ferber was initially incredulous. American musicals in the twenties, including those by Kern, were frivolous affairs; stories were excuses for song and dance, not dramatic situations generating musical feeling.[40] Though the music and book he and Oscar Hammerstein II came up with ultimately opts, like *The Jazz Singer*, for a "happy ending" that reconciles family, love, and career, not found in its original literary source, it made history as "the first American musical to tackle an explicitly serious social subject without reducing it to embarrassing claptrap" (Mast 1987, 59). That subject, of course, was race.[41]

Edna Ferber's novel did not ignore race. But neither did it place race, as Kern and Hammerstein would do in several key songs, at the emotional center of a thirty-year history of popular entertainment forms. It is as if the addition of actual melos to the frequently cited spirituals that punctuate Ferber's text[42] opened up the musical to a melodramatic power of expression unattainable in the novel. As Lauren Berlant (1996) has noted, the musical versions of

Show Boat substitute a "genealogy of entertainments" for the national history of black–white relations. All of the songs but one are imitations of musical forms popular in the period covered by the narrative (1890–1927). Even the actual spirituals and work songs cited in the novel's text are represented in the musical by white-authored popular songs that imitate these forms. Yet even with its escapist romance that happily reunites the (white) principals in the final scene, *Show Boat*'s ability to utter the ugly word "miscegenation" on stage represents a distinct departure from the frivolity of all previous musicals and the first significant movement toward a new "realistic" integration of song, story, and racial theme that is now the norm for modern musical theater.[43]

It is in *Show Boat*, then, that we see the birth of the modern American stage musical. But which *Show Boat*? As with *Uncle Tom's Cabin*, there are a bewildering number of versions: the 1929, 1936, and 1951 films, as well as the 1928 and 1993 revivals of the musical, but I will attempt to center my discussion on the 1927 original production, whose influence on the subsequent musical was formative and which, in many ways, parallels *The Jazz Singer*.[44] However, since stage plays are so ephemeral, and since there is no full recording of this production, and no published book, I will frequently rely upon the 1936 James Whale film produced by Universal for material details of performance and staging. I do this because it includes many performers from the original production and because it remains the most faithful of all the film versions to that production.[45]

An Integrated "Space of Innocence"

One way of understanding *Show Boat* in terms of the tradition of black and white melodrama we have been tracing is to imagine the story of Uncle Tom overtaken by a happy ending in which little Eva grows up, marries the man of her dreams, is abandoned by and then reunited with her wayward love, and all the while Tom, instead of suffering his own travails, is relegated to the sidelines singing soulful accompaniments of "Old Folks at Home." Lauren Berlant is certainly correct when she points out that *Show Boat* displaces a much more historically significant story of miscegenational love and black toil with an insipid story of white romance. Such is the great disappointment of the musical *Show Boat*'s second act that consigns its African-American characters to what Berlant calls a "petrified obsolescence" while the white characters embrace the future (Berlant 1996, 402).

Nevertheless, for all its problems and disappointments, there is still much to be studied in the way music and race intersect in this work. For if what Berlant calls the "fantasy bribe" of happy-ending romance for white people can be seen today as a displacement from the "real" story that lies just beneath the surface, it may be worth scratching that surface. Looked at today, it is

obvious that the most melodramatically engaging and the most musically affective parts of *Show Boat* are the "black" parts. Harold Prince's 1993 revival
attempted to stage the show in such a way as to reverse Berlant's judgment:
now it is the white parts that seem stuck in "petrified obsolescence" while the
black roles, though woefully undeveloped, seem prescient. But even in 1927,
it was the presence of race as "realistic" theme that drove the innovations of
this new form of "the musical." If that musical form then fails to live up to
the potential it has permitted audiences to glimpse, it is still important to
acknowledge the new kinds of racial legibility it made possible. Thus while
much of what follows is deeply informed by and indebted to Berlant's essay,
I will be less interested in condemning *Show Boat*'s evasions and displacements of racial themes and more interested in placing *Show Boat* within the
larger trajectory of the history of melodramatic constructions of racial virtue.
As with *The Jazz Singer*, this examination will lead to an investigation of the
complex nature of the melos (Rogin's "white noise") that makes its melodramatic constructions of virtue possible.

Like *The Jazz Singer*, *Show Boat*'s melodramatic recognitions of virtue
are primarily accomplished by a white character whose success as a performer
is due to her expropriation of a "black" melos associated with the afflictions
of slaves. Magnolia's virtue is recognized in the novel through her ability
to recapture the folk authenticity of her years on the show boat performing
melodrama and singing "coon songs." The central "space of innocence" of
this folk authenticity is depicted in the novel in a brief scene in the Cotton
Blossom kitchen—which Kern and Hammerstein later develop into a memorable moment of integrated black and white music-making. In the novel, the
child Magnolia, not unlike "Mass'r" George in *Uncle Tom's Cabin*, basks in
the glow of interracial amity in what feels for all the world like an "old
Kentucky home."[46] In this kitchen, Magnolia joins in, singing with Jo and
Queenie, with "her head thrown slightly back, her eyes rolling or half closed,
one foot beating rhythmic time to the music's cadence. Her voice was true,
though mediocre; but she got into this the hoarsely sweet Negro overtone—
purple velvet muffling a flute" (92). Though her forbidding mother, like Jakie
Rabinowitz's father, objects to the singing of "nigger songs," it is clear that
Magnolia's real inheritance will come from Jo(e) who, had he been born
some fifty years later, "might have known brief fame in some 'Club Alabam'
on Broadway" (Ferber 1994, 93).[47]

Accounts of Jerome Kern's enthusiasm for adapting Ferber's novel suggest that it was the central metaphor of the show boat itself—he called it "a
million dollar title" (Bordman 1978, 276)—that struck his fancy. Already by
the 1870s—the era of the novel's beginning—show boats were nostalgic repos-
itories of the archaic entertainment forms of both melodrama and minstrelsy.[48]
This nostalgia for a simpler form of travel and entertainment dovetailed neatly

with minstrel-filtered memories of the antebellum "old Kentucky home" and with the dominant cultural form of that era, the "Tom" show.

On this show boat where "stories of slaves stolen, sold, restolen, resold and murdered" are told and retold, and where Magnolia has memorized parts ranging "from Simon Legree to Lena Rivers" (77), Jo and Queenie, who in the novel have been purchased like slaves, right along with the boat, offer the first echo of the Tom story. Their kitchen, as we have seen, echoes the idyllic, racially integrated space of Tom and Chloe's cabin. On stage, the singing stevedore chorus, played in the 1927 production by the Negro Jubilee Singers, are free men, but in most stagings their work toting bales of cotton echoes the toil of slaves. Julie, the mixed-race and furtively "passing" leading lady of the show boat, offers an amalgam of the ravaged Cassy and the passing-to-escape Eliza. Pete, the jealous bargeman who exposes the secret of Julie's mixed race, is a two-bit Simon Legree, resembling that villain both in his intolerance of black humanity and in his lust for a light-skinned black woman. Parthy, Magnolia's eternally forbidding New England–reared mother, is a more hard-hearted version of Aunt Ophelia. Finally, Magnolia's father, the henpecked, diminutive Cap'n Andy, is the kindly slave master transformed into an early culture industry "master of ceremonies" whose living room doubles as the stage. His domain, aptly named the Cotton Blossom, resembles nothing so much as a free-floating plantation adapted, as the plantation itself had long been adapted in the familiar Tom show, to the production of entertainment instead of cotton.[49]

Like Tom's Kentucky home, the show boat is the traditional "space of innocence" of black and white melodrama—the place from which the Africanist figures (and their more prominent white counterparts) are cruelly separated (like Julie) or to which (like Jo and Queenie) they faithfully cling. Like *The Jazz Singer*, the place of performance becomes conflated with the virtues of home.[50] The show boat stage/plantation/home thus resembles Tom's Kentucky home in both its racial inclusions—the interracial amity of its music performed by black and white performers and characters who often sing together—and exclusions—in the banishment of Steve and Julie for the crime of miscegenation. For in the segregated, post–Civil War South depicted in *Show Boat*, the idealized "make believe" world of the show boat itself must nevertheless pull into a specific historical, Jim Crow port. In the Kern and Hammerstein musical that port, in Act 1 Scene 1, is the levee of Natchez, Mississippi, circa 1890. Immediately, a black male chorus working on the levee piling up bales of cotton sings the opening number: "Cotton Blossom."[51]

Kern and Hammerstein's musical seems acutely aware that its very representation of the apartheid of black and white life on the Mississippi is accomplished through the quasi-integration of its own performers. Although the white and black choruses of the opening number do not mix and mingle among themselves, inhabiting, as the segregated world depicted demands, different regions of the stage, it was still extremely rare in 1927 for a Broadway musical to have a mixed cast.[52] The more common practice on Broadway in the twenties was the newly popular all-black review and the perennial all-white review (whose music might now occasionally be written by black talent and whose performers might still don blackface).

Like Universal Picture's nearly contemporaneous production of the film version of *Uncle Tom's Cabin* (Harry Pollard, 1927), which introduced the black actor James B. Lowe in the part of Uncle Tom (see Chapter 3), the 1927 stage *Show Boat* represented an equally significant moment of integration of black and white performers. This "realistic" representation of racial conflict on a stage where blackface was still a frequent practice suggests some of the anomaly of the painfully slow integration of American show business. Nineteen twenty-seven thus represents an odd convergence of blackface "Africanist" roles, like that of Jolson in *The Jazz Singer*, with roles played by "real" blacks in *Show Boat* but themselves mixed, incongruously, with whites in blackface.[53] Indeed, the 1927 Ziegfeld production of *Show Boat*, for all its innovative integration of white and black choruses and principals, also starred Tess Gardella, an Italian-American blackface performer whose stage name was Aunt Jemima, as Queenie, Joe's wife. Gardella played opposite the first Joe, the African-American performer Jules Bledsoe.[54]

The 1936 film, starring Hattie McDaniel as Queenie, eliminated the peculiarity of a black actor playing opposite his blackface wife. However, it did not eliminate blackface altogether, adding a new number, written especially by Kern and Hammerstein for the film, for Irene Dunne as Magnolia to sing in blackface as part of the show boat's minstrel "olio" (Fig. 4.8). This promiscuous mix of black and blackface elicited no comment from contemporary reviewers. However, if these discrepancies were not noted, the power of Joe's song, and of the performer who inhabited the role, was. That power, for which critics struggled to find the right words in an era before "black power," is arguably what would eventually lead to the elimination of the blackface tradition. For once characters like Queenie and Joe had been played by actual black performers, and once they had begun to inflect these stereotypically blackface Africanist roles with their own individual personalities, there would be no turning back.

James Baldwin has commented on the process by which black performers have struggled against the limited roles they have been given:

> It is scarcely possible to think of a black American actor who has not been misused: not one has ever been seriously challenged to deliver the best that is in him. The most powerful examples of the cowardice and waste are the careers of Paul Robeson and Ethel Waters. If they

Figure 4.8 Magnolia (Irene Dunne) sings "Gallivantin' Around" in blackface on the stage of the Cotton Blossom. (*Show Boat*, Universal, James Whale, 1936).

> had ever been allowed really to hit their stride they might immeasurably have raised the level of cinema and theater in this country. . . . What the black actor has managed to give are moments, created, miraculously, beyond the confines of the script; hints of reality, smuggled like contraband into a maudlin tale, and with enough force, if unleashed, to shatter the tale to fragments. The face of Ginger Rogers, for example, in *Tales of Manhattan*, is something to be placed in a dish and eaten with a spoon—possibly a long one. If the face of Ethel Waters were placed in the same frame, the face of Little Eva would simply melt: to prevent this, the black performer has been sealed off into a vacuum. Inevitably, therefore, and as a direct result, the white performer is also sealed off and can never deliver the best that is in him, either. (Baldwin 1976, 121)

Baldwin asserts the terrible waste of black performers in American film and theater despite the existence of "miraculous moments," of which some of the musical numbers of *Show Boat* are prime examples. However, he portrays the struggle to achieve authenticity as a war between realism and the confectionary maudlin tale—symbolized here by the reference to Little Eva. Yet if melodrama is a dynamic mode that incorporates realism, then the pure opposition between realism and melodrama misconstrues the actual process by which "black" reality has become visible and audible to white and black audiences alike.

Much of the time, *Show Boat* does seal off its black and white performers into vacuums. But in the places where it does not, there is an (unequal) exchange that does not so much "shatter" the tale, as Baldwin insists, as creep into it, creating new standards of black performance, making possible revolutionary integrations—of audience, cast, and characters—that *The Jazz Singer* so strenuously avoided.[55] Black–white racial conflict comes to a head in *Show Boat's* first scene. Amidst the hoopla of Cap'n Andy's introduction of the troupe to the admiring crowd, Pete, unaware that Julie is of mixed race, vents his fury at her for giving the brooch he had given her to Queenie, "a nigger." Soon he finds himself in a fight with Steve, Julie's jealous white husband. Though Cap'n Andy covers up by pretending the fight is a preview of the melodrama to be played that night, the basic racial tensions that will animate the first half of the work have been introduced.[56] On the very show boat where *Uncle Tom's Cabin* is part of the repertoire and where "stories of slaves stolen, sold, restolen, resold and murdered" (Ferber 1994, 84) are basic fare, a Legree-like villain grows jealous of the happiness of a couple we will soon learn to be mixed race.

Meanwhile the main romantic plot—the equivalent of Ginger Roger's face in Baldwin's formulation—follows the time-honored pattern of countless operettas, introducing Magnolia to the dashing riverboat gambler Gaylord Ravenal. They sing the romantic duet "Make Believe," celebrating the confusions between real life and performance. Since the two musical numbers that follow, "Ol' Man River" and "Can't Help Lovin' Dat Man," are the heart and soul of the work's racial melodrama, and since both numbers augment the presence and melodramatic virtue of characters who remain rather shadowy in Ferber's novel, they will be examined closely below.

"White Noise"

"Ol' Man River" occurs at the end of Act 1, Scene 1. Joe wanders slowly on stage carrying a sack of flour.[57] (Joe is played by Jules Bledsoe in the 1927 production and by Paul Robeson in the 1928 London revival, the 1932 Ziegfeld revival, and in the 1936 film.) His wife, Queenie, berates him for his slowness, calling him "the laziest man that ever lived on this river." Magnolia then calls down to tell him she cannot wait to tell Julie about the handsome gentleman she has just met. This is Joe's cue: "Ask Miss Julie! might as well ask old man river what he thinks—he knows all 'bout them boys." Sitting down on a bale, and beginning to whittle, Robeson launches the song's verse in his deep bass in a low-key, almost meditative fashion (Fig. 4.9).[58]

Figure 4.9 Joe (Paul Robeson) launches the verse of "Ol' Man River." (*Show Boat*, Universal, James Whale, 1936)

> Dere's an ol' man called de Mississippi
> Dat's de ol man dat I'd like to be
> What does he care if de world's got troubles?
> What does he care if de land ain't free?

From the mouth of the "laziest man that ever lived on this river" we hear a surprising mix of serious complaint and stoical philosophy. Singing of an anthropomorphic river representing enviable power over, and indifference to, the troubles of a land that "ain't free," Joe duplicates the tune, but not yet the lyrics or the faster rhythms, of the black complaint that began Act 1, Scene 1 with the song, "Cotton Blossom." After this introductory verse, the refrain begins very slowly:

> Ol' man river,
> Dat ol' man river,
> He mus' know sumpin'
> But don't say nuthin'
> He jes' keeps rollin'
> He keeps on rollin' along. (A)
>
> He don't plant taters,
> He don't plant cotton

An' dem dat plants em'
Is soon forgotten
But ol' man river,
He jes' keeps rollin' along. (A)

You an' me we sweat an' strain
Body all achin' an' racked wid pain
Tote dat barge! Lift dat bale!
Get a little drunk an' you land in jail. (B)

I git weary
An' sick of tryin'
I'm tired of livin'
an' skeered of dyin'
But ol' man river
He jes keeps rollin' along. (A')

"Ol' Man River" has been described by Richard Dyer as the "ultimate white person's spiritual" (Dyer 1986, 87). In making this argument Dyer would seem to agree that its music is a commodified, white-authored imitation of blackness that we have seen Michael Rogin call "white noise" (Rogin 1996, 115).[59] As a popular song posing as a spiritual, Dyer argues that it fails to capture the deeper nuances of the experience of slavery and racism. Instead, it simply constructs a folk image of the "unchanging, unchangeable fate of the black people." Expressing "the basic emotional tone that whites heard in spirituals and in Robeson's voice—sorrowing, melancholy, suffering," the song nevertheless lays the cause of this suffering at the door of nature in the river's indifference and not where it belongs, Dyer argues, at the door of the white boss (Dyer 1986, 87).

I do not quarrel with the general argument that Joe, Robeson, this song, and the whole of *Show Boat*'s narrative are, as Lauren Berlant also suggests, removed from the specifics of history, slavery, and racism (Berlant 1996, 401). Nevertheless I think that Dyer is confusing the function of spirituals with the more pointed and specific complaints of work or protest songs.[60] This confusion allows him to blame what he sees as the failure of the song to express the authentic pain and anger of historically situated African Americans on being sold out to popular, "white" musical forms that fail to capture the "real" pain, sorrow, and resentment of their historical situation (Dyer 1986, 87).

Dyer is right in many ways: "Ol' Man River" *is* a white person's version of a spiritual, written by upper-class, highly assimilated Jews. The song became a hit in an era when authentic spirituals had already been enjoying a revival of interest by both white and black audiences. But rather than take the song to task for its failure to be "authentic," we might ask: what does "white person's spiritual" mean? If it can be seen to imply in its white creators something of the "double consciousness" that W.E.B. Du Bois once argued constituted the conflicting mix of cultures animating the "souls of black folk" (Du Bois 1989, 3), then it may be possible to see and hear not simply the evacuation of the "true" spiritual but the warring hybridities that feed the melos of the popular American musical melodrama. To do this, we need to understand something of the standard thirty-two-bar structure of the conventional American popular song as it had been formulated by composers like Irving Berlin, George Gershwin, and Jerome Kern since the early teens.

The thirty-two-bar chorus expanded the simpler melodic idea of earlier songs—such as Stephen Foster's eight-bar minstrel songs ("Old Folks at Home") or his sixteen-bar ballads based on Irish and Scottish models ("Beautiful Dreamer")—into a musical structure that supported more complicated verbal patterns of rhyme and more complex turns of thought. In "Ol' Man River" an introductory verse recalls the melody, if not the "con brio" tempo, of "Cotton Blossom" (Dere's an ol' man called de Mississippi"). Next, the familiar chorus, sometimes also called the refrain, begins an eight-bar tune, united with tight rhymes setting forth the most familiar and hummable portion of the work (the A stanza, beginning with the words, "Ol' Man River"). The song repeats this structure exactly in a second eight bars ("He don't plant taters"). A "release" from this pattern is offered in the rising melody of the B stanza ("You an' me we sweat an' strain"). A final stanza (A') then repeats the first with a slight modification and in the rising crescendo of the middle section.

There is nothing particularly novel in Jerome Kern's use of the thirty-two-bar structure. Irving Berlin's "Blue Skies," from *The Jazz Singer*, is a classic example of this already well-established AABA form. With some variation, this structure became the standard for American popular song until rock music's more primitive (and once again black-inflected) form displaced it in the sixties.[61] Structurally, then, "Ol' Man River" *is* a modern popular song in the AABA form. But it also evokes qualities similar to the simpler spiritual: first, and most obviously, in its use of Negro dialect; second, in the folk brevity and simplicity of the lines of its A stanza, which nearly repeats the first line twice ("Ol' man river/ Dat ol' man river"); finally, in the absence of end rhymes in the last two lines of the first A stanza that makes us wait until the second A stanza for the only true end rhyme ("cotton" and "forgotten," borrowed from Dan Emmet's minstrel song, "Dixie," adopted by the Confederacy).[62] While it is possible to see these echoes of minstrelsy as a betrayal of the "black authenticity" of the spiritual, Stephen Foster's sad minstrel songs were themselves integrated into the spiritual programs of the Fisk Jubilee Singers, who first popularized spirituals in America and Europe. Kern and Hammerstein were thus not duplicating minstrelsy but refashioning and complicating an already racially marked musical heritage that included minstrelsy.

The overall tone of the " 'Ol' Man River" refrain, as Dyer notes, suggests human frailty and resignation in the face of the river's inhuman strength and endurance. The release (B stanza), like the ascending middle of the two A stanzas, introduces a brief moment of rising resentment and anger formed, as Lauren Berlant notes, out of Joe's direct address to the "ex-slave peasantry" of stevedores: "You an' me we sweat an' strain . . ." (412). In this section, the angry imperatives quoted from the white boss's command to work—"Tote dat barge! Lift dat bale!"—illustrated in Whale's film by an image of a shirtless, toiling Robeson, is eventually diffused by the pathetic, falling final lines of the B section—"Get a little drunk an' you land in jail"—illustrated by a high-angle shot of a chagrined Joe in straw hat entering jail. The concluding mood of the song could thus be described as pathetic resignation following brief anger. As we shall see, however, something more complex happens when Joe and the chorus of stevedores sing together.

On stage, this happens after Joe's solo is applauded.[63] The verse recommences with the same words with which the musical opened, the black complaint of "Cotton Blossom":

(Joe alone:)
Colored folks work on de Mississippi
Colored folks work while de white folks play
Pullin' dos boats from de dawn to sunset,
Gitten' no rest till de Judgment Day. (Verse A)

But now, instead of launching into the familiar chorus as before, the verse expands, putting off its return to the theme of the endlessly rolling river, extending its complaint about black toil as the chorus of stevedores joins in with a new energy:

(Chorus of stevedores:)
Don't look up an don't look down,
You don't dast make de white boss frown;
Bend yo' knees an' bow yo head,
an' pull dat rope until yo're dead. (Verse B)

With rhythmic cadences that echo the stevedores' original complaint from "Cotton Blossom," but this time pointedly naming the source of complaint in the "white boss," the stevedores (arrayed behind Joe in the 1936 film) vividly prolong and detail the depiction of the constraints under which they toil (Fig. 4.10).[64] And they do so in eight measures of verse which echo both the release (B) section of the chorus ("You an' me we sweat an' strain") and the earlier song, "Cotton Blossom," with which the musical began. This tight interweaving of verse and chorus, of complaint and resignation, gives this imitation spiritual a striking complexity and ambivalence. Neither fully resigned to suffering nor fully admiring of the enduring river, the song moves from envy in the first section of the verse, "Dat's de ol' man dat I'd like to be," to a poignant desire to escape in the last:

Figure 4.10 Joe sings "Ol' Man River" with the chorus of stevedores. (*Show Boat*, Universal, James Whale, 1936)

> (Joe alone:)
> Let me go 'way from de Mississippi,
> Let me go 'way from de white man boss.
> Show me dat stream called de river Jordan,
> Dat's de ol' stream dat I longs to cross! (Verse A)

In contrast to the energy, anger, and tight rhythms of the stevedores, Joe now slowly and plaintively introduces the traditional "other river" of spirituals in the form of a return to the A section of the verse ("Let me go' way") that will then lead back to the A section of the chorus ("Ol' man river"). At this point in the song the complex weaving of the ABA verse with the AABA thirty-two-bar chorus permits a mixture of articulations that go beyond both the longing to return to the Lord typical of spirituals and the singing about work typical of work songs. By the time Joe returns to the original refrain, its mixture of complaint and resignation has been strengthened and deepened.

While Joe's first solo rendition of the song—before the addition of the extended verse—is rousing in all stage performances (in the Harold Prince revival starring Michel Bell as Joe, it never failed to elicit wild applause), this second run-through, with the new verse leading back to the familiar chorus, stops the show.[65] Certainly one reason for the wild enthusiasm in the 1993 revival is the degree to which its performance and staging now seem to express,

Figure 4.11   The shirtless, toiling Robeson "totes that barge" in James Whale's montage from "Ol' Man River." (*Show Boat*, Universal, James Whale, 1936)

however briefly, something today recognizable as "black power." In the 1936 film, Paul Robeson's expressions of anger are accompanied by intercut montages that (often too literally) illustrate the toil and sorrow (Fig. 4.11). Although at one point Robeson raises a briefly clenched fist, the pose is not held. It is further softened by the seated posture from which he delivers the song and a concluding smile that seems designed to reassure white audiences of a Joe returned to the easygoing persona with which he began.[66] In contrast, the 1993 Toronto-originated revival of *Show Boat* that later toured the United States makes a point of eliminating most of the dialogue referring to Joe's laziness, delivers the song from an upright position, and emphatically does not end with a smile. Post–civil rights era Joes have become more hardworking, serious, and angry, but few have had the sheer charisma of Robeson, who initially did the most to extend the Tom stereotype.[67]

It would be a mistake, however, to judge the power of the song on a quantitative measurement of degrees of militancy in its staging and delivery. To do so would give the post–civil rights era Joes the decided advantage, but it would miss the impact of seeing even a smiling Joe singing this song, interacting with a Negro chorus on a Broadway stage still so used to the melos of blackface. Indeed, it seems more appropriate to consider that this racial melos may have had the same kind of revolutionary impact as the blackface incarnation of Tom singing "Old Folks at Home" in the Aiken-Howard blackface production. In both cases, what audiences—white and black—heard and saw was a "black" man singing with feeling and longing for a southern river associated with America's rural past (the Swanee and Mississippi). Both the minstrel "home" song and the song personifying the enduring power of the mighty Mississippi offer an emotional power couched in longing associated with the sorrows of slaves and their still-unfree descendants. Neither song offers a pure and authentic expression of African-American experience. Both are "contaminated" by their commodifying (Irish minstrel and Jewish Tin Pan Alley) influences. But in this very "contamination," both in their time achieved a pathos that moved white and black audiences to recognize the Americanness and sympathize with the suffering of the black man. The fact that one of these quintessential black Americans wore burnt cork while another did not is perhaps less significant than the fact that both sang songs in which Jewish-American songwriters fused an idea of black folk music and spiritual with their own hybridized musical traditions of ballad and Tin Pan Alley popular song.

Although critics at the time seemed hardly aware that they were witnessing a historic transformation from blackface to black performance, they nevertheless recognized something different in the performance of Paul Robeson: "Mr. Robeson has a touch of genius. It is not merely his voice, which is one of the richest organs on the stage. It is his understanding that gives 'Old Man River' [*sic*] an epic lift. When he sings it out of the cavernous depths of his chest his face is a mask for the humble patience of the Negro race and you realize that Jerome Kern's spiritual has reached its final expression" (*New York Times*, May 20, 1932). Though this critic—Brooks Atkinson—has no vocabulary for the intimations of "black power" hidden in the performance, the contrast between the image of power figured in the "cavernous depths of his chest" and the awareness that "humble patience" can be a mask, captures, as a blackface Tom's rendition of "Old Folks at Home" had before it, an unprecedented seriousness and expressivity in the performance of blackness.

What American audiences—black and white—see and hear in "Ol' Man River" is thus best understood not as a definitive break with a vile Africanist minstrel stereotype, but as an extension of Uncle Tom–inflected pathos through a musical amalgamation of Tin Pan Alley pop with minstrelsy and spiritual. Adapting Ferber's novel, in which Joe is a very minor character, they give him a song and a presence that far exceeds his narrative role. Within the tradition of black and white racial melodrama a new musical expression of African-American pathos was born. "Ol' Man River" became an instant standard of the American popular song repertoire. Performed by everyone, from Frank Sinatra to Sun Ra, it nevertheless remained primarily associated with Paul Robeson during his subsequent concert career.[68] In its context in *Show Boat*, however, "Ol' Man River" stands frustratingly alone, "sealed off into a vacuum" to which black performers are so often confined.[69] Consigned to the background, narratively, with no place to go, it nevertheless gives voice to emotions that had never been voiced on the mainstream stage or in film by a black performer. Its "miraculous moment" is never purely a matter of Robeson's indelible performance but also what this performance did with music and lyrics of a song that unprecedentedly "integrated" the canon of songs of American musical theater, bringing a new power, tension, masculinity, and expressivity to the performance of blackness.[70]

173

If the innovation of Kern and Hammerstein's integrated musical theater is to have created songs that grow naturally out of character and situation, then the failure of this great song is that its unprecedented depth of feeling, which surpasses that of any of the white characters in the show, along with its specific relation to racial oppression, has no further narrative issue except in the link formed between Joe and Julie through an exchange of looks. Increasingly, Joe and his song dissipate to become a mere leitmotif marking the passing of time as the comparatively trivial family melodrama of Magnolia, Gaylord, and Kim is played out against the background of black toil and sorrow.

The second great "race" song in *Show Boat*'s first act fares a little better in becoming "integrated" into the narrative of the musical. "Can't Help Lovin' Dat Man" is an imitation blues number that expands and dramatically deepens Ferber's depiction of interracial idyll in the kitchen of the Cotton Blossom. It makes Magnolia's instruction in the soulfulness of black music the occasion of a rousing interracial anthem in which whites and blacks come close, for the first time in an American musical, to singing the same song.[71] Like "Ol' Man River," the number is prompted by an initial conversation with Magnolia regarding her meeting with the young stranger. Julie, like Joe, is suspicious of the young man. She worries aloud to Magnolia: "Once a girl like you starts to love a man it ain't so easy to stop." When Magnolia asks if Julie could stop loving Steve, Julie initiates the chorus of "Can't Help Lovin' Dat Man," initially skipping the introductory verse:

> Fish gotta swim, birds gotta fly
> I gotta love one man til I die
> Can't help lovin' dat man of mine. (A)

> Tell me he's lazy tell me he's slow
> Tell me I'm crazy, maybe I know,
> Can't help lovin' dat man of mine. (A)

Helen Morgan, a white singer-actress, originated the part of Julie in the Ziegfeld production and performed it on stage for two decades. In the 1936 film she begins the song in her distinctive tremulous soprano at the bottom of the stairs to the kitchen (Fig. 4.12). A camera tilt reveals Queenie (Hattie McDaniel) at the top of the stairs about to descend into the kitchen. She looks startled and vaguely suspicious, asking, "How come you all knows that song? . . . I didn't never hear any body but colored folks sing it—it sounds funny for Miss Julie to know it." Then, almost as a challenge, she asks, "Can you sing the whole thing?" (Fig. 4.13)

At first fearful of Queenie's recognition of the song (and through it of Queenie's recognition of her mixed race), Julie then defiantly accepts the challenge, this time including the song's more bluesy introductory verse:

> Oh listen sister,
> I love my mister man
> And I can't understand
> Dere ain't no reason
> Why I should love dat man,
> It mus' be sumpin'
> Dat de angels done plan.
>
> Fish gotta swim, birds gotta fly
> I gotta love one man til I die
> Can't help lovin' dat man of mine. (A)
>
> Tell me he's lazy tell me he's slow
> Tell me I'm crazy, maybe I know,
> Can't help lovin' dat man of mine. (A)
>
> When he goes away, that's a rainy day
> But when he comes home
> That day's fine, the sun will shine. (B)
>
> He can come home as late as can be
> Home without him ain't no home to me
> Can't help lovin dat man of mine. (A)

Like "Ol' Man River," "Can't Help Lovin' Dat Man of Mine" is a Broadway show tune in AABA form posing as a traditional black musical idiom, in this case the blues. It is constructed as a piece of "black" wisdom printed in the vocal score, in Negro dialect (e.g., "dat," "dere," "gotta"). Where "Ol' Man River" is a song of complaint filled with male wisdom about the lack of freedom and the constancy of work sung among black men, "Can't Help Lovin' " is a song of complaint whose lyrics suggest an address by one black woman to another ("Oh listen sister").

"Can't Help Lovin' " is sung here by Julie—the apparently white star of the show boat—in a fashion that suppresses many of its "blacker" idioms. As a warning-initiation to the love-struck Magnolia, it first seems to be a "black" song applied to an apparently white situation. The song is thus narratively prompted by the primary white love story and it is returned to that story in

Figure 4.12 Julie (Helen Morgan) begins to sing "Can't Help Lovin' Dat Man." (*Show Boat*, Universal, James Whale, 1936)

Figure 4.13 Queenie (Hattie McDaniel), suspicious that Julie knows a "colored" song, challenges her to sing the whole song. (*Show Boat*, Universal, James Whale, 1936)

the second act, where it is reprised by Magnolia. However, its apparent racial posing of a white woman singing a black song soon takes on added resonance. For when Queenie notes that "it sounds funny for Miss Julie to know it," she means that what really seems "funny" is not the familiar phenomenon of white "posing" to sing a "black" song, but the suspicion, apparent in Queenie's first hard look at Julie when she recognizes the song, of a much more dangerous, and criminal, "passing" as white (Fig. 4.13).

The performance of this song thus takes on special resonance in a double display of posing as black *and* passing as white. Where whites who pose as black intentionally exhibit all the artifice of their performance—exaggerated gestures, blackface make-up—blacks who pass as white suppress the more obvious artifice of performance. Passing is a performance whose success depends on not overacting. Julie has gained the privileges of whiteness—the ability to perform as leading lady opposite a white leading man, the ability to be married to that leading man—by not calling attention to the difference between herself and the role she plays.

Helen Morgan was a white chanteuse who specialized in torch songs sung perched on, or against, pianos. There was nothing "black," or even bluesy, in her thin soprano, still posture, and relatively proper diction that played down the "dere"s and "dat"s of the song. However, she could convey infinite pathos, and even at a young age her face and voice suggested deep dissipation and ruin. In performing this song she stands very still, first holding on to the stairs (Fig. 4.12), later holding on to a chair, and finally sitting on a table. The one thing she resolutely does not do in any of these postures is precisely what Queenie, Joe, and Magnolia, and eventually a whole chorus of black dancers, seem not to be able to keep from doing: shuffling, swaying, and dancing to the song's rhythm. Where Queenie, Joe, and Magnolia all represent various degrees of exaggerated *posing as black*, Julie's restraint offers the contrast of *passing as white*. In a song about the involuntary nature of love, involuntary rhythms invade the performance to bring out the "blackness" of Kern and Hammerstein's pseudo-blues—rhythms that Julie herself resists, but which the infectiousness of the song itself "can't help" but bring out in everyone else.[72]

Queenie and Joe's separate reactions to the song are privileged in matching close-ups in Whale's film. Standing behind Julie on the stairs leading down to the kitchen as Julie recommences the whole song, Queenie's ample, stereotypical "mammy" body begins to pick up the song's rhythm, moving cheerfully down the stairs in a shuffle, tending to the stove according to the song's rhythms, rolling her eyes from side to side. Queenie's shuffling movements exaggerate the infectious rhythms that accentuate the "colored" origins of the song. As Julie reaches the final refrain ("He can come home as late as can be") a slow-moving, apple-munching Joe appears at the top of the stairs, coming home late himself to Queenie. Joe, too, recognizes the song, exclaiming, "Why, that's my favorite song!"

A song that began as Julie's quasi-tragic warning to Magnolia about the dangers of indiscriminate loving—prompted by her own love of Steve—now becomes an opportunity for a sly, down-and-dirty comic blues complaint by Queenie about her own indiscriminate love of Joe. Reformulating and expanding the verse, she too begins from the top:

177

> My man is shif'less,
> And good fer nuthin' too,
> He's my man just the same!
> He's never round here
> When dere is work to do. (A)
>
> De chimbley's smokin',
> De roof is leanin' in,
> But he don't seem to care,
> He kin be happy
> Wid jes a sip of gin.[73](A)

To which Joe interjects sheepishly:

> Why you all talk 'bout gin?

And to which Queenie answers:

> I even love him
> When his kisses got gin.

The chorus is then repeated with Queenie, Joe, and Julie all singing together and, in the Whale version, separate shots of Negroes on the wharf dancing along. During this rousing, upbeat performance—very different from the tragic resignation with which Julie began, Magnolia becomes the center of attention as she begins to imitate a shuffling, "darkie" dance. Joe's admiring exclamation approves of her black posing—"Look at dat little gal shuffle!" and the whole interracial group emerges from the kitchen to the deck of the show boat, where they join the dancing Negroes on the shore, to take a comic bow.

What begins as a serious torch song by Julie for Steve, with its submerged pathos of the tragic mulatta doomed to a proscribed love, moves into a more comic mode as a celebration of Queenie's love for the "shif'less" but endearing Joe. All traces of the serious Joe of the previous "Ol' Man River" now vanish. In its up-tempo, "ragging" form, the song becomes the occasion for what in 1927—an era of newly popular all-black Broadway musicals—was a rare moment of performative integration. It may seem natural enough, in retrospect, that a torch song sung by a "passing" mixed-race woman should performatively evolve into a more blatantly black idiom like the blues, especially when audiences would soon discover that the originating singer possesses black "blood." Under such conditions we would expect the inherent "blackness" of the song to emerge. Indeed, Queenie's insistence that Julie demonstrate knowledge of the more bluesy verse ("Oh listen sister") instead of the more European chorus ("Fish gotta swim"), along with her own variation and expansion of that verse ("De chimbley's smokin'"), obviously exaggerates the "blackness" of the song.

However, this extreme emphasis on the "blackness" of the song and the infectious black posing it elicits in Magnolia may yet serve another purpose. In becoming an overtly "black" female blues song, and in shifting its focus from Steve to Joe, the song deflects attention from the interracial love that is its raison d'être. For if the white Steve is "dat man" whom Julie cannot help but love, then her song about him will prove, once the audience knows her story, to be a mixed race love song. No wonder that Steve himself is not present during its singing and that the song's focus so quickly shifts to Joe. No wonder, too, that Julie's second-act torch song, "Bill," pointedly avoids reference to Steve even when the narrative explicitly states that it is abandonment by her "husband" that has led Julie to drink.[74]

In a musical littered with no less than three love duets between its white principals—"Make Believe," "Why Do I Love You?," and "You are Love"—the absence of a love duet between the doomed lovers, Julie and Steve, is striking. That Steve himself is the only principal character in the main plot of Show Boat with absolutely no music to sing suggests the extreme nature of the musical dilemma Kern and Hammerstein faced when they introduced two sympathetic characters engaged in interracial love. To give musical expression to the melodramatic virtue of this love would be to give virtue to a sexual and emotional relation that directly challenged long-established boundaries between black and white. Yet not to give expression to this love would be to deny sympathy to a melodramatic situation that evolves out of black and white racial melodrama's investment in the virtue of racially beset characters.

As we have seen, Kern and Hammerstein's solution to the dilemma of representing miscegenation was, like The Jazz Singer, to walk a fine line between the acceptable expression of interracial sympathy inherited from the Tom tradition and the taboo relation of interracial love excoriated by The Birth of a Nation. In The Jazz Singer this meant displacing the potential sexual energy of interracial love songs between Mary and Jakie into the blackface performance of mammy songs. These songs diverted attention away from interracial love, celebrating instead mammy songs of intraracial mother-son love. In Show Boat, however, black-white interracial love was both more taboo and more directly expressed by the narrative. Not surprisingly, then, it deflects potential musical expressions of interracial love into more acceptable forms, as when "Can't Help Lovin' Dat Man" becomes a celebration of black on black love, or, later, into Julie's torch song for an unseen and racially unspeci-fied "Bill."

Staging the Audience: Integration, Segregation, Miscegenation

The narrative, as opposed to the musical, expression of the above tensions surrounding interracial love comes to a head in the melodramatic astonish-ment of what has come to be called the "miscegenation scene." The scene takes place very much as written in Ferber's novel.[75] During a rehearsal of the old-fashioned melodrama, *The Parson's Bride*, the more "realistic" melodrama of Ferber, Kern, and Hammerstein's miscegenation story intrudes.

As Steve and Julie rehearse their stilted lines, Steve receives warning that the sheriff is coming. According to an apparently predetermined plan, he then opens a knife, pulls the blade across Julie's finger, and drinks her blood (Fig. 4.14). Julie sinks in a near faint, Magnolia screams, and, true to melodramatic convention, all "stand astonished." Immediately, "the sheriff of melodrama" (Ferber 1994, 109) enters. From this point until the end of the scene, Whale's film calls attention to the audience of Negroes forming at the windows of the theater who have come to see the "real," racial, melodrama playing out on the show boat stage.

The sheriff formally accuses Cap'n Andy of having a "miscegenation case" on board, defining the term one-sidedly as a "case of a Negro woman married to a white man." But Steve objects: "You wouldn't call a man a white man who had Negro blood in him, would you?" On cue, the sheriff answers that in the state of Mississippi, "one drop of Negro blood makes you a Negro."[76] Steve then prods everyone on stage to agree to the literal truth that he has considerably more than "one drop" of black blood in him. Foiled by the Cotton Blossom troupe's conspiratorial refusal to "nominate" the evil miscegenation of Julie and Steve's relation, the sheriff nevertheless threatens to prosecute an equally proscribed though less taboo case of racial integration among the players and orders the "black" couple to leave the boat for their own safety.

Only the naive Magnolia dares argue that Julie and Steve remain with the troupe. She does so by insisting that Julie should not be punished for what she "can't help," though given Julie's previous song there is a certain blurring of what Magnolia means Julie "can't help"—loving Steve or being of mixed

Figure 4.14   The "miscegenation scene": Steve drinks Julie's blood to take on a black identity and escape the charge of miscegenation. (*Show Boat*, Universal, James Whale, 1936)

race. These confusions—between the "fault" of being black and the "fault" of being in love with the wrong person; between the illegal act of miscegenation and the less serious, but still illegal act of integration—are typical of the moral obfuscations of melodrama in general and of the conflicted attitudes of black and white racial melodrama in particular in the Jazz Age. As in *Way Down East*, this melodrama is ambivalent about the nature of the "wrong" for which its victims suffer. Miscegenation, which white supremacists saw exclusively in black and white terms as the sinister end (and ultimate goal) of integration, is rendered sympathetic, in the time-honored fashion of melodrama, through the virtue that accrues to victims who "can't help" certain things. At the same time, however, miscegenation law is covertly upheld through the banishment of the couple from the narrative once the racial nature of their relationship is revealed.

Legally, miscegenation is defined as "intermarrying, cohabiting, or interbreeding of persons of different races" (Saks 1988, 39; Pascoe 1999). Antimiscegenation laws persisted in most states—not only in Mississippi—until the Supreme Court held them unconstitutional in 1967 (Saks 1988, 40). Especially relevant to all film versions of *Show Boat* is the fact that the legal ban on miscegenation was echoed by the ban on its representation in Hollywood during the era of the Hollywood Production Code (effectively 1929–52). The key words of the 1934 version of the code—Hollywood's first censorship document with enforcement teeth—remarkably echo the definition of miscegenation offered by the sheriff in *Show Boat*: in both, the term "miscegenation," which can refer to sexual relations between a wide variety of different races, is immediately qualified as a "sex relationship between the white and black races" alone.[77]

Under the prohibitions of the Production Code, the very existence of a mixed-race character on the screen became problematic proof of the prior "crime" of miscegenation. Such characters automatically opened up the vexed question of with whom this mixed-raced person should mate. For if the person "looked" white, a black mate would offend the white supremacist eye, yet if the white-looking person "was" black—in the essentializing way miscegenation's discourse of blood saw it—a white mate would offend miscegenation law. The 1934 version of Fannie Hurst's *Imitation of Life* (John Stahl, 1934), for example, whose subplot included a passing mulatta but which did not represent any miscegenational "sex relationship," was heavily censored by the Joseph Breen Production Code Administration for depicting miscegenation "in spirit, if not in fact!" in its focus on the passing character, Peola (Courtney 1997, 211). It is all the more curious, then, that the 1936 *Show Boat*, released two years later under the same code prohibitions, did not raise the ire of censors, for its passing character, Julie, did depict the "fact" and not just the "spirit" of a "sex relation" between a white man and a black woman.[78]

The easiest explanation might be that the Production Code censors were only really exercised about the actual, as opposed to the fictional, mixing of races. In other words, *Imitation of Life* (1934) caused consternation while the 1936 *Show Boat* did not because Freddie Washington, the actor who plays Peola, was of mixed race while Helen Morgan, who plays Julie, was not. Thus Washington's physical presence in the cast, even without the narrative depiction of "sex relations" in that film, was much more destabilizing to the conventional black and white polarities of Hollywood representation than was Morgan's fictional presence in *Show Boat*, which did have a narrative depiction of "sex relation" to the degree that Julie and Steve are represented as a couple in love. *Imitation of Life* thus seems to have introduced a more troubling version of the complex crossracial dynamics of passing than *Show Boat* did to Hollywood censors. At any rate, while a flurry of letters and eventual narrative change was generated by the former, no serious objection was raised by the latter.[79]

But perhaps the deeper explanation for these inconsistencies derives from the unstable status of the "crime" of miscegenation itself. This "crime" is actually relatively new; it was not recognized during slavery so long as it was a case of a white man and a black woman. Only after the end of slavery, when persons of mixed blood began to have a stake in property rights and inheritance from their predominantly white fathers, did miscegenation become a "crime." At this point it began to be formulated not as the mixing of white and black (or yellow and white or brown and white) people, but as the mixing of "blood." The reason for the law's shift away from the observation of visible color to what Eva Saks calls an invisible "discourse of blood" was to establish blood as a symbol of race that could function autonomously of visual observation in the case of "light-skinned" Negroes. Genealogy—and its instrument, the famous "one drop" rule referred to by the sheriff of this melodrama—was made the determinant of race, marking former slaves as a genetic underclass, whatever appearances might say (Saks 1988, 40–48).[80]

Of course the great flaw in miscegenation law from a white supremacist perspective was the fact that the very "blood" that works so hard in this system to essentialize race is not itself visible. The invisibility of "blood" could permit a person like Julie to pass until her true genealogy was exposed. The melodramatic theatrical model of this particular *coup de théâtre* dates back to Dion Bouccicault's 1859 stage melodrama *The Octoroon*, where the possession of "black blood" becomes cause for the heroine's suicide, always a handy way to dispose of the problem.

In *Show Boat*, when Steve drinks Julie's blood he both exposes the absurdity of miscegenation law's "discourse of blood" by making its metaphorical and invisible blood visible, *and* he gives the metaphor a strange validity by literalizing it. Substituting temporary ingestion for inherited possession, Steve both makes a mockery of the hallowed importance of blood, exposing its metaphor as just that, *and* he literalizes the metaphor, joining his fate to Julie's through a tie of blood.[81] Of the many ways in which whites gain virtue by performatively posing as black in this work, Steve's negrophilic "posing" is the most disruptive of the boundaries of the color line that *Show Boat* simultaneously challenges and upholds. For unlike Magnolia, he poses as black without performing as black, without joining the exaggerated blackface tradition.[82] His pose, performed out of love for a mixed-race woman, is the only one the text cannot accommodate musically. His vampiric gesture of sucking Julie's blood signals a willingness to fully become black in the eyes of the world, all the while subversively insinuating that race is a thoroughly unstable quality, neither a question of blood nor a question of visibility. Melodramatic astonishment followed by utter banishment from the narrative seems to be the text's only possible reaction.

If we consider the fact that New York audiences of 1927 were themselves sitting in theaters that had only recently been racially integrated and that they were watching black and white performers on stage who were also, before their very eyes, *being* integrated, then we begin to see the compelling fascination of this work in its own time and despite its inability to continue the story of race. Add to that the fact that these performers were themselves acting out

Figure 4.15   The perspective of the black audience on "the show" from its position in the segregated balcony. (*Show Boat*, Universal, James Whale, 1936)

a melodramatic moment of astonishment at the very "crime" of miscegenation and see how very resonant the racial thematics of the work must have been.

All stagings of this scene in the twenties and thirties, including James Whale's 1936 film, place Joe in the balcony high above the action looking down upon it. A photo from the 1928 London production—the first to include Robeson—shows the white principals to the left, dark-clad Negroes to the center and right watching the scene, and Joe in white high above as the most significant witness of the racial apartheid that expels Julie from her show boat home. Joe's position in the balcony does not simply serve the purpose of isolating and highlighting his presence, like a Greek Chorus, or even a Greek God. It also places him in the same position of the segregated Negro audience during the performances of the show. In both the 1929 and 1936 versions of the film, brief scenes introduce the point of view of the black audience high up in what was called "nigger heaven" (Fig. 4.15). While the anonymous black audience in the balcony watches the "olio" concert that follows the show, featuring, in Whale's film, Magnolia in blackface (Fig. 4.8), Joe watches the much more compelling melodramatic spectacle of Steve's unmusical posing as black and Julie's failure to continue to pass as white. In Whale's film the couple's banishment is marked by their slow exit down the aisle of the theater away from the stage on which they can no longer appear together, while Joe, the racially knowing, empathic, and isolated black witness, sadly bids "Master Steve" and "Miss Julie" goodbye from his "segregated" vantage point in the balcony. If this expulsion quite literally clears the decks of the show boat for the formation of a second—all white—couple who will replace Julie and Steve as leading lady and man on the Cotton Blossom, it also ironically marks it as a wedding-like procession that further bonds the interracial couple.

Both musical play and film self-consciously stage the internal audience of the miscegenation scene in ways that dramatize segregation as a felt evil. The Ziegfeld audience thus experiences Jim Crow as the wrenching apart of what had heretofore been Cap'n Andy's "happy family." This audience may well have felt liberally superior to the enactment of a form of segregation that was, in its very own practices of theater-going, beginning to fade into history. In the deep South during slavery, audiences attended the same theater in segregated sections; on stage, only whites performed. As we have seen, the presence of slave audiences in theaters in the antebellum era was one reason for banning *Uncle Tom's Cabin* in southern theaters (Dorman 1967, 233). Usually black theater patrons were confined to the balcony, as depicted in the brief shot in Whale's 1936 film (Fig. 4.15). Segregation was also the norm on Broadway before the Jazz Age. The main floors of Broadway theaters remained exclusively white until the 1921 production of the all-black show *Shuffle Along* began seating African Americans in the orchestra—though only in the back third. Succeeding "black" shows produced on Broadway during the twenties loosened seating restrictions until they gradually disappeared (Woll 1989, 50–52, 72, 73). Movie audiences, on the other hand, remained rigidly segregated, especially in the South. This persistence of segregation among film audiences is undoubtedly one reason why the 1929 film version excised the miscegenation plot altogether.[83]

In the racial victimization of this banishment, so like the classic banishment from *Way Down East* discussed in Chapter 1, melodramatic virtue is recognized in the suffering of the banished couple even as they are covertly punished, as Anna in Griffith's film is covertly punished, for a forbidden sexual relation. But where Anna's banishment and suffering provides the occasion for a rescue in-the-nick-of-time that washes her clean and reinstates her as a "virgin," Julie and Steve's banishment and suffering provides no such reinstatement in the narrative. Tacitly, then, this racial melodrama recognizes a "stain" that its narrative, unlike the narrative of the fallen woman, does not know how to wash clean. Permanently sullied by this public recognition of their forbidden love, there is no snow storm and raging river (despite the narrative opportunities) to simultaneously cleanse and punish them.[84] Their banishment is thus banishment from the story altogether and an opportunity for Magnolia and Gaylord to carry out a much more acceptable version of the "forbidden" love story, with Gaylord's gambling substituting weakly for race as the narrative "problem."

Just as the (mostly untold) story and the (mostly unheard) music of Julie and Steve's miscegenational relation gives resonance to the told story and heard music of Magnolia and Gaylord's relation, so again in the second act the untold story and unheard music of Julie's abandonment by Steve gives depth and meaning to Magnolia's abandonment by her luckless husband. *Show Boat* is punctuated, at midpoint in each of its two acts, by the pathetic, processional exit of this self-sacrificing passing woman. If the first exit is against her will, the second is a noble and willing sacrifice for Magnolia who, we are asked to believe, needs Julie's job as a chanteuse. Both, however, effectively remove the mixed race woman from the narrative while infusing the white heroine with her suffering virtue.

The original stage musical of *Show Boat* ends, unlike the novel, with the happy reunion of Gaylord and Magnolia gazing fondly upon their now-grown daughter performing on stage as a flapper. An antiquated but still grand Magnolia and a humbled, returned Gaylord reunite in admiration of a triumphant apparition of their daughter as modern woman, while Joe reprises "Ol' Man River" for the last time.[85] As in *The Jazz Singer*, approving parents join an audience of Americans that recognizes the virtue of their performing and assimilating children. Where Tom and anti-Tom racial melodrama had previously recognized racial virtue in suffering and deeds, the melos of racial melodrama in the Jazz Age now recognizes a virtue of racial suffering presented in musical performance. In *The Jazz Singer* and *Show Boat* whites learn to appropriate the distilled essence of black suffering in song. Posing as black is the instrument of their success on stage, and blackface becomes the emblem of that success in *The Jazz Singer*. In *Show Boat*, however, it is a different matter. In this work blackface has become part of the antiquated past, like theatrical melodrama. Both blackface and theatrical melodrama cede to up-to-the-minute inventions like radio and bobbed hair. Yet both also live on—transmuted into a white posing as black that no longer needs blackface and into a form of musical theater and film that has integrated music and narrative. And just as Jack Robin's blackface song, "Mammy," came to stand for the reconciliation of the now-assimilated Jewish-American family once the intransigent Orthodox father had passed on, so "Ol' Man River" came to stand for the old-fashioned eternal, American values supporting the triumphant white family.

If *The Jazz Singer* represents the triumph of the assimilating son over the old-world father, *Show Boat* represents a less traumatic, but perhaps more truly modern triumph of a headstrong daughter over an intransigent, spoilsport mother. Both this Jewish father and straitlaced New England mother present impediments to an assimilating show-biz success. Success in both is achieved through promiscuous minglings that come ultimately to define being American. Jakie's father says, "Stop," and the flow of "jazz" music (and spontaneous speech) freezes. But the Jewish mother recognizes the virtue of the old world in the new and the music flows again. Magnolia's forbidding New England mother tries to put a stop to the singing of "nigger" songs in the show boat kitchen, but the infectious pleasure of the music wins out under the encouragement of the indulgent father, who perpetually tells his black-posing daughter to "smile." In each case, the spoilsport, "orthodox" parent is no match for the forward march of the American culture industry that grounds the virtue of its new stars in the racial suffering of the now-distant past of slavery. The pathos of racially marked suffering gives depth and seriousness to their otherwise all-too-frivolous triumphs. Thus, while neither work can overtly endorse the interracial love that flows transgressively from the racial sympathy of the "Tom" tradition—whether between white woman "gentile" and Jewish man, or between black woman and white man—the integrationist ethos that animates each leads toward the covert expression of precisely this love.

Edna Ferber's novel ends, unlike the musical, with all the principals dead except Magnolia and her daughter Kim, now a famous actress on what had come to be called the "legitimate" stage—the new stage of "Ibsen and Haupt-mann, and Werfel, and Schnitzler, and Molnar, and Chekhov" (302). Magnolia, who has just buried her mother and decided to return to her river origins, magnanimously gives her daughter Parthy's fortune "made out of this boat in the last twenty-five years" (301). Kim is enthusiastic about the new "American Theater" she will be able to build. Magnolia considers the term "American Theater" and offers her trademark smile: "She looked a trifle uncomfortable, as one who has heard a good joke, and has no one with whom to share it" (302). The reader knows, however, what Kern and Hammerstein's musical would successfully translate into musical terms: that the real "American The-ater" is the theater of melodrama and that racial conflicts have always provided it with its deepest resonance.

5 Rewriting the Plantation Legend: Scarlett "Totes a Weary Load"

The head must bow and the back will have to bend

    Wherever the darkey may go

A few more days, and the trouble all will end

    In the field where the sugar canes grow

A few more days for to tote the weary load,

    No matter 'twill never be light,

A few more days till we totter on the road,

    Then my old Kentucky Home, good-night!

        —Stephen Foster, "My Old Kentucky Home"

Melodrama, as we have seen, needs to establish the virtue of an uncorrupted "space of innocence" (Brooks 1995, 29). In American racial melodrama this space is typically an idealized version of the rural southern home that at various moments in American history has been fancied by the nation as a whole as constituting our national origins, our "roots." As Grace Elizabeth Hale (1998, 295) writes, the "South," a "place of not now," is a "space of safety and mooring for whatever we imagine we have lost." At the same time, however, and especially due to the legacy of slavery, this lost home "space of innocence" is also a space "of horror" (295).

In the decade of the Great Depression, American popular culture would wax even more nostalgic over the traditional virtues of the agrarian southern home than it had in Stephen Foster's day, to the point of reviving its most controversial symbol of white mastery: the plantation. Long after the ravages of the Civil War and Reconstruction had swept through Georgia, Margaret

Figure 5.1 Tara as it appears toward the beginning of David O. Selznick's *Gone With the Wind*. Scarlett and Gerald gaze at their plantation home. (*Gone With the Wind*, 1939, Turner Classics)

Mitchell and David O. Selznick erected, each in a different way, a monument to this home in the form of Tara, the northern Georgia plantation named after the ancient seat of the Irish kings that stands proud at the end of both novel and film (Fig. 5.1). Even Dixon and Griffith's Progressive Era paean to the virtue of the old South had not ventured such an apparently unapologetic celebration of the economic system of chattel slavery for which this plantation home stood.

It is conventional, of course, for home to be associated with the feminine and the maternal. In the popular, "sentimental" tradition of lady novelists, home is Heaven, while in the high art literary tradition, where masculine heroes flee home to "light out for the territory" of action and adventure, home is Hell (Fiedler 1982, 150–53). In the tradition of black and white melodrama, however, the conventional gendering of the melodramatic "haven in a heartless world" was reversed very early: while the dark-skinned male Uncle Tom provided the pathos of longing for home, his light-skinned female fellow slave Eliza provided the exciting action of escape. Later critics have viewed the maternal passivity and domesticity of Uncle Tom as an emasculating "desexing" of the African (American) male.[1] However, it was precisely this feminization and domestication of Tom that gave Stowe's novel and many of its subsequent stage versions the power to do battle with reigning stereotypes of oversexed, virile minstrel caricatures of antebellum culture.

When Thomas Dixon and D. W. Griffith inverted the racial polarities of *Uncle Tom's Cabin* to create their own "anti-Tom" racial melodrama, they were also inverting well-entrenched gendered and raced polarities of the good **189** home. *The Birth of a Nation* reinvested sympathy in a racially beset white home by dramatizing the spectacle of white women victimized by black "beasts." Dixon and Griffith rewrote Stowe's racial family romance to idealize the white masculine heroes who defended the purity of the white woman and a "pure" line of succession from white father to white son. Thus, although a melodramatic home "space of innocence" is central both to the "Tom" and "anti-Tom" melodramas, they cannot simply be equated with the tradition of feminine, sentimentalized pathos.[2]

Indeed, a closer look at the role of home in the ongoing tradition of racial melodrama we are tracing suggests that while its variously raced and gendered victim-heroes may embrace an abstract ideal of home, they rarely stay there themselves. Whether they flee bondage, like Eliza, are sold down river, like Tom, march off to war like the Cameron brothers, go to Chicago like Magnolia, or go to Atlanta to raise money for taxes like Scarlett, these heroes, black and white, male and female, are better at making dramatic homecomings than they are at staying home.[3] Though Ben Cameron returns home, the antebellum world he left is, as Margaret Mitchell would later put it, "gone with the wind." The force of the *Clansman/Birth of a Nation* narratives would be to restore something of the feeling and the mythos—if not the actual architecture—of that agrarian southern home. However, in the restless modernity of the Jazz Age, and in the social upheaval of the Great Depression that followed, the melodramatic, home "space of innocence" became an abstract locus of nostalgia located even less in the actual South than in Hale's imaginary South "inside us." In these works, upwardly mobile, assimilating white protagonists flee the restrictions of old-fashioned homes that have become unliveable and then imitate Uncle Tom in nostalgically longing for what they have lost.

In *The Jazz Singer* and *Show Boat*, for example, white protagonists have it both ways: they assimilate to mainstream, white, bourgeois society and they emotionally come home in their music. This music forges a link between their spontaneous and natural qualities as performers and the virtue of the true, long-suffering "Old Folks at Home"—the "Mammies," the "Queenies," and the "Joes" whose very lack of social mobility makes them seem permanently attached to the rural southern home.[4] With *Gone With the Wind*, however—and especially with David O. Selznick's 1939 blockbuster film—an entire nation—indeed large parts of the western world—would adapt a regional story of the South as an allegory of national identity and adopt the southern plantation as its own "old Kentucky [in this case, Georgia] home."[5]

This chapter investigates the "moral legibility" of the southern home as figured in Margaret Mitchell's 1936 novel and David O. Selznick's 1939 film. Though novel and film have assumed almost mythic status, neither has received the kind of attention its monumental impact on American culture would seem to demand. Film scholars have been especially negligent in fathoming the reasons for the popularity of this most beloved of American movies, taking for granted its power but often only to deride its seeming anachronisms, especially as a throwback to Griffith's *Birth of a Nation*. GWTW remains in many ways the middlebrow film lover's guilty secret: the film we love but know we shouldn't. Its study has been given over to historians who document the grandeur and folly of the heyday of the studio system (and David O. Selznick's peculiar place as producer-auteur within it), and buffs who lovingly reproduce the artifacts surrounding the film's making.[6] No major history of American cinema gives it more than passing mention.[7] One reason for this striking silence about a film that has repeatedly been acknowledged in polls and box-office figures as one of the best-loved films of all time is its idyllic picture of slavery and apparent resuscitation of the plantation legend. Unlike *The Birth of a Nation*, which has been much studied as both art and ideology despite, and lately because of, its indefensible racial politics, GWTW has been little investigated as either art or ideology. If the story of its making, of its epic size, star-studded cast, two directors, and seventeen writers has been told repeatedly, it may be because critics working within the critical strictures that have valued the economy and balance of the "classical Hollywood cinema" have not known how to situate this most grand and excessive of black and white (now in color) racial melodramas.

Something of the same fate has met Margaret Mitchell's novel, although here feminist critics of popular culture have done a better job of beginning to fathom its themes of race and gender.[8] By and large, however, Mitchell's novel has been subject to a similar cultural disdain, despite its enormous popularity. In an early review that set the tone of northern, liberal reactions, Malcolm Cowley described the novel as no less than "an encyclopedia of the plantation legend" (Cowley 1983, 19). It is worth quoting his review, which is also a parodic summary, for a concise statement of the stereotypes that have caused liberal intellectuals to dismiss the work.

> The big white-columned house sleeping under its trees among the cotton fields; the band of faithful retainers, including two that quaintly resemble Aunt Jemima and Old Black Joe; the white-haired massa bathing in mint juleps; the heroine with her seventeen-inch waist and the high-spirited twins who come courting her in the magnolia-colored moonlight with the darkies singing under the hill—then the War between the States, sir, and the lovely ladies staying behind to nurse the wounded, and Sherman's march (now the damnyankees are loot-

ing the mansion and one of them threatens to violate its high-bred mistress, but she clutches an old horse pistol and it goes off bang in his ugly face) then the black days of Reconstruction, the callousness of the Carpetbaggers, the scalawaggishness of the Scalawags, the knightliness of the Ku Klux Klansmen, who frighten Negroes away from the polls, thus making Georgia safe for democracy and virtuous womanhood.

Cowley's parody is both amusing and apt in its description of the outward trappings of the "moonlight and magnolias" school of fiction. Yet these trappings miss the very heart of Mitchell's tale and its power to move readers because, like so many other critics, Cowley had no way of acknowledging, except by parody, the power of its melodrama.[9] His survey omits the central dual love stories between Scarlett, her old-fashioned cavalier ideal Ashley, and her modern opportunist reality Rhett. It also fails to observe that no helpless heroine of the "plantation legend" tradition would so aggressively save herself by blowing off the face of a "damnyankee," let alone exult in the act the way Scarlett does afterward. Indeed, Cowley is so disdainful of the slick, mass appeal of the novel, associated in his mind with the same kind of feminization of American literature that had led serious critics to disdain Stowe, that he fails to see what an entirely different form of feminization Mitchell carries out. If it is true that the outward similarities of the plantation legend and *Gone With the Wind* are striking—in both works former slaves and poor whites grow licentious during Reconstruction; in both works a white woman is threatened by a black man and the Clan rides to avenge her—it would be a mistake, however, to believe that *Gone With the Wind* simply gave a new lease on life to the myth of white female virtue and black bestiality so familiar in Dixon and Griffith. While the specter of the "black beast" still had an important function in the white supremacist imagination as a rationale for Jim Crow laws and continued scapegoating of African Americans, by the 1930s this vilification of the black man could no longer serve the same function. Nor could it continue to serve as an easy rationale for a practice of lynching that was finally receding.[10]

The mythic vilification of the black male, once so instrumental, as Jacquelyn Dowd Hall (1993, 151) has noted, in keeping white women "in their place," could not continue to perform this function in a work whose deeper appeal lay in its portrayal of a rebellious father-identified Irish girl who flouted all tradition. Such a woman, we can be sure, was not going to stay in her "proper" place in a Kentucky, Georgia, or any other American home.[11]

It is thus only with the increase in historical distance that Scarlett O'Hara, the southern belle with green eyes, flirtatious manner, and seventeen-inch waist, may seem to fit easily into the mold of the "plantation legend." Scratch her but a little, however, and you discover a woman with more affinity with her restless Jazz Age counterparts, Jakie Rabinowitz and Magnolia Hawks Ravenal, than with her southern sisters. Like them, she is the upwardly mobile child of scrappy immigrants who have made their way in a new land. Like them, she grows nostalgic for a southern home and an "old-world" tradition that she herself has rejected.[12] And like them, her story is one of thwarted love and successful career. Scratch her but a little more, however, and we find that her resolution to survive all manner of social and economic upheaval marks her as a product of the generation of women who lived through the Great Depression.

Perhaps most importantly, however, Scarlett derives whatever melodramatic virtue she possesses from a southern home that does not ultimately reside, as Malcolm Cowley would have it, in the plantation romance of "moonlight and magnolias," but in that home's ability to appropriate a new kind of blackface. We should not be deceived, then, by Mitchell's reproduction of the outward form of the anti-Tom narrative with its antebellum picture of Paradise, and its Reconstruction picture of the Fall. *Gone With the Wind* is deeply attached to the myth of the "good" southern home, but it constructs that home very differently from preceding versions of the Tom and anti-Tom melodramas of black and white.

Little Lady, Big Book, Bigger Film

The one incontrovertible fact about *Gone With the Wind*—novel and film—is its size. The 1,036-page book published in 1936 sold a million copies in its first six months, won a Pulitzer Prize the following year, stayed on the best-seller list throughout the decade, and was soon a worldwide publishing sensation that has still not abated. Sales have now reached nearly thirty million, averaging over five hundred thousand copies a year (Rose 1979, 4; Taylor 1989, 1–2).[13] Indeed, the novel's only rival in popularity was the publishing sensation of the previous century by that other great "lady" novelist, Harriet Beecher Stowe. Both novels found immediate disdain among serious literary critics and both novels entirely transcended—Henry James would say "leaped"—the conventional categories of literature to become ubiquitous, transliterary media events. If Stowe's novel "convulsed a mighty nation" by stirring sympathy for the lowly slave, GWTW stirred a new kind of sympathy for the disappearing way of life of the slaveholders.

Like Stowe, Margaret Mitchell was an unlikely celebrity author. An Atlanta "housewife"—though significantly also a former newspaper woman and Jazz Age flapper whose mother had been a suffragette—she began to write her long novel about "Pansy O'Hara" in 1926. Her ostensible reason for writing was a broken ankle that prevented her from continuing her career in a journalism. But the story of the ankle and the idle housewife who jokingly took up writing "the great American novel" was also a way for the self-deprecating author, dutiful wife, and daughter to mask her very real ambition and monumental labor behind the pretense of ill-considered amateurism (Pyron 1991, 234). All her life Mitchell was deeply at odds with conventional notions of feminine duty. Her novel was a monument to those contradictions. She wrote the last chapter first and generally proceeded in reverse order, finally writing the first chapter shortly before publication in 1936. When Macmillan publisher Harold Latham visited the South in search of manuscripts in 1935, his hospitable, obliging tour guide and society matron host, Peggy Mitchell, was rumored by friends to have written a book. Latham inquired several times, but each time Mitchell claimed to have no manuscript. Finally, just before Latham left, she gathered up the dusty, messy chapter envelopes of her still incomplete book and presented them to an astonished Latham (Pyron 1991, 301).

Many recountings of the novel's phenomenal success are marked by the kind of masculine condescension shown to "little lady" novelists who, like Stowe, presume to meddle in world-historic events. And just as Abraham Lincoln could not resist his famously condescending remark to Harriet Beecher Stowe—"So this is the little lady who made this big war" (Adams 1989, 8)—so other male readers could not reconcile the small size of Mitchell with the large size and effect of her book. It may not have helped that in Margaret Mitchell's case the "lady" was physically even littler than Stowe and the book even bigger.[14]

As with Stowe, too, it was the subsequent media event of the leap of the novel into another form, with David O. Selznick's 1939 lavish, star-studded, much-hyped Technicolor film that fully captured the imagination of the nation, making Scarlett O'Hara as much a household word as Uncle Tom had been before her. *GWTW* was, as everyone knows, the most expensive, longest (3 hours, 46 minutes) "event" in motion-picture history. It would go on to win eight Academy Awards, including the first one for an African American, and it would gross over $300 million. And like the novel, the film had "legs." Sold to television in the late 1970s, it generated 110 million viewers in its first screening—more than any other single television program in history. Significantly, that record would stand until the appearance of Alex Haley's *Roots* miniseries in 1977. To put this media ubiquity in perspective it helps to understand that Selznick's film has been seen by more people than the entire population of the United States.[15] And it has recently turned up as the number four film in the American Film Institute's 1998 poll of the best (e.g., most popular) American films of all time (behind *Citizen Kane, Casablanca,* and *The Godfather*).

The only previous film with this kind of impact had been that other famous film about the Civil War and Reconstruction, *The Birth of a Nation.*[16] But where *Birth* had had phenomenal impact on the medium, it did not endure as a popular film over subsequent decades. *Gone With the Wind*, which did endure, had a somewhat lesser impact on the medium. It was a precursor to what would come to be called the "independent producer system"—the system in which an individual producer, rather than a studio, was responsible for selecting, shaping, and selling a single title. This independent system of production, pioneered by United Artists, David Selznick, and Samuel Goldwyn, often for special "prestige" pictures, would eventually replace the more factory-oriented, mass-produced studio system. Although the producer system was an important innovation, it cannot be said to have had as comparable a shaping effect on the medium as *Birth of a Nation*'s transformation of the nickelodeon.[17]

Selznick's film turned a wildly popular regional novel into a national media event that took the nostalgic appeal of the southern "lost cause" as a basis for a new, middle-class, white national identity. An America emerging from the depths of the Depression, beginning to face the fact of war in Europe—and thus a greater need for national unity—experienced the event of this film as a new discovery of its "roots" in the complexly constructed "good" of the plantation home. *Gone With the Wind* thus universalized for all white Americans the romance of southern history as the American story of nation-making at the same time that it constructed an entirely new kind of American hero in selfish-headstrong-greedy Scarlett.

At issue therefore is not simply the novel and film's benign portrayal of the antebellum South with nary a whip or chain in view, but the more central question of how the southern home that was rapidly becoming the mythic origin of Americanness itself was racially understood. When Scarlett comes home to Tara after the burning of Atlanta she finds a ravaged plantation still cared for by its loyal house slaves after all the field hands have run off. Mammy, Pork, and Prissy attempt to carry on their usual duties as "house niggers" (the film softens the term, spoken by Pork, to "house workers") until Scarlett insists they work, as she herself will work, in the fields (Mitchell 1936, 416–17). But where Scarlett's work in the fields is ultimately liberating, freeing her from the narrow constraints of southern bellehood, it offers no such liberation to the former slaves.

Later, when Scarlett and Rhett set up house in the ostentatious mansion on Peachtree Street, Mammy, Pork, and Prissy are there again, suitcases in hand, ready to care for the home, looking for all the world like a black nuclear family.[18] Where this new home, and new bourgeois life of conspicuous consumption represents an enormous change for Scarlett, it seems to represent no change at all for Mammy, Pork, and Prissy, who go right on caring for their white home and former masters as if they were its slave "family." The fiction of both Mitchell's novel and Selznick's film would thus seem to be that while white people fight wars, lose their wealth, and rebuild a new economy, the culture of black servitude grounded in familial love provides continuity with the past. Thus, even as the world outside grows ever more white supremacist and segregated, the home of the black mammy appears constant.

We have seen that the political punch carried by Harriet Beecher Stowe's "big book" was the "moral reframing" (Hanne 1994, 89) of slavery accomplished by taking African (Americans), for the first time in American popular culture, as objects of sympathy instead of fun. But how shall we understand the nature of the punch carried by Mitchell's "big book," given the very difficult nature of her selfish, willful, and none-too-bright heroine and the concomitant portrayal of African Americans as loyal "house niggers" both before and after slavery? In short, how does GWTW "fit" into our ongoing saga of black and white racial melodrama? In answering this question I will distinguish between Mitchell's often meticulously realistic (though still thoroughly melodramatic) novel, which offers a historically grounded image of the Georgia locales, and Selznick's more glamorous and romantic Hollywood version. The difference between these two versions is probably best symbolized by Mitchell's description of Tara, the O'Hara plantation, as a plain and simple northern Georgia country home, decidedly without the grandeur of white, neoclassical columns, and Selznick's Technicolor version of the same with glorious columns, swelling music, and blood-red sunsets (Fig. 5.1). However, I will attempt to discuss novel and film together, rather than in separate sections, because, despite levels of realism, they ultimately cannot be separated in popular memory and imagination.

195

The Pathos of "Too Late!"

An initial answer to the question of how to place GWTW in our trajectory of the melodrama of racial victims and villains might turn to that point three-fourths of the way through the novel, during the ravages of Reconstruction when, according to the pattern of the Dixon-Griffith negrophobic, plantation legend, Scarlett is attacked (while riding in her buggy through Shantytown) by "a big ragged white man and a squat black negro with shoulders and chest like a gorilla."[19] "The negro was beside her, so close that she could smell the rank odor of him as he tried to drag her over the buggy side. With her one free hand she fought madly, clawing at his face, and then she felt his big hand at her throat and, with a ripping noise, her basque was torn open from neck to waist. The black hand fumbled between her breasts, and terror and revulsion such as she had never known came over her and she screamed like an insane woman" (780).

By placing Scarlett O'Hara in the traditional "plantation legend" role of the white woman victimized by the "black beast," Margaret Mitchell pays unmistakable homage to her "anti-Tom" predecessors. Yet the whole interest of placing Scarlet in this role of the endangered white woman facing the proverbial "fate-worse-than-death" is that she is emphatically not the innocent virgin of the Dixon-Griffith tradition but a coolheaded, calculating profiteer who is, at the very moment of the attack, seeing after financial interests in her lumber mill and callously supervising convict laborers.[20]

Even the "bodice-ripper" cliché of the scene is not entirely what it seems. In an earlier passage (in a scene not reproduced in the film), the white partner of the attacking Negro had already informed his accomplice that Scarlett's money could probably be found in her "bosom." It is money Scarlett pursues when she flouts convention by riding alone in Atlanta's most dubious neighborhoods to look after her lumber mills. And it is money the attackers seek in the novel, not her precious white womanhood.[21] Nearly every woman in the novel except Melanie condemns Scarlett for her brazenness in driving alone through Shantytown and for her Simon Legree–like greed in hiring convicts to work in her mill. They also regret the Clan retaliation her brazenness has made "necessary," not, of course, for the destruction it wreaks on the poor blacks and whites who live in Shantytown, but for endangering the lives of the husbands and fathers who carry it out.

Although Scarlett is punished for this transgression by social ostracism, and she exhibits, in its aftermath, what may be her only sincere remorse, her infraction is of a patriarchal white code that believes—as Scarlett never does, and as the novel and film never do—that a southern white woman's place *is* in the home. It is precisely this conflict over the place of woman, in the old and the new South, that both the novel and (to a somewhat lesser extent) the film address. Mitchell's female readers, especially those who took up the book during the years of World War II, seemed to have found in it a compelling expression of ambivalence about their place in the war and postwar world.[22] Especially in its literary form, *Gone With the Wind* wants to have it both ways, insisting on the virtue of a feudal past where men, women, and slaves knew their place while simultaneously engaging in the excitement and competition of a (social Darwinist) capitalist future where men and women (but not former slaves) engage in a sexual and economic will-to-power.[23]

Consider, for example, those aspects of the novel that Cowley's parodic summary omits (and some of which Selznick's film softens): in the course of the novel Scarlett O'Hara Hamilton Kennedy Butler marries three times, gives birth to three children, delivers Melanie's baby alone, buries her mother, father, daughter, and two husbands, "sells" herself in marriage to pay debts, and presides as head of the house over former slaves and family members. She also loses both of the men she loves—the one that she thought she loved and the one that she recognizes, too late! that she actually does love. Despite her losses, she grows strong and endures. If she is an antebellum southern belle, she is also a thirties revision of the flapper.[24] It is the unresolved tension between her conventional desire to serve the man of her dreams and her modern compulsion to control and master everything else—that makes her such an apt hero.

Subsequent generations of readers fascinated by Scarlett may, in fact, have found the deepest source of their fascination in her near-pathological inability to recognize what she really wants. Thinking she loves the traditional cavalier Ashley, she fails to see that she really loves the rogue and scalawag Rhett; thinking she will live out the high ideals and morality of her French-bred aristocratic mother, she actually embraces the scrappy survivalism of her Irish immigrant father. This amazing self-ignorance produces, in both novel and film, what must be the most excessively prolonged tension in the melodramatic dialectic between "too late!" and "in the nick of time!" in all of melodrama. This tension, I argue, is a key aspect of the work's phenomenal popularity.[25]

197

Since *Gone With the Wind* is not a melodrama whose pathos and action lead to a final suspenseful climax of exciting escape or rescue of the *Way Down East* or *Birth of a Nation* variety, it is important to understand the peculiar nature of the tension played out between its melodrama of "too late!" and "in the nick of time!" We have seen that typically this tension exists in the form of suspense built upon timing: the dynamic delays that endlessly put off resolution by cutting from one incomplete action to another. In *Way Down East* (see chapter 1), for example, we saw that behind the immediately prolonged anxiety about whether or not it is too late for rescue lies the deeper question of whether it is possible to return to the mythic time before it was "too late!"

Physical action, however, in the form of chases, escapes, and rescues, is not the only form suspense can take. In *The Jazz Singer* we saw how the dynamics between "too late!" and "in the nick of time!" was transposed into musical terms.[26] Ambivalent endings that are both too late *and* in the nick of time prevail in the Jazz Age and Depression-era melodramas in the absence of more conventional chases and rescues.[27] In *Gone With the Wind* a pattern of too-late homecomings is established first in Chapter 24, when Scarlett, Melanie, her new baby, and Prissy endure the journey through the cadaver-strewn countryside to go home to Tara. Sick of war and of carrying the burden of those (like Melanie and Prissy) weaker than she, Scarlett longs for home. Escaping the siege of Atlanta with the help of Rhett Butler, she cannot wait to return to the comfort of her mother and Mammy. After a long and arduous journey, a weary and hungry Scarlett arrives home to find her mother dead and Mammy herself weak and lost.

This pattern of too-late homecoming is repeated at the end of the novel when Scarlett, again bereft and weary, this time by the death of Melanie and the belated discovery that Ashley has feet of clay, rushes home in search of the maternal comfort that she has been dreaming about throughout the novel.

The suspense, by this point, is nearly intolerable, though not in an action-melodrama way. It is suspenseful because we know so acutely by this point how Scarlett O'Hara has persistently failed to recognize the virtue of those who love her. Indeed, for nearly a thousand tantalizing pages of the novel, and for nearly four hours of screen time, this willful heroine has put off the hard thinking that would force her to reevaluate her belief that virtue lies in the valiant bravery and heroism of the "old world" Ashley, with whom she would be ecstatically happy if only Melanie were out of the picture. She persists in this belief despite her own obvious relish in the crass competition and materialism of the "new world" represented by Rhett Butler, despite the fact that numerous signs of Rhett's love are offered and despite the fact that Melanie consistently shows herself to be Scarlett's only true friend.

Scarlett's excruciatingly delayed recognition of what the reader (and viewer) has long known finally begins in the novel on page 1000 in a scene at Melanie's deathbed: "Why, oh, why, had she not realized before this how much she loved and needed Melanie?" In prose that uncannily reworks, to very differently gendered ends, D. W. Griffith's memory of his father's phallic sword—the sword that Michael Rogin argues was eventually used to castrate the threatening black beast in *The Birth of a Nation*—Scarlett recalls that hot summer day at Tara when she shot the intruding Yankee. Melanie had dragged herself to the top of the stairs, wielding a sword she could hardly lift but fully ready to fight fiercely to defend herself and the children (Fig. 5.2). At that moment, Scarlett had (however briefly) recognized that weak, shy, frightened Melanie was every bit as strong as she. "And now, as Scarlett looked sadly back, she realized that Melanie had always been there beside her with a sword in her hand, unobtrusive as her own shadow, loving her, fighting for her with blind passionate loyalty, fighting Yankees, fire, hunger, poverty, public opinion and even her beloved blood kin. . . . Scarlett felt her courage and self-confidence ooze from her as she realized that *the sword which had flashed between her and the world* was sheathed forever" (1000; emphasis added).

"Too late!" Scarlet recognizes that what she had perceived as weakness was actually strength, the "terrible strength of the weak, the gentle, the tender hearted" (1001). The phallic sword—the sword that Rogin has shown to be the emblem of white supremacist paternal power in Dixon and Griffith—here "becomes a flashing vision" between two women. "Too late!" Scarlett proceeds to the further recognition that Ashley, the supposed dashing hero of her prolonged romantic fantasies and the proper bearer of the sword, is the one who is truly weak and frightened as he faces the prospect of life without the "steel-spined" Melanie.[28] "As once before, in the moonlight at Tara, drunk, exhausted, she had thought: 'Burdens are for shoulders strong enough to carry them.' Well, her shoulders were strong and Ashley's were not. She *squared her shoulders for the load* and with a calmness she was far from feeling, kissed his wet cheek without fever or longing or passion, only with cool gentleness"

Figure 5.2 Physically weak, Melanie pulls herself to the top of the stairs, dragging a sword, to fight the Yankees with Scarlett. (*Gone With the Wind*, 1939, Turner Classics)

(1003; emphasis added). Now that the dream of Ashley has faded, and the reality has sunk in that once again she must be the strong one to shoulder the "weary load" (1006) of responsibility, Scarlett wanders out into the misty night and feels an overpowering yet inchoate need to go home. "Home" at this point is literally the ostentatious mansion on Peachtree Street where Scarlett and Rhett live, a place that had never been a true home to either. In the course of traversing the five blocks between Melanie's house and her own, panic overtakes her and she finds herself running wildly—as she has in countless nightmares—away from a nameless dread and toward an elusive and vaguely defined homey destination. To her surprise, that home turns out to be the lights of her own house: "Home! That was where she wanted to go. That was where she was running. Home to Rhett! . . . Now she knew the haven she had sought in dreams, the place of warm safety which had always been hidden from her in the mist" (1008).[29]

Scarlett, as her creator was the first to admit, could often be a trifle simple.[30] Certainly much condescension and irony has been expended by critics who grow impatient with her fickle, out-of-joint loves. But I suggest that there is a special melodramatic value to the painfully slow manner in which Scarlett gradually, and much "too late," recognizes her love for the man with whom she has all along been living. For if there is exciting action in *Gone With the Wind* on a par with the most gripping action-based melodrama, it is not in the conventional, action-packed escape from Atlanta that occurs midway through the book and film. Rather, it is in the temporal suspense—the infinite delay—built up through Scarlett's frequent and obtuse deferrals of thought over hundreds and hundreds of pages. This obtuseness is finally released into action the moment she leaves Melanie. At first she moves automatically, heading blindly in the mist. Later, overcome by panic, she runs toward a light that seems to represent the safety and warmth promised, but never realized, by her nightmare. Recognizing for the first time that it is Rhett and her own home that represent the safety for which she has longed, Scarlett is suddenly running purposefully to rescue something that she only at that moment realizes it is important to save.

In these near-final pages the "good" home is at least momentarily separated from all the trappings of the antebellum past. It is opportunistic Rhett, the cynical, unsentimental, future-embracing, blockade-running, entrepreneurial Atlantan, not the backward-looking, planter gentleman Ashley, she seeks. Played in the film by Clark Gable—the one role in the film for which there was never any doubt about whom to cast—Rhett, not Ashley, now defines the safety and security of home. And Rhett's animal-like, overpowering sexuality—the sexuality that once pleasurably ravished her—is suddenly recognized as the true object of her desire. In one fell swoop the idealized image of the gentle good old days is supplanted by a more vital past that will soon also, with Rhett's frank confession that he no longer gives a "damn," be "gone with the wind."

Foiled in her attempt to regain the recent past of her life and "home" with Rhett, Scarlett *then* falls back on Tara—the antebellum "plantation legend" of Cowley's parody. Thus, at the end of both novel and film, the plantation home that prevented characters like Ashley from facing the future, and which she herself had done the most to kill off, is invoked as the melodramatic "space of innocence": "She thought of Tara and it was as if a gentle cool hand were stealing over her heart. She could see the white house gleaming welcome to her through the reddening autumn leaves, feel the quiet hush of the country twilight coming down over her like a benediction, feel the dews falling on the acres of green bushes starred with fleecy white, see the raw color of the red earth and the dismal dark beauty of the pines on the rolling hills" (1024). This nostalgic image of the rural southern home, with its "avenue of dark cedars," jessamine bushes and "fluttering white curtains," would not be complete without the comforting dark human presence that complements the "dark beauty of the pines" and "dark cedars" of the Georgian home: "And Mammy would be there. Suddenly she wanted Mammy desperately, as she had wanted her when she was a little girl, wanted the broad bosom on which to lay her head, the gnarled black hand on her hair. Mammy, the last link with the old days"

Figure 5.3 Tara as it appears in the last shot of the film, with Scarlett now alone. (*Gone With the Wind*, 1939, Turner Classics)

(1024). The last pages of the novel thus rush breathlessly from one belated "recognition of virtue" to another. Lost in the mist, Scarlett confuses romantic love with love of home. Rushing away from the misrecognized Ashley to the too-late recognition of Rhett, she finally falls back upon the image of the old plantation home and the security of the love of Mammy. Like Jakie Rabinowitz, she turns from the vicissitudes of romantic love to the fixed constancy of a "Mammy" who will always recognize her as "her baby." From the comfort of Mammy's arms and "broad" bosom Scarlett hopes she will regain the strength to reconquer Rhett; "After all, tomorrow is another day."

Yet the reader knows from her previously "too late" emotional homecoming to Tara after the burning of Atlanta that the solace she seeks in Mammy and in home will ultimately elude her, that she herself will have to provide whatever strength is needed to fight her future battles. Thus a seductive image of home emerges powerfully at the end of the novel. In the film this image quite literally pictures Scarlett, much as she had been pictured at the beginning with her father, gazing from a distant hill under a giant tree at the "red earth" of Tara (Fig. 5.1, 5.3). This image gives her the strength to once more embrace the future. As if acknowledging the illusory status of the image, Mitchell writes that Scarlett feels "vaguely comforted, strengthened by the picture." It is indeed a pretty picture of home and stability that proved necessary to generations of southern women even as they forged a future grounded on their ability to move, as Mitchell herself had moved, beyond its walls.[31] Out of the comfort and strength of this nostalgic illusion Scarlett paradoxically moves forward by appearing to go back. "With the spirit of her people who would not know defeat, even when it stared them in the face, she raised her chin. She could get Rhett back" (1024).

Mammy and Tara are thus the means to an end that Scarlett has been seeking and, in spite of herself, achieving, all along: a middle-class female agency rooted in the ideology of the rural southern home but overreaching its confines. Historian Grace Elizabeth Hale has shown how white southerners experienced Confederate defeat and Reconstruction as an abrupt break with the rural household way of life. While other parts of the nation experienced a more gradual dismantling of the rural household, southern white women determined, well into the next century, to see their actions as the preservation of old social structures against Yankee aggression, rather than the building of new ones. Urban middle-class lives and values were thus paradoxically modeled on the celebration of a supposed continuity with the agrarian past. The figure of continuity with that racially integrated, rigidly hierarchical, agrarian past and the racially segregated urban future was the mammy.[32]

Scarlett's Mammy functions as a spokesperson for aristocratic plantation values. She does so most famously in the "corset scene," which offers a contradictory image of force-feeding and enforced starvation. Lacing up Scarlett's seventeen-inch waist so tightly that she can barely breathe, Mammy then forces her to eat her breakfast, not so much to nurture her, however, as not to show an unladylike appetite at the barbecue before her many beaux (Fig. 5.4). In Scarlett's visit to Rhett dressed in the green velvet curtains that were all that remained of the splendor of Tara, Mammy not only has sewn the dress but provides the disapproving chaperone who assures Scarlett of a cover of respectability while she undertakes to fleece a scoundrel. At every important moment of Scarlett's life a loyal if disapproving Mammy is there to demand adherence to ladylike standards of behavior that Scarlett will repeatedly flout. And when she does flout them, Mammy will be there, to tell her that "it ain't fittin.' "[33]

In the passage quoted above in which Scarlett suddenly longs to return to Tara, it may seem that the return to Tara represents a return to her long-lost mammy as well: "And Mammy would be there. Suddenly she wanted Mammy desperately. . . ." Yet in both the novel and the film Mammy—that "link with the old days"—has only rarely been absent from Scarlett's side. Indeed, while the passage deliberately gives the impression that Mammy has been vegetating, along with the jessamine bushes, dark cedars, and cotton at Tara, in fact, in both novel and film she is right there at that moment with Scarlett, the busy major domo of the garish, nouveau-riche house on Peachtree Street. Mammy's faithful adherence to values that Scarlett has long ago abandoned masks the enormous changes that have taken place between "the old days" and the new. For it is the very institution of the southern

Figure 5.4   The "corset scene." Mammy both feeds Scarlett and restricts her appetite. (*Gone With the Wind*, 1939, Turner Classics)

mammy that has made possible the mobility and agency of the new life Scarlett lives as the owner and manager of thriving lumber mills.

Because southern mammies in the post–Civil War era crossed the line between the increasingly segregated places of whiteness and blackness, white southern women were able to "cross the gender line between the white home and the larger world" (Hale 1998, 106). With a black servant in the home, white women could both remain ladies and at the same time more fully exercise the privileges and authority granted by white skin. Yet because Scarlett's mammy is associated mythically with "the old days" and the old ways of the aristocratic plantation, we tend not to notice how that association actually permits Mitchell to "read the white middle-class present back into the romanticized antebellum southern past" (Hale 1998, 261).

By standing for home as the source of Scarlett's strength found in "the old days," Mammy thus serves to obfuscate the fact that this home, this past, this white relation to the virtue of blackness is "gone with the wind." The end of the novel and (with some modification, to be explored below) the end of the film leave us differentially suspended between two possibilities: the mature knowledge that it is too late to revive whatever virtue is to be found in either the Reconstruction or the antebellum past and the irrational hope that this slippery virtue can still be rescued, "in the nick of time." Like *The Jazz Singer* and *Show Boat*, GWTW wants to have it both ways.

The novel prolongs Scarlett's disorientation as she moves from Melanie's death to the slow recognition of her love for Rhett in the journey she makes through the night's mist. In this misty landscape, Scarlett is a lost girl seeking the refuge of a home more fundamental than romantic love. In the film, of course, she is somewhat more simply the romantic heroine returning to the man she realizes she loves. Indeed, the film makes only a halfhearted attempt to build the suspense of her realization.[34] Although Tara and home loom just as large at the end of the film as in the novel as the place of refuge and solace, it looms differently and without the icon of Mammy. Instead of Scarlett's evocation of longing for Mammy's "broad bosom," the film provides a montage of male voice-overs all speaking to Scarlett of Tara:[35] a fragment of Gerald's famous speech about the virtue of land (discussed below); a portion of Ashley's speech to Scarlett that the earth of Tara is "something you love better than me"; Rhett's wisdom that it is "from this you get your strength, the red earth of Tara." Thus in place of the maternal, racially marked home, the film offers the "authoritative tones of three white men" (Taylor 1989, 173). A collective male wisdom tells the wandering woman to go home. Though Scarlett accepts this wisdom and rises up hopeful that Tara will offer her the refuge she needs to reconquer the world and Rhett, we already know that she, no more than Jakie Rabinowitz or Magnolia Ravenal, will not be able to stay there.

The "Weary Load"

If, as I have so far argued, *Gone With the Wind* does not simply embrace the "moonlight and magnolias" virtue of the antebellum, "plantation legend," but constructs a much more ambivalent tension between the aristocratic languor of the "old days" and the bourgeois energy of the new southern home, then what "home" virtue does it ultimately recognize?[36] If it is not precisely Tara the plantation, then it is "the red earth," "the land" on which it sits that constitutes Scarlett's "true" virtue and strength. Land comes to represent an absolute moral good for our otherwise morally dubious heroine. Early in the book and film, when Gerald O'Hara tells Scarlett his plan to leave Tara to her, Scarlett begins to explain that she doesn't want it, that "plantations don't amount to anything" (38). Her father interrupts her in a speech that the film will partially repeat in voice-over at the end: "You mean to tell me, Katie Scarlett O'Hara, that land doesn't mean anything to you? Why land is the only thing in the world worth working for, worth fighting for, worth dying for, because it's the only thing that lasts" (quoted from film, nearly identical in the novel).

Thus Gerald O'Hara, the Irish immigrant displaced, as we are told in the novel, from his original homeland where his family had been reduced to tenancy (and where the novel tells us Gerald had impetuously killed the rent collector), recasts the love of plantation into a more elemental love of land. Gerald insists on his pride in being Irish, reminding Scarlett that she is Irish too and that "to anyone with a drop of Irish blood in them the land they live on is like their mother. . . . There's no getting away from it if you're Irish." In the film these words extolling the connections of blood, land, and race are uttered as father and daughter pose on a hill under a giant oak, against the red earth (which Selznick had actually dyed for the occasion) and a blood-red sunset, with the soaring strains of "Tara's Theme" sounding from Max Steiner's score. At the end of the scene when the camera pulls back a dramatic distance to reframe Scarlett and Gerald as tiny figures against land and sky (Fig. 5.1), with the plantation home now small in the distance, Gerald assures Scarlett that the love of the land will come to her. Just how it comes to her, and how the stated virtue of Irishness becomes linked to an unstated, but emotionally felt, virtue of blackness, is the key to understanding how the antebellum plantation acquires a folk virtue in the melodrama of black and white.

Throughout the course of novel and film there is an almost systematic testing of the aristocratic virtues of the old South. With each testing, there is a reduction of those ideals to a more basic, elemental connection to home and land. As early as page 209 Ashley Wilkes begins the first reduction when, in a letter home to Melanie, he rejects the original catch phrases—"King Cotton, Slavery, States' Rights, Damn Yankees"—for something that, to him at least, seems more real: his home, "Twelve Oaks . . . how the moonlight slants across the white columns and the unearthly way the magnolias look, opening under the moon. . . . Darkies coming home across the fields at dusk, tired and singing and ready for supper. . . . The old days, the old ways I love so much but which, I fear, are now gone forever" (209).

However, Ashley's rejection of jingoistic cliches for a more sentimental memory of home is hardly the novel's, or the film's, final word on the true virtue of the old South. Indeed, his letter remains the very embodiment of the "moonlight and magnolias," "singing darkies" cliché that Mitchell wrote against. Gone With the Wind emphatically rejects the bogus virtue of Ashley's "old days" and "old ways" just as it ultimately rejects the hangdog, impotent nobility of Ashley himself. Instead, as we have seen melodrama consistently do, both novel and film reject one older melodramatic cliché for a newer, more modern melodrama in tune with the energy of Scarlett's realistic lessons in survival. And it finds this expression, not in Ashley's abhorrence of the "dirt" of war, but in Scarlett's physical encounter with real dirt. This encounter, which is also, in the novel especially, an encounter with blackness, constitutes her elemental learning of her Irish immigrant father's lesson on the importance of "the land."

As we have seen, when Scarlett returns to Tara after the siege of Atlanta with Melanie, Melanie's baby, and the dim-witted slave girl, Prissy, she finds her mother dead and the survivors on the "shrouded," denuded plantation helpless and childlike.[37] As in Atlanta, it falls upon her unwilling shoulders, in the much-quoted words of Stephen Foster's song, to "tote the weary load" necessary for survival. Even Mammy, whose bosom she gratefully embraces, seems lost without Miss Ellen. In both novel and film this survival is literal: the extended family of house "servants," hungry child, and bereft white folks need food. In the novel Scarlett makes the difficult journey to Twelve Oaks—the Wilkes family's former plantation—to search for it. In the burnt-out ruins of what was once the grandest of plantations, she desperately forages for food. In a scene that is the very antithesis of the forced-feeding (made possible by the labor of slaves) "corset scene" (Fig. 5.4), a hung-over, voracious Scarlett, dressed in Mammy's calico sunbonnet, surveys the ruin of the plantation. She finds a garden patch that had not yet been raided of its vegetables near a row of whitewashed cabins in the former slave quarters. Sitting down in the furrows, she digs into the earth with her hands, pulls up and devours a dirty radish. "No sooner had the lump gone down than her empty stomach revolted and she lay in the soft dirt and vomited tiredly" (420).

Here, then, is a very "down-to-earth" encounter with Gerald's exalted "land" so important to his and Scarlett's Irish identity. But here too is a complex reworking of a racialized fantasy of nourishment whereby the child who was once nourished at the breast of her mammy, and whom we saw in a battle of wills with that same mammy over how much to eat for breakfast in the corset-lacing scene, now must take on the mammy function of feeding herself and others. In the novel, this encounter with the red Georgia soil functions in direct contrast to Ashley's pretty picture of a plantation home with darkies singing and laughing in the background.[38] In both instances, however, it is striking how necessary a background presence of "darkies" is to the perception of the "good" of the scene. In Ashley's case they are *heard* in the background. In Scarlett's more realistic case they are *smelled* in close proximity: one of the contributions to her nausea is the "faint niggery smell" emanating from the cabins.[39] Yet the physical proximity of her suffering to that of the now-absent slaves gives her a new strength derived from the virtue of their past suffering. In contrast, Ashley's distance, signaled by his removed auditory perception of their minstrel-like happiness, only dooms him to a disempowered nostalgia. It is thus in the melodramatic "realism" of this picture of a former southern belle on hands and knees, dressed in the bonnet of her mammy, puking her guts out on the red Georgia soil, that Scarlett's more authentic, earthy, slave-like virtue, so different from Ashley's nostalgia, is, quite literally, grounded. After retching, she "lay weakly on her face, the earth as soft and comfortable as a feather pillow" (420). And now, for the first time in the novel, too sick and weak to move, Scarlett does not put off thinking:

For a timeless time, she lay still, her face in the dirt, the sun beating hotly upon her, remembering things and people who were dead, remembering a way of living that was gone forever. . . . When she arose at last and saw again the black ruins of Twelve Oaks, her head was raised high and something that was youth and beauty and potential tenderness had gone out of her face forever. What was past was past. Those who were dead were dead. . . . Throughout the South for fifty years there would be bitter-eyed women who looked backward, to dead times, to dead men, evoking memories that hurt and were futile, bearing poverty with bitter pride because they had those memories. But Scarlett was never going to look back. . . . Hunger gnawed at her empty stomach again and she said aloud: "As God is my witness, as God is my witness, the Yankees aren't going to lick me. I'm going to live through this, and when it's over, I'm never going to be hungry again. No, nor any of my folks. If I have to steal or kill—as God is my witness, I'm never going to be hungry again." (421)

By sinking into the elemental dirt of a slave cabin, by losing all illusions about lost causes, about moonlight and magnolias and "happy darkies," by becoming herself like the suffering, toiling, and "toting" "niggers" who once lived in these cabins, rather than by being herself simultaneously fed and constricted by "house niggers" (Fig. 5.4), "Katie Scarlett O'Hara" finally connects with the strength of her Irish roots and her immigrant father's lesson about the good of the land. From that strength she rises up, like Antaeus, with a newfound virtue that comes from the land and its "folks."

Selznick's film, however, is once again less explicit about the racial components of Scarlett's connection to the plantation home. In the film a hungry, bereaved, and dazed Scarlett wanders out into the devastated land surrounding Tara, digs for and eats a carrot, and very discreetly vomits in silhouette—we hear a cough that becomes a sob and see a convulsed body lean toward the earth and fall to the ground. Silhouetted against a blood-red sunset that obscures both dirt and vomit (Fig. 5.5), she then rises up from the ground to deliver the words quoted from the novel above (Fig. 5.6). Yet even in such a sanitized, comparatively deracialized, scene, even without Mitchell's depiction of the "nigger smell" from the cabins and without slave garb in the form of Mammy's sun bonnet, Scarlett nevertheless is seen to pass briefly before the burnt-out slave cabins—cabins that had no previous visibility in the film at all (Fig. 5.7). Against this background Scarlett is thus seen, even in the film, to brush up against the poverty and toil of slaves and to "tote the weary load."

Indeed, before going out to the ruins of the garden, and after facing up to the helpless infantilism of her father, she encounters each of the house's former slaves in turn. First Mammy—the same Mammy who had insisted that Scarlett not go hungry to the barbecue—asks her how they will feed the sick

Figure 5.5   Scarlett begins to rouse herself after vomiting into the dirt. (*Gone With the Wind*, 1939, Turner Classics)

Figure 5.6   Scarlett vows never to be hungry again. (*Gone With the Wind*, 1939, Turner Classics)

Figure 5.7   The burnt-out slave cabins Scarlett passes while searching for food.
(*Gone With the Wind*, 1939, Turner Classics)

folks and new child. Where the ample-figured Mammy had once forced Scarlett to eat more than she wanted—while contradictorily constricting her waist and warning her not to reveal her true appetite (Fig. 5.4)—now a starved Scarlett is asked to provide for the former slaves who once fed her. From spoiled belle of the plantation, she herself becomes the weary forager for food. Either way, however, Scarlett seems to either get too much or too little food.[40] Prissy next complains that she cannot take care of the sick folks and the new baby. Finally Pork helplessly asks her who will milk the cow, since "we'se house workers."

Scarlett escapes the house to the "land" that will give her strength. In rising up from this land after first sinking into it, the film thus contrasts her difference from the helpless slaves. While they complain, she resolves to "never go hungry again." Where the novel gives her strength through her association with the slave cabins and its dirt, the film exalts the difference of the strong white woman's resolution. Neither grants the former slaves the courage and initiative to endure or to feed themselves. In both cases, however, the residual aura of the perception of their past endurance lends virtue to the white woman who is viewed as their salvation.

Connected to the land, in imitation of, but also improving on, the endurance of slaves, Scarlett shoulders her burden, and takes up her "weary load."

Figure 5.8 Scarlett and her sisters work in the fields before burnt-out slave cabins. (*Gone With the Wind*, 1939, Turner Classics)

We can only wonder in *Gone With the Wind* about the lives of the former slaves who have fled the cabins from which this "niggery" smell emanates. Indeed, the film seems frequently to place the laboring Scarlett, wearing what we recognize from the novel to be Mammy's bonnet, adjacent to these empty burnt-out cabins when she forces her sisters and herself to work the fields (Fig. 5.8). As we have seen, the only African (Americans) whose lives matter in this work are the upper-class house slaves and the one field hand, Sam, who have fully identified with the aristocratic ambitions of their former owners: Mammy, who for all her warmth, humor, and good sense absurdly goes on worrying about Scarlett ruining her lily-white hands; Pork, who, facing starvation, absurdly worries about his status within the family;[41] and Prissy, whose dim-witted caricature of "good breeding" turns out to make her completely useless at every moment of crisis, including the infamous moment of Melanie's delivery of a child.[42]

Improbable as it may seem, it is selfish-headstrong-greedy Scarlett O'Hara who, in these moments of crisis, appropriates the moral legitimacy of the suffering slaves inherited from *Uncle Tom's Cabin* via the Jazz Age tradition of whites posing as black. And, as in *Uncle Tom* and its Jazz Age inheritors, this appropriation of virtue takes a musical form. Early in the novel's depiction of the Civil War, at a party at Aunt Pittypat's, Scarlett is sent to the piano to rouse the spirits of guests who have grown anxious and testy arguing about the war. She tries one white sentimental ballad after another, but their uncomfortable references to dead and dying Confederate soldiers fail to rally the group. Finally Rhett suggests "My Old Kentucky Home," and though it too is described as "none too cheery," Stephen Foster's song about a black slave nearing the end of his life recalling the good of his "old Kentucky home" finally pulls the anxious whites together. The portion of the song that the novel quotes is taken from the end:

> Just a few more days for to tote the weary load!
> No matter, 'twill never be light!
> Just a few more days, till we totter in the road!
> Then, my old Kentucky home, good night! (291)

Foster's ballad will recur (in different forms in both novel and film) each time Scarlett must muster the strength to endure. As we have already seen with respect to both *Uncle Tom's Cabin* and *The Birth of a Nation*, the use of Foster themes is entirely conventional in any musical evocation of the antebellum and Civil War eras. Composer Max Steiner's score for *Gone With the Wind* would, in fact, utilize a wide variety of Foster tunes.[43] However, the use of this particular Foster song, written in 1852 as a direct result of Foster's reading the first serialized version of *Uncle Tom's Cabin*, has a special resonance.[44]

In its first appearance in the novel the song has a generalized application to the weakened and "tottering" South about to give up the ghost before Sherman's onslaught. Soon, however, it appears in the mouth of Prissy, who sings the song during the siege of Atlanta when Melanie is close to giving birth. Scarlett harshly hushes her, afraid of its "sad implications" (343).[45] Later, however, after the once-boastful Prissy confesses her ignorance of "birthin,' "— and after a furious Scarlett has slapped her hard—the song's rhetoric of sorrowing virtue transfers from the unworthy, flighty slave girl to the suddenly worthy Scarlett, ennobled by her ability to "tote the weary load" the slave girl cannot. "For a moment Scarlett stood still, looking up, listening to the low moaning [Melanie's birth moans] which had begun again. As she stood there, it seemed as though a yoke descended heavily upon her neck, felt as though a heavy load were harnessed to it, a load she would feel as soon as she took a step" (360). Stepping into the yoke, Scarlett shoulders the "weary load" and takes over the "birthing" function that in the "old days" would properly belong to an experienced Mammy.[46] Suddenly authoritative, she orders Prissy to bring the proverbial boiling water, towels, and so forth, and sets to work delivering the baby. Thus Prissy's childlike immaturity makes possible Scarlett's maturity, and the rhetoric of the song makes possible an articulation of a more responsible, if unwilling, bondage. Margaret Mitchell, no less than Harriet Beecher Stowe, was at least unconsciously aware of the affinity between nineteenth-century white women and their slaves. As disenfranchised persons with no rights, white women and black slaves were liminal beings who derived whatever power they had from the moral virtue of their very powerlessness. Foster's song, applied here to slave and white woman, both acknowledges this similarity and steals the better part of this virtue for the white woman. Later in the novel, when Scarlett returns to Tara and falls into Mammy's arms, Mammy quotes the "weary loads" lyrics, causing Scarlett to recall the words of the song once again: " 'No matter, 'twill never be light'—she took the words into her tired mind. Would her load never be light? Was coming home to Tara to mean, not blessed surcease, but only more loads to carry? She slipped from Mammy's arms and, reaching up, patted the wrinkled black face" (409). Once again, Scarlett takes over the "Mammy" function, this time to comfort her very own Mammy, shouldering yet another "weary load."

The deployment of both the lyrics and the music of "My Old Kentucky Home" in *Gone With the Wind* thus takes on a special meaning. Max Steiner, for example, made note of the song and its curious connection with Prissy: "I have often wondered why Margaret Mitchell should have gone to the length of mentioning it, but in any case I knew it would not be amiss if I wove that melody into my score for scenes in which Prissy has a part" (Ussher 1983, 167). Steiner thus instinctively understood not that Prissy herself had any special nobility—quite the contrary—but that the pathos of music associated with slaves in general could be transferred, through Prissy's failures, from her unworthy shoulders to Scarlett's.

The travails of the Civil War thus permit a "plantation legend" southern belle to wear a kind of Jazz Age metaphorical blackface. Indeed, in a scene not reproduced in the film, Margaret Mitchell literalizes this blackface. While the motley family of former masters and slaves wards off starvation at Tara, a raiding party of Union Soldiers arrives. Resourcefully hiding the gold stolen from the dead Yankee in the baby's diaper, Scarlett cannot prevent the burning of their cotton and the attempted burning of Tara. But she and Melanie fight side by side against the fire, finally beating it down to save the house. Afterward Scarlett looks at Melanie's smiling, singed face made black by the smoke: " 'You look like a nigger,' murmured Scarlett. . . . 'And you look like the end man in a minstrel show,' replied Melanie equably" (462).

Almost systematically, then, this selfish, unreflective heroine earns respect either by taking over the natural, close-to-the-earth, biological functions of slaves or by connecting with earth, dirt, and blackness. In this way, the Depression-era Irish heroine, no less than the Jazz Age Jewish hero, becomes a representative American through yet another form of posing as black. Recent scholarship has commented on the process by which the Irish, who had once fled caste oppression and a system of tenancy that made their conditions in Ireland like those of slaves, suffered many of the conditions and stigma of African Americans. Upon immigration to the United States the Irish were often thrown together with slaves, and often used for labor in the South too dangerous to risk the life of a valuable slave. In popular culture the Irish became stock figures of fun, not unlike blackface minstrels, many of whom, as we have seen, were played by Irish bohemians most familiar with the culture of free blacks. Yet the Irish eventually lost the stigma of racialized identity to "become white" and gained a mobility that African Americans could not attain.[47] In becoming white they repudiated black. Yet even as they lost this social and material connection to blackness, they appropriated tokens of sentimentalized black virtue that were every bit as important to their constructed white identity as the nostalgic lip service to the aristocratic values of the plantation legend.

That this appropriation of black virtue was both important and conscious to Margaret Mitchell is evidenced by the fact that her favorite of several working titles for the novel was not *Gone With the Wind*, imposed much later by the publisher, but a quote from Stephen Foster's "My Old Kentucky Home," "Tote the Weary Load" (Pyron 1991, 281). Indeed, it is significant that Chapter 24, in which this phrase turns up the most, is precisely the chapter, along with the beginning, that had long eluded Mitchell and was not written until after the stock market crash of October 1929. It was this chapter, telling the story of Scarlett's first "too late" homecoming to find her mother dead and the plantation desolate, that would speak the most to the generation of the Great Depression.[48] In each of Scarlett O'Hara's "slave" functions—delivering a baby, foraging for food, working in the fields, becoming blackened in putting out a fire, selling herself for taxes—Scarlett, the Jazz Age/New Deal, middle-class democrat below the surface of the southern belle, is seen to work even harder than her former slaves. Thus does Scarlett, by the strange logic of a democratic culture seeming to embrace its aristocratic past, appear to have earned the right, retroactively, to the virtue of the "old plantation."

For all *Gone With the Wind*'s presumed debt to Dixon, Griffith, and the "plantation legend," for all its glorification of the southern "lost cause," for all its one-sided view of aristocratically identified faithful darkies and scorn and hatred for emancipation, it cannot be considered a work primarily cast in the *patriarchal* mold of white supremacy. Dixon and Griffith's insistence on the importance of racial purity, their heroic defense of an "Aryan birthright" so importantly linked to the cloistering of white women and so necessary to the maintenance of an unbroken line of succession from white fathers to white sons, is a matter of little or no importance in a work in which women are recognized as the true heads of households, the important line of racial descent is between a father and daughter, and virtue descends from the suffering of black slaves. Despite its outward trappings, *Gone With the Wind* is much more indebted to the crossracial posings of a mongrelized Jazz Age where the important lines of succession and connection are between mothers and sons (Jakie and his Jewish "Mammy") and fathers and daughter (Cap'n Andy and Magnolia). Neither patriarchy nor racial purity matter much in a work where blackness functions as a virtue to be emulated (and appropriated) by an upwardly mobile white daughter.

The central paradox of *Gone With the Wind* is its linking of two contradictory nostalgias: an overt nostalgia for the aristocratic, agrarian ways of the "old South" and a more covert nostalgia for the strength, virtue, and endurance of oppressed races (Irish and black). These two nostalgias constitute the essence of both the "Tom" and the "anti-Tom" racial melodrama. The apparent resolution of tension between these two forms of the melodrama of black and white are, I argue, the deepest source of the work's abiding popularity. Jakie Rabinowitz and Magnolia Ravenal assimilated as Americans through crossracial posing. Scarlett O'Hara becomes an even more representative American heroine for the Depression era by linking her Irishness on the one hand to an aristocratic "plantation legend" golden age and on the other hand to the suffering of black slaves. Though she does not overtly don blackface the way the Irish immigrants before her had done in the North, she, like them, is a product of cultural and racial mongrelization.

The reader may have noted that much of the best evidence of Scarlett's racial mongrelization comes from the novel rather than the film. It seems that David O. Selznick's liberal fear of producing an "anti-Negro film"—his decision to make sure that the "Negroes come out decidedly on the right side of the ledger" (Selznick 1972, 188)—necessitated many excisions of direct black and white racial conflict and connection from the novel. In the Shantytown attack on Scarlett, for example, carried out in both novel and film by a white and black man together, the black man leads the attack in the novel while a white man leads it in the film. Similarly, while the novel describes the revenge on Shantytown taken by Ashley, Frank, Dr. Meade, and other members of the Ku Klux Klan, the film informs us of the attack but excises mention of the Klan. Even the word "nigger," which figures prominently (and with historical accuracy) in the novel, especially in the mouths of low-class whites and blacks, is banned in the film. Thus Rhett's observation that Scarlett's calloused hands reveal her to have been "working like a nigger" (569) becomes in the film "working like a field hand," losing yet another sense of Scarlett's racialized connection to the land. Nor, as we have seen, does the film show Scarlett puking her guts out and groveling in the dirt of a slave cabin at Twelve Oaks prior to taking her memorable resolve to "never be hungry again." The film makes its point of Scarlett's return to the land, but at the expense of connecting that land to the toil and sweat of slaves.

In general the film omits racial detail in favor of gorgeous sunsets and pretty pictures. These excisions blunt the racial melodrama of the film compared to the novel. While they were designed to lessen the racial tensions between blacks and whites that might, as Selznick put it, "come out as an unintentional advertisement for intolerant societies in these fascist ridden times" (Selznick 1972, 188), they also had the unintentional effect of lessening the link to black suffering that I have argued is the covert source of Scarlett's virtue. Although Selznick's fear of offending Negroes, at the very moment war against fascist (and racist) nations was looming in Europe, shows the degree to which black viewers were now beginning to matter to film producers and exhibitors (e.g., the degree to which a black national presence could no longer simply be conjured away as it had been at the end of *The Birth of a Nation*), it also shows the degree to which the film was incapable of depicting the desires and aspirations of black subjects apart from the desires and aspirations of their former masters. If Mitchell and Selznick could not demonize blacks as Griffith and Dixon had done, neither could they depict them as independent and suffering subjects, with destinies apart from those of their masters, as Stowe had done.

Obviously the cumulative effect of the absence of a black subjectivity with its own interests, and the excision of many overt racial components of the novel, is to weaken the intensity of the racial melodrama of the film compared to the novel. Ironically, the more Selznick's good intentions toward Negroes were implemented, the more Scarlett's mixed emotions of rage, impatience, and protectiveness toward Pork, Prissy, Mammy, Uncle Peter, Big Sam, and other blacks were eliminated. The result was a general whitewashing of the theme of race altogether and an unintended accompanying idealization of the plantation legend Mitchell had done so much to debunk.

It would be wrong to assume, however, that Selznick's liberal "whitewashing" simply negates the racial melodrama of the novel. It would be wrong for the simple reason that in the kind of study I am attempting to carry out—in which works exist in various versions and in profound dialogic relation to previous works—it is futile to make too fine a distinction between one version of a work and another. Textual scholars may make meticulous comparisons, individual viewers and readers may passionately prefer the film to the novel or the novel to the film, but the *Gone With the Wind* I have been trying to evoke here encompasses novel, film, theme music, appropriation of popular songs, and all subsequent rereadings and reviewings.[49]

In this century, *Gone With the Wind* is the popular racial melodrama that has most intensely and most consistently carried on a life in more than one medium, this time in novel and film. Like *Uncle Tom's Cabin*, then, it cannot easily be pinned down to a specific text. But unlike *Uncle Tom's Cabin*, which existed singly on the page and multiply on the stage and then equally multiply in film, *GWTW* exists in these two forms alone.[50] Any memory of the novel, no matter how contradictory, feeds into the memory of the film and vice versa. As a "state of vision, of feeling and of consciousness" it both transcends, while fully inhabiting, its novel and film form.[51]

So if I cite the many ways the film elides the novel's covert racialization of Scarlett, I must qualify these observations with the recognition of the futility of ever really separating the experience and memory of the novel from the experience and memory of the film. Thus the film's physical embodiment of Scarlett rising from the earth of Tara (Fig. 5.5), while softening the novel's linguistic connection between slave cabins, dirt, and Scarlett's assumption of the "yoke" of virtue, nevertheless lends a spectacular, if glamorized, vividness to a white assumption of virtue in a more generalized and less specific "racial" context. This virtue registers differently in the film, in the mutual recognitions of strength and responsibility demonstrated between Hattie McDaniel's Mammy and Vivien Leigh's Scarlett, or in the gesture with which Mammy raises her skirt to reveal to Rhett the red petticoat he once gave her that now functions as a sign of her newfound respect for him.

"The Winds of Change"

In what way was *Gone With the Wind* a story for African Americans? Let us consider the experiences of two young black viewers at the occasion of the film's opening. In 1939 the future Malcolm X was in the seventh grade in Mason, Michigan, where he attended a screening of *Gone With the Wind*. He later wrote in his autobiography, "I was the only Negro in the theatre, and when Butterfly McQueen went into her act, I felt like crawling under the rug" (Haley 1964, 32). In that same year, on December 15, at the gala premiere of the film in Atlanta, the ten-year-old Martin Luther King, Jr., took part in the city's gala pageant celebrating the film. On the City Auditorium stage, where the Junior League was holding a "Gone With the Wind Ball" for the film's stars and important (white) dignitaries, King sang, dressed as a slave, in the Ebenezer Church choir, under the direction of his mother, Mrs. Martin Luther King.[52]

Malcolm Little felt racial shame sitting among whites in an integrated northern theater watching the film that would seem to define an America poised between depression and war. We do not know what Martin Luther King, Jr., felt portraying a happy slave in the Atlanta pageant. But we do know that he would not be able to actually see the film until it opened several months later in a black theater, for the Atlanta Loews' Grand, where the premiere was held, had no black section (Bernstein 1999, 24). The fussy pageantry that surrounded the Atlanta premiere represented the quintessence of southern segregation. (Neither Butterfly McQueen nor Hattie McDaniel, for example, was invited to the premiere, and McDaniel's photograph was even removed from the program listing the film's players [Thomson 1993, 322]). We know as well that King's father was attacked by other black Baptist ministers for participating in a function that was not only segregated but, perhaps more importantly, an occasion for sinful dance and drink (Branch 1988, 55).

The Reverend Martin Luther King, Sr., had not been able to refuse the opportunity to share some of the glory of the Atlanta premiere for his church and choir even at the expense of acting the charade of happy darkies. His rift with other ministers over the propriety of participating in the film's glory was typical of the film's reception in the black community at large. While some, like Malcolm Little, would cringe at the stereotypes, or like W.E.B. Du Bois dismiss the film as "conventional provincialism about which Negroes need not get excited" (Cripps 1993a, 364), others, like Martin Luther King, Sr., or Hattie McDaniel, *would* get excited and make the most of their designated roles in the (segregated) action and take pride in what accomplishments were available. Still others would note that Selznick had at least eliminated the word "nigger" and representations of KKK revenge.

Historian Thomas Cripps writes, in an essay that gives this subsection its name, "By standing astride a moment between the Great Depression and a world war during which American social attitudes changed, in part prodded by forces released by war-time propaganda calling for national unity across ethnic lines, the movie provided a punctuation mark between the last era in which racial matters were considered to be purely local and a new era when they resumed a role in national public policy" (Cripps 1983, 137). Clearly, *Gone With the Wind* was a long way from being in the forefront of social change. Yet, within the limits set by their roles, the black actors, like McDaniel—who knew those limits well having already been there three years earlier playing Queenie in the film version of *Show Boat*—did what they could. For these small inflections they tended to receive high praise in the black press. One paper, for example, admired the modernity of the relationship of mutual admiration between Mammy and Rhett (Cripps 1993a, 146). On the other hand, many dressy premieres for black bourgeois audiences were marked by picket lines. But these lines were always crossed and by the time McDaniel won her Oscar, the black community had given general acceptance to a film that, if it had not depicted any heroic rebellion or sustained black subjectivity, at least had avoided the racial villains of the plantation legend.

Every bit as important as the portrayals before the camera was what went on behind it. Here the "winds of change" were blowing harder. A delegation of blacks on the set threatened to walk off unless racially segregated restrooms were eliminated. Butterfly McQueen's vociferous objection to one of Vivien Leigh's overly forceful slaps—"I'm no stunt man, I'm an actress"—would cut in half the number of times Scarlett would slap Prissy in the film compared to the novel (Cripps 1983, 144). Los Angeles was clearly not Georgia, and the black actors had to learn their southern accents just as Gable and the imported British talent did.

It almost seemed as if the real issue for African Americans had to do with the degree to which their lives and subjectivities could be seen to be included in the nation that was being defined in the Mitchell-Selznick celebration of America's new-found southern "roots." In 1939 there seemed to be some modest possibility for inclusion. For if the South was once again being defined as the essence of what the nation was, then its treatment of African Americans could become, as it had become in the wake of Stowe, a matter of national concern. Ambivalence about this inclusion of African Americans in national identity goes to the very heart of the film's appeal to a nation on the eve of a war that would encourage Negroes to extend their social gains even as it refused to integrate its troops. To the degree that the film seemed, at this moment of hesitation between old apartheid and new wartime opportunity, to halfheartedly include them as Americans, African Americans accepted its lies, and the masks they were to wear, as better than those of previous eras.

It would not be until the 1950s that a new melodrama of black and white would rewrite the script of white and black virtue on the national stage. In this new melodrama, racially beset black victims would again, like Uncle Tom, occupy central stage, displacing white women victims and white male rescuers of the plantation legend. This time the "media event" would not be the public reception of a novel and its transformation into a film, nor a nostalgic representation of the past. Rather, it would be highly conflicted representations of the civil rights movement, a spectacle that "transformed the blackface performance of black inferiority into a ritualized enactment of black subjectivity and moral supremacy" (Hale 1998, 293). For the civil rights movement was nothing if not a black and white racial melodrama whose nonviolent tone of "moral supremacy" represented a significant reworking of the Christian values of the original Tom story. Where Uncle Tom's startling innovation had been to demand the recognition of black humanity in a culture and a society that gave little thought to black rights, now a white supremacist nation was belatedly being asked to recognize the rights of black *citizens*.

The spectacle of stoically suffering blacks murdered, hosed, beaten, spit upon, jeered at, attacked by dogs, denied the right to sit at the lunch counter or in the front of the bus, denied the right to drink at the drinking fountain, to swim in the swimming pool, or to attend the university had the same kind of power of moral reframing that Tom's suffering had once had.[53] The Simon Legrees of this melodrama—the white governors, sheriffs, and school administrators who defied federal orders to integrate—found themselves up against one enemy they could not beat: the African American's ability to play out their morally superior roles as victims before the glare of national media, especially the newly arrived medium of television. Television, as we shall soon see, would turn out to be the next medium to provide a home for that indefatigable **219** "leaping fish."

6 Home Sweet Africa: Alex Haley's and TV's *Roots*

If there was no fictional black and white melodrama with anything like the galvanizing appeal of the civil rights movement, that is because this struggle was itself a galvanizing racial melodrama beside which mere fiction seemed to pale. As we shall see in this chapter and the next, the post–civil rights era would increasingly locate its most convulsive forms of black and white racial melodrama in reality-based forms. In the decade of the 1970s this move away from fiction to "fact" was most dramatically played out in the form of Alex Haley's family saga, *Roots*. Published for the first time in its entirety in 1976, the year of the nation's bicentennial, *Roots* sold a million and a half copies while still in hardback, won the Pulitzer Prize for nonfiction and the National Book Award, and was eventually translated into twenty-four languages. Not since Margaret Mitchell's *Gone With the Wind* had there been an American publishing sensation like it. Like *GWTW* as well, Haley's book became the most significant media event of its age, when it was immediately adapted to television, the mass medium that had now replaced film as the most pervasive.[1] As a twelve-hour, eight-part television miniseries, it would break all previous television viewing records—significantly, including the previous year's broadcast of *GWTW*. *Roots* virtually paralyzed the nation, closing restaurants and movie theaters for eight consecutive nights in January 1977. Here, then, was a new kind of "leaping fish" boldly transforming, and lending new significance and seriousness to, the medium of television.

Where *GWTW* had told a southern story of slavery and after, with which the (majority white) nation had powerfully identified, *Roots* told the story of slavery from an African-American, post–civil rights perspective. The strikingly original phenomenon of *Roots* as both book and film was that for the first time blacks and whites together would powerfully identify with the pathos and action of an African-American–authored work about African-American heroes.[2] That the saga of an African-American family could now be seen as a representative American experience is eloquent testimony to a civil rights movement that had finally made black Americans simply Americans. After the civil and legislative gains of this movement, African Americans could no longer be excluded, as they had effectively been excluded as significant subjectivities in mass popular culture since *The Birth of a Nation*, from the "imagined community" of the American polity. Despite the fact that segregation, lack of equal opportunity, and prejudice would continue to be deeply rooted in American culture, the story of a black family, like the stories of the Hawkses, the Rabinowitzes, and the O'Haras, could finally be, as the book's subtitle had it, *The Saga of an American Family*.

I shall argue in what follows that this saga gripped the broad American public, black and white, and every other ethnicity, because it was an Afrocentric revision of *Uncle Tom's Cabin* on the one hand and of *The Birth of a Nation* and *Gone With the Wind* on the other. These seemingly contradictory melodramas of black and white had come to stand, by the time of Haley's writing, as stark oppositions in a majority white culture in a post–civil rights America. In revising the central "Tom" story of the suffering slave, Haley was simultaneously incorporating and criticizing the civil rights tradition that had used moral supremacy and martyrdom as the means to integration. At the same time, in revising the reactionary "anti-Tom" story of the "bad nigger," Haley was simultaneously incorporating and criticizing a "Black Power" tradition that eschewed martyrdom for more virile expressions of separatist black pride. His melodramatic saga of origins would thus use racial melodrama to negotiate the tensions between the King tradition of integration and the Malcolm X tradition of separatism in an attempt to "solve" the endemic problem of a divided racial and social identity.[3]

Alex Haley's "leaping fish" rewrites both the Tom and the anti-Tom myths through the story of the man Haley claims as his ancestor: the proud Mandinka warrior, Kunta Kinte. The book's main story tells how in the late eighteenth century, this young warrior, having recently completed his manhood training, went out one day to chop wood for a drum. Kidnapped by white slave traders, brutally ripped from the shores of his edenic African home, plunged into the horrors of the Middle Passage, Kunta Kinte arrives in Virginia, where he is rechristened with the slave name Toby. Refusing to accept both his slave name and status, Kunta Kinte fiercely resists, running away four times. When he is finally prevented from running by the brutal amputation of part of his foot, he acquiesces to his fate as a slave, and "plants his seed" in the alien American soil through "marriage" to Bell, a "big house" cook. He then passes on the knowledge of African heritage to his daughter, Kizzy. In the next generation, Kizzy is sold away from her parents for helping a fellow slave to escape. Her new master rapes her, and the son of this "union," Chicken George, is a cockfighter who eventually earns his freedom. After emancipation, Chicken George leads his family to Tennessee, the new "home" where Alex Haley himself will eventually be born. Each new descendent of Kunta Kinte is told the story of his or her African ancestry in a familiar litany that recounts the story of the loss of the good African home.

Though the tale loses vividness and force as the generations continue, finally becoming little more than a list of generations following the turn of the nineteenth century, it nevertheless reaches a rousing melodramatic conclusion when it arrives at the time of Haley's writing. At this point, after Haley has narrated the event of his own birth and has begun to write in the first person, the story of the Kinte line becomes the story of the writing of *Roots*. Recalling the occasions when he himself heard the tale of the farthest-back relative, "Kin-tay," "the African" who, when out chopping wood to make a drum, had been kidnaped into slavery, Haley then briefly tells the tale of his own life. This life, in contrast to that of his farthest back ancestor, is one of successful assimilation via a career in the Coast Guard. Later, he becomes a journalist for *Reader's Digest* and *Playboy*, and the famous ghostwriter for *The Autobiography of Malcolm X*.

As Haley moves closer to recounting the events that led to the actual writing of his book, the direction of the tale reverses: in place of a sad-ending melodrama of loss that moves from the Eden of Africa to the Hell of America, he offers a happy-ending melodrama leading back to the recovery of the Edenic African home. Thus *Roots*, the book, is actually a double narration, moving forward as a chronicle of American history and backward to a retrieval of the mythic lost "home." The happy ending of this second, backward-moving, story accomplishes what the primary, forward-moving, story of the generations that flow from Kunta Kinte cannot: the "rescue" and recovery of the melodramatic "space of innocence" through Haley's heroic efforts as a genealogical journalist. The following is an abbreviation of how he tells this second tale.

In the course of his own "rootless" wanderings as a peripatetic journalist, Haley describes coming across the Rosetta Stone in the British Museum. This stone, inscribed on three sides with different languages—one of which was once mysterious hieroglyphics—became the key to much of humankind's earliest history when a scholar was able to prove that the inscription on all sides was of the same text. On the model of this stone, Haley believed he might be able to crack the code of his own family's earliest history and connect with its farthest-back ancestor, called simply "the African." By using the few African words that had been passed down in the family's story of the African ancestor, Kunta "Kint-ay," who had gone away from his village one day to chop wood to make a drum, he eventually matches these words to an oral litany recited by an African griot.

When Haley arrives in Juffure, in the Gambia, to hear the genealogical recitation of the griot, a crowd of curious "jet black" Africans surrounds him. Looking at his own comparatively light skin, he feels himself to be a hybrid. "I felt somehow impure among the pure; it was a terribly shaming feeling" (677). He is immediately rescued from this shame and impurity, however, by the events that follow the tale of the griot hired to recite the ancestral history of the Kinte clan. When the griot, through translators, finally arrives at an account of a certain Kunta who went away from his village to chop wood for a drum and was never heard from again, Haley is dumbstruck. He shows his interpreter his written account of the family oral history told to him by his grandmother. As the words on the different sides of his personal Rosetta "stone" match, Haley tells his readers that the audience of seventy Africans listening to the griot recognize that, hybrid or not, light-skinned or not, Haley is one of them. His shame vanishes as the Africans recognize him, and he recognizes them, as of one and the same people.

A spectacular scene that performs a mutual "recognition of virtue" follows.[4] First, the women recognize him. Young mothers thrust their babies into his arms in a ritual later explained to Haley as a ceremonial "laying on of hands" that enacts the identity of their flesh—"Through this flesh, which is us, we are you and you are us!" (680). Then it is the men's turn. They take him into their bamboo mosque and surround him in postures of prayer. Finally, when he is about to depart from another, much larger, village where news of his experience has spread, Haley recounts an even grander melodramatic recognition of virtue, when he finds himself mobbed by a crowd that cries out to him, hailing him in the name of his African great-, great-, great-, great-, great-, great-grandfather: "Meester Kinte! Meester Kinte!" (681). Haley writes: "Let me tell you something: I am a man. A sob hit me somewhere around my ankles; it came surging upward, and flinging my hands over my face, I was just bawling, as I hadn't since I was a baby. 'Meester Kinte!' I just felt like I was weeping for all of history's incredible atrocities against fellowmen"(681). The involuntary sob that this scene of "homecoming" wrenches from Haley is the melodramatic recognition of his own racial virtue as it is linked to the virtue and suffering of his ancestor and all the generations in between. Haley's sob is all the more meaningful as he, an assimilated, urbane, light-skinned Negro, made initially uncomfortable by his racial hybridity, finds himself "hailed" by the name of his pure black African ancestor by other black Africans. It is simultaneously the ("too late") recognition of what his ancestor lost—home, fatherland, freedom—and its belated regaining ("in the nick of time"). In hailing him through the name that becomes his "proper" patronymic once he answers it with his monumental sob, Haley finds himself nominated (in Peter Brooks's sense) and interpellated (in Althusser and Fanon's sense) by the name-of-the-father (Lacan's sense) that slavery had stolen from him.[5] Thus the name-of-the-father is symbolically restored to the African-American descendent robbed of his patronymic. We must note however, that this name, which constitutes the book's ultimate recognition of an (African) virtue and which gives Haley access to an African purity that his light skin belies, is itself a hybrid of African patronymic ("Kinte") and Anglo-American address ("Meester").

In one fell swoop Haley finds himself recognized both as a proud, "pure" African *and* as a racial victim robbed of the home he never had, his "home sweet Africa." By apparently retrieving the place in his ancestral life that represents the mythic time before it was "too late," Haley appears to recover his racial virtue as an African and to compensate for a two-hundred-year diaspora through what might be called a positive application of the "one-drop rule." The emotional discovery of this home in these last pages of his book enables Haley, like Marcel Proust in the *The Past Regained*, to retrieve a lost past and write the very book we have been reading. But where Proust claimed the recovered past of his childhood and adolescence in the name of a highly individualized bourgeois experience, Haley redeems what David Chioni Moore (1994, 10) calls the crime of history by "claiming an entire continent for an entire unmoored people." Racial pride and racial victimization are the entwined virtues of Haley's recognition. To best understand how these recognitions operate within the previously white-authored tradition of black and white racial melodrama, we need to look closely at their relation to the related myths of Tom and anti-Tom.

An Afrocentric Uncle Tom

The story of the proud Mandinka warrior Kunta Kinte, who four times attempts escape, works hard to differentiate itself from the story of the humble Christian, Uncle Tom, who prides himself on having always been found "on the spot" for his master.[6] However, any attempt to tell the story of African slavery in America cannot help but be determined by what Toni Morrison has called the "master narrative" of American fiction; and, for better or for worse, *Uncle Tom's Cabin* constitutes the original negrophilic strain of the white-authored "master narrative" of slavery.[7] Consider that both works establish racial virtue and pride through their African protagonist's racial victimization in prolonged scenes of beating. Both works show their heroes resisting the power of the white master—Tom, by refusing to tell of the escape of Cassy and Emmeline and by giving his body, but not his soul, to his master; Kunta Kinte, by repeated escapes and prolonged refusals to acknowledge his slave name. Tom's resistance is, of course, nonviolent. Twice in the novel he is offered an opportunity to run away; twice he urges others to go but stays put himself. Kunta Kinte, on the other hand, runs so often and fights so fiercely that he is finally given a choice between castration and the removal of part of his foot. His choice to retain his sexual organs and to lose the organs of flight is ultimately the choice of regeneration in the alien "home."[8] But of course this choice to keep his sex organs takes on a much deeper meaning within the context of a "Tom" figure who had become, ever since the emergence of black power movements, the very figure of emasculated docility. The choice to retain virility is thus both the choice that makes the *Roots* story of generation possible and the symbolic retention of a virile alternative to the "desexed" Uncle Tom. African identity is linked in this choice of virility. Thus, where Tom's strength comes from a humble and feminine Christian forgiveness, Kunta Kinte's strength comes from a combination of his warrior status and a Moslem superiority toward Christianized slaves who have lost their pride. A generalized version of this racial and cultural pride—if not the specific Moslem religion—is ultimately what is passed on to each new generation privileged with the memory of its connection to the original "African."

Perhaps most significantly, however, both works attempt to forge happy endings by leading their surviving heroes (Eliza, George, Cassy, Topsy in *Uncle Tom*; Alex Haley himself in *Roots*) back to Africa in melodramatic recognitions of their "roots." Indeed, the problem of African-American identity that this movement "back to Africa" appears to "solve" is ultimately nothing less than the location of the melodramatic home "space of innocence" for a people who had never been fully welcome in the American home to which they were transplanted.

Stowe had given both a comic and a heroic dimension to the dilemma of home and origin in the character of Topsy, who is so ignorant of her provenance that she cannot tell Aunt Ophelia who made her: "I spect I grow'd. Don't think nobody never made me" (Stowe 1983, 210).[9] George Harris echoes the same dilemma, but on a more elevated note of pathos, when he writes a letter to a friend announcing his intention to embrace Africa (specifically Liberia) as his true home. His reasons, however, carry none of the emotional force of Haley's more dramatic recovery of his African homeland. Although George acknowledges that his race has as much "right to claim the American republic as the Irishman, the German, the Swede" (610), he spurns this right in favor of what Arthur Riss (1994) calls the racial nationalism, and racial essentialism, of a morally superior, uniquely African country. Casting his lot with "the oppressed, enslaved African race" (608), George effectively also casts his lot with a maternal Africa against a paternal Anglo-Saxon America. His reasoning is his own sympathy and love for the fleetingly known black mother who once cared for him and his repudiation of the absent white father who never acknowledged him: "My sympathies are not for my father's race, but for my mother's. To him I was no more than a fine dog or horse: to my poor heart-broken mother I was a *child*. . . . When I think of all she suffered. . . . I have no wish to pass for an American, or to identify myself with them" (608).

George cannot "recognize the virtue" of, or be recognized as virtuous by, the white father, since the "one-drop rule" of blood renders him one hundred percent African. Because the even more distant black male ancestor is lost to him through the institution of slavery, George chooses a maternal (and Christian) version of Africa as the good home. As we saw in Chapter 2 this choice constructs a notion of familial origin grounded, not simply in relations of blood, but in relations of race. In Stowe's brand of romantic racialism, race ultimately replaces paternity as the ultimate mark of belonging to a family.[10]

Of course the great problem with Stowe's argument for Africa as the maternal, racially inflected, home is that it does not function this way within her narrative. Home remains, despite George's arguments, throughout the Tom *and* the anti-Tom tradition of black and white racial melodrama, that poor but honest slave cabin where "the sun shines bright" and where "darkies" "tote the weary load" of racial victimhood. Since neither Stowe, nor any of her theatrical or film adaptors, ever found a way to bring George Harris either physically or emotionally home to Africa (recall that even in the novel we only see him planning to go there), Kentucky—or some other agrarian southern home—continues to function as the felt locus of innocence in all adaptations of Stowe's novel and in all other versions of the Tom (and even the anti-Tom) stories. As a result, the problem of racial origin and identity that Stowe so neatly "solves" in her novel remains emotionally unresolved in the responses of her readers and theatrical and film audiences. The "South within us" continued to rule as the melodramatic locus of feeling, and as long as it did, home was a problem for African-American audiences and readers of the tradition. Despite the racial essentialism that would define all descendants of Africans as belonging to the "family" of Africans, the association between the American southern home and the African slave cabin had become so strong that there would ultimately be no dislodging it.[11]

Whatever else one might say about this enormously popular but controversial writer, eventually accused of plagiarizing material and fudging historical chronology, Alex Haley's stroke of genius was to locate the home and begin his narrative in a place that was every bit as exotic and foreign to his readers as the rural southern home was to Stowe's predominantly northern readers, or, later, to white readers and viewers of the Jazz Age and Depression era. In all cases the nostalgia was for a rural, southern, "black" home that had never really been known to whites and that could not be idealized by blacks. Haley's story of the long lost, but symbolically regained African home captured the imagination of countless readers of all races and ethnicities.[12] Yet the ultimate function of *Roots* would not really be to provide African-American readers with a nostalgia for the African home they had never known and an African identity they could thus assume. Rather, as we shall see, the appeal of this image of the African home would ultimately permit African-Americans to achieve a more covert reconciliation with their more mundane American one. **227**

Haley begins his tale in the idealized West African village of Juffure, where young boys chase rainbows, herd goats, and are indulged by their mothers until, at the age of seventeen, they undergo a ritual "manhood training" involving circumcision and the assumption of their role as virile warriors and hunters, above women. Young Kunta Kinte is no ordinary villager. He is the proud descendent of Karaiba Kunta Kinte, a wandering holy man who saved the village in a time of drought and then settled there. After a hundred and fifty pages of village life told from the point of view of the boyhood and adolescence of this "noble savage" living in close harmony with nature, the reader grows familiar with the ways of an "Africa" remarkably (and anachronistically) untouched by white colonization, in which white men, "Toubobs," are only frightening rumors.

By the time Kunta Kinte arrives at the Waller plantation in Spotsylvania County, Virginia, the docile ways of slavery, so familiar in American culture through both the Tom and anti-Tom traditions, have been effectively defamiliarized. Haley makes certain of this by painstakingly recounting all events from Kunta Kinte's often excessively naive "African" point of view.[13] Thus home— that mythic, Christian, maternal "space of innocence" about which everyone from Uncle Tom to Magnolia Hawks to Jakie Rabinowitz to Scarlett O'Hara had sung—is no longer located in the South. It has been transferred into an equally mythic, but now Moslem and patriarchal "home sweet Africa."

Roots thus poses an answer to the dilemma of Topsy and George's origin in *Uncle Tom's Cabin*. Native-born African Americans had been treated as if, like Topsy, they had just "grow'd." Given the improper patronymics of white "fathers" who were often also sexual violators, black slaves had been, as Hortense Spillers (1987, 66) has provocatively put it, "ungendered." Arguing that the middle passage constituted a moment in which "all social and human differentiation" is eradicated in the interest of delegitimating the rights of personhood and citizenship, Spillers maintains that slaves, male and female, were robbed of both maternal and paternal functions in order to be rendered nonsubjects (78).[14] But if the "ungendered" black male slave was deprived of his manhood through his inability to own "his" women, he was also, as we have seen, given a certain measure of humanity through the feminized suffering attributed to the popular icon of the Uncle Tom.

Gender, whether eradicated or exaggerated, posed complex problems to African-American citizenship. The exaggerated marks of gender as attributed to African Americans by white supremacist culture could cut both ways. In one instance the comic hypermasculinity of the Africanist minstrel figure could disprove humanity; in another instance the feminine suffering of the Christian slave could prove a humanity that had revolutionary repercussions in the quest for citizenship. The burlesqued hypermasculinity of blackface minstrels certainly discredited the personhood of African men and women, but as we have seen, the "Uncle Tomitudes" that produced empathy for an Uncle Tom worked melodramatically to assert the subjectivity of racially victimized persons. If African Americans were deprived of the traditional attributes of patriarchal gender that marked the humanity of white (male) citizens, it was only through unorthodox versions of gender—the black woman actively fleeing bondage, the black man passively dying in it—that resistance occurred. The one thing African Americans could not be, of course, were carbon copies of conventional (white) nineteenth-century citizens.

It is against the history of all these "perverse" twists of gender and race that *Roots* works to establish the emotional validity of the black African patriarch and progenitor. Haley thus offers an emotionally powerful mythic "solution" to Daniel Patrick Moynihan's (1967) pathologizing report on the matriarchy of the black family.[15] In place of Stowe's matriarchal family melodrama, in which identification with mother Africa is the only recourse in the face of the white father's denial of paternity, Haley's secondary narrative refashions a patriarchal family melodrama in which a restless, wandering, uprooted son (Haley himself) "rescues" his contaminated race by finding the racially pure lost black father.[16]

Although the racial purity of this recovered black father would seem to lead, as Stowe wished to lead her black characters, back to an Africa construed as the one true home for the race, its real effect in the year of America's bicentennial was quite the opposite. The recognition of virtue of the lost African ancestor leads his descendants, and by implication many American descendants of Africans, to a paradoxical acceptance of the fact of racial hybridity and the American locus of home.

This acceptance is made possible, I think, because Haley is writing the modern equivalent of what David Chioni Moore (1994, 4) calls a foundational, sacred text, telling people where they come *from*, not where they must *go*. *Roots* was written in the aftermath of a period of convulsive political and social events that had finally made African Americans equal citizens before the law. The American civil rights movement of the sixties had achieved this citizenship through stagings of its own melodramas of black and white in which noble black citizens suffered at the hands of villainous white supremacists at voting booths, public schools, and lunch counters. In this new melodrama the "return to Africa" was not offered, as Stowe offered hers, or as Lincoln offered his, as a *political* solution to the place of Africans in American society but as an *emotional* solution to the melodramatic problem of the "space of innocence."

Figure 6.1   Kunta Kinte, captured and chained, shows both resistance and suffering. (*Roots*)

The post–civil rights era context for the reception of Haley's book is crucial to the new version of Uncle Tom that Haley writes. For where Stowe had been concerned to establish the simple humanity of the "objects" owned, traded, and mistreated by the "patriarchal" institution, Haley—for all his capture of the imagination of Africa—is finally more concerned with the question of how these former objects could continue to live in America as manly citizen-subjects in what remained a white-dominated culture. In revising the most volatile, racially charged moments of what Leslie Fiedler likes to call "inter-ethnic flagellation" in Stowe's work, Haley goes directly to the "root" scene of the melodrama of black and white. But his narration of these repeated white-on-black beatings occurs in the aftermath of a time when spectacles of black victimization had already been recognized as the cause of the delegitimization of white supremacy and, conversely, as the legitimization of African-American rights. Furthermore, since these beatings and oppressions occurred on the body of a slave who repeatedly ran away, they no longer appeared to mire African-American identity in the now-dreaded passivity, and femininity, of the "Tom." Instead, played out against the proud foundation of paternal African identity, these icons of enslavement became a new source of black male pride in their ability to illustrate struggle in suffering, as the image of Kunta Kinte's first enslavement in *TV Roots* illustrated (Fig. 6.1).

What *Roots* did for its African-American readers and viewers is thus not unlike what blackface and a song about "Mammy" in *The Jazz Singer* did for Jews: it offered identification with an exoticized blackness, ennobled through suffering, whose actual purpose, however, was ultimately to forge an *assimilated* American identity. The African home presented in *Roots* is no less exotic, no less idyllic, no less foreign to modern American and African American sensibilities than the rural cabins or moonlit plantations of the previous Tom/anti-Tom traditions were to the bulk of their readers and viewers. Indeed, for the first time in American popular culture's "master narrative" of racial melodrama, African Americans were invited to identify and sympathize with racially victimized Africanist figures in much the same way white Americans had long been doing. Through this circuitous route of identifying with an exotic Africanness that was precisely what they were not—and who, except an extreme minority of Black Muslims, could call themselves pure black, non-pork-eating "Mandinka" warriors?—African Americans in the post–civil rights era assumed their own distinctive American identity. "Posing as black" now became not just the prerogative of white Americans seeking to find themselves in the racial other, but the prerogative, indeed the duty, of African Americans themselves. Only now, "posing as black" walked a fine line between the abject suffering of the feminized Tom and the newly masculinized, but still ennobled-through-suffering, *African American* who took his place.

An Afrocentric Anti-Tom

Kunta Kinte is a Mandinka warrior who is ultimately defeated by white domination. When he realizes he will never see home again, he belatedly "plants his seed" in the foreign land. The story of *Roots* is the story of how repeated generations of what is always viewed singularly as the Kinte line will make this foreign place home. After the birth of Kizzy, Kunta Kinte reflects, "Though it was a girlchild—which must be the will of Allah—it was nonetheless a child, and he felt a deep pride and serenity in the knowledge that the blood of the Kintes, which had coursed down through the centuries like a mighty river, would continue to flow for still another generation" (340). But when the grown Kizzy is sold away to another master, Kunta Kinte loses his connection to home that the perpetuation of his bloodline had offered. Remembering an African custom of preserving the dust of the footprints of a loved one to ensure that loved one's return, he seizes the dust of Kizzy's footprint and runs to his cabin to find a container for it. Seeing only the gourd in which the pebbles marking each month of his fifty-five "rains" of life are measured, the sudden recognition of how long he has been in slavery makes him realize the futility of the old custom. At this moment, the continuity between the markers of time past (the pebbles) and the marker of his extension into time future (the dust of Kizzy's footprint) is brutally ruptured. Kunta Kinte hurls the dust into the air and the gourd to the ground. Pebbles and dust scatter in a powerful metaphor of diaspora (427).

When Kunta Kinte throws the dust of Kizzy's footprint into the air, he loses his connection to an idyllic, patriarchal, and aristocratic era that is now every bit as "gone with the wind" for him as the patriarchy and aristocracy of the old South would later be for the Confederacy. Marking the end of the temporary accommodation Kunta Kinte had made with slavery is the abrupt termination of his point of view and its transfer to his daughter Kizzy. In a sense, the "real" story of slavery told from the slave's point of view—the familiar "American" story of enslavement that moves toward freedom, the story of descent through the mother and not the father—begins here with Kizzy's almost immediate violation by her new white master, Tom Lea. This sexual violation of the black mother and the subsequent establishment of the mother-centered black family marks the end of the patriarchal lost paradise. From this point on, Kizzy and all her descendants can only attempt to keep faith with the distant memory of the African past and its patriarchal ancestor, "the African."[17]

The story of *Roots* falls into the tripartite pattern made familiar by the plantation legend: the first part consists of the idyllic picture of a patriarchal African paradise; the second is the Fall from this Paradise in the Hell of the Middle Passage and slavery; the third is a slow progress toward a regained Paradise.[18] Within the picture of the Fall there are highly qualified moments of triumph usually depicted with the birth of each new child (Kizzy, Chicken George, the various children of Chicken George) and the always-moving moment when the family's African history is passed on to each of them. The slow progress to Paradise Regained is accomplished through Chicken George's exceptional prosperity and, after emancipation, his Moses-like leadership of the clan in a wagon train to the "promised land" of Tennessee. Here the family prospers and produces its second rescuer in the person of Haley himself, whose genealogical detective work makes the connection to the lost African ancestor not only a source of family pride and identity, but a source of pride and identity for all African-American people.

Of course, what is Paradise to *The Birth of a Nation* and the plantation legend—the antebellum era—is the Fall to the African. Nevertheless the structure is similar: Kunta Kinte's African home, Juffure, corresponds to the idealized "moonlight and magnolias" of the antebellum era. Indeed, both of these homes offer representations of slavery that are relatively benign.[19] Haley's description of the Middle Passage and the enslavement that robs the aspiring African patriarch of all that he is corresponds, in the plantation legend, to the story of the devastation of the Civil War and Reconstruction eras. Finally, emancipation and the recovery of racial pride in the reconnection with the past corresponds to the rise of the Ku Klux Klans and the restoration of white supremacy.[20] Haley's recasting of the anti-Tom plantation legend is made pos-

232

sible by the adoption of a longer historical lens than that afforded by the familiar antebellum/Civil War and Reconstruction/KKK progression. In the year of America's bicentennial, this imagination of a pre-slavery Paradise and a post-slavery, post–civil rights Paradise Regained finally rewrote — as no other African-American work had been able to rewrite — the master narrative of black and white melodrama.

The close structural parallels between a "plantation legend" story of the loss and restoration of white supremacy and pride and a story of the loss and restoration of black power and pride speaks not simply to the phenomenon of reverse racism, with black power substituting for white. For as we have begun to see, Haley's *Roots* is an Afrocentric revision of both Tom *and* anti-Tom. As a version of both, it ultimately leads neither back to Africa, nor to African separatism within the United States, but *through* the melodramatic return to Africa to an accommodation with African-American racial hybridity. Thus if *Roots* is, as one critic (Rose 1979, 2–3) has claimed, a black version of *The Birth of a Nation* and *Gone With the Wind*, it is not a simple reversal of the plantation legend's moral and racial polarities.[21]

The comparison between *Roots* and the plantation legend grows more compelling when we consider their similar attempts to enshrine idealized, aristocratic, and patriarchal ways of life as myths of origin. Consider, for example, that both works are obsessively concerned with preserving an uninterrupted line of succession between fathers and sons. It is the retrieval of this line of succession — the perpetuation of the racially pure patriarchal seed — that Haley, as much as Dixon and Griffith, wants to ensure. And it is the interracial rape of the racially pure woman by the "wrong" race that is seen to brutally interrupt this succession. But here, of course, the similarity ends. For where the rape of the black woman by white masters was the norm of the antebellum South, the rape of the white woman by the black man was the fantasmatic exception: white men fantasized the specter of the "black beast" lusting after the white woman *in order* to keep black men and white women in their place; in contrast, black men, both slave and free, had no power to protect "their" women from real or imagined sexual assault. There is no equivalent of the Ku Klux Klan ride-to-the-rescue for the black woman.[22]

All the more reason, then, for the *Roots* narrative to navigate a longer, and more circuitous, generational route to the melodramatic *deus ex machina* of rescue. Thus, where Griffith and Dixon offered the rides of the Clan to save the endangered white women as the exalted actions of white action-heroes "to save a nation," Haley's inability to depict the rescue of the endangered woman leads to the construction of something more meaningful. For if he could not narratively prevent interracial violation, he could at least try to redeem it over time: first in the family's survival with a modicum of its original, aristocratic pride intact; second in its repeated refusals to succumb to a sentimental attachment to any of the various "homes" of enslavement;[23]

and third in its ability not to be paralyzed by anger toward white power but, instead, to get on with the generational business of capitalizing on its aristocratic self-conception and, through that conception, to prosper.

Prevented from depicting rescues "in the nick of time" à la Dixon and Griffith, *Roots* offers in compensation two complex retroactive "rescues" that **233** are all the more poignant because they are both painfully "too late!" In the aftermath of historical crimes that have already taken their toll on the black family and that cannot be undone because they are already registered in the racially mixed "blood" of the next generations, this "too late!" rescue occurs first when Chicken George, the son of Kizzy, "fathered" by her white master, Tom Lea, finally returns from England to claim his wife and eight grown children. George's return appears to occur just in time to save the family from dispersal in the aftermath of emancipation. He is welcomed joyously, assumes leadership with much fanfare, and, like Moses, leads them to a place he has billed in advance, in George's typical hyperbole, as "de promised lan" (647).

While this late appearance of the perennially absent African father seems to want to make up for all the previous absences and disconnections suffered by each generation, there is something a little hollow about it. For one thing, Chicken George is no longer necessary to the family, whose leadership has long since been taken over by his son Tom, who is both steady and present. His presence at this point in the narrative is simply symbolic. He is a titular head of a family, and a story, that wants desperately to believe in the power of the African patriarch. Yet, as if to belie this power, George's act of rescue is neither dramatic nor suspenseful. We never learn, for example, how he acquired the land in Tennessee. Within four pages of this 688-page book, the family has built its wagon train and reached its "promised land."

We have already seen, of course, that the much more dramatic rescue to occupy the end of the narrative is that performed in the book by Alex Haley himself in discovering the griot who recounts the words that match his family's oral history. In this symbolic rescue of the memory of a whole people, it is far "too late" for any individual to be literally saved. Indeed, the pathos of this rescue-redemption of the past resides precisely in the fact that it does come "too late!" to have made a difference in the lives of previous generations. The lives that it does make a difference to, however, are those of contemporary readers who might, like Haley himself, be tempted to forget about the heritage lost to slavery.

Roots's story of the heroic recovery of the idealized memory of Africa passed on from generation to generation made the "Tom" story of black oppression by whites newly viable for a post–civil rights, post–Black Power population of African Americans, because it replaced the "old Kentucky" (rural southern) home with a new "space of innocence." But, as we have seen, this memory of the lost, "true" home does not lead merely to a substitute nostalgia for Africa; rather, it makes possible a deferred cathexis, suspended over several generations, to the new, post-slavery Tennessee home—a home that we are given to understand most closely resembles the ideal, cohesive, self-reliant, patriarchal community that had been the Juffure, if not of history, then of Haley's wishful imagination.[24]

234

Alex Haley's relocation of the home "space of innocence" to home sweet Africa is thus a means to the ultimate goal of finding an *American* home that is not burdened with the baggage of the fatherless, mother-centered heritage of slavery. Like *The Birth of a Nation, Roots* wants to assure the racial purity of a line of succession passed on from father to son; unlike that work, it cannot rescue the women whose "protection" would ensure that succession. What can be rescued, however, is the wishful "memory" of a pure and singular African root, onto which varieties of other roots (of the Irish-American master Tom Lea, for example) have been violently grafted. The accomplishment of *Roots* is to have exalted the impossibly singular root of the past African heritage over the multiple roots of American hybridity, even as it accommodates to a future hybridity and assimilation.

Black Power and Civil Rights

As many commentators have noted, Alex Haley's connection to the Afrocentric home could not have been forged without a contemporary model of the non-Christian, patriarchal African who held himself aloof both from the "toubob" and from the ordinary Christianized slaves who had lost their connection with "father" Africa. For Alex Haley that model was Malcolm X—the proud Black Muslim who, like Kunta Kinte, refused to bear the patronymic of the white slave-owning father.[25]

Malcolm X was fond of accusing assimilating Negroes, like Martin Luther King, Jr., or like Haley himself, of being "Uncle Toms." The Black Power movement of the sixties had been marked by a concerted determination to reject the Christian role model of the Tom in favor of the violent "bad nigger" first projected, as Fiedler notes, by Dixon, Griffith, and Mitchell, later reembodied and reappropriated in Richard Wright's (significantly named) Bigger Thomas, and then developed as a revolutionary figure of Black Power in writers and activists like LeRoi Jones, Eldridge Cleaver, Huey Newton, and the Black Panthers.[26]

The Black Power movement of the late 1960s had repudiated the integrationist quest of Martin Luther King's "dream that one day on the red hills of Georgia the sons of former slaves and the sons of former slaveowners will be able to sitdown together at the table of brotherhood." In place of King's dream of brotherhood, Black Power advocates offered what would for some become a more compelling dream of purging white influence and celebrating the separate and unique virtues of a black African identity. Malcolm X, who was the most articulate early proponent of this position, began his political career as a Black Muslim separatist. Like Kunta Kinte he despised the smell, look, and culture of the enslaving "toubob," or what Malcolm called the "white devil." As Leslie Fiedler puts it, "Even as the living Haley ghostwrote the *Autobiography*, Malcolm X, from beyond the grave, ghostwrote what is most authentic and moving in *Roots*—the story of Kunta Kinte" (Fiedler 1982, 224).[27]

Fiedler argues that Haley's Black Power story of the proud African was ultimately an expression of revulsion from the "Melting Pot Americanism" of the last decades, leading to the purchase by countless descendants of immigrants of genealogical charts delineating their connection to home countries that were "as suspect as Haley's own" (Fiedler 1982, 228). While I agree with Fiedler about the suspect nature of Haley's genealogy, I do not agree that *Roots* finally represents a rejection of an assimilated, hybrid Americanism. I have been arguing, to the contrary, that the celebration of a refigured Afrocentric, masculinized, but still racially victimized "Tom" was not a rejection of African-American assimilation, but ultimately the very means to it.

Reading Haley's ghostwritten account of Malcolm X's trip to Mecca, for example, one cannot help but be struck by its similarity to the epiphany Haley describes when he is hailed by fellow Africans as "Meester Kinte!" after hearing the griot's account of his family history. Repeatedly, Malcolm is struck by the interracial brotherhood of pilgrims. On the plane are "white, black, brown, red, and yellow people, blue eyes and blond hair, and my kinky red hair—all together, brothers! All honoring the same God Allah, all in turn giving equal honor to each other" (Haley 1976, 323). Ashamed that as a Muslim minister in the Nation of Islam, he does not know the proper ritual of prayer, Malcolm is nevertheless overwhelmed by the cohesion of the racially and culturally disparate groups united in worship. He is especially moved by the white Muslim worshipers who extend themselves to the "Muslim from America." He undergoes a radical transformation in his outlook toward "white" men as a result.[28]

Where Alex Haley's racial epiphany derives from being recognized as African by Africans more "pure" than he, Malcolm's racial epiphany derives from being recognized as a fellow worshiper of Allah regardless of race. Though Haley's epiphany is of the racial connection between pure and mixed-race Africans and Malcolm's epiphany is of the possibility of a broader, less color-conscious collectivity of Moslems, they are both realizations of a larger interconnection of races. This epiphany of human recognition is paradoxically achieved in both cases through reconnection with a pan-African racial "home." Both men tell stories of black pride and black separatism that glorify Africa as the racially grounded, essentialist, singular root of good corrupted by white hegemony. At the same time, however, both men use these stories of the black "root" to negotiate a circuitous acceptance of the much more hybrid and multiple "black Atlantic" home.[29] And, of course, Alex Haley is the controversial "author" of both stories.

Malcolm X was assassinated soon after his trip to Mecca. He never had the chance to put his new insights to the test. Some would even say that the threat of these more pluralistic, less racially essentialist insights were the very reason for his murder. Alex Haley's *Roots*, published over a decade later, might be viewed as the popular culture application of those insights. But where *The Autobiography of Malcolm X* is an important book, still read and discussed by historians, politicians, and black and white intellectuals of every sort, *Roots*, while still a very popular book that sells much more briskly than the autobiography, and while still a classic in Afrocentric circles, has long since ceased to be discussed by mainstream scholars of any race. Why has the book that sold more than any other African-American narrative ever written been dropped so precipitously by scholars and intellectuals?

The Embarrassment of *Roots*

All the books, films, and media events discussed in this work have become, in one way or another, embarrassments to modern readers, viewers, and thinkers. In most cases this is due to the fact that the racial content that once made them seem new and daring became antiquated. Nothing dates like last year's, or last century's, black and white racial melodrama. Indeed, *this* year's racial melodrama often arises from the need to counter or update last year's. *Roots* is no exception; as we have seen, it is the Afrocentric answer to *Uncle Tom*, *The Birth of a Nation*, and *Gone With the Wind*. Yet unlike these fictional works, which claimed to be the morally legible racial "truth" of the eras they depicted, Haley's book was based on supposed fact. The book that once spent five months on the *New York Times* best-seller list in the category of nonfiction, the book that won the Pulitzer Prize for nonfiction and spawned a television series that would, the following year, transform the possibility (if not the reality) of television itself, would soon be dropped like a hot potato. This is not to say that it would cease to be popular. The book would continue to sell, the miniseries would be rerun, and Haley himself would receive the keys to many cities and be treated as a living legend. But the intellectuals and leaders who had initially championed the work soon grew silent when Haley's great claim to have traced his family back to the single "root" ancestor proved untrue. Not only did he fudge dates and evidence that put in question the accuracy of his genealogical connection to "the African," but he plagiarized many passages from other works.[30] Many influential readers who enthusiastically embraced Haley reacted subsequently with silence.

Harriet Beecher Stowe, Thomas Dixon, and Margaret Mitchell had all fought skeptical critics who had challenged the authenticity of their stories.[31]

But where these writers were upholding the spirit of "truth" in their fiction, Haley, who promised, but never published, a defense of his sources, was upholding the more rigorous authenticity of fact. Until his death he would maintain that he had actually traced his ancestors back to Africa. Haley's bridge to the past had promised to redeem the very crime of history; "he claimed an entire continent for an entire unmoored people" and in so doing he created a kind of "sacred text" (Moore 1994, 10). Haley was not content to tell a fiction that needed to be told; he had to claim that he was the unique individual to have made the connection in time back across the Middle Passage. As that unique individual, his mystique has remained strong, but the price he paid was the loss of respect among intellectuals, leaders, and scholars, many of whom are resentful of a *Reader's Digest* writer who became a folk hero on the basis of a lie.

In the tradition we have been tracing, the "original voice" of the writer is less important than the melodrama of racial victims and villains. We may choose, as Helen Taylor (1993, 58) does, to see Haley as an African-American griot deeply in tune, as was the African griot who recited to Haley, with what his audience wanted to hear. For this reason alone the power of *Roots* is worth examining and the silence that now surrounds the text worth breaking.[32] I have tried to show that this construction of a heroic African identity as the rooted identity of African Americans was one way of accommodating and compensating for hybridity. There is no actual rooted identity, in Africa or anywhere else, except as selective and retroactive affiliation constructs it. If the genealogy narrated in the book is true, then Alex Haley is part Irish. Haley chooses to ignore the Irish part of his family tree and to trace an origin to a singular and pure African because the melodramatic icon of home has been so troubled for African Americans. What he does with the Africa of the past, however, is no different than what Margaret Mitchell does with the Georgian plantation that is "gone with the wind": he constructs a locus of virtue out of the needs of the present.

If *Roots* succeeded in appropriating the melodrama of black and white for vast sections of the mainstream American audience, we must overcome cultural disdain and confront its popularity as a "middlebrow" phenomenon. Culture critics are very adept at analyzing both the high and the low of culture but, as David Chioni Moore suggests, the popular middle often escapes them. Popular enthusiasm for the colossus that was Alex Haley's *Roots*—and indeed for the colossal celebrity that was Haley himself—has not waned in the face of scholarly indifference, any more than popular enthusiasm for the colossus of *Gone With the Wind*—and the celebrity that was Margaret Mitchell—has waned before the indifference of serious literary and film scholars. But if we are to grasp the real colossus that was *Roots*, we must come to grips with its adaptation to the little box that replaced movies as the most important source of mass-produced, popular spectacle.

TV Roots

Roots could have been adapted to a number of media (stage, musical stage, film), but it is significant that it was adapted to the one medium with a reputation for a lack of seriousness and that had previously paid little attention to serious dramas about African Americans. Television was now in a position to grant this (melo)drama more exposure than any other.[33] This new version of black and white melodrama was in a position, in turn, to grant new moral legitimacy and seriousness to the medium of television. The effect was not unlike that moment a hundred and twenty-five years earlier when the popular stage melodrama suddenly took on national political significance when it demonstrated that the African (Americans), who had been conventional figures of fun, could also be figures of pathos. Just as the stage version of *Uncle Tom's Cabin* galvanized the empathy of middle- and working-class white audiences used to laughing at comic black stereotypes and brought a middle-class respectability to the melodramatic stage, so *TV Roots* galvanized a national audience used to laughing at comic blacks in television sitcoms and brought a middle-class respectability to television.

In what came to be called "Haley's Comet" (*Time*, February, 1977), African Americans were newly recognized as a people who had lost their home. The white majority recognition of this home "space of innocence" lost to the slave constituted a galvanizing interracial "recognition of virtue" especially significant to the white audience. This "recognition of virtue" was inextricably linked in the popular imagination to the "new" incarnation of black and white melodrama in a medium that, like the American stage in 1852, had previously viewed African Americans as sources of "Negro fun." In other words, the melodramatic recognition of virtue was not confined solely to the represented suffering of black characters but in both cases as well to a new-found virtue of the medium itself. With *Uncle Tom's Cabin* the mid-nineteenth-century stage took on a new middle-class respectability and moral seriousness to which its blood-and-thunder tradition had not previously aspired. With *TV Roots* Newton Minow's "vast wasteland" of television momentarily achieved its own high moral seriousness as it replaced the familiar "flow" of ordinary programs with eight consecutive nights of a single story. Viewers fought blizzards to be home in time to catch the show. Urban black viewers and white suburbanites alike rushed to see the program. Henry James's "fish" had "lept" once again.[34]

Because *Gone With the Wind*'s marginalization of African-American subjectivity and aspiration had ruled for so long as the dominant mass-culture spectacularization of the antebellum and postbellum eras, the mass audience had no popular vision of African-American history beyond the portrayal of loyal darkies and occasional renegades. From 1939—the initial release of Selznick's film—to 1976—the year its appearance on television broke all previous records for audience share—GWTW ruled as the dominant culture's "version" of the melodrama of black and white. Yet this version was rapidly becoming anachronistic as the civil rights movement rewrote the text of America's racial melodrama and as African Americans began to place themselves at the center of a maelstrom of history.

The dominant white, middle-class television audience had witnessed much of the melodrama of this movement, from the Montgomery bus boycott to the dogs of Birmingham through the 1965 Watts riots where black rage finally exploded. Through television news and special reports, many viewers had come to see the virtue of racially beset black citizens deserving equality of rights before the law. But through this same medium they had also come to fear the wrath of an aroused African-American populace. Now, popular television entertainment was not only catching up with the news, it was selling a story whose very appearance on television was itself news—a news "event" of an emphatically post–civil rights nature. ABC's purchase of Haley's book in advance of publication was a first in television history. Thus, even though the miniseries appeared three months after the book's publication, the proximity of publication and airing constituted an almost collaborative multi-medium "event" whose only parallel was the "event" of David O. Selznick's much slower (three-year) transformation of Margaret Mitchell's novel. *TV Roots* was thus a unique amalgam: part docudrama (in its purported basis in the facts of Haley's family history), part prime-time soap opera (in its serialization over eight consecutive nights), and part made-for-TV movie (in its observation of one- and two-hour formats adapted to the requisite number of commercial interruptions).

The acquisition of the still unpublished book by ABC was facilitated by David Wolper, a veteran television producer with a track record in documentaries and historical subjects, who acquired the rights and then pushed hard for the innovative television miniseries.[35] He then hired veteran television writers with experience in both the relatively new form of the made-for-TV movie and the tried-and-true dramatic series to begin adapting the still-unpublished drafts of Haley's book. It is easy to "blame" the gross concessions that *TV Roots* made to the majority white audience by hiring exclusively white writers who had made their reputations, like William Blinn, on made-for-TV movies like *Brian's Song* (1970) or the series *Starsky and Hutch*.[36] But to do so is to presume a purity and authenticity of content that, as we have seen, black and white melodrama never possessed in the first place.

Broadcast television circa 1977, no less than popular stage melodrama circa 1852 (or the stage musical circa 1927), needs to be understood on its own, "middlebrow," terms. And those terms consisted, in the case of *TV Roots*, of an episodic adaptation of the format of the uplifting melodramatic values of "made-for-TV movies" where the human soul is often seen to triumph in the face of affliction and adversity. *Brian's Song* (Buzz Kulick, 1971), from a teleplay by William Blinn, is often cited as a "milestone of excellence" (Maltin 1999) among made-for-TV movies and one of the first to have a serious black character (Billy D. Williams as Chicago Bears football star Gale Sayers). *The Autobiography of Miss Jane Pittman* (John Korty, 1974) is similarly cited and was, in addition, the story of a 110-year-old ex-slave. Starring Cicely Tyson, this latter work had already proved to television advertisers that quality made-for-TV films, in the mode of high seriousness, centered on the wisdom of long-suffering slaves, could be a commercially viable phenomenon for the mainstream audience. Indeed, Cicely Tyson had already proven that an African-American star could occupy the center, not just the periphery, of a television drama, crossing over to the majority white audience. Tyson's presence in the African episodes of *Roots*, playing Kunta Kinte's mother, was thus at least as reassuring to white producers as that of the other familiar (white) faces inserted into the narrative to reassure television viewers.

It is all too easy to deride *TV Roots*'s lack of fidelity to Haley (who was himself grossly unfaithful both to history and to the historical record of his family saga), or the producer's many concessions to the majority white audience. It is equally facile to take the reverse tack and praise the remarkable breakthrough it represented in the representation of African Americans. It is more valuable, I think, to ponder the ways in which a relatively new, profoundly commercial, mass medium shaped yet another version of the long-playing American melodrama of black and white, this time in a post–civil rights era.

To watch all twelve hours of *TV Roots* is to be initially struck by the adaptation of the distinctive rhythms of melodramatic pathos and action to the measure of broadcast television. Consider the arresting opening sequence of episode 1, which begins dramatically with Cicely Tyson as Kunta Kinte's mother, struggling to give birth while standing as the father-to-be paces outside. After a successful delivery, and a discussion of the child's name, we cut to a gorgeous sunset followed by a starry night sky where, to the strains of Quincy Jones's Africanesque music, the father holds the naked child high up into the starry sky and names him: "Kunta Kinte, behold the only thing greater than yourself!" A camera flourish that pulls back in a crane shot reveals Omaro and infant framed against the starry sky and the African soil. It is a flourish not unlike those moments in *Gone With the Wind* when Scarlett stands, first with her father and then alone, on a rise near Tara and the camera cranes up and back to reveal the epic grandeur of "the land."

Both Selznick's film and *TV Roots* exalt an idealized land that is home. Indeed, the African countryside is as lush and green as Selznick's California imitation of Georgia—not surprisingly, perhaps, since this episode was actually shot, unlike the others, near Savannah, Georgia. Kunta Kinte's father paces near a beautiful river, animals and children frolic in the credit sequence, and women with naked breasts (a first for broadcast television in this era) are seen from a discrete distance. Both Selznick's film and *TV Roots* end with powerful visual and musical flourishes paying homage to their different homes. But where the camera pullback and musical flourish that end part 1 of *GWTW* conclude nearly two hours of screen time that have lavishly established the way of life of the old South, to be followed by a leisurely intermission, the camera pullback in *TV Roots* punctuates seven minutes of screen time followed by a commercial.[37] Although this idyllic picture of "home sweet Africa" will occupy subsequent screen time, it is never made familiar the way rural Georgia is made familiar in *GWTW* or the way the village of Juffure is made familiar over the first thirty-three chapters (150 pages) of Haley's book. Indeed, so eager were the anxious producers of *TV Roots* to get the story "out of Africa" and onto more familiar American territory (populated with familiar white personalities) that this first seven minutes is immediately followed (after the commercial) by a quick scene in "Annapolis, Maryland, 1715," where a white character never mentioned in Haley's book, Captain Davies, is hired to command the slave ship that will soon transport Kunta Kinte to the new world.[38] The entire first episode is thus marked by a restless intercutting between brief idyllic scenes in Africa and scenes of Captain Davies taking command of his ship, sailing to Africa and purchasing a cargo of slaves.

241

Two factors seem to be at work here in the different rhythm of *TV Roots*: the need to provide frequent mini-climaxes, called "act curtains," before each of the six commercial interruptions that would mark the seventy-five minutes of drama of the two-hour episodes,[39] and the worry that a totally African story, without white faces in it, would put off white viewers. Writers William Blinn and Stan Marguiles, who crafted the first draft of Haley's story for television, are responsible for the policy of introducing conscience-stricken, or at least uneasy-looking, white characters, played by familiar white television actors early on in the story. While these characters—mostly slave traders, slave owners, or overseers who racially victimize Kunta Kinte and his descendants—are not exactly sympathetic, their roles as villains are considerably softened when incarnated by such TV-friendly faces as Ed Asner (*Lou Grant*), Lorne Greene (*Bonanza*), Robert Reed (*The Brady Bunch*), and Chuck Connors (*The Rifleman*). As producer Brandon Stoddard put it, "We made certain to use whites viewers had seen a hundred times before so they would feel comfortable" (Bogle 1989, 340).

Ed Asner is the extreme case. He is given an important role as the conscience-stricken Captain Davies of the slave ship that transports Kunta Kinte to Annapolis (Fig. 6.2). Haley never names this captain or gives his moral dilemma any thought. In *TV Roots* Davies's naive acceptance of the post of captain without fully understanding the nature of the job permits viewers to identify with an essentially decent man whose reluctant involvement in the slave trade leads to his tragic fall. Davies first gazes in wonder at diagrams of

Figure 6.2   Ed Asner, as Captain Davies, reassures white viewers that the story is also about the tragedy of whites. (*Roots*)

black bodies crammed into the ship's hold; later he stares horrified at thumb-screws to be used to torture the "cargo"; finally he becomes fully complicit in the institution of slavery when he guiltily accepts his first mate's offer of a nubile woman slave as his nightly "belly-warmer." As a conscience-stricken white presence fully appreciative of the horrors of slavery, yet unable, by the mistaken beliefs of his time, to believe in the humanity of slaves, Davies be-comes, in his own way, a tragic victim of racism, a ruined man who eventually turns to drink.

Where Alex Haley had had little interest in characterizing the "toubobs" who enslaved, transported, and profited from slaves, *TV Roots* was no more able to keep the story focused on its black victims than George Aiken, Stowe's stage adaptor, had been able to keep the comic white figures of Gumption Cute, or Marks the Lawyer, from "lightening" up and altering the tone of Stowe's story. *TV Roots*, no more than the stage *Uncle Toms*, could not trust its white majority audience to identify with the sufferings of slaves. That the white majority audience did so identify was, in both cases, a surprise to the showmen—P. T. Barnum and George Howard in the 1850s; David Wolper and Fred Silverman in the 1970s—who took a chance on the material.

Bets were also hedged in the use of audience-friendly, well-known black television stars, often more associated with song and dance than drama (Cicely

Figure 6.3 O. J. Simpson, as a traveling African chieftain, is amused by Kunta Kinte's seriousness. (*Roots*)

Tyson as Kunta Kinte's mother, Ben Vereen as Chicken George, Leslie Uggams as Kizzy). Perhaps the most audience-friendly of all these was episode 1's first-listed star, who had volunteered, no matter the pay, for whatever role he could get: O. J. Simpson. That O. J. Simpson made his first "dramatic" appearance in this televisual version of the melodrama of black and white is no small irony given his starring role some twenty years later in television's even more "reality-based" continuation of black and white melodrama.[40] According to a 1976 poll, Simpson, the famous Buffalo Bills running back and first black crossover athlete-celebrity, was America's most popular personality. He flew to Georgia for one day's shooting (Wolper and Troupe 1978, 60). Like Ed Asner, Simpson provided a reassuring familiarity for black and white viewers alike, lest the African sequences seem "too dark, in both tone and skin tone." Simpson plays a chieftain traveling with his daughter, Fanta, whom Kunta Kinte "meets cute" when he awkwardly barges into their camp during his "manhood training." In a vignette designed to showcase Simpson's speed as a running back, he chases after the fleeing Kunta Kinte, effortlessly passes him, then gracefully places him in a head tackle and steers him to a stop. After a comic interrogation in which the worldly and sophisticated man shows amusement at the seriousness of the aspiring Mandinka warrior (Fig. 6.3), Kunta Kinte apologizes and continues on his quest.

The episode, which has no basis in Haley's book, signals to white and African-American viewers alike that the apparent foreignness of the exceedingly patriarchal, Moslem, primitive African milieu, not to mention the extreme seriousness of a story whose hero is about to become a slave, will not be too heavy-going. With a knowing wink the episode introduces a budding romance absolutely foreign to Haley's narrative and the reassurance that even an ethnographic representation of African "manhood training" can be trumped by the presence of the one African-American popular personality to have crossed over into the mainstream.

A related case might be made for the presence of the popular writer and personality Maya Angelou in the role of Kunta Kinte's grandmother, Nyo Boto. This role does occur in Haley's book, but it is transformed in ways that make the patriarchal gender politics of a West African Moslem village oddly reminiscent of a down-home African-American matriarchy. In the book Kunta Kinte goes to visit his beloved grandmother after undergoing his manhood training, hoping to reestablish his close relation to her. He finds, as he has already found in his relations with his mother and younger brother, that he must give up demonstrations of affection for the more distanced respect he now commands as a man. Nyo Boto, as she should be, is cold and gruff with him: "He wouldn't understand until much later that her rebuff had hurt Nyo Boto even more than it did him; she had acted as she knew a woman must toward one who could no longer seek comfort at her skirts" (112). In the miniseries, however, Maya Angelou is a commanding presence, towering over Kunta Kinte in a blue turban and sheath. She catches him gleefully rejoicing in the acquisition of his own private hut, and with a paddle and a tongue-lashing cuts him down to size (Fig. 6.4). In a voice far deeper than Kunta Kinte's own, and speaking, like Simpson, in clear African-American accents, without a trace of the faux African accents the other African characters use, she warns: "You can grow as tall as a tree and I will *still* be your grandmother!" Reminding him that Allah is still considered greater than he, she insists that he make himself useful to his mother and brother. Women still rule, Angelou's performance seems to say, so don't take all this patriarchal Africanism too seriously.

TV Roots also goes to some lengths to establish conventional seventies television gender roles of male action and female romance. As we have already seen, Haley's book makes a point of portraying Kunta Kinte as actively resistant to slavery. The television series follows suit and makes the young Kunta an impetuous hero. The most striking instance of his heroic struggle is shown in the slow-motion sequence depicting his first moment of enslavement on the beach in the Gambia (Fig. 6.1). This prolonged depiction of the young, proud African (LeVar Burton) twisting and turning to struggle against the utterly foreign chains offers an impressively kinetic substitute for the more conventional iconography of a bowed and weary suffering slave. The suffering

Figure 6.4   Maya Angelou, as Kunta Kinte's grandmother, gives him a tongue-lashing. (*Roots*)

of bondage is here portrayed as active resistance rather than passive accep-tance.[41] However, more conventional depictions of male heroism against the foil of female passivity follow. In a later episode, in one of Kunta Kinte's many escape attempts, he arrives at the plantation where Fanta—the "love interest" manufactured out of the encounter with O. J. Simpson's daughter—is now a house slave. Improbably, he urges Fanta to escape with him. When she re-fuses, they argue and the noise of her voice alerts the white overseers to Kunta Kinte's presence, leading to the capture that this time will cost him his foot. Thus *TV Roots* complements, in its own way, Haley's project of rewriting the gender politics of *Uncle Tom's Cabin* by firmly placing a female "Eliza" figure back in the traditional place of the woman who stays "at home" and by placing the "Tom" figure in the role of the heroic male who would, if he could, escape.

As *TV Roots* aired over eight consecutive nights, it imperceptibly shifted its tone from the self-important epic family drama of the first episodes to a final episode that resembled nothing so much as an African-American episode of *Bonanza*.[42] One reason for this shift in tone was the abandonment of Haley's ending. As we have seen, the last part of Haley's book downplays the conven-tional mechanisms of melodramatic action in favor of a more Proustian genea-logical recovery of the lost African past. Under the influence of Haley, who was a consultant on the television production, the original plan for the script of *TV Roots* had been to intercut the drama of Haley's recovery of his past—with Haley playing himself—along with other pertinent events, such as the assassination of Malcolm X, into the main story. However, a simpler, singular chronology was eventually chosen when writers deemed the intercut version too distracting (Wolper and Troupe 1978, 48–49).

Once the writers had abandoned Haley's complex genealogical "rescue of the race" via the return to, and recovery of, Africa, they opted to expand the final episode into a more conventional rescue-escape. Since *TV Roots*, unlike the book, had gotten itself so quickly out of Africa in the first place, the retrieval, on any level, of "home sweet Africa" could no longer be the point of the narrative. The point now was to make the drama of the family's escape to Tennessee exciting and to somehow make this act count as a meaningful "rescue" of the race. Although I believe the episode fails to do this—even on its own television drama terms—the failure is instructive. For it offers the fascinating spectacle of an Afrocentric television drama attempting to rewrite the end of *The Birth of a Nation*. Only this time the heroic rescue of the white family by the Clan becomes the heroic rescue of the black family *from* the Clan.

Where Haley's book positions the return of Chicken George to his family as only a pro forma rescue, leading them to "de promised lan" of Tennessee, we have seen that the action of this rescue as pictured in the book is neither dramatic nor suspenseful and that the home that matters is the increasingly distant but ever-more idealized Africa. Chicken George, as his name perhaps implies, is not the heroic male figure who saves his family from continued slavery; he is simply a link in the chain of the process that keeps the memory of "the African" progenitor alive.

The final episode of *TV Roots*, on the other hand, attempts to stage an exciting rescue by the black father of his sons. In Chicken George's long absence his family remains, even after emancipation, as sharecroppers on "Master" Harvey's land. Some of the sons want to leave but Matilda, Chicken George's wife, and his son Tom insist they stay united as a family until their Daddy returns. This much is in Haley's book. In Haley's version Chicken George returns soon after this family conference and without further ado leads them in a wagon train to Tennessee. In *TV Roots*, however, George's return is delayed. Immediately after Lincoln's assassination, "night riders" begin to terrorize the family in an effort to get them to abandon the land they are farming. Tom, Chicken George's eldest son, goes to the local sheriff with information on who is doing the terrorizing. The corrupt sheriff warns the ringleader, a drygoods store owner played by Lloyd Bridges (another familiar white television face). The upshot is a scene that rewrites Ben Cameron's "inspiration" for the Clan disguise in an antiheroic mode.[43] Informed that Tom has proof of the identity of the night riders, the store owner, who happens to be holding an empty flour sack and a cigar, burns an ominous hole in the

Figure 6.5 A hooded night rider whips Chicken George's son, Tom, before the friendly George Johnson takes over the task. (*Roots*)

sack with his cigar. Cut to a group of men on horseback with sacks over their heads and burnt out eyeholes calling Tom out of his cabin at night for a whipping. Without ever directly naming the KKK, and by positioning their marauding as the villainous threat to the black family, the final episode of *TV Roots* revises *The Birth of a Nation* and, to a lesser degree, the *Gone With the Wind* image of the heroic clan. Instead of heroic southern men defending white women, we see a band of land-greedy crackers terrorizing black families huddled in their cabins.

The night riders' whipping of Tom takes a curious turn, however, when Ol' George Johnson, the white former friend of Tom's family but now the overseer of their work as indebted sharecroppers, takes over the beating (Fig. 6.5). The kindly, diminutive George pretends to cruelty and takes over the whipping in order to save Tom from a beating that we are given to understand might otherwise kill him.[44] The decision to stage a whipping of a free black man by night-riding crackers opened up a highly sensitive iconography no longer safely distanced in the antebellum past. Though the scene takes place in the South, the scene looks like the iconographically more familiar televisual world of the West (partly, of course, because these later episodes were shot, like most television of the era, in southern California). The iconography of interracial violence is always incendiary. Indeed, we have seen how this single

image of the black man beaten by the white was the galvanizing first installment—in Harriet Beecher Stowe's "picture" of the martyred Christian slave—
of the American melodrama of black and white. It is perhaps not surprising,
therefore, that when it appeared outside the historical context of slavery, and
in the more familiar television context of a Reconstruction-era rural town, that
television writers were especially careful to "balance" it with the figure of the
kindhearted and innocuous flagellator, George Johnson. The figure of George
is at pains to demonstrate, against the grain of its black/white, victim/villain
Manichaean binarism, white virtue in the very act of whipping.

George Johnson had been a minor poor white character saved from starvation by the kindness of slaves in Haley's book. In this final episode of *TV
Roots*, however, he and his wife, Martha, become important characters who
suffer alongside the slaves and former slaves and help to redeem the sins of
whites. Their shared suffering is offered as a reassurance to white audiences
against the incendiary potential of interracial violence. We need to come to
grips, however, with what sort of reassurance such an obsessive restaging of
the Tom beating offers. Flagellation in this case depicts a scene in which
things are not as they seem and yet are as they seem—in which master and
slave are in their "proper" historical places and yet not in their places—since
the white man's beating also rescues the black man from a worse fate: a beating unto death.

As in all beating fantasies—that is, in spectacles of beating offered up as
personal daydreams or forms of popular entertainment—the question worth
asking, we have learned from Freud, is where to locate the onlooker. How
does he or she identify in the fantasy? Freud's answer is that the viewer can
be many places at once, sadistically identified with the beater, masochistically
identified with the one who is beaten, or more neutrally situated as an onlooker. This fantasy seems ingeniously, if also transparently, designed to
allay the guilt of seventies white audiences who might identify with the beater
and the rage of black audiences who might identify with the beaten. Tom
suffers by the whip and George, in an interesting twist on the conventional
role of the sadist, suffers by having to wield it. It is surely accidental, but no
less resonant, that the pair of this beating fantasy are named Tom and George.
When Uncle Tom was beaten to death by Simon Legree, he was rescued
"too late" by Mass'r George, the son of his original master. George had vowed
to save Tom when he grew up. Arriving too late to save him, but not too late
for the beaten slave to die in his arms, young Mass'r George is Stowe's reassurance against interracial hatred. Here another master George, one who knows
he is only acting as master, *does* rescue his Tom but perversely by also giving
him a beating.

In the aftermath of this beating, George's wife, Martha, attempts to
soothe Tom's angry son, who is now ready to kill all whites for the whipping

he has seen his father receive. Martha answers, "Then you might as well shoot me.... That's what happens when you start killin' people for being white. Hate 'em for what they done, not for being white. Me and mine is white but we love you—if you'll let us love you." Officially, this expression of white love of black is meant to compensate for the pain of whipping, but there may also be a sense in which it proves that demonstrations of white love can be very painful.

It is precisely at this dire moment, when Tom's wounds are being dressed, his son is preparing for race war, and the patient Tom himself has finally taken up a gun to shoot the next white man who attacks his cabin, that Chicken George returns. A knock is heard at the door and Tom cocks the gun ready to shoot. When the door opens, the intruder turns out to be none other than the long-awaited and long-lost "Daddy." Quite literally, then, Chicken George's belated homecoming rescues his family from a race war that would have been suicidal. Significantly, however, it also rescues the miniseries from taking very seriously the images of interracial beating it had just conjured. For once the lost patriarch has returned, and as if to allay any lingering anxiety about the incendiary possibilities of such interracial violence, the last twenty minutes of the final episode becomes a strangely lighthearted charade bordering uncomfortably on minstrelsy.

To be sure, it is a minstrelsy of ironic black obeisance to white power that ends in the triumph of the black man who poses as dumb. Certainly it represents an odd shift of tone from the original melodramatic mode of high seriousness to the comic stratagems that outfox the crackers, though it is perhaps no different, in its way, than Stowe's way of giving Simon Legree his comeuppance in ghostly hauntings. Once home, the wily Chicken George devises a charade that exaggerates his family's comic inability to stand up to white power. Drawing upon his experience gained in the Civil War, Chicken George's "military operation" exploits their appearance of helplessness. The once proud Tom humbles himself before the ringleader of the night riders, and George Johnson once again plays the role of the cruel overseer who lords it over his black workers, lulling the night-riding store owner and evil senator (Burl Ives) into thinking the uppity blacks have been put in their place. The charade works, mules are extracted from the store owner for the family's getaway, and, after several halfhearted moments of action in which first the blacks and then the whites and then the blacks again get the drop on their adversaries, Chicken George's family, in league with George Johnson and his wife, win the day and set off for "de promised lan." Thus, unlike the book, *TV Roots* turns its final episode into an elaborately plotted rescue-escape that relies heavily on the wiley patriarch's ability to outsmart the whites.

Once in Tennessee, high on a hill with his extended family, Chicken George, with the aid of Tom, recites the litany of the story of Kunta Kinte for the last time. By this time, however, the lesson that is passed on is not so much the pride of the African, and of the African past, but his very American-inflected, and now civil rights–inflected, dream of freedom. The dream is given iconic shape by the sight of the family's wagon train in the new land. In familiar-sounding phrases, George tells how the African gave the dream of freedom to his daughter Kizzy and how she passed it on to him: "Hear me old African—the flesh of your flesh has come to freedom. You is free at last. We is free." It is only at this definitive end point of the story of Kunta Kinte's family that Alex Haley finally appears, walking down a road, reciting the rest of the genealogy that leads up to his own existence, concluding, "And these things I learned, I wrote in a book called *Roots.*"

Thus *TV Roots* skirts the book's Proustian theme of the past recaptured, focusing instead on an image of a land that has not yet been turned into a home, a land that holds the promise of Martin Luther King's dream of being "free at last" but that does not yet have any cabins built on it. It is this land without roots and without history that the end of *TV Roots* asks its audience to believe is "promised." It is a deep irony that the author of a book called *Roots* is himself pictured in so unspecific a location. Despite Chicken George's purchase of land there is no (home) land celebrated in the episode's conclusion. Indeed, in the tension between Malcolm X and Martin Luther King that we have seen to animate Haley's writing, *TV Roots* leans emphatically toward the more assimilationist King. But in so leaning, in presenting a safer, less African-rooted integrationist picture of African-American identity, *TV Roots*—like no other melodrama of black and white we have studied—fails to visualize the crucial figure of home in any one place. Indeed, as we have seen in this final episode, the evasion of Africa as the rhetorically important root leaves the family curiously unsituated, like Haley himself, at the end.

Earlier, as Chicken George and his wife, Matilda, set out with the rest of the family in their wagon train to Tennessee, Matilda looked back sadly at the former slave cabins where she had lived the last fifteen years. Chicken George anticipates her sadness, respecting her apparent feelings of attachment to the only "home" she has known. But Matilda does not produce the anticipated nostalgia. Though she has fond reminiscences of babies born and loved ones buried, she responds to George's statement that leaving is hard: "Hard! Ain't nothin' hard about being happy. This ain't never been our home. It never belonged to us no way. This here's Mass'r Harvey's nigger quarters!" It is on a joyous note of escape, then, that the wagon train leaves the cabin homes behind. Thus black and white racial melodrama as authored, finally, by an African American definitively rejects the rural southern cabin that was Uncle Tom's home, but its televisual mass-media translation cannot find an image to replace what it rejects. The result is an enfeebled rescue in which what is rescued and who does it (Chicken George shares whatever heroism he has with the kindly and equally unheroic George Johnson) is never as clear as it was in *The Birth of a Nation*. Without the strong shadow of "the African" and without the icon of the home "space of innocence," this version of *Roots* loses its energy in compromise. Its accomplishment, however, is to have brought African-American heroes and self-rescuers to the briefly "serious" medium of television.

251

7 Trials of Black and White: *California v. Powell* and *The People v. Orenthal James Simpson*

Introduction

The most familiar and generative icon of the American melo-drama of black and white has without question been that of the beaten and enslaved black man. Ever since Harriet Beecher Stowe enshrined her vision of the sins of slavery in the icon of white hands inflicting wounds on a black body, a paradoxical power was discovered: the very injury that enslaved the black noncitizen became a recognition of virtue that conferred humanity—and eventual citizenship—on the slave. Stowe, and the "Tom" tradition that followed, turned slave narratives into popular commodities, converting the spectacle of black suffering into a melodramatic power (Fig. 2.3). Less than a century later, at the height of the movement for civil rights, the Reverend Martin Luther King, Jr., invoked the power of this racial melodrama when he proclaimed: "We will no longer let you beat us with your clubs in the dark corners. . . . We will make you do it in the glaring light of television" (Garrow 1978, 111).

The "Tom" beating vision—the spectacle of interracial violence that be-comes visible as an infringement of humanity and rights—features the display of black suffering and white force. It is a media-dependent show, needing the pulpit, the stage, the film, or the "glaring light of television" to melodramatize the villainy of slavery and the virtue of slaves, the villainy of segregation, the virtue of black men and women seeking rights. Thus it was only when beatings became deployed as public spectacle—first in the Tom story proper, or later in the televisual struggle for civil rights featuring such "moving pictures" as white police attacking peaceful black demonstrators (Fig. 7.1)—that the power of the beating vision to redress the very suffering it displayed became manifest. From Harriet Beecher Stowe's fictional vision of a beaten and bleeding slave, through the media glare of the civil rights movement, to Alex Haley's vision of his ancestor beaten, enslaved, and ripped from the shore of his native land (Fig. 6.1, 6.5), the beating or mutilation of the black male body has been the generative icon of black and white racial melodrama.

On the night of March 3, 1991, a twenty-five-year-old black man by the name of Rodney King was pursued by police for speeding and running red lights on California Highway 210. When the Los Angeles Police Department took over the arrest begun by the California Highway Patrol, King was brutally beaten by at least four police officers. An eighty-one-second amateur videotape shot by George Holliday, whose apartment balcony was situated across the road from the beating, shows the officers repeatedly striking him with their batons (fifty-six blows), stunning him twice with an electric Taser Gun and delivering miscellaneous kicks (Fig. 7.2). After the beating King suffered from a split inner lip, a partially paralyzed face, nine skull fractures, a broken cheek bone, a shattered eye socket, and a broken leg.

When the video was broadcast first on local and then on national news programs, viewers of all races joined in condemning the police.[1] Rodney King was no Tom-like saint—he was drunk, he had evidence of marijuana (though no PCP) in his blood, he was speeding, he was in violation of parole, and unlike the faithful Tom he did not remain willingly "on the spot" to endure his pain. His beating nevertheless registered powerfully within the iconic Tom-tradition of the black man abused by illegitimate white force. Not since police dogs were unleashed on civil rights demonstrators in Birmingham, Alabama, had the whole nation cringed at a comparable media image of interracial violence.[2] Played against the new political background of the dismantling of affirmative action programs aimed at redressing the past wrongs of discrimination, Rodney King's visible suffering lent him a virtue akin to that of nonviolent civil rights protestors. In the alchemy that confers morality on suffering victims, he gained a strange authority. Indeed, after the riots had destroyed much of South Central Los Angeles, following the verdict that had found the police not guilty in the beating, King would capitalize on that authority, pleading for peace: "Can we all get along?"[3] Only the beaten black man—not the city's black mayor and certainly not its discredited white police chief—had the kind of moral authority to make this plea effective.

However, if this spectacle of a black man cruelly beaten by white police recalled the long and shameful history of slavery and Jim Crow lynching,

Figure 7.1 White police in Atlanta arrest black demonstrators in 1963. (Magnum Photos Inc., Danny Lyon)

Figure 7.2   Rodney King is beaten in the George Holliday videotape. (*Rodney King: What the Jury Saw in California v. Powell*)

Holliday's video was not the direct cause of the riots that would follow. Rather, it was only when this beating scenario became evidence in a court of law, and when this court of law failed to find the police guilty of the beating, that race riots erupted. Indeed, when the interracial beating first appeared in the "glaring light of television," there was a remarkable consensus to condemn it.[4] There was faith on the part of African Americans and civil rights–conscious whites, Asians, and Hispanics that at last hard evidence of racist police brutality in nonwhite communities had been captured and made visible (Watts 1993, 241). There was hope that "the glaring light of television" would expose discriminatory police practices and bring the perpetrators to justice. However, when yet another archaic component of the melodrama of black and white was brought to bear, in an "anti-Tom" defense, to explain the police officers' fear of the animal strength of the "black beast" they had beaten, it became starkly evident that diametrically different, "raced" perceptions of the spectacle of the beaten black man were possible.

The beating of Uncle Tom portrayed on stage and page throughout the antebellum era had resulted in sectional divisions between North and South, contributing to the causes of the Civil War. The 1991 beating of Rodney King resulted in riots characterized by twentieth-century racial, rather than nineteenth-century sectional, conflict. However, this riot differed from previous race riots in its focus on the failure of justice for African Americans. The chant "no justice, no peace" exemplified the rioters' specific contestation of a judicial system with a double standard for whites and blacks. Behind African-American anger at the "King" verdict stood yet another trial, that of a South Central Los Angeles Korean convenience store owner who had, on March 16, 1991, two weeks after the beating of King, shot and killed a fifteen-year-old black high school student, Latasha Harlins, for allegedly stealing a bottle of orange juice. This interracial violence, too, was captured on videotape in the store surveillance system.[5] In November 1991, roughly five months before the verdict in the King beating, Soon Ja Du, the grocery store owner who shot Harlins, was found guilty of murder but sentenced only to probation. Thus, although black and white victims and villains still governed the main contours of the melodrama, in the last decade of the twentieth century racial and ethnic resentments far exceeded any simple black/white binary.

Nevertheless, the key to racial divisiveness in this case remained the realization that in the ritual contest of an American jury trial, the all-too familiar spectacle of the beaten black man was perceived differently by white and black citizens. The verdict in the trial of the police who beat Rodney King—*California v. Powell*—was a crystallizing event in which many African Americans who had viewed the video as "moral capital in a racial struggle" (Watts 1993, 241) were forced to realize that even so blatant an example as this would not result in justice. Indeed, they were forced to realize that, for the jurors with the power to decide, it had transmuted to an entirely different story of whites who were threatened by the contemporary inheritor of the (anti-Tom) scenario of the threatening "black beast."

At this point, and at this point only, the televised spectacle of Rodney King's beating by white police elicited a furious outpouring of violence manifested in looting, burning, and the destruction of businesses perceived to feed off African-American and Latino disadvantage. This violence constituted what I choose to call a race riot.[6] It was instigated by African Americans but joined by a large contingent of Latinos. Since the targets of the riot were just as often Asian-American shopkeepers as whites, this riot, like the trials that precipitated it, was not like the black/white riots of previous eras, although its most immediate precipitating cause was initiated by the perceived black/white conflict of the "King" verdict.[7] It is important to recognize, however, that what actually put people in the streets was never the simple "raw truth" of what the video saw, but, rather, the deeply paranoid, but also deeply accurate, reaction of people of color to the failure of whites (as symbolized by the predominantly white jury in the case) to be moved to sympathy by the spectacle of the beaten black man. For it was only when the tape of the beating became key evidence in a trial whose predominantly white jury *refused to see* the racial villainy of the beating—who refused to see the beating as a trauma whose injury needed to be redressed by the law—that the tape, *as failed evidence in a trial*, became the motive for racial unrest. It was thus the failure of the "Tom-story" to work its familiar magic within the venue of a court of law—the fact that the demonstration of "a state of injury" was not viewed, as it had been during the movement for civil rights, as immediate proof of a denied citizenship—that sparked the violence.

257

Thus until the first jury in the trial of the police in the beating of Rodney King delivered its verdict, it seems possible to say that there was something like a popular consensus about the prima facie interpretation of evidence: the Los Angeles police were caught on videotape using excessive force in the beating of Rodney King. Much the same thing could be said about the later trial of O. J. Simpson: prima facie evidence suggested that Simpson had left a "trail of blood" from the scene of the murder of his former wife and Ron Goldman to his Rockingham home.[8] This is not to say, however, that a color-blind justice was perverted in the case of each trial by the introduction of racial perspectives.[9] Rather, it is to say that initially the perception of interracial violence as seen through the "Tom lens" seemed predetermined in the trial of the police who beat King, and initially the perception of interracial violence as seen through an "anti-Tom" lens—the lens that would immediately operate to darken O. J. Simpson's mug shot on the cover of *Time* as soon as he was a suspect in the case—seemed predetermined in the Simpson case.[10]

However, when the juries in both cases delivered verdicts that flew in the face of the "Tom" consensus in the trial of the police and the "anti-Tom" consensus in the trial of Simpson, the melodramatic plot thickened to create a new public judgment of the juries themselves. In the new atmosphere of trial mania, the American public, having become engaged as trial watchers as never before, felt structurally entitled to judge not only the guilt of the defendants but the racially inscribed guilt of the jurors as well. The "white" jury in the suburban Simi Valley trial of the officers who beat King[11] and the predominantly "black" jury in the Simpson trial[12] were perceived by large numbers of the public, and not only by their racial opposites, as racially motivated villains who refused to see the obvious evidence before their eyes, and who refused to be properly moved by the abundant evidence of interracial violence. Nevertheless, the most dramatic responses were bifurcated along black and white racial lines: black outrage at the 1991 "white" verdict that found the police in the Rodney King beating not guilty ended in riots that left much of South Central L.A. decimated. White outrage at the 1995 "black" verdict finding Simpson not guilty ended in a more law-abiding, but no less devastating, sort of indirect violence: the abandonment of the moral need to redress the wrongs of blacks, whether by voting for Newt Gingrich, moving away from the city, or ending affirmative action.[13] In both cases, black people, and black neighborhoods, have suffered the more serious consequences.

What thus began as public consensus regarding the evidence in both trials ended in a kind of racial Rashomon, the dramatic widening of a "gap in the perception between blacks and whites" (Felman 1997, 773). Each jury read against the grain of an already racially inscribed lens, finding an "anti-Tom" story where initial consensus saw "Tom" and finding a "Tom" story of the racially beset black man where initial consensus saw "anti-Tom." Here, then, was a new version of the long-running melodrama of black and white. In the climactic verdict of the O. J. Simpson criminal trial, watched on the morning of October 3, 1995, by 142 million viewers—more than the previous record set by the final episode of *Roots*,[14] and starring one of the featured performers of that earlier work—the melodrama of black and white became a melodrama of the differences in black and white perception. These perceptual differences were manifest in the public reception of the divergent, yet structurally similar, verdicts putting into place a *mise-en-abyme* of racially invested judgment: raced juries judging facts, trial watchers judging the raced judgment of juries. Finally, there is the subsequent phenomenon of the embittered reactions to the reactions: "black indignation at white anger at black jubilation at Simpson's acquittal" (Gates 1995, 56).[15]

It is not my goal in what follows to accuse or defend the system of justice that has led to this racially divided impasse. Rather, my goal is to more deeply understand the phenomenon of racial melodrama as it assumed the form of a highly mediated trial that was, in part, a reaction to a previous trial and as factions of the public began to see themselves as more legitimate judges of racial victims and villains than the juries themselves. Let us begin by asking, then, about the particular kind of media event that the confluence of Rodney King and O. J. Simpson represented. What were these trials? In what way is a trial already a melodrama and how did America's peculiar history of entertaining itself with stories of racial victims and villains transmute to courtroom racial melodrama?

A "Live" Media Event: Trials in Black and White on Color TV

Trials have always been important flashpoints in American history. Scopes, Hauptmann-Lindbergh, Sacco and Vanzetti, Leopold and Loeb—each in its time was deemed a "trial of the century." Media circuses around trials are not new, either. Indeed, moving image cameras and radios were a familiar feature of popular trials and were not restricted until after the previous media excess of the Lindbergh kidnapping trial.[16] Race trials have been especially important tests of the nation's ability to define itself as a democracy. Dred Scott, the Scottsboro Boys, Emmett Till, *Brown v. Board of Education, California v. Bakke*—all were race trials that have crucially defined the rights of racial minorities in their respective eras. Fictional films of race trials—*The Cheat* (1915, Cecil B. DeMille), *Sergeant Rutledge* (1960 John Ford), *To Kill a Mockingbird* (1962, Robert Mulligan), *A Time to Kill* (1996, Joel Schumacher), *Amistad* (1997, Steven Spielberg), *The Hurricane* (1999, Norman Jewison)—have offered a distinctive subset of movie entertainment rooted in both "Tom" and "anti-Tom" thematics. In the post–civil rights era, the classic version of the race trial has been Harper Lee's 1960 novel *To Kill a Mockingbird*, followed in 1962 by a popular film directed by Robert Mulligan. In this story a black man is falsely accused of rape by poor white southerners, and a noble white defense attorney endures the scorn of his racist neighbors to defend him. Both novel and film are now required in high schools across the nation. They constitute what we might call the contemporary national consensus version of the Tom story. It is a story typically told from either a safe historical or geographical distance, permitting the racial victims and villains to be clearly marked as figures out of a racially prejudiced time (the past) or place (the deep South). We can tell by his sweat in the overheated southern courtroom that the white man has falsely accused the black man. We know that even if justice is not done, that we, as audience-jury, will feel righteously condemnatory about the racial injustice—it is southern, it is archaic. If put in the position of jury we can be certain that we would judge more fairly.

Given the confluence of anxieties over the trial of the police in the beating of Rodney King with the trial of O. J. Simpson in the double murder of Nicole Brown and Ron Goldman, this familiar, fictional form of racial courtroom drama was overtaken by something that was both absolutely new and at the same time very familiar to American culture: the endlessly commented upon, soap opera–like unfolding of an actual trial, broadcast live on television over its fifteen-month duration. The televised spectacle of the trial was new in the sense that televised trials were new to American popular culture. The William Kennedy Smith and Menendez brothers trials of 1993 helped prepare the way for the televised celebrity defendant trial—Smith because of his link to the Kennedys, the Menendezes because they were rich, cute, and based their defense on prior child abuse. Yet even before these televised celebrity trials, trials were familiar ritual forms that as Carol J. Clover (1998) has argued, inform and structure popular American entertainment at the deepest level.

Black and white fictional courtroom drama would continue to be a form of popular entertainment. *A Time to Kill, Amistad,* and *The Hurricane* are recent, moderately popular examples. But the racial melodramatics of works like these would be entirely eclipsed by the more compelling unfolding of a real trial, broadcast "live" into the living rooms, bedrooms, sports bars, and waiting rooms of America. Just as the fictional melodrama of black and white had been eclipsed by the real drama of civil rights in the late fifties and by Alex Haley's merger of fiction and history in the seventies, so the seemingly endless "flow" of the televised Simpson trial became the crucial new medium for black and white racial melodrama in the nineties.[17]

Although the Simpson trial took place in a specific courtroom in downtown L.A., fragments of its "text" were everywhere: on the evening news, in the television and print media tabloids, on all the talk shows, in the endless commentary of experts and nonexperts alike, and, eventually, in the dozens of books written by even its most peripheral participants. Just as the newly expanded melodramatic stage was most central to the phenomenon that was Uncle Tom in the 1850s, so the televised proceedings of the trial emanating from the lone Court TV camera was most central to the phenomenon that was "O. J." in the nineties. Broadcast live on CNN for 631 hours of direct coverage (not counting commentary) and on the cable channel devoted exclusively to trials, Court TV, for over a thousand total hours during a period of fifteen months, as well as on many local network stations, the trial of O. J. Simpson was the central platform from which this new racial melodrama achieved a new kind of cultural ubiquity. The trial "leaped" from the courtroom to the airwaves, and seemed to exist, as Vincent Bugliosi (1996, 27) put it, "in the air"—in the very Zeitgeist of late-twentieth-century America.

In the early 1980s, the Supreme Court had issued a number of rulings that resulted in the admission of television cameras in many courtrooms. In an electronic age, a televised trial was simply presumed to be an extension of the will of the Founding Fathers, who had always "intended" trials to be open to the public. By the early nineties, Court TV was eagerly obliging this "will." A number of high-profile celebrity cases aired live and in their entirety, with accompanying legal commentary—including William Kennedy Smith and the Menendez brothers (1993).[18] *California v. Powell*, the trial of one of the officers in the beating of King, was among those also broadcast live on Court TV in 1992 for over 150 hours. Without a celebrity defendant, however, and until its shocking verdict, it did not attract the same widespread interest as the following year's celebrity-driven trials.[19]

What exactly is a televised trial? The answer bears importantly on the elusive medium of television itself. John Fiske argues that televised media events are distinctly postmodern, hyper-real phenomena in which there is no longer a clear distinction between a "real" event and its mediated representation.[20] Daniel Dayan and Elihu Katz (1992, 4–5) further define media events as television broadcasts that differ markedly from the everyday genres, interrupting the normal flow of broadcasting and everyday lives to produce highly ritualized "live" events. Television differs importantly from film in its ability to transmit events as they occur, to evoke a presence and immediacy impossible in film. This presence and immediacy contributes to its impression of continuous "flow," and to what Jane Feuer (1983, 15) has called "segmentation without closure." Although the medium of television does not always exploit its ability to transmit live events, Feuer argues that the "ontology of the television image" is inherently supportive of at least the impression of immediacy and presence. Television has thus been seen to fulfill itself most when it broadcasts "live" and in real time (Feuer 1983, 13–15). Certainly it fulfills itself as a *mass* medium. The nearly 150 million television viewers who watched the Simpson verdict were an audience measured not as film or theater audiences are measured, in terms of cumulative numbers of viewers over time, but in terms of a single event of simultaneous witnessing. Of course, such an audience is never present "at" the event and can never be assembled in any one place. Nevertheless, the sheer size of these audiences force us to understand the special nature of public events that are "celebrated" in these ways. While the home viewing situation is a far cry from the cafes and salons of Jurgen Habermas's famous description of the public sphere, it may well constitute whatever version of a public sphere that exists in contemporary society.

The televisual event becomes, through the very fact of being televised, a kind of "performance" of the event (Dayan and Katz, 1992, 92–93). The essence of that performance consists of the equality of access that compensates for the loss of what Walter Benjamin (1968) calls aura—by allowing, for example, the home audience to see more of the event from a closer distance than, say, witnesses at a royal wedding situated along the route of its procession can possibly see. (In the case of the televised jury trial, whenever the jury leaves the courtroom the home audience "stays" and hears the arguments, for example, about whether detective Mark Fuhrman's use of the word "nigger" is relevant to the case.)

The television viewer of the media event is thus afforded a totalizing vantage point along with instantaneous interpretation that attempts to compensate for the loss of presence. The live broadcast, displayed in real time, continuous with the time of its viewers, is a continuum that cannot be edited in any of the usual ways.[21] It exists in the particularity of its ceremonial and ritual form (in this case, the adversarial Anglo-American trial). But that adversarial form is exacerbated by the media event's compulsion to make each instant of this time significant, in ways that it would never be to one simply attending the trial in person. Thus continuous interpretation and commentary, in which experts "scored" the performance of the prosecution and the defense for each day, provided viewers with temporary closure for each day's testimony.

Media events can be anything important enough to interrupt the normal flow of television broadcasting. Funerals of heads of state and of celebrities, catastrophes such as the Challenger explosion or the California earthquakes, public hearings, presidential debates, the Olympics—all are examples of (more or less) live media events that (more or less abruptly) interrupt the normal flow of broadcasting. The 1977 broadcast of *TV Roots* was, as we have seen, a quasi-media event: though not live, it interrupted the flow of regular programs and normal routines of eating to bring a previously recorded event to the television public.

The Simpson trial was a media event whose interruption of normal daytime television programming was in itself so prolonged that it took on, for over a year, its own quasi-regular rhythms. The fifteen-month period during which the Simpson case was so insistently "in the air," not to mention the second trial, which, though not televised still managed to be on television (see below), represented an astonishing investment of viewer time. It was a media event that drew into its orbit the history of other recent "race" trials. These included, most obviously, the 1992 Rodney King verdict and its incendiary aftermath; the trial of Damien Williams (one of four black men accused of beating white truck driver Reginald Denny during the riots that reacted to the "King" verdict);[22] and the trial of Soon Ja Du.

What is it, then, about the American jury trial that made it possible for this "leap" into the melodramatic mainstream of popular entertainment? First there is the fact that the American trial is, in many ways, inherently a melodrama. As Alan Dershowitz (1980, xv) puts it, a trial is a cross between a "soap opera, spectator sport and morality play." Successful trial lawyers are those, like Dershowitz himself, who know how to work the popular entertainment value of the form. As yet another observer of the form puts it: "The trial has a protagonist, an antagonist, a proscenium and an audience, a story to be told and a problem to be resolved, all usually in three acts: plaintiff's case, defendant's case, and the third act, consisting of the summations, charge and rendering of the verdict" (Simonett 1966, 1145). Most importantly, the Anglo-American trial always positions its audience as a jury, whether it is one or not, and entrusts that audience with arriving at a judgment (Clover 1998, 257). Cultures that do not have an adversarial system of oral argument before a jury, namely the various civil law systems of the European continent and Scandinavia descended from Roman law, have less melodramatic trials.

The Anglo-American jury trial originated in the illiterate tribal world of Germanic Europe, where oral arguments were presented to laymen summoned for a concentrated period of time to judge their peers. In contrast to the system descended from Roman law, its adversarial structure "played" to a jury occupying the place of an audience that is asked to adjudicate between starkly opposed stories. In the spinning of these adversarial stories something like an "aesthetics of astonishment"—the *coup de théâtre* that suddenly reverses the direction of the proceedings—is produced. This moment of astonishment is the privileged melodramatic moment encouraged, if not always realized, by the adversarial system. In an adversarial "one-performance play" before a jury-audience, the staging of a moment in which the defendant for example, tries on a blood-stained glove is irresistible.[23] As in melodrama, mute signs and gestures are seen to speak more eloquently, and more "truthfully," than language.[24]

In addition to these obvious melodramatic features involving the display of evidence as dramatic signs of guilt or innocence, much has been made of the other "soap opera" components of trials. In the Simpson trial we can cite the simple fact that the daily airings came, for many people, to replace their regular soaps. Like those daytime melodramas, it was a multiple "family saga" with villains and victims, glacial pace, meandering twists of plot, pregnant pauses, paucity of action, and abundance of talk, and with cuts to commercials during recess or after dramatic pieces of testimony.[25] If actual soap opera—whether of the daytime *Days of Our Lives* variety or of the prime-time *Dallas* variety—is an especially protracted form of family melodrama, then it is not surprising that these distinctive "soap" features helped the trial play so compellingly despite—but perhaps also because of—its legalistic longueurs.

263

However, it remains to determine the more precise ways in which the Anglo-American jury trial feeds into melodramatic entertainment. Here, Carol J. Clover's recent work on the trial movie and the "adversarial imagination" of American popular culture proves particularly insightful.[26] Clover argues for the generative cultural power of Anglo-American jurisprudence as an engine for the production of (what I call melodramatic) narrative. The prosecution's job is to tell a story based on the evidence that X happened (e.g., Rodney King was brutally beaten by racist police; Nicole Brown and Ron Goldman were brutally murdered by a jealous O. J. Simpson). The defense has the job of proving that the prosecution's story is wrong, and it therefore argues a different story: Rodney King threatened to overpower the police with every move; L.A. police framed Simpson for murders he did not commit. Its obligation is to show reasonable doubt about the prosecution's story by arguing any number of examples of "not X" (Clover, forthcoming, chapter entitled "Law and the Order of Popular Culture"). Thus, a process of dialectical argument, in which the art of rhetoric flourishes, spins warring stories in an effort to determine a highly contingent "truth."

Whereas the more inquisitorial, European trial aims at a philosophical, idealistic, one-sided notion of truth that is "absolute and independent of the world of sense—Plato's truth," the dialectical, argumentative, rhetorical truth arrived at in the Anglo-American system is "a truth of exhausted possibilities" achieved after all the stories spinnable by the prosecution and the defense have been spun (Clover, forthcoming, chapter entitled "Doubt"). The process of arriving at the "truth of exhausted possibilities" entails a rhythmic alternation between the building up and dismantling of one story after another. Each story spun by the prosecution and even more so by the defense is a provisional hypothesis to be tested by the process of proof. Juries try out these stories to see what they can and cannot explain. As jurors and trial watchers, we temporarily suspend judgment. Sometimes the most paranoid, the most melodramatically "astonishing" story can win out over more ordinary truths. Truth, in the pure philosophical sense, is almost never what an Anglo-American trial produces.[27] The system aims simply at the contest between the least doubtable of stories. Melodramatic stories of wronged innocence are very often the entertaining by-product of this scrupulous attempt to give each side, as the saying goes, "its day in court."

Melodrama, however, wants its audience to believe in something more than the truth of "exhausted possibilities." Like many contemporary critics of the jury trial, melodrama longs for a more pure and absolute sense of truth. It wants to believe in the virtue and innocence of suffering victims. Contrary to what popular trial watchers may feel, however, it is never the job of a jury trial to prove innocence. Innocence, like truth, is legally unrecognizable in the Anglo-American system. A jury acquits a defendant if it has "reasonable doubt" about the prosecution's case for guilt. Acquittal is never an outright testament of innocence. Melodrama, on the other hand, seeks what Peter Brooks calls the "recognition of virtue" through a stark opposition of good and evil. Anglo-American jurisprudence stages an equally stark dramatic conflict between opposed narrative explanations of fact. But the jury's verdict is a highly provisional and contingent "truth" that functions merely as the basis for future legal proceedings and for future argument. Where melodrama believes that a more deeply spiritual truth and innocence will win out, often through the expression of inarticulate signs, the Anglo-American jury trial simply believes it has an adequate system of choosing the least doubtable of stories.

The defense in a trial thus does not set out directly to prove the innocence, or virtue, of its client. However, when the Anglo-American trial becomes the vehicle of Anglo-American entertainment, the subtle distinction between innocence and reasonable doubt about guilt can easily get lost, especially when, in the process of raising reasonable doubt, the defense puts in play a paranoid story of wronged innocence and frame-up. And when a narrative of wronged innocence and frame-up also has recourse to familiar scripts of racially beset victims and racially motivated villains, racial melodrama—playing into deep-seated feelings about the moral legibility of race in America—meshes with the adversarial system of American justice to produce the melodramatic "race trial." When the defense in the trial of the police who beat Rodney King spins the story of beleaguered police as a "thin blue line" protecting citizens from the likes of the animalistic Rodney King, or when the defense in the Simpson trial spins the story of O. J. Simpson as victim of a racist police conspiracy and planted evidence (and of Colombian drug lords who killed the two victims), the epistemological limits of the Anglo-American jury trial uneasily mesh with the quest of melodrama to reveal all.[28] A trial cannot express the totality of truth beneath the surface of reality; it cannot offer a pure recognition of virtue. A trial is a place for law, reason, and fact. However, the adversarial structure of the American jury trial can often treat juries like audiences of a melodrama. Moving them to sympathy is a necessary part of "winning" a case. Thus, as the many "trials of the century" have shown, the adversarial structure can lend itself to Manichaean, "black and white" expectations.

Consider the case of jury constitution. The phrase "all-white jury," used to describe the Simi Valley jury in the trial of police in the beating of Rodney King, conjured up a history of African-American exclusion from the processes of American justice going back to the trials of the Scottsboro Boys in the 1930s.[29] Just as the trauma of the King beating evoked the past trauma of the whippings of slaves, so the exclusion of black jurors in the change of venue from Los Angeles to Simi Valley evoked the past trauma of African-American exclusion from the processes of American justice.

265

The whole history of American race relations—of police discrimination and brutality in Los Angeles, of unfairly constituted, nonrepresentative juries—was similarly brought to bear on the Simpson case, overdetermining the playing of what prosecutor Christopher Darden called "the race card."[30] This metaphor of a wild, cheating card that would contaminate an otherwise supposedly race-neutral realm of objectively weighed evidence assumed that the previous terrain of the case, and of the "King" case that so informed it, *had* been race-neutral. The claim itself was part of the inflammatory, adversarial rhetoric of the case.[31] As we saw in the introduction, the fact that it was Chris Darden, an African-American prosecutor, chosen at least partly because of his race, who made an argument that only a black prosecutor could make, demonstrated how very far the Simpson case had always been from race neutrality.[32]

One reason so many people became addicted to the daily playing of the race card in the Simpson trial was thus the historically overdetermined repetition of melodramatic racial trauma so deeply bound up in the American justice system. As we have seen, the term "playing the race card" was used to stigmatize the introduction of race into the case. Yet, arguably, what was lacking in the prosecution's case was precisely an ability to confront the melodrama of race directly, to acknowledge how much race cards are always in play. Such a strategy might have been able to defuse the defense's paranoid story of racist cops planting evidence against a black defendant. However, once police officer Mark Fuhrman had been tarred by the brush of racism, he, along with the evidence he had to offer, was unceremoniously dropped by the prosecution. No effort to defuse the damage done to the case by the "discovery" of his racism was made. Thus the prosecution tacitly acknowledged the validity of the defense's "race card" even as it accused the defense of cheating by playing it. Such is the complexity of an official ideology of color blindness which demands that all concerned act as if race does not exist. In the absence of structural reforms to eliminate white dominance and black subordination, however, race did color judgment in the case.[33]

When "color blindness" is viewed as not only the goal, but also as the necessary practice of racial justice, "playing the race card" can appear to be cheating. Within a legal system in which all races are presumed to have formal equality before the law, any appeal to race can seem, like the appeal to melodrama, illegitimate and outmoded.[34] Yet precisely because equality before the law has not been reached, these supposedly outmoded appeals to supposedly outmoded racial fears and paranoias make gripping drama. Racial villains and victims deemed archaic thus return in new guises. Simpson's athletic and social success, his historic crossing of the color line to sell products to white and black audiences alike, his possession of a Brentwood mansion where African Americans had once been barred, his possession of a white wife where miscegenation had once been a crime, made him seem race neutral. The fact that his white wife, exclusive Brentwood home, and biracial children had not previously been "issues" worth mentioning—though they had always been compelling visual facts to be noted—was apparent proof of that neutrality. But because "color blindness" was never an accomplished fact, Simpson's race now emerged as an inchoate but morally significant fact that, if it could not directly be spoken, "colored" the entire trial. Race became legible as a mute melodramatic sign—whether of guilt or innocence—just as Rodney King's race became an issue, from the moment he became a fugitive from justice. Simpson's case—now haunted both by the unrecognized "Tom" scenario of police brutality and racism and by the "anti-Tom" scenario of the "black beast" lusting after the white woman—could be read both ways. The scenario of black victimization was spoken directly by the defense. The scenario of the "black beast" was rarely spoken directly.[35] But if it was not speakable, it was acutely visible in all the images of the Simpson marriage and its once-glamorous, now demonized, interracial couple.

Just as the beating and trial of Rodney King had taken place within what Judith Butler (1993, 15) has called a "racially saturated field of visibility," so, too, did the trial of O. J. Simpson take place within a similarly saturated visible field.[36] One of the lessons of the King beating trial had been that the jury was led to see the victimized body of King as itself the source of danger—that there was no neutral "color blind" reading of the visible field. King was interpreted as perpetually threatening to beat the police who beat him; this threat, embodied in the sight of the powerful black male body, made his beating defensible in the eyes of both white police and white jurors. In the visual field, which evokes race without having to directly speak it, the black male body can be viewed as dangerous, threatening, and sexual, *or* as passive, victimized, and downtrodden. The prosecution, relying much too confidently upon the evidence of the videotape that clearly showed King being beaten, presumed that it had impartial evidence in no need of further interpretation. To watch *California v. Powell* is to understand how the prosecution failed to make its case precisely because it had what it thought was incontrovertible *visible* evidence. Commentators during the trial praised the prosecution for their restraint in not making race an issue (Court TV, second day); yet in not making race an issue, in acting as if justice could be "color-blind," they let stand the way race was already in "the field of the visible" for the defense. This failure actively to read the visual field—to invoke the melodramatic "Tom" lens of the suffering black male body beaten by white masters against the "anti-Tom" lens of the defense's presentation of King as a threat—is arguably the reason for the prosecution's failure.

267

Raced Demeanor

In the American courtroom the jury box is typically situated just to the side of the witness stand, affording the jury an opportunity to see the face of a witness from the closest possible vantage point. An adversarial trial offers the jury an occasion for the intense examination of the face and gestures of witnesses and of the defendant who sits at the defense table. Lawyers call the effect of a witness or defendant's appearance under this close scrutiny "demeanor evidence," and it is crucial to a trial. Demeanor is also basic, as Carol Clover shows, to trial movies. Juries and audiences scrutinize demeanor for the most subtle signs of lying—a blink, a twitch, a pause that is a fraction too long or too short. Seeing from the perspective of the jury is most importantly a matter of scrutinizing the demeanor of potential liars.[37] In trial movies proper, this faith in the power of demeanor to reveal whether a witness is lying manifests itself in the repeated and sustained close-up. Clover calls this cinematic fascination with the close-up of the possibly lying face the "polygraphic look," relating the unique faith the American system of jurisprudence puts in lie detectors that measure changes internal to the body with its equally unique faith in the jury's ability to judge the visual evidence of demeanor.[38]

Demeanor evidence is one of the important justifications for a jury trial and an important reason for the jury trial's existence as popular entertainment. And it is in the jury trial's faith in the ability of jurors to read the external, visual signs of demeanor that we may locate the trial's connection with melodrama's quest for moral legibility in a post-sacred universe.[39] Demeanor represents the fascinating paradox of the Anglo-American jury trial. While the trial's adversarial structure of permutating story-spinning denies the possibility of knowing an absolute, philosophical truth, the trial process nevertheless believes the power of demeanor to reveal a perceptually visible truth. Demeanor evidence holds out a compensatory hope that some kind of singular truth will out, that inarticulate signs—the very signs we have seen to be key to melodrama's will to recognize virtue—will succeed where the dialectic of argument fails.

But what is the special role of demeanor when the already intense scrutiny of face and body demeanor becomes an additional scrutiny of racialized bodies? What happens, in other words, when the irrational signs of guilt or "innocence" are put in relation with equally irrational, intersected scripts of

Figure 7.3 The courtroom camera lingers over its famous defendant. (*Court TV: The O. J. Simpson Trial, Volume Two: The Prosecution*)

race and gender? What happens when new forms of media make the reading of raced demeanor available not only to the privileged readers of demeanor placed in the jury box but to a whole nation of trial watchers who can now view this raced demeanor in close-up from the same perspective as the jury? And finally, what happens when the raced demeanor of the jury itself—the faces that are never seen in a televised jury trial—are brought into play through other means?

If the Simpson trial was about anything, it was about a national fascination with the demeanor of its famous defendant (Fig. 7.3). O. J. Simpson had been the the premier running back of his time. With the capital of this fame, he became the first black American athlete to cross over to white product endorsement (Hertz) and to a career in Hollywood as an actor (recall his cameo as a princely African in *TV Roots*) (Fig. 6.4).[40] In all of these roles, Simpson was admired less for his acting than for his relaxed, sometimes cocky congeniality. His "good looks and cheerful demeanor" had already earned him rich dividends from the moment he left the University of Southern California to play for the Buffalo Bills (Toobin 1996, 49). His arrest in the murder of his blond ex-wife was a shock that had already sparked an earlier televised media event, in the form of the famous "low speed" chase across several southern California freeways with police in pursuit of an apparently suicidal Simpson holding a gun to his head. Throughout this event (discussed below), Simpson was treated as a special celebrity. Indeed, Simpson was the most famous person in U.S. history to be put on trial for murder. This fact alone made the case compelling news. However, the fact of Simpson's celebrity was immediately linked to the visible but often unspoken "fact" of his race, and the word "tragedy" was frequently invoked to describe what seemed to be his fall from grace.[41] The famous *Time* mug shot that digitally darkened his skin, froze his movement, and wiped the confident smile off his face represented a radical reversal of the smiling athlete who had so gracefully faked out opponents or leaped with casual ease through airports.

The demeanor of this charismatic, and now emphatically "black," celebrity was, finally, the most compelling reason the American jury-audience could not stop watching the Simpson trial day after long day.[42] Though Simpson never took the stand in his own defense, opportunity to scrutinize his face and body language was abundant during the give and take of the courtroom ritual dialectic: whenever the defense spoke, Simpson was visible in the background. Indeed, the defense complained bitterly that the courtroom camera fixated entirely too much on Simpson during the course of the trial. This fixated gaze perpetually posed the enigma: was this a smiling villain under whose affable facade lurked a wild beast, or a genuinely friendly, falsely accused African American? Avoiding sight of the jury, yet approximating its point of view by broadcasting from a camera position above and behind it, the camera followed the action of the trial in the distinctive scanning gesture of the Court TV camera. When not fixed on the Seal of the State of California located above the judge—and to obviate any possible view of the jury entering or exiting the courtroom—this camera would take in the events of the trial in one continuous shot, tracing a semicircle from above and behind the jury box. The most frequent resting place of the camera tended to be the witness box, to the immediate right of the always unseen jury box. From there it could pan left to frame the judge, further left to frame the defense table (and its fascinating defendant), further left to frame the table of the prosecution. It could then reverse the direction of the pan to return to any of these prior positions. It could also pan back and forth between any two positions—typically between the defense and the prosecution. What it could not do, however, was conventional shot-reverse-shot editing that requires two camera setups. The distance between any two positions would always be measured by a pan whose unseen approximate point of view was always that of the invisible jury box.[43]

At the end of the defense table, at the furthest distance from the jury and its scanning eye—though still easily captured in close-up by the camera's long lens—sat Simpson, who would be caught reacting in the background whenever the camera was trained on the defense. Sometimes, however, the camera would linger over his reactions to arguments or testimony, not framing the main action but framing instead his reactions and participation (Fig. 7.3). The constantly scanning camera afforded an opportunity to examine Simpson's demeanor, first under the sway of the prosecution's case, then, in the trial's "second act," under sway of the defense. Indeed, the quite literal "swaying" of the camera produced an almost visceral effect of the influence of first one and then the other side of the courtroom. Finally, the two warring stories reached a crescendo in the "third act" summation in which both sides told their tales with abundant visual and auditory aids. In all of this rhythmic swaying from one story to the next, from one place in the courtroom to another, and from direct examination to cross, the television audience had ample opportunity to scrutinize a black male body whose race had now become an unspoken yet palpable factor in both the prosecution's and the defense's case.

So hypnotic was this viewing experience, with its alternating rhythms of examination and cross-examination, that it was repeated, in a debased form, in the second, civil, trial, which did not permit cameras in the courtroom and so resorted to staged reenactments of the previous day's testimony. Televisual watchers of this trial found themselves reduced to watching vaguely look-alike actors impersonate the familiar cast of characters.[44] Uncannily, an identically placed camera scanned the action from precisely the same position as the televised first trial. As staged reenactments, these courtroom scenes could have been shot in conventionally dramatic shot-reverse-shot cinematic style. It could have revealed what everyone in the courtroom, and everyone in a trial movie, can already see, namely the jury. It could also have edited out the inevitable longueurs of the testimony. But the continuous, semicircular panning rhythm of the televised "live" trial was by this time so familiar, so much a part of the racial melodrama of demeanor, that these staged reenactments precisely duplicated the laborious pans of the real courtroom camera, scrupulously avoiding any sight of a jury. An O. J. look-alike gave the audience-jury a chance, once again, to scrutinize raced demeanor (Fig. 7.4).

Against Simpson's demeanor, the defense pitted the demeanor of his dead wife—victim, according to the prosecution's story, of Simpson's insane jealousy. "Testifying" from beyond the grave, in recordings of her 911 calls to police during episodes of spousal abuse, Nicole Brown was potentially the most powerful "witness" in the case, to the degree that she could be evoked in the courtroom. In addition, police photos of her battered face were also displayed. These photos, placed by Nicole Brown in a bank vault, were an uncanny reminder of her own belief in the power of her demeanor to speak to Simpson's guilt (Fig. 7.5). Although these pictures and sounds did not equal the "caught in the act" dimension of the Rodney King beating, it was chilling evidence of the violence of her past relations with Simpson.

To establish the evidence of spousal abuse, Nicole Brown's sister, Denise Brown, was called by the prosecution to testify. Except for her dark hair, Denise Brown bore a striking resemblance to her blond sister. The testimony of this still-grieving sister seemed to offer the prosecution a chance to evoke the

Figure 7.4   O. J. look-alike in reenactments of the O. J. Simpson civil trial. (*E! Entertainment*)

Figure 7.5   November 25, 1996: Nicole Brown's battered face "testifying" raced demeanor from beyond the grave. (*Court TV, California v. Simpson*)

Figure 7.6 Denise Brown, sister of Nicole, on the witness stand. (*Court TV, California v. Simpson*)

physical presence of its absent victim. She was examined by Christopher Darden and cross-examined for the defense by Robert Shapiro. She wore black on both days of her testimony, fingered a large gold cross on the first day, and frequently cried. Yet her demeanor did not seem to win sympathy with the predominantly black and female jury (Fig. 7.6). As "the white girl's white sister" (Clark 1997, 290), who had made no bones about her belief in Simpson's guilt, she was too clearly intent to vilify Simpson from the outset. According to lead prosecutor Marcia Clark, instead of aiming for an "understated sincerity" that would go "easy on the tears," prosecutor Darden lost control of his witness, who immediately began to vent about distant incidents of Simpson's sexual brutality. For example, Darden asked Brown about an early incident in which Simpson had grabbed Nicole's crotch and asserted: "This is where babies come from and this belongs to me" (291). Since no foundation for this evidence had been laid, objections were sustained, a sidebar was held, and Judge Lance Ito instructed the witness to stick to relevant issues closer to the date of the crime. Other incidents were related that allowed Brown to describe the altered demeanor of Simpson when he became violent or verbally abusive toward his former wife.[45] When Brown shed climactic tears at the (theoretically) optimum moment of a late Friday afternoon—when the jury would have the memory of her tears resonating throughout the week-end—the prosecution seemed to have scored a victory with her testimony. However, the testimony apparently registered as heavy-handed prosecutorial staging rather than as sincere grief.

Darden's failure to capitalize on this witness cut short the domestic violence portion of the prosecution's case when Marcia Clark saw that it was not playing with the jury (Toobin 1996, 279; Clark 1997, 292). One reason Brown's performance failed with the jury, along with prosecutorial mishandling of her testimony, is what Jeffrey Toobin (1996, 274) has called her "unmistakable hard edge." If Denise Brown seemed an ideal witness for the prosecution because of her uncanny ability to embody her victim sister's suffering, she also had the potential to mirror the many ways in which the "rich white bitch" did not fit the role of ideal victim to a predominantly female, African-American jury. For even though Nicole Brown Simpson was without a doubt the victim of both murder and spousal abuse, the prosecutors failed to forge a strong enough connection between these two forms of victimization. The injury to the white woman victim was ultimately trumped by the seemingly greater injury to a possibly framed black man. White women trial watchers—the group most offended by the verdict—may have seen those same hard edges in the demeanor of Denise Brown, but her testimony still seemed "true" to them. However, the adversarial opposition between warring narratives—prosecution spinning a tale of a jealous husband with a short fuse; defense spinning a tale of racist cops framing a good black man—forced the jury to choose between two opposed forms of victimization: one based on gender, one based on race.

A crowning irony of prosecutor Darden's attempt to use Brown's demeanor to win the jury's sympathy for her sister is that it inadvertently gave the defense a chance to produce exculpatory demeanor evidence for Simpson. When Darden asked Denise Brown to comment on Simpson's demeanor on the night of the murder—when she and the rest of the Brown family had attended a dance recital for one of the Simpson children—Brown had testified that Simpson was not himself, that he had a "bizarre" and "faraway look" in his "glazed-over, kind of frightening, dark eyes" (Court TV, February 3 and 6, 1995). On cross-examination, however, defense attorney Shapiro was then able to show the jury a videotape, taken by chance by a vacationing stockbroker who recognized Simpson outside the recital. The tape showed a happy family scene with Simpson and the various members of the Brown family embracing. Denise Brown herself was even shown embracing a warm and familial Simpson. Thus, the videotape showing the well-known public persona of the congenial "O. J." as paterfamilias, engaging in friendly relations with his in-laws the very night of the murder, ultimately trumped the sounds and images from beyond the tomb of the beaten wife and the virtuous victim demeanor of the "white girl's white sister."

The American jury trial has been widely criticized for its "bread and circus" sensationalism, yet as critical race theorist Patricia Williams has suggested, we need to take its sensational ritual form seriously: "Perhaps it would do us good to own up to the fact that racial passion plays, from the Scottsboro Boys to the Clarence Thomas hearings, have emerged as a uniquely American art form, like jazz—our own stylized form of Kabuki theater. However, reading those passion plays as symbols of a legacy of trauma is a task that few in the popular media have deemed worthy of sustained attention" (Williams 1997, 280). Because of the tendency to "leap" from one medium to the next, culture critics have not always recognized the importance of the melodramatic form operating in such "racial passion plays." Thus they have seemed, as Williams puts it, "unmoored" and "unreclaimed as ritual" (280). However, with the arrival of black and white melodrama into the intensely ritualized medium of the Anglo-American jury trial comes the ability to see what has been at stake in the American racial melodrama all along: the construction of moral legibilities out of deep-seated guilt. And this ritual, as Williams notes, revolves precisely around a racialized "legacy of trauma."

In order to solidify our understanding of these "racial passion plays"—in order to claim them *as* ritual—the final section of this chapter offers an analysis of some of the most iconic and highly ritualized moments of the Simpson and "Rodney King" trials in their resonance with the stylized "America Kabuki" heritage of previous black and white racial melodrama. My goal is neither to exhaust the analysis of these trials, nor to disparage the oddities of the Anglo-American jury trial, but simply to analyze some of their most intensely iconic moments from the perspective of the black and white racial melodramas that have been most in play throughout this book. I want, in other words, to claim the deepest possible ritual connections between these trials and the entire trajectory of the American melodrama of black and white in order to understand both the persistence of racial melodrama and its transmutation here into a new form.

An Iconography of Interracial Violence

Both the "King" and Simpson trials involved the dramatic display of black and white beaten bodies (Fig. 7.1, 7.7, 7.5). Shoshana Felman (1997, 745) has argued that there is a powerful "cross-legal" nature to these trials in which one jury conjures up another. Either unwittingly or by design, the Simpson trial recapitulated the memory, the themes, the legal questions, and the arguments of the King beating trial. Felman argues that what distinguishes historic trials is precisely the propensity to repetition—one trauma repeated, in a new way, in another. The Simpson trial, which seemed to present to its jury a stark choice between two forms of victimization—the gendered (though I would

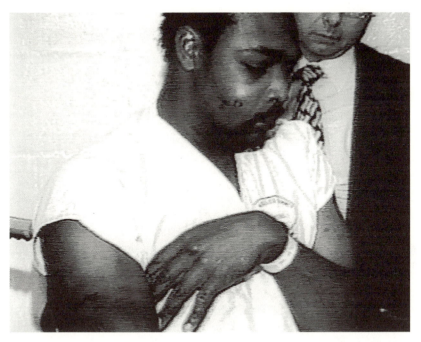

Figure 7.7 Rodney King's wounds exhibited. (*Rodney King: What the Jury Saw in California v. Powell*)

add also racial) victimization of Nicole; the racial victimization of Simpson—conjured up the "ghost" of the King beating trial and delivered a verdict that "answered" the "King" verdict. Where the King beating verdict had failed to recognize King's racial victimization by white police, the Simpson verdict went overboard in recognizing real or imagined police misconduct. Felman's point is that within the adversarial structure of Anglo-American litigation, the warring traumas of the Simpson trial—victimization based on gender, victimization based on race—could not be seen in their totality (Felman 1997, 744). What critical race theorists call the intersectionality of race and gender is invisible to the either/or arguments of law and to the similarly structured Manichaeanism of melodrama. There is thus a "cultural blind spot" at the intersection of these two injuries. The Simpson jury did not accept the domestic violence (gender) evidence as relevant and, in that lack of acceptance, the jurors were seen by many trial watchers to repeat the trauma of the Rodney King beating trial in inverse fashion—to reenact, in other words, an inverse form of racial violence.[46]

Black fury at the King verdict was grounded in the evidence of race-based violence that had been discounted by its jury. White fury at the Simpson verdict was grounded in the trauma of (predominantly but not exclusively) gender-based violence discounted by its jury. We have seen how, in the Simpson trial, the "race card" scenario of police violence toward the black man trumped the "gender card" scenario of gendered domestic violence. This is not to say, however, that racial victimization trumped gender victimization altogether, since the narrative frame of gender-based domestic violence, as we have already seen, was already covertly intersected by race. It is to say, however, that there appeared to be no way for juries, prosecutors, and defense attorneys to acknowledge the intersection of the history of raced and gendered injuries in the case. All they could do was pit one raced or gendered form of injury against another as if a legal win for blacks could only result in a loss for women and vice versa. As so often before, it was as if "all the men were black and all the women white" (Crenshaw 1997, 145–51). As soon as Simpson was charged with murder he could no longer be simply a husband with a history of spousal abuse; he became a black husband with a white wife, the jealous Othello, a man with "glazed-over, frightening . . . dark eyes" who beat her. Thus gender and race were already in play, already intersected, long before the supposed "race card" was introduced into the trial. However, in the adversarial format there was no way to acknowledge this intersection.

In contrast, it might seem as if, in the King beating trial, racial victimization alone was in play. On closer scrutiny, however, we can see that from the very beginning, and probably at its very root, victimization was based on both race and gender. Again, however, it was not directly articulated in the course of the trial. Consider the important testimony of Melanie Singer, the California Highway Patrol officer who, with her husband-partner, Timothy Singer, originally pursued and stopped Rodney King. Singer (Fig. 7.8) was a key witness for the prosecution in the state trial and, somewhat ironically, a key witness for the defense in the federal trial. In both cases, she testified that the Los Angeles police officers who took over the arrest used excessive force. In particular, she testified that Officer Lawrence Powell hit King several times in the head with a power swing of his baton *before* the George Holliday videotape began to capture the beating. Under prosecution examination, Singer explained how she and her husband-partner had stopped King and initiated the arrest, but were pushed aside by L.A.P.D. Sergeant Stacey Koon, who proceeded to stun King with two shots of an electronic Taser gun, after which the police under Koon beat him.

Singer described the chase after King, which was eventually joined by cars from the L.A.P.D. after Singer had radioed for help. As the "primary unit" engaged in the pursuit, it was that pair's job to arrest King. Under examination by prosecutor Terry White, Melanie Singer indicated that although she had requested help from L.A.P.D. units, she had at no point relinquished control over the arrest. When Rodney King's white Hyundai with two passengers finally pulled over, and King exited the car, Timothy Singer ordered King to put himself prone on the ground. When King moved away from the car as if to do so, he dropped his right hand behind his body where Melanie Singer

Figure 7.8   California Highway Patrol Officer Melanie Singer testifies about the King beating. (*Rodney King: What the Jury Saw in California v. Powell*)

could not see it. Alarmed that one of his hands was not visible, and not having had a chance to see if he was armed, Singer drew her gun. She testified that she "told him to get his hands away from his butt. I could not see where his hand was. And at that time he turned his complete body around to where his rear end was facing me. He grabbed his right buttock with his right hand and shook it at me" (Court TV, second day of trial).

Singer then repeatedly told King to place himself prone on the ground. When he did not comply, the L.A.P.D. officers on the scene gathered around yelled at King "to do what she says." When King at least partly complied (he put himself on the ground but not fully prone) Singer approached him, gun in hand, to handcuff him. At this moment Sergeant Koon yelled at Singer to "get back, we'll handle it." It was then that he shot King twice with the Taser gun and Officer Powell hit him with his baton. As Melanie Singer testified: "Officer Powell came up to the right of him and in a matter of seconds he had out his baton and he had it in a power swing and he struck the driver [King] right across the cheek bone, splitting his face from the top of the ear to the cheek bone." (testimony from Court TV's *The "Rodney King" Case: What the Jury Saw in California v. Powell*). When the prosecutor asked her if there was "any reason for the strike to the head," Singer answered, "In my opinion, no, sir." Strikes to the head (or groin) are strictly forbidden uses of

278

"deadly force" in police procedures. Singer later stood to demonstrate the "power swing" that split open King's face. When she stood, the six-foot Singer towered over the prosecutor (and later over defense attorney Michael Stone). In cross-examination, the defense attempted to show that Singer was wrong about the blow to the head, since King's face had not been split in the exact manner she described and since the video had shown no clear blows to the head. She answered, "I saw what I saw, sir."

According to her testimony, the point at which Sergeant Koon intervened in Singer's arrest of King was soon after he saw a sexually provocative black man shaking his "butt" at a white woman. Apparently unaware that the very word "butt" had been introduced by Singer herself in order to get King to reveal the side of his body that was not visible to her, Koon seemed to perceive King's gestures toward Singer as sexual provocation. This is how he describes his intervention in his book, *Presumed Guilty*: "Melanie Singer . . . shouted at King to show her his hands. Recognizing the voice as female, King grinned and turned his back to Melanie Singer. Then he grabbed his butt with both hands and began to gyrate his hips in a sexually suggestive fashion. Actually, it was more explicit than suggestive. Melanie wasn't so much fearful as offended. She was being mocked in front of her peers. . . . Control and common sense were cast aside. Melanie's Jane Wayne and Dirty Harriet hormones kicked in. She drew her pistol, and advanced to within five feet of the suspect" (Koon and Deitz 1992, 33–34).

In the unedited manuscript of this book Koon offered a slightly different version, stressing what he imputed to be Singer's white feminine "fear of a Mandingo sexual encounter" (Fiske 1996, 145). He explained, in an interview after his acquittal in the state trial, what he meant by these words, eventually eliminated from the book: "In society there's this sexual prowess of blacks on the old plantations of the South and intercourse between blacks and whites on the plantation. And that's where the fear comes in, because he's black" (*Los Angeles Times*, May 16, 1992). This improbable imputation of the six-foot-tall and highly professional Singer's *Birth of a Nation*–style sexual fear of King, at the moment he was surrounded by no fewer than eight highway patrol persons with drawn guns, helps explain Koon's precipitous, Clanlike, ride to her rescue.[47] But it is worth noting that in these accounts Koon wildly vacillates between two competing images of the white woman cop: one casts her, somewhat improbably, in the Lillian Gish role of defenseless white woman cringing before the "black beast," while the other casts her as a trigger-happy Dirty Harriet, trying unsuccessfully to fill a man's shoes.

Clearly the white male sergeant can't decide between vilifying the white woman for acting like a man or attributing to her the virtue of the racially beset white woman of anti-Tom melodrama. Interesting also is the fact that the film entitled *Mandingo* (1975, Fleischer), to which Koon seems to allude, and which he is old enough to have seen, is not a film about a defenseless white woman raped by a black slave, but is itself an anti-anti-Tom revision. It is the story of the white wife of a plantation owner who is killed by her husband for having seduced a slave.[48]

As the only significant woman in the case, Melanie Singer's role in both trials became inordinately important as the place where gender intersects with race. Although the dilemma of this intersection could not be directly spoken in the courtroom, it had much to do with how the jury interpreted the raced demeanor of King. In the first, state, trial Singer was cast by the prosecution as the reasonable good cop who saw no reason for the beating that ensued. Her testimony was precise and authoritative but not particularly dramatic and obviously did not move the jury. In the federal civil rights trial that followed in March and April 1993, Singer was not called by the prosecution but, ironically, by the defense aiming to discount her claim that she had seen Powell strike King in the face. The strategy backfired when Singer, the tough professional, broke down on the stand and wept, blurting out in an agonized voice, "There is no doubt in my mind that he struck him in the face. I will never forget it until the day I die" (*Los Angeles Times*, April 18). At this point in the second trial, Singer's testimony functioned to desexualize the butt-grabbing anti-Tom beast and recast him in the Tom role of helpless victim. Ironically, however, it also functioned to sexualize her, not as the defenseless white woman victim of King's "Mandingo" sexual aggression, as in Koon's erroneous imagination, but as the empathic female cop who broke ranks with the "thin blue line" mentality to weep, like Harriet Beecher Stowe before her wept, over the victimized black male body.[49] This time her sympathy registered with the jury. In a trial that had only seemed to have a "race card," Melanie Singer's weeping proved that there was a "gender card" as well.[50]

Iconographies of Chase, Escape, and Rescue

Stacey Koon had cast himself in the role of Melanie Singer's white rescuer from a misremembered "Mandingo-like" scenario of the sexually aggressive black man. The police beating of the black man seems to have originated, in Koon's mind at least, as an exciting rescue of white womanhood. But what are the other elements of melodramatic action that hovered over these two intersected trials? In Chapter 1, I argued that melodrama combines the pathos of suffering with the action of exciting chases, escapes, and rescues that occur either too late or in the nick of time. Trials, however, are mostly devoid of the kind of exciting action that fills so much American popular entertainment. Action in a trial necessarily belongs to past events that are brought to light and elucidated by the trial's process. Recapturing and interpreting the evidence of past events can be the trial's most exciting action.

Figure 7.9 The low-speed "chase" after the Bronco on the Los Angeles freeways. (*Court TV: A Question of Evidence: The O. J. Simpson Hearing*, 1994)

The most exciting events of the King beating and the O. J. Simpson trials—apart from the actual crimes themselves—were the two police chases of African-American male suspects on southern California freeways. The chase after Rodney King was high speed, unmediated (the beating, not the chase, was captured on video), and eventually became evidence in the trial. The chase after O. J. Simpson, on the other hand, was "low speed"[51] (a cortege of police cars followed Simpson and friend Al Cowlings at a respectful distance, ultimately escorting him home), excessively mediated (nationally televised throughout the evening of June 17, 1994), and, despite the fact that it demonstrated Simpson's suicidal frame of mind, was strangely never admitted as evidence in the trial (Fig. 7.9). Ironically, King's low-end car (a Korean-made Hyundai) gave the police a run for their money, while Cowlings's powerful white Bronco never even exceeded the speed limit.

Simpson had failed to turn himself in to Los Angeles police when he was charged in the dual murders and had taken off in the Bronco driven by Cowlings. Reports by Cowlings to police on a cell phone said that Simpson was suicidal and had a gun to his head. Rodney King, driving drunk with a car full of friends, had failed to pull over when he was observed speeding. The celebrity accused of murder may have been attempting to flee the country and was certainly fleeing the media,[52] but he was simply followed by police until he arrived back at his Rockingham home. The poor black man on parole who attempted to flee the police was, in striking contrast, brutally beaten and arrested. It is impossible not to compare these "dual road hunts" (Felman 1997) and the different relations of the two suspects to the law that pursued them.

The O.J. low-speed "chase," which ritualized the very action of the chase, thus recalled Rodney King's more action-packed high-speed chase. In both cases, however, the most deeply embedded prior story—the story that stands behind all the stories, and the icon that stands behind all the other compelling iconography—is that of fugitive slaves "running" from the law that enslaves them.[53] We saw in Chapter 2 that it was the the passage of the Fugitive Slave Act, as part of the Compromise of 1850, that had moved Harriet Beecher Stowe to write her abolitionist novel. While conventional stories about fugitive slaves featured heroic males fleeing the laws that made them chattel in the South, Stowe had radically reversed gender to make her heroic fugitive a woman. The Fugitive Slave Act had disturbed many antislavery northerners because it made them complicit with southern slavery, legally compelling them to return them to their masters. The Fugitive Slave Act thus contributed to a legal and constitutional crisis about the place of African (Americans) in the American polity. The most famous of these fugitives was Dred Scott. In 1857 a majority of southern justices on the Supreme Court had ruled, in *Dred Scott v. Sanford*, that the slave family of Dred Scott, which had not actually run away but whose master had moved them to free states, could not be free in those states. The court ruled that "the African Negro race" were "beings of an inferior order [who] had no rights which white men were bound to respect" and that they did not "belong to the family of nations" (Nash 1990, 495).

O. J. Simpson, in contrast, was a wealthy man whose celebrity had, by all accounts, allowed him to enjoy more freedom, and more exemption from the law, than most people of any race.[54] Nevertheless, from the moment his car appeared surveilled by helicopter on television, "on the run" from police, O. J. Simpson, through his "cross-legal resonance" with Rodney King, acquired some of the moral legitimacy of the fugitive slave (Felman 1997, 767). His famous history as the Heisman Trophy–winning running back, the fleetest man in football, whose skill as a runner had been featured in an impressive cameo in *TV Roots*, lent resonance to this, the most important "run of his life."[55] The fugitive excitement of this run was enhanced for national audiences who watched the chase on national television, and who, ignorant of southern California freeways, did not know—as local L.A. stations did—that the televised part of the "chase" was leading not away from home but back to it (Toobin 1996, 106; Bugliosi 1996, 101).

Approximately 95 million Americans watched some portion of this "chase" culminating in Simpson's arrest. It was this "chase," Jeffrey Toobin argues, that precipitated a tabloid murder into an international incident.

Through its exciting action, television viewers were first hooked by the story. Though watched by considerably fewer viewers than the 142 million who would eventually watch the verdict, it was nevertheless watched by more viewers than had seen that year's Super Bowl (Toobin 1996, 106). Reactions to the chase seemed to begin with what Peter Brooks would call "general astonishment." The nation as a whole stood "astonished" at the live spectacle of a well-loved media personality and once-great athlete running, if not exactly *from* the law, then before it. Gradually, this general reaction would begin to vary according to class, race, and gender. Jeffrey Toobin argues that response very quickly broke down into discrepant black and white displays, with poor black neighborhoods demonstrating enthusiastic solidarity along the sides of the road and on overpasses, shouting and holding signs that read "Go O. J.!" and "Save the Juice" and with upscale white neighborhoods demonstrating little or no enthusiasm.[56] However, Toobin's account of black enthusiasm and white indifference to the run cited above strangely omits notice of the cheering young white men caught up in the excitement of the chase. Nor does it recognize the significance of the fact that even Los Angeles District Attorney Gil Garcetti, whose office had charged Simpson in the first place, and who oddly became one of the live commentators on ABC describing the freeway chase, seemed to empathize with the fugitive, saying, "We're all sharing a very painful experience."[57] Two points are worth noting, however; few women, white or black, were cheering; nor did anyone cheer the police.

The run of the black man "in the face of the law" (Felman 1997, 767) elicited an almost knee-jerk response of support by black as well as white men. It does seem, however, that it was at this moment that the black community began to reidentify with O. J. Simpson—the man who had once said "I'm not black, I'm O. J.," the man who had claimed to have escaped race—as a raced victim. This is the case, despite the fact that the "chase" itself could easily be construed—had the prosecution ever cared to make the argument—as a sign of guilt.[58]

It is a peculiarity of the form of a melodramatic trial that the exciting action of a chase or rescue can never be, as in conventional melodrama, the climax of the story. In place of the ritual suspense of chase, escape, or rescue, a trial provides an entirely different ritual of suspense: the waiting for, and the reading of, the verdict. Verdict readings take place in courtrooms where verbal displays of approval or disapproval are taboo. All the more reason, then, for the melodramatic text of muteness to take over as defendants, defendants' families, defense attorneys, and prosecutors register mutely eloquent postures of relief and vindication or sorrow and outrage. These exaggerated gestures are almost pure moments of theatrical melodrama, functioning much like the tableaux of the nineteenth-century stage. Because the verdict in the Rodney King case took the public by surprise, its reading did not itself register as a memorable iconic moment, though its aftermath of rage certainly

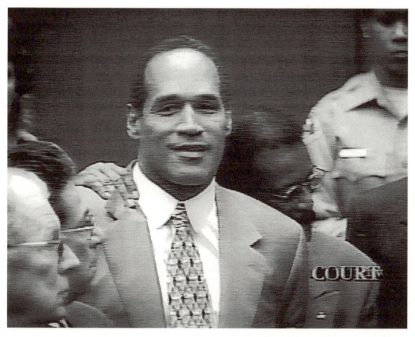

Figure 7.10   O. J. Simpson and his defense team react to the verdict. (*Court TV: The O. J. Simpson Trial, Volume Four: Closing Statements and Verdict*)

did. The not-guilty verdict in the O. J. Simpson case, however, partly because it was viewed as caught up in the melodrama of the previous "King" verdict, was the most viewed moment of television in all the medium's history. Every detail of the response of the defendant and his defense team was remembered and analyzed, since, true to form, the camera remained trained on Simpson. Viewers could thus observe the way Simpson exhaled and half smiled, the way Johnny Cochran standing behind him first slapped his shoulder and then rested the side of his head on the back of Simpson's shoulder (Fig. 7.10); the way, in another view, Kim Goldman, sister of Ron Goldman, let out a howl of pain, and finally, in a gesture of "raced demeanor" that was not seen by the television camera but was much commented on by the media, the way one black juror, upon exiting the courtroom, raised his fist in what some interpreted as a black power salute and others saw simply as the pleasure of being set free.

Verdicts close a trial. However, in the Anglo-American adversarial jury trial they often can offer but a provisional sense of closure that holds only until the sequel of a new trial on appeal. The "sequels" in the case of the "King" and Simpson trials were, in fact, not retrials on appeal but rather new legal avenues of redress. In the case of the trial of the police in the beating of Rodney King, the criminal state verdict led to the federal trial that accused police of violating King's civil rights. This time the verdict was against the police, although the sentences imposed were the minimum. In the case of Simpson, the first trial was followed by a civil suit brought by the Goldman and Brown families that accused Simpson of wrongful death. This time, too, the verdict was guilty. Both "sequel" trials played out much of the same evidence but in each case for reduced stakes. Neither sequel verdict canceled the original verdict. Nor did they have the same galvanizing, racially divisive effects in the general population. The effect, rather, was like an uncanny repetition of familiar material but with different outcomes, setting "straight" the outrage of the first trials but not healing the racial divisions that had been exposed by each.[59] Thus the "rescue" of each sequel trial came melodramatically "too late" to repair fully the damage done by the initial "wrong" verdicts.

Home Sweet Home: Black and White Melodrama's First, and Last, Icon

Melodrama needs a home. Home is the "space of innocence" for its many virtuous victims. Black and white racial melodrama originates in the homey virtues of Uncle Tom's cabin, which render familiar the American "family values" of the African slave. In an era when even many abolitionists (Stowe included) preferred Liberia to Kentucky as the proper home for African slaves, the humble cabin of Uncle Tom worked, against official ideology, to make Tom and his cabin seem quintessentially American. In addition to idyllic flowers, good cooking, nostalgic melos, and interracial amity, a portrait of a black George Washington hangs on the wall in Stowe's "picture" of a happy evening in Tom's cabin—a symbol of the slave's loyalty to things American. Since the icon of home is essential to establish the virtue of racially beset victims, it was no surprise, then, that Dixon and Griffith's "former enemies of north and south" found themselves uniting in protection of their "Aryan birthright" within the confines of this symbol of humble virtue. We have seen throughout this book that the humble home of the black paterfamilias has been ingeniously reworked in the Jazz Age for assimilating whites as a kind of floating plantation in *Show Boat* and as a Lower East Side Jewish home in *The Jazz Singer*. In the next decade, this icon of home would boldly shift to the nostalgicized plantation of *Gone With the Wind* but refunctioned there as a democratic picture of "land and people." In a post–civil rights era, since nostalgia for the good home could never be, for African Americans, the place of slavery, home sweet Africa took over the iconic function as the space of innocence, leaving the ongoing melodrama of black and white without an indigenous locus.

The image of home in black and white racial melodrama is both necessary and deeply fraught in both the Tom and anti-Tom traditions. Tom's cabin,
for all its warmth and cheer, was never his. His bondage leads him to a series
of less and less homelike homes until he finally lands in the Gothic hell of
Legree's Red River plantation. In contrast, the vehemence of Dixon's original
"anti-Tom" message was precisely aimed at refuting the notion that Africans
could ever find a home in America.[60] In both the "Tom" and the "anti-Tom"
narratives, there is a Gothic anti-home marked by the specter of miscegenation: Legree's run-down mansion where he cohabits with his African concubine; Lynch's miscegenational proposal to build a "black empire" with the
white Elsie Stoneman as his Queen.

285

At its deepest level, the icon of O. J. Simpson's Brentwood mansion resonated with the tension between the melodramatic and the Gothic image of
home: that of the happy racial amity figured in Stowe; that of the racial and
sexual violence figured in Dixon and Griffith. Just as Uncle Tom's cabin took
on an iconic significance out of all proportion to its actual importance in the
story, so the seven-bedroom, six-bath house located at 360 N. Rockingham
had an iconic significance out of all proportion to its importance in the trial.[61]
Though it was grand, with swimming pool, tennis court, family room with
built-in glass trophy case, and guest house with an air conditioner that once
went bump in the night, the Brentwood mansion was frequently described
as homey and warm, welcoming and friendly.[62] Rockingham, the symbol of
Simpson's active, outdoor, relaxed southern California lifestyle, the home in
which he had lived for twenty years, was his pride and joy. It was there that
he married Nicole Brown (and it was also there that one of his children from
his first marriage drowned in the swimming pool). Even when the jury visited,
he acted as genial tour guide. Simpson's wives, children, and houseguests
came and went, but the home was always his. In describing the 1989 incident
of spousal abuse that ended in police coming to the house, Simpson accused
Nicole of "tearing up my house" (Toobin 1996, 61).[63] And whatever Simpson's
initial intent in taking off in the Bronco with Al Cowlings, the televised part
of his "run" from justice was, unlike that of the fugitive slave, never anything
but a run toward home.[64]

Indeed, part of O. J. Simpson's celebrity during the long cold years he
played football for the Buffalo Bills in the 1970s was grounded in his oft-
voiced desire to become a free agent in order to return to his southern California home. Sold "downriver" to unglamorous and working-class Buffalo, Simpson was like a modern-day slave trying to buy his freedom.[65] Ever since he
had been a delinquent kid in Potrero Hill, San Francisco, and Willie Mays
did him the honor of trying to keep him out of trouble by showing him around
his home, Simpson had been fixated on the symbolic value of the grand
home.[66] But where Willie Mays had endured racial discrimination in acquiring his home, Simpson had encountered no difficulty acquiring his. Nor was

there any reported flack in his marrying a white woman and raising a biracial family. Like Simpson himself, Rockingham purported to be a carefree, effortlessly integrated symbol of the good life.

At the time of Simpson's arrest, Rockingham sported numerous photos of white female movie stars and a nude portrait of Simpson's then-girlfriend, Paula Barbieri, over the fireplace in his bedroom. But when part of the defense's case entailed a field trip by the jury to both Bundy (Nicole's condominium and the scene of the crime) and Rockingham, Johnny Cochran, with the help of Simpson's daughter by his first wife, transformed the playboy mansion into the home of an upstanding black family man. Simpson ordered flowers for throughout the house, an American flag on the flagpole, and a fire in each fireplace. The pictures of white women came down and a silver-framed picture of Simpson and his mother was placed on the bedside table. Color photocopies of Simpson's black family were also framed and hung. As a crowning touch Johnny Cochran had Norman Rockwell's famous painting, *The Problem We All Live With* (1964), of a black schoolgirl walking to school surrounded by federal marshals, placed at the top of the stairs.[67] The jury trooped by no fewer than twenty-seven pictures of Simpson, his black family, and his black friends (Schiller and Willwerth 1996, 371–74).

The transformation of Simpson's Brentwood mansion was an obvious attempt to recapture aspects of a familial black identity Simpson had long ago shed. At the same time, however, it represented a telling erasure of the integrationist ethic expressed by the Norman Rockwell painting so prominently displayed by Cochran. Indeed, the very blackening that transformed Rockingham paralleled, in Tom-story counterpoint, the anti-Tom blackening of the *Time* mug shot. In both instances a kind of blackface is imposed. In the first instance, the blackening of Simpson connotes a Tom-like racial virtue; in the second instance, an imposed, literal blackface connotes a racialized guilt. Both instances made it impossible for Simpson, after being charged in the murder, to resume the apparently race-neutral persona he once seemed to—but of course never fully did—inhabit.

It is instructive to consider the changing representations of Rockingham in each of Simpson's subsequent homecomings after his two trials. Homecoming, as we have seen repeatedly throughout this study, is a familiar trope of melodrama. It is the happy or melancholic ending where the space of innocence is regained. *The Birth of a Nation*'s famous homecoming remains one of the most emotionally wrenching set pieces of all American cinema, despite our knowledge that the home space of innocence is premised on the exclusion of African Americans as full citizens. Indeed, we have seen in the Tom tradition that the pathos of the fugitive slave is his very lack of a home. Dred Scott could not have any home but that of slavery. Despite the fact that his cabin provides the icon through which the virtuous American home is established, Uncle Tom's only home is with his maker. *Roots*, as we have seen, can only locate the good home in Africa. O. J. Simpson, in strong contrast to all these other Tom-style heroes, represented the quintessentially free, and quintessentially "at home," black man in an integrated world. Police not only did not harass him, they consistently turned the other way at his transgressions, initially even after he became a suspect in the double murder.

Simpson's homecomings after each of his trials focused first on his continued enjoyment, and later on his loss of enjoyment, of this home. After the acquittal in the criminal case, Simpson and his entourage were driven in two white vans (echoing the white Bronco of the low-speed "chase") to his Brentwood home. Like the "chase," this ride too was covered by helicopter and televised. And like the chase, Simpson was cheered by motorists and bystanders along the way. This time, however, the supporters were mostly blacks. Back "home," his joyous return was marred by white neighbors holding up signs of "Murderer" or, more tellingly considering the fact that he *was* home, "Go Home, Murderer." Simpson's homecoming included a party for friends, family, and attorneys that was every bit as mediated, in its own way, as the televised trial had been. Lawrence Schiller, author of Simpson's jailhouse autobiography and coauthor of the chronicle of the Simpson defense, had sold first rights to photos of a victory party to the tabloid *Star* for a six-figure sum, half the proceeds of which went to Simpson. Though some white friends were present, in particular the ever-loyal Robert Kardashian, the picture painted of the party, both in the photos published in *Star* and in Schiller's journalistic account, was of black solidarity and white recoil: many white celebrants moved away to avoid being photographed with Simpson.[68] Thus Simpson's enjoyment of home was muted by a now quite visible racial divisiveness. Simpson's black attorneys attended and enjoyed the party, with Johnny Cochran leading a chorus of "Amazing Grace," while his white attorneys—Shapiro, Scheck, and Neufield—were pointedly absent (Schiller and Willwerth 1996, 681–83).

As white backlash set in, Simpson would find himself closed out of high-paying media interviews and increasingly confined socially to the black community he once eschewed. His second homecoming to Rockingham, on February 4, 1997, after the civil trial that found him guilty in the wrongful deaths of Nicole Brown and Ron Goldman—and ultimately liable to pay $33.5 million in damages to the families of the victims—was a much more somber affair. Simpson was driven by his bodyguard to Baskin-Robbins, where he picked up cookie-dough ice cream for his children, whose custody he had previously won from their white grandparents. Greeted by his children as well as his older children from his first wife and his sister, Simpson now really was the black paterfamilias whose identity had once been stage-managed by his lawyers. However, media attention was now focused on the pathos of his mixed-race children, doomed to learn of the verdict in a civil suit finding their father guilty of killing their mother.[69] In this light, Rockingham—Simpson's "good" home—was increasingly characterized as troubled, besieged, and doomed. Indeed, press accounts seemed to relish in the more and more circumscribed life Simpson led, confined to his "gilded prison" watching "highlight reels from his football glory days," making occasional forays into the still-welcoming African-American community, playing golf on public links, no longer welcome at his country club (*Newsweek*, February 17, 1997, 31). Rockingham, no less than the cabin of the Anglo-Saxons at the end of *The Birth of a Nation*, was now racially besieged.

The next time O. J. Simpson would make national news was again in relation to his home, when Rockingham was placed on the market in November 1997 to pay Simpson's mounting debts. As the realtor who put the house on the market put it, there had never been a house "with this much media coverage." With the house up for sale and empty, it was now possible for the media to investigate the icon in which so much fantasy had been invested. Though the now-empty house had been spruced up, repainted, wall-papered, and generally modernized—even replacing the famous air conditioner in the guest house—press reports dwelled on the "eerie reminders" of the past, in particular, the one room the realtor had not been allowed to spruce up during renovations: Simpson's study. "It's the one room we were never allowed in while Mr. Simpson was still here. . . . We don't know what was in there," said the realtor. "And we never will," commented the *Los Angeles Times* reporter, as if Simpson's ghost was already haunting the house (*Los Angeles Times*, November 16, 1997).[70]

Not surprisingly, no one wanted to buy the four-million-dollar now-Gothic mansion. Though the property was eventually sold, the new owner leveled it to make way for a new home. So the next, and last, time that 360 N. Rockingham Avenue made national news was the day (July 29, 1998) the wrecking ball demolished it (Fig. 7.11). Neighbors and press alike turned out to see the bulldozers tearing down the once grand home. Denise Brown, who happened to be in the neighborhood, attended the demolition to exult: "Simpson is slowly but surely being demolished. This was his pride and joy" (*Los Angeles Times*, July 30, 1998). "Rockingham is history," Simpson himself was quoted as saying, while a neighbor claimed the justice in seeing "malignant things . . . cut away" (*San Francisco Chronicle*, July 30, 1998).

What is the nature of this grim satisfaction taken by neighbors, public, family of alleged victims, and press in this icon of a ruined home? Certainly there is a sense that this destruction of a home that had once been so celebrated offered the only possible payback to the famous owner who had seemingly gotten away with murder. As one neighbor put it: "The man has not paid." In an ostentatiously materialistic southern California world, and in the context of a civil suit that had precisely demanded that Simpson "pay" for his crimes, the destruction of Rockingham offered far more than the sale of prop-

Figure 7.11   The destruction of O. J. Simpson's Rockingham home, "Rockingham Rubble." (*Los Angeles Times*, July 30, 1998, front page, Ken Lubas)

erty to pay damages. It offered an added surplus of symbolic payment: symbolically wrecked in the "Rockingham Rubble" was Simpson's former place in the wealthy white community. His home—the opposite of Uncle Tom's humble cabin, but on some level the fruition of the racial amity Tom's home had once represented—had symbolized the assimilation of an upwardly mobile African-American hero. Now it seemed to symbolize the end of white good will toward that assimilation. Behind it stood the beginning of the end of affirmative action in the state of California and soon throughout the nation.

In black and white melodrama, homes have been deployed as symbols of integration and racial amity (Tom learning to read from his young master, George Shelby, Jr.; Magnolia learning that she "Can't Help Lovin' Dat Man" from Julie and Queenie). They have also been deployed as symbols of apartheid (the humble cabin appropriated to white supremacist ends in Dixon and Griffith). In the post–civil rights era, this apartheid vision of home had become officially anathema. Integration, diversity, and multiculturalism are embraced as social goods. Segregation, racial purity, and white supremacism are social evils. Yet no icon of home has represented the good of black and white amalgamation, no white and African-American "space of innocence" has captured the imagination the way Tom's cabin or Magnolia's show boat once did. No true African-American homecoming has been forged in the iconography of American culture on American soil. Now, at the end of the millennium, against the background of the dismantling of affirmative action measures that had been designed to redress past societal discrimination that had prevented many African Americans from being "at home" in America, the wrecking of this famously assimilated African-American home took on a special resonance as a return-of-the-repressed revenge on one of the few blacks to have obtained this symbolic home.

I do not mean to argue that the overcharged destruction of Rockingham spelled the end of actual African-American assimilation and upward mobility in American culture. I do mean to argue, however, that the Simpson trial now seems permanently linked in the public imagination with a bitter legacy of white *ressentiment* against the perceived "advantages" won by blacks or by any racial or ethnic category of peoples. Thus I would argue that it coincided significantly with an ethos sanctioning the dismantling of affirmative action across the nation.

This perception, symbolized by O. J. Simpson's wealth, celebrity, wife, and home, is perhaps the trial's most serious repercussion. *Ressentiment*, as Friedrich Nietzsche (1956, 127) defines it, is a form of moralizing revenge that is endemic to liberal societies and particularly felt by the weak toward the strong. In this case we observe a peculiar instance of an advantaged racial majority finding it possible to perceive themselves as if they were an aggrieved minority. Affronted by the advantages granted Simpson as a person of color by a jury sensitive to past injustices toward persons of color, white *ressentiment* is exercised against this icon of home.

In this most recent chapter of the melodrama of black and white, resentful whites saw themselves as injured by the behavior of O. J. Simpson just as surely as the white thirty-six-year-old unsuccessful applicant to U.C. Davis medical school, Alan Bakke, had felt injured by the special minority applicants with lower grade point averages accepted into the school over him. Significantly, Bakke did not challenge any of the white students with lower grade point averages who were also admitted over him. Nor did he challenge the enrollment of students admitted because their parents had either attended or given money to the school. In a decision of the Supreme Court, which ordered Bakke's admission to medical school, Justice Lewis Powell argued that although whites could not be considered to constitute a minority likely to suffer invidious discrimination, they might nevertheless *perceive* affirmative action programs that gave preference to minorities as a denial of equal rights that would amount to "invidious discrimination." Ever since the Bakke decision in 1978, affirmative action programs designed to bring the number of minorities into higher education to offset the long-standing effects of white privilege have been gradually chipped away, culminating on July 20, 1995 — just two months before the Simpson verdict—in a vote of the regents of the University of California to end affirmative action at all of its campuses.[71] This action, taken against the opposition of faculty, students, and administrators, ended all attempts to give preferences to historically disadvantaged racial or ethnic groups. Its immediate effect was a dramatic drop in African-American and Latino students admitted to the university.

291

This new sense of white injury feeding the animus against affirmative action was radically different from that experienced by Jim Crow racists who felt threatened by the possibility that black men might enjoy the rights of property, education, and citizenship and ultimately enjoy potential sovereignty over "their" women. O. J. Simpson was the beneficiary of the civil rights movement. He had long been in possession of that property, education, and citizenship and, let us not forget, of a white woman as wife. Indeed, it was the loss of that woman that, according to the prosecution's theory of the case, was the motive for the crime. When the jury failed to convict, whites as a group became the resentful angry spectators of Simpson's life. Seething with a racialized resentment that could no longer find expression in lynching or the refusal of equal rights, these resentful whites took pleasure in the loss of Simpson's privilege as symbolized by the loss and destruction of his home. Thus Simpson became, as Kimberlé Crenshaw (1997, 97) puts it, "a new symbol in a reconfigured vision of racism." In this reconfigured vision there is a denial of overt racial prejudice. It is never the race of the black man that appears to offend; it is the spectacle of his impunity, his arrogance, and, most significantly in the context of the challenge to affirmative action, his possession of what he appears not to deserve to possess: a luxury home and a white woman.

To the extent that Simpson can still play golf and enjoy his family and home, he seems to have won in the adversarial, Manichaean structure of black and white melodrama. To the extent that he cannot do so, he seems to get a measure of the punishment he never received from the criminal courts. While Simpson's race is rarely spoken about, it is a ghostly presence in every story about him, and the underlying reason for all the resentment. We have only to compare the media treatment of Klaus von Bulow—the Danish aristocrat whom many believe to have equally gotten away with murdering his American heiress wife (and who, like Simpson, was also defended by Alan Dershowitz)—to the seething resentment expressed against Simpson. The white pleasure taken in the ostracism of this black man is not the same racism that fueled the ride of the Clan to rescue a cabin, nor is it that which fueled the apotheosis of Scarlett's beloved Tara. But neither is it "color blind"—it is a melodramatic feeling of moral outrage that not just any murderer walks amongst us, but a black villain.

All the Blacks Are (Still) Men, All the Women Are (Still) White, but the Jury Has Spoken

The verdict in the Simpson case has led some critics to declare a crisis in justice. The jury system itself has come under special attack in the wake of a verdict that generated such racial division.[72] One of the most aggressive and far-reaching attacks was made by Jeffrey Rosen (1996). Turning his attack on the verdict into a larger attack on African-American susceptibility to conspiracy theories and on critical race theory's embrace of racial storytelling as a way to redress past injustice, Rosen argues that a reliance on storytelling usurps reason and the rule of law. Citing the Simpson defense as a casebook example of the flaws of critical race theory in fanning the flames of African-American conspiracy theory, he derides the racial storytelling that cast police in an elaborate and unlikely plot to plant Simpson hair and fiber evidence. "The point is that this trial took place in a world that had transcended facts. The insidious genius of the defense strategy was to act on some of the central premises of critical race theory: that racism is institutional and endemic; that there is no need to prove individual acts of intentional discrimination to establish that an African American defendant has been victimized by racism" (39).

Rosen is clear that this breakdown of justice and reason took place with a jury that "looked nothing like America—or like Los Angeles County, which is only 11 percent black" (36). That jury, as we have seen, was composed of eight African-American women, one black man, one Latino man, and two white women. During jury selection Johnny Cochran sought to empanel as many African Americans as possible. Since Marcia Clark disregarded focus group advice that black women resented Nicole Brown and were sympathetic to Simpson, she unwisely did not challenge these jurors, believing that they would be sympathetic to the issue of spousal abuse. Thus Cochran did not object when Clark chose black women jurists and Clark did not object when Cochran did the same. The result was a jury that did not look like America, a jury with a disproportionate number of black women and a complete absence of white men.

My interest in discussing the raced and gendered nature of this jury and verdict is not, like Rosen, to comment on its failure to recognize the "truth" of the case but to situate the verdict within the history of the melodrama of black and white and the many possible ways of playing "the race card." In this light, the absence of white men and the presence of black women takes on enormous significance. For African-American women to find themselves the significant triers of fact in the Simpson case was to become the judge of a racial melodrama that had long written them out of its "primary psychic roles." Although Henry James fondly recalled his childhood memory of *Uncle*

Tom's Cabin in the image of Eliza's ordeal on the ice, it was Tom's "staying put" and subsequent beating death that endured in the tradition, not, as we have seen, the exciting action of the black woman's escape, nor even the drama of her virtuous suffering.[73] The black male and the white male, as both villains and victims, have remained central to this melodrama while the white female has gradually become the *only* woman. Black women had been pushed to the margins as Mammies or disappearing tragic mullatas.[74]

293

To be a visible victim in black and white racial melodrama is, as we have seen, to be worthy of citizenship. As feminist theorists Lauren Berlant, Wendy Brown, and Robyn Wiegman have all shown, the minoritized body is caught up in a rhetoric of injury in which the quest for liberation often translates to an opportunity to show one's wounds.[75] In the case of *The People v. Orenthal James Simpson*, however, the wounds of the white woman were decisively trumped by the wounds of Rodney King and the long, shameful history of injustice toward black men. If, as Shoshana Felman puts it, the history of the failure of justice in the beating of Rodney King haunted the O. J. Simpson trial and made it impossible for the jury to see with any degree of empathy the injury of the white woman, then we need to understand what it means that it was African-American *women* jurors who rendered this verdict. For this was a group whose own wounds have been increasingly erased from the melodrama of black and white. It is regrettable, therefore, but not too surprising, that the verdict in the Simpson trial represented the revenge of black women on what they perceived to be the white woman's privileged occupation of the role of victim. Indeed, the failure of this jury to find Simpson guilty may have had much more to do with resentment toward Nicole Brown than with paranoia about racist police planting evidence.

Invoking racial stereotypes that are also aesthetic stereotypes, Patricia Williams argues that the case would never have attracted the attention it did had Nicole been "overweight or dark-skinned"—or even if she had had "bad hair." Acting out a fascinating mix of sympathy for Nicole Brown's situation as a woman along with resentment that it was her race and blond beauty that incited all the concern for her murder in the first place, Williams draws the lesson that the failure to see how race and gender intersect is a cultural blindness that afflicts us all (Williams 1997, 290–91).

In the rigid binary of victimization by race and gender, there has seemed to be no place for the intersected victimization of black women. The point is not to excuse a verdict grounded in emotion and racial storytelling. It is, however, to understand its logic within the rhetoric of black and white melodrama. For example, it seems fruitless to attempt to defend this verdict, as Nikol Alexander and Drucilla Cornell (1997) have done, as reasonable. It seems more valuable to recognize that it was no more color-blind than the "verdict" in the Senate's confirmation of Supreme Court nominee Clarence Thomas over the charges of sexual harassment leveled by Anita Hill. If ever there was a moment when the melodrama of black and white might have included the victimization of the African-American woman, it was at Thomas's Senate Judiciary Committee hearings. But Hill's dilemma proved inassimilable to the dominant paradigms of race and gender discrimination. The white male "jury" that sat in judgment of that "case" could only perceive victimizations based on race (in which case all the blacks are men) or gender (in which case all the women are white). They could not perceive victimization based on both race and gender; they could not perceive the insidious way Thomas had cast Hill in the role of the white women who falsely accused black men of rape and brought about their lynching; they could not perceive, in other words, black female sexual abuse by a black man. Instead of heeding Hill's claim and coming to see the intersected nature of the black woman's victimization, the all-male, all-white Judiciary Committee "jury" vilified Hill and allowed Thomas to play the "race card" of his supposed "high-tech lynching."

Jeffrey Rosen (1996) is correct to say that the Simpson trial took place in a world that had transcended facts. Prior injustice to black men seemed sufficient in this case to convict the police rather than Simpson; evidence, logic, objectivity all flew out the window once Mark Fuhrman was exposed as a racist and the story of police conspiracy gained credence in the jury's eyes. However, Rosen's verdict that "we will be blind to color or we will be blind to justice" (40) seems wrongheaded. We will achieve a better justice to the degree that we are aware of color and gender (and class) as factors that impinge on justice. This does not mean that we should cynically play one "card" against another, but that we must equip ourselves as a culture with the tools to understand the melodramatic stories of race, gender, and class that do, inevitably, sway both audiences and juries. The Simpson jury was caught, as was Christopher Darden, between what Kimberlé Crenshaw (1997, 104) calls an institutional expectation to perform as if color-blindness prevailed and the recognition that it did not. It does us no good at all to blame this jury, to portray them as unworthy of these rights of citizenship, when they did much the same thing, for almost no pay and a complete loss of respect, that the Senate Judiciary Committee did for a great deal of pay and considerable acclaim.

As Crenshaw (1997, 154) notes, if we confront the different narrative frames of "the black man caught within a potentially racist criminal proceeding" and "the white woman brutalized by her black obsessor," it seems obvious that the first would seem more compelling to a black female jury. What we need to better understand is not the phenomenon of irrational black women blind to evidence carrying out racial payback, but the phenomenon that has placed these women on the margins of the melodrama of black and white in the first place. Why is their only role to choose between feeling sympathy either for the victimization of the black man or the white woman?

It is curious, given the obvious preponderance of African-American women on the jury, and the obvious fact that a "race card" of racial victimization was pitted against a gender card of spousal abuse, that neither side thought of inviting an African-American woman lawyer to plead the case before the predominantly black and female jury. Marcia Clark, the lead prosecutor who had made her reputation prosecuting male stalkers of women, and who had willingly accepted black women on the jury in the expectation that they would be moved by Nicole Simpson's history of beatings by Simpson, could not move what she called the "Twelve Stone Faces" of the jury. I would argue that it was the general neglect of the perspective of the African-American woman, throughout the long history of these melodramas of black and white, that created those stone faces in the first place.

Conclusion
Our Melodramatic Racial Fix

In Chapter 1 we learned that Harriet Beecher Stowe was once thoroughly taken aback by the notion that she had been transfixed by a work of art tarred with the adjective "melodramatic." Contemporary Americans are similarly confounded by the notion that melodrama might be the aesthetic form to which they most deeply respond. Like Stowe, we prefer to duck the term, or at least to claim that it has no current relevance. We have no trouble agreeing today that *Uncle Tom's Cabin* and *The Birth of a Nation* are outmoded examples of racial sympathy and antipathy toward African Americans, or that of the Jazz Age's "posings as black" and "passings as white" are regressive, or that *Gone With the Wind* whitewashes southern history. Even *Roots*'s reconsideration of Tom and anti-Tom from an Afrocentric perspective seems today blatantly overdetermined by its desire to overturn these earlier racial melodramas. If we "appreciate" any of these works today, it is more often for their technical or formal innovations than for the thematics of racial melodrama that once drove them. However, if "yesterday's" outmoded racial melodramas seem hopelessly retrograde, "today's" racial melodramas, as the recent example of race trials in the nineties has shown, prove uncannily gripping. I have been arguing throughout this book that it may not be accidental that the most innovative, form-breaking works of American mass culture have been what I call melodramas of black and white. Every time we are ready to bury the supposedly archaic mode of melodrama it has a way of rising from the ashes. The only difficulty is in keeping track of the many, sometimes unlikely, places where it takes hold.

When I began this project I was under the illusion that I would be able to circumscribe the study of black and white racial melodrama within the medium of film. However, there were two drawbacks to this approach. First, by beginning with the medium of film, I was arbitrarily cutting off the full cultural history of the interplay of the stereotypes of racially constituted good and evil, whose most important inaugural moment was in the mid-nineteenth century appearance of Uncle Tom on the melodramatic stage. Second, by beginning with the racial melodrama that made film a legitimate medium— *The Birth of a Nation*—and its bad old stereotype of the animalistic black man lusting after the white virgin, it became all too easy to blame the negrophobia of Dixon and Griffith on their deployment of "old-fashioned" melodrama itself, as if the "intrinsic" realism of cinema might be able to correct such melodramatic contrasts of absolute good with absolute evil.

The realization that an equally melodramatic, negrophilic Uncle Tom stood behind (and was in continual dialectic with) the anti-Tom of Griffith's film meant that it became imperative to study the larger context of American race melodrama as a whole, both before the advent of film as a dominant medium and long after television had become the new locus of melodramatic "moving images." For, as we saw in the very first chapter, melodrama is not a static, archaic, stereotyping and non-realist form, but a tremendously protean, evolving, and modernizing form that continually uncovers new realistic material for its melodramatic project (Gledhill 1987, 31). It therefore needs to be studied in those places where it has made a difference in the American national imaginary: in the ongoing conflicts of racial virtue and villainy that have taken place in the melodramas of black and white. By admitting this larger context and multimedia perspective, it has been possible to trace a genealogy of the constructions of racial virtue and villainy across the broad workings of the melodramatic imagination in theater, musicals, film, popular fiction, and popular "non-fiction," as well as in media events like the Simpson trial, over a hundred-and-fifty-year history.

Seen in this light, *Uncle Tom's Cabin* was not simply the most influential novel of the entire nineteenth century; it was also, and more importantly, the revival of theatrical melodrama in a new, morally uplifting form that found an unexpected moral legibility in the vision of the suffering slave. And similarly *The Birth of a Nation* was not simply a reaction to and refutation of Stowe; it was also the one work of American film to establish the seriousness, moral legitimacy, and social power of the new medium through the deployment of a melodramatic thematics of race. It accomplished what Dixon's novels and play had only dreamed of doing, and it did so by mixing racial melodrama's Manichaean oppositions of good and evil with the dynamism and novelty of a new medium.

In the Jazz Age, yet another wrenching of the signs of racialized virtue and villainy occurred in the new relevance and seriousness of the stage and film musical. Here elements of the negrophilic Tom melodrama were appropriated through song to the trials and tribulations of newly assimilating white ethnicities. *The Jazz Singer* and *Show Boat* refigured white sympathy for suffering slaves in serious, pathos-filled musicals about white characters who pose as black and black characters who pass as white. During the Depression, another kind of wrenching of the signs of racial virtue lent moral weight and significance to the otherwise flighty and selfish adventures of Scarlett O'Hara, reviving in new ways the image of the good plantation home. Like *The Birth of a Nation* before it, *Gone With the Wind* took the nostalgic appeal of the southern "lost cause" and lost home and made it the basis of national longing. An America emerging from the depths of the Depression, beginning to face the fact of war in Europe, experienced the "event" of this film as a new discovery of its "roots." As we have seen, however, the combined effect of this novel and film did not simply reproduce the negrophobia of Dixon and Griffith. Rather, it appropriated the virtue of suffering slaves to the upwardly mobile daughter of an Irish immigrant.

And so it has gone, with each animation of a new form of black and white racial melodrama also constituting a refiguration of the signs of racial virtue and villainy. If there is a gap in the argument of this book, it is in its lack of an account of the workings of racial melodrama in the era of civil rights. During this period black subjects, for the first time in American history, became the "authors" of black and white melodrama by self-consciously orchestrating the spectacle of their victimization at the hands of white supremacist authority. The civil rights movement was the moment when African Americans began to fashion their own role according to a self-conscious awareness of the power of the public spectacle of racialized suffering. It was also the moment when the melodrama of black and white moved from the domain of fictional text to historical events. After its impact, and even though fictional racial melodramas would continue to proliferate, the most convulsive melodramas of black and white would prove to be those (with at least a claim to be) based in fact. Unfortunately, this vastly important and richly documented historical movement, so crucial in American history, has proved beyond my powers to contain within a tidy chapter. It should be apparent, however, that the civil rights movement could not have achieved what it did without adapting the negrophilic Tom story, even as it attempted to modernize it and masculinize it with new forms of courage and power.

With *Roots* we have seen how the melodrama of black and white was refigured in a post–civil rights era. Rewriting both negrophilic sympathy for the suffering Tom (while radically remasculinizing this figure) and rewriting negrophobic antipathy for the vilifying anti-Tom of *The Birth of a Nation* (by celebrating a patriarchal purity of the male line of descent), Alex Haley's "nonfiction" revised and refigured elements of both traditions. His melodramatic saga of origins, and its TV adaptation, negotiated the tensions between the King tradition of integration and the Malcolm X tradition of separatism to "solve" the problem of a divided racial and social identity. However, where Haley's bicentennial birthday present to America had precipitated an unprecedented unity of black and white feeling for the suffering of the African, the confluence of the "Rodney King" and O. J. Simpson trials pulled these black and white audiences back apart, making the raced viewing from separate "Tom" and "anti-Tom" lenses the very heart of their experience.

299

One important aspect of the story of the American melodrama of black and white in mainstream mass culture is the painfully belated assimilation of an African-American viewpoint, into what was once—in both Tom and anti-Tom forms—an entirely white supremacist cycle. Blacks had been shunted to the edges of the frame, literally made to disappear in a whitening of the screen at the end of *The Birth of a Nation*; with civil rights and *Roots*, however, African Americans finally gained a stake in the cycle—not just as Mammies and Joes but as active figures in their own right. While the presence of an African-American perspective from within the melodrama of black and white has meant that new dimensions of racial sympathy and antipathy have developed, it has by no means meant the end of the Tom/anti-Tom dialectic. Tom stories of racial persecution are still being rewritten from a black perspective both in mass cultural forms as well as in more high art or "experimental" venues (cf. Bill T. Jones's dance *Last Supper at Uncle Tom's Cabin*, or Robert Alexander's play *I Ain't Yo Uncle: The New Jack Revisionist 'Uncle Tom's Cabin'*, in which Harriet Beecher Stowe is taken to task by her characters for the mess she has made of black roles).

Black-authored Tom revisionism thus coexists with white-authored anti-Tom revisionism (the Rodney King beating defense or the Willie Horton political commercials). What stays the same is the elastic mode of melodrama. Melodrama has proven key to understanding the ways in which American mass culture "talks to itself" about the relations between race and gender. It is through the Manichaean logic of good and evil and of victim and villain that melodrama recognizes virtue, expresses the inexpressible, and reconciles the irreconcilables of American culture.

So what, finally, can we conclude about the importance of the mode of melodrama in this study of the melodramas of black and white? We have seen that, contrary to the beliefs of many film critics, melodrama is neither an inherently masculine nor an inherently feminine form, even though the interplay of feminine pathos and masculine action are central to it. We have also seen that it is a democratic, modern form that believes it is on the side of the weak and oppressed against the power of the strong. However, melodrama's democratic "propensity to side with the powerless" (Vicinus 1981, 130) has not prevented it from being employed by resentful whites whose own sense of powerlessness dangerously exaggerated the perception of a black threat to white hegemony. Neither an inherently racist nor an antiracist form, melodrama has effectively been utilized to both ends. Its key, however, is not simplistic, "black and white" moral antinomies, but what stands behind them: the quest to forge a viscerally felt moral legibility in the midst of moral confusion and disarray. Melodrama is organized around a paradoxical quest for a full articulation of truth and virtue at precisely those junctures where truth and virtue are most vexed. It operates, as Peter Brooks (1995) notes, in the register of the special eloquence of the "text of muteness"—in metaphor, picture, and gesture. Ever since pantomime with music appeared on the French stage in the original "melodrames," melodramatic pictures, gestures, tableaux, and music have strained to articulate a virtue that lies beyond the power of words.

Here may lie the special link between melodrama and the melodramatic form of contemporary discourses of race and gender in American culture. For if melodrama can be understood as a perpetually modernizing form whose real appeal is in its ability to gesture toward inexpressible attributes of good and evil no longer expressible in a post-sacred era, then this quality could explain why race has been such a prime locus of melodramatic expression. For race has precisely become an "occulted" moral category about which we are not supposed to speak, yet which, far from disappearing, has remained as central to popular thought and feeling as it was in the mid-nineteenth century. In a post–civil rights and post–affirmative action era, Americans are enjoined to be color-blind, not to notice race. Now that we are supposed to live in an achieved era of equal rights for all, race has joined the category of the officially inexpressible. Mentioning it is considered in bad taste, a cynical ploy, "playing the race card." Increasingly, however, it is within the irrational, fantasmic, and paranoid realm of the melodramatic "text of muteness" that race takes on a heightened mode of expressivity as a dialectic of feelings—of sympathy and antipathy—that dare not speak its name. The mere appearance of the black male body on the film or television screen, for example, creates a heightened expectation for the expression of extreme good or extreme evil. This expectation exists at the level of the mute signs of bodily expression, gesture, and demeanor. All the expressive means of melodrama are brought to bear upon the hyperexpressive body of the black man, in melodramatic configuration with the body of the white woman, and the white man.[1]

Throughout this book, I have resisted the temptation to discuss the many peripheral melodramas of black and white that have contributed to the tradition I have been tracing, but which have not had the same kind of galvanizing influence as the texts and media events treated in these pages. This has meant shunting aside many important theatrical melodramas and musicals.[2] It has also meant shunting aside a great many films that might profitably be understood within this tradition, among them *Imitation of Life* (1934, 1959), *Pinky* (1949), *Home of the Brave* (1949), *The Defiant Ones* (1958), *Sergeant Rutledge* (1960), *To Kill a Mockingbird* (1962), *In the Heat of the Night* (1967), the *Die Hard* and *Lethal Weapon* films of the '80s and '90s, *Mississippi Burning* (1988), *Glory* (1989), *Do the Right Thing* (1989), *Grand Canyon* (1991), *Malcolm X* (1992), *Nightjohn* (1996), *A Time to Kill* (1996), *Rosewood* (1997), *Amistad* (1997) and many more. Because these films have neither radically changed national feeling about race nor innovated new forms of media, they have not figured in this study.

301

In this conclusion, however, I would like to indulge in a brief discussion of two popular films made in 1999, both of which have received Academy Award nominations as I write, and both of which prove, should anyone still need convincing, that Tom and anti-Tom variations of the melodrama of black and white continue to be necessary to the way mass American culture "talks to itself" about race.[3] These works are not the extraordinary melodramas of black and white that I have been tracing, but mere ordinary examples. I make no claim for the special importance of these films as racial melodramas or as works of film art, but I do want to stress, by way of ending, how they demonstrate the enduring power of black and white melodrama to forge crossracial recognitions of virtue in a heightened emotional register in ever-shifting historical contexts. That context, I will argue, is precisely the ongoing dialectic of Tom and anti-Tom in the era of post–civil rights, post–affirmative action America and in the aftermath of the impact of the previous chapters' "trials in black and white." As we saw in the last chapter, the entertainment form of the race trial has nearly usurped fictional courtroom racial melodrama. Who needs *To Kill a Mockingbird* when we have these true-life trials? Nevertheless, the fictional courtroom race melodrama persists and deserves new attention in the wake of the national trauma of these "trials of black and white."

The Hurricane (1999, Norman Jewison) is a literal courtroom drama. It climaxes in a verdict of not guilty delivered on appeal to the long incarcerated middleweight boxer, Rubin "Hurricane" Carter, falsely convicted of murder in 1967 and not exonerated until 1985. *The Hurricane* operates in the *Roots* tradition of the proud, self-reliant, seething black man, aggressively rewriting both Tom docility and the paranoid white fantasy of anti-Tom threat. *The Green Mile* (1999, Frank Darabont) is also about a black man falsely convicted, incarcerated, and executed. It is the fictional story, based on a Stephen King serial bestseller, of a seven-foot-tall black giant awaiting execution on death row in a Louisiana penitentiary in 1935. John Coffey (Michael Clarke Duncan) is to be put to death for the rape and murder of two blond little girls found bloodied in his arms. Although the film does not actually show the trial that convicts the black man, it replays alternate versions of the evidence, putting the audience in the position of an ideal jury. We are privileged to learn, however—as the real jury did not—the truth of Coffey's innocence and the circumstances that convicted him. *The Green Mile* is thus a trial movie without a trial that nevertheless takes us through the paces of the adversarial spinning of stories from a defense and a prosecutorial point of view.[4]

Both films are in the mainstream of the negrophilic Tom tradition. They address the problem of an all-white justice that prefers to frame or accept circumstantial evidence of black male guilt rather than investigate white evil, as if to remind us, in the wake of the resentful white backlash against the Simpson verdict, that it is white juries who have carried out the vast majority of miscarriages of justice. Rubin Carter and his fan John Artis are framed for the murder of whites in a New Jersey bar; John Coffey is not framed, but because of circumstantial evidence his guilt in the rape and murder of two little white sisters is simply assumed rather than proven. In *The Hurricane* the true villain is the New Jersey detective Della Pesca (Dan Hedaya), who first arrests Carter as a juvenile offender and, like Inspector Javert in *Les Misérables*, proceeds to hound him the rest of his life, eventually framing Carter for the murders in the bar.

In *The Green Mile* it is not the prosecutor but the defense attorney who performs this villainous role. Paul Edgecomb (Tom Hanks), the condemned man's kindly jailor-executioner, pays a visit to the attorney who defended John Coffey. In a harrowing scene, this attorney (Gary Sinise), who at first appears to be a just man, launches into a story of a mongrel dog. The dog is likened to a "niggra" that you keep around "because you think it loves you." At the end of the interview the attorney dramatically reveals the mutilated face of his young son bit by such a mongrel dog. At this point it suddenly becomes clear that the fair-minded, loving father who defended Coffey is also a hate-filled racist who believes fervently that "niggras" are dogs. Thus both films pin their unjust verdicts on hate-filled administrators of justice whose racism forms part of a personal vendetta against the animality of black men. Both films then pose the question of whether interracial love is possible in the wake of such white villainy.

In *The Hurricane*, blaming the miscarriage of justice on a single Simon Legree villain meant foregoing the opportunity to tell the true story of how the prosecution built a theory that Carter and his "accomplice" John Artis had committed the murders out of revenge for a prior murder of a black man by a white man.[5] Thus, as is typical in melodrama, the more systemic villainy of the justice system is not depicted, while the lone, personal, melodramatic villain, behind whom stands the memory of Mark Fuhrman, is. Similarly, in *The Green Mile*, it is the resentful, scapegoating defense attorney who is the personal villain, rather than the totality of Louisiana justice circa 1935. Indeed, all the authorities of the justice system we see in this film, except for the racist defense attorney, are kindly, just men. But what is especially revealing in the racism of the defense attorney is its peculiar sense of betrayed love as the animus behind his hate. His Nietzschean resentment of the "mongrel" is grounded in the shock and hurt of the discovery that the dog he thought loved him could attack his child. The rest of the film will work miracles to prove this lawyer wrong.

The possibility of interracial love is thus very much on the mind of both films in the bitter aftermath of the "Rodney King" and O. J. Simpson trials. "Hate put me in prison," says Rubin Carter to the young black man working with three liberal white Canadians for his release; "Love's gonna bust me out." Love in this film is both interracial—it includes the white Canadians—and intraracial—it features the troubled black youth who adopts Carter as a surrogate father. *The Hurricane* thus operates both to express and to soothe black anger by showing that there is both race hatred *and* selfless interracial love. It also operates to soothe white guilt by showing that the judicial system can correct its errors and cancel out the hate of the rogue cop.

Both films can be accused of answering the question of the possibility of interracial love with a rather facile, liberal affirmation. However, what interests me is the way the entire legacy of the Tom and anti-Tom melodramas of black and white are invoked and, once again, reconfigured to new historical contexts in order to answer the post-O. J. question of interracial love and hate. Of the two films, *The Green Mile* offers the most outlandish reconfiguration. As we have seen, *The Hurricane* presents the now-familiar post-*Roots* revision of Tom's Christlike docility in the figure of the proud, righteously angry black man who, like Kunta Kinte, resists becoming a docile slave. In Denzel Washington's assured and underplayed Academy Award–nominated performance, we appreciate the ultimately futile effort Carter makes to cut himself off from the love of family and friends on the outside in order to be hard enough to survive on the inside. In contrast, *The Green Mile* embraces the Christlike docility of the Tom figure, playing this meek stereotype off the seven-foot, three-hundred-pound, hypermasculine body of Michael Clarke Duncan's John Coffey.

John Coffey's complete lack of anger toward the system that executes him extends in a direct line from the Tom tradition. It is worth asking why, in an era in which the figure of the Tom has been so thoroughly discredited by blacks and whites alike, such a Tom-like hero has been resuscitated in the exaggerated body of a black giant. The answer is not simply that white American audiences still need to be reminded of the humanity of Africans the same way they were reminded by the Christlike docility of Uncle Tom. Rather, a reconfigured version of the Tom scenario still seems to be necessary to perform melodrama's moral legibility. In this case, Coffey's virtue and docility works, in conjunction with his hypermasculine physicality, to allow the film (and novel) to safely reenact all the worst anti-Tom scenarios of the paranoid white racist imagination, apparently in order to disavow them. It is remarkable, in fact, just how often Coffey's virtue puts him in a position of reenacting all the worst anti-Tom fantasies of black sexual threat.

Consider Coffey's miracles. The first occurs after he has been incarcerated in Edgecomb's death-row cellblock, named the "green mile" for the green linoleum along which the "dead men" make their last walk. Edgecomb, a kindly white jailor who takes his duty of conducting smooth and swift executions seriously, and who anachronistically displays no prejudice against his seven-foot-tall black prisoner, suffers from a painful urinary infection. Coffey lures Edgecomb to his cell, where he grabs him in what at first appears to be a sexual attack, placing his hand on his crotch. The light grows bright and something magical passes between Coffey and his jailor, leaving Coffey with the pain and suffering that was once Edgecomb's. Coffey then emits the evil humors of the illness in the form of a large swarm of insects from his mouth. Whatever his miraculous healing power consists of, it requires Coffey to embrace the pain, to "take it back" by absorbing it into his own capacious body, reemitting it orally, in a grand Stephen King *coup de théâtre*, as swarming insects.

Soon Edgecomb urinates with enormous relief and, in a comic sequence not found in King's novel, makes love to his wife no fewer than four times that night, later coyly telling Coffey that his missus was pleased by his cure, "several times." Thus potency passes from the black man to the white through this ritual "laying on of hands." If love — both the possibility and the fear of interracial love — is in fact the burning question that black and white racial melodrama is "talking to itself" about in these two films, then *The Green Mile* is the film that most wants to prove the virtue of a selfless, uncarnal black love. It does so, however, by placing its black and white bodies in the most compromising positions, staging the same homoerotic fear it wishes to disavow.

Realizing that Coffey is more saint than sinner, Edgecomb concocts a plan to bring him into contact with the wife of his warden, whose brain tumor has transformed her from a sweet-tempered middle-aged woman to a foul-mouthed harridan. Audaciously springing Coffey from death row late one night, Edgecomb accompanies him to the warden's home. Facing down the warden's shotgun, Edgecomb leads Coffey to the bedridden victim with long blond hair in a white nightgown. She greets him at one moment with obscenity — "Don't come near me, big fucker!" — and at another moment with kindly sympathy for his scarred arms. Coffey kisses her forehead and then her mouth, reenacting every white racist's worst fears of the black sexual attack on the white woman. This interracial kiss seems to want to master prophylactically the white man's fear of black men's sexual threat to "his" woman, as if to cure him of thinking of the black man as a sexual threat. Like the compromising touch to Edgecomb's penis, it disavows the very forbidden desire it enacts, while asserting transcendent purity in the face of lurid, interracial carnality.

"Sucking" up all the woman's pain—and in the process her "dirty" mouth—into his own, Coffey works his miracle under the kindly gaze of Hanks's Edgecomb and the astonished gaze of the warden. The house shakes, the woman's skin clears, and another cure is accomplished. Now it is the wife's turn to initiate contact: she walks over to Coffey, places her St. Christopher medal around his neck, and, reaching way up, embraces him. Once again, the kind of contact that would drive a conventional white racist to murder is provocatively offered up under the guise of a sublime form of transcendent love. This melodramatic spectacle of a black man embracing, and "taking back," the suffering of whites is thus repeated even more obsessively than in *Uncle Tom's Cabin*. It is worth asking, then, why American audiences appear to have warmed their hearts to this story.

Coffey's miracle entails repeated, ritualistic, prophylactic enactments of interracial sexual threats that ultimately function to master white fear and paranoia. In this fantasy, the white woman becomes the sexually obsessed harridan that the white man fears she might become if corrupted by black flesh. But—miracle of miracles—it is precisely the contact with that black flesh that cures the woman of her carnality. Neither a threat to the white man's phallic power nor to the white woman's purity, John Coffey's miracles are there to prove—his defense attorney's claim to the contrary—that the "mongrel" will not screw his master's wife or rape his children, despite what some might infer from his hypermasculine body.

The film's final miracle is not another cure, but in this courtroomless courtroom drama it provides miraculous insight into the circumstantial evidence that convicted Coffey. Inadvertently touching the condemned man in the next cell, Coffey has a vision that allows him to see that it is this man who committed the crimes for which he himself is about to be executed. Coffey uses his powers to orchestrate the premature execution of this condemned man at the hand of a villainous guard. By way of explanation, Coffey then offers Edgecomb his hand, and through this touch Edgecomb attains a true vision of the crime in cinematic flashback that we see this time as well. We learn that what had looked like the rape of two young white girls was another attempt, this time failed, to "take it back."[6]

So much for the black hero's superhuman efforts to rescue whites: now what about the white hero's efforts to save the falsely accused black man? Having ascertained Coffey's innocence, what does Tom Hanks's Paul Edgecomb do to prove *his* love to the black man? This is where this already strange film gets even stranger. When Edgecomb asks Coffey if he wants to run away, Coffey, like Uncle Tom, has no interest in escape. Escape is futile to a Christian martyr fatigued by life's ugliness. It thus remains for Edgecomb to make us feel good about this execution. Of what does this good feeling consist? Certainly it is not happiness; it is a feeling of empathy and recognition of the virtue of the other that permits a good feeling about oneself. This does not mean that Edgecomb is morally exempt from culpability in Coffey's execution. However, in his own sympathetic feelings for the condemned man's suffering, we are invited, perversely, to excuse the violence of the execution since we are led to believe that if anyone else carried it out, it would only **306** hurt more.

Edgecomb asks Coffey what he can do to make him happy before he dies. In a departure from the novel, Darabont's film has him answer, "Ain't never seen me a flicker show." Cut to John Coffey, open-mouthed in reverent awe before the image of Fred and Ginger singing "Heaven, I'm in heaven," in the "Cheek to Cheek" number from *Top Hat* (1935, Mark Sandrich). Back-lit from the projector beam, sitting alone in the prison auditorium, John Coffey murmurs, "Angels, just like up in heaven." Instead of escape, Coffey is given Depression-era American escapism. He will now be ready to die happy if he can only negotiate the trials of the electrocution itself. Indeed, electrocution, "with love," operates in this film much like the last-minute legal rescue that frees Rubin Carter. The greater or lesser humanity of this execution becomes the sole arena with which we are to measure the white virtue of John Coffey's jailors.

Because the procedures of execution by electrocution have become familiar over the course of this nearly three-hour film, highlighting no fewer than three examples, one of which is horribly botched due to the sadism of one of the guards, we are thus in a position to judge a "good" as opposed to a "bad" execution. John Coffey's execution will prove to be "good." But the very fact that we are engaged in such judgments at a time when the death penalty is under attack for having put to death a disproportionate number of innocent black men—as DNA evidence is rapidly proving—suggests that this film is addressing deeper levels of white guilt than the execution of one black martyr in Louisiana.

When Coffey first enters the electrocution chamber, he cringes, losing his nerve before the hate exuded by the family of the victims. But Edgecomb and his team of loving, professional executioners tell him to feel their love instead. Coffey does and can proceed to withstand his execution. When asked if he has anything to say, he apologizes, not for what he has done, since he is innocent, but, much worse, "for what I am"—by which we can only imagine that he means a black giant whose very bodily existence frightens paranoid white racists. When it is time to put on the hood that will cover his face, Coffey again shows fear—like a little child, he is afraid of the dark. Edgecomb leaves off the hood, his one small act of resistance. The execution then takes place, with Edgecomb and his men hiding their tears.

What are we to make of such an interracial act of violence in the name of interracial love? It is as if Master George, at the end of *Uncle Tom's Cabin*, not only failed to rescue Uncle Tom, but wielded Simon Legree's whip in the final beating—with love. It is also as if the relative kindness or brutality of that whiplash were now the only possible measure of white virtue. Like Coffey's cure, we are meant to see that what looks like evil—white guards in a Louisiana prison operating an electric chair to execute an innocent black man—is, no less than Coffey's apparently violent embrace of the two raped and murdered white girls, a misrecognition of virtue.

307

We have seen this kind of white-on-black violence construed as kindness before, in the television adaptation of *Roots*, when the kindly and innocuous George Johnson whipped Chicken George's son Tom in order to prevent a more brutal whipping from a racist night rider. With friends like these, we might say, black men in the negrophilic melodrama of black and white hardly need enemies. As in *TV Roots*, this revision of the white beating of the black man operates to contrast the sadistic, vengeance-seeking crackers who taunt Coffey and tell him they hope it hurts with the loving professionals who hate their job but do it. Either way, the black man gets beaten and executed. The lesson for the black onlooker may very well be that white love, no less than white hate, can hurt every bit as much.

How a still-majority white America is to carry out the incarceration and execution of more and more African-American men, while still feeling virtuous, seems to be the deeper issue at stake in this new twist on the "trial" movie produced in the wake of nineties "trials in black and white." O. J. Simpson's not-guilty verdict, no less than Rubin Carter's, are the great exceptions to the general rule of black incarceration and execution. The familiar answer of *The Hurricane* is belatedly to rescue the falsely accused black man; the less familiar, more audacious, and frightening answer of *The Green Mile* seems to be to make white Americans feel good about putting him to death. Both films are designed to deliver the moral—spoken aloud in *The Hurricane*—that "not all white people are racists" and that "not all black people are murderers." These may not be the most useful lessons for America's fraught history of racial relations, but they are the kinds of lessons that arise directly out of the resentments raised by the King and Simpson trials.

We can legitimately ask why, in *The Green Mile*, John Coffey is never seen working his miracles for fellow African Americans, only for whites. Even Uncle Tom suffered for the "sin" of aiding his fellow slaves. We can also ask, in both films, why it is not the justice system but only the personal villains who are exposed, when surely the pressing issue before the nation is how to introduce real "moral legitimacy" into a corrupt and thoroughly unequal system of justice. We can also ask why it is not possible to tell a story that situates the black man somewhere in between Rubin Carter's righteous anger and John Coffey's abject apology for being who he is. But we already know that the reason is melodrama in general, and Tom and anti-Tom melodramas in particular. As the very logic of the excluded middle, melodrama cannot tell the story of the middle ground.

Conclusion

We have seen over and over that a predominantly white America needs to believe in its own virtue vis-à-vis either the extreme suffering or the extreme villainy of the black male body. Much in both these films is thus predictable. What is striking, however, in *The Green Mile* is the remarkable extent to which the establishment of white virtue rests upon a paradoxical administration of pain and death to the black body. We discover in this film the hidden, insidious logic of the white sympathy extended to the Tom figure: the beating scenario that we have seen invoked in order to establish the humanity of the slave—originally against the antebellum belief of the slave's lack of humanity—contains a deep aggression, a violence that is necessary to the achievement of the Tom's virtue all along. Stowe, no less than Stephen King and Frank Darabont, meant well within the limits of the form of racial melodrama. But the cost of this melodramatic virtue is high: it must act out the very violence that it wants to deter. The suffering of the black man thus becomes necessary to the vision of his humanity. Though white viewers want to think that their crossracial sympathy is a reaction to a violence that is external to themselves, the inescapable logic of the dialectic of the melodrama of black and white is that violence is necessary both to keep the black man in his place *and* to generate the recognition of virtue that seeks to get him out of this place. This is why, in the melodramatic racial imagination, Tom and anti-Tom have been chasing each other's shadows so continually throughout American popular culture. Tom and his alter ego will go on being beaten, it seems; the only real difference is how white and black Americans feel about it.

It is conventional to ask, at this belated point in such an analysis, what can be done? What is a culture critic who studies melodrama to *do* about it? One route, the one most taken, is to blame the stupidity of a public that still buys into melodrama. Consider the following critical despair uttered by a reviewer at the *New Yorker*: "'The Green Mile,' as perhaps you've gathered, is about good and evil, miracles and redemption, and I sat through it in a misery of embarrassment and irritation, increased by the sure knowledge that the movie will give comfort, and possibly even strength, to millions of people. The writer-director Frank Darabont has achieved precisely that combination of the uncanny, the violent, and the stupid which seems to operate like a Mickey Finn on the hard common sense and good humor of the American public" (November 20, 1999, 108).

It might seem natural, then, to conclude this book with a call for an end to the melodramatics of race, with a call for shared responsibility and reasoned solution over the Manichaean adversarial circling of victims and villains that is both a violation of "common sense and good humor." Not unreasonably, this is what Bill Nichols (1994, 39), writing about the melodramatics of the Rodney King beating trial, did by calling for a "break with the identificatory frame that binds us as spectators to a crime in terms of moral outrage rather than social change." Nichols also calls for a break with the "narrative strategy" of news reporting that develops "suspense, anxiety, and catharsis rather than investigation, contextualization, and transformation." He calls as well for a break with the "dramatic curve that constantly runs outrage to ground, short-circuiting efforts to move beyond the frame of immediacy to those structures and patterns responsible for the production of immediacy, sensation and closure." In other words, Nichols calls for a collective decision to rupture the narrative frame and emotional power of melodrama.

309

Nichols is entirely right when he argues that justice—whether for Rodney King or for O. J. Simpson, or for Rubin Carter or John Coffey—cannot be satisfied within the melodramatic frame of a trial. Real, transformative social praxis will necessarily exceed that frame. But what if the very "structure and pattern" that produces "suspense, anxiety and catharsis" is the same structure and pattern that produces our very sense of justice? What, in other words, if melodrama is deeply ingrained in the habit and tradition of American culture? If so, it will not be possible to break the narrative frame of melodrama by calling either for common sense, or for more Brechtian forms of rupture. Such calls have been made in the past, but the popular "vernacular" of American melodrama is far too powerful, far too moving, far too much a part of the very essence of drama itself (Bentley 1964), and far too nimble in its ability to "leap" from form to form, to be eschewed by popular storytellers or image producers. In other words, there are, unfortunately, deeper reasons for the existence of a film like *The Green Mile* than the stupidity of an American public consuming films as if they were "Mickey" Finns, and we have explored many of them in this book. Calls for the end of melodramatics almost never account for the deeply embedded nature of the form or for the profound melodramatization of the stories white and black Americans tell themselves about racial villains and victims.

If I have tried not to make this book a rehabilitation or defense of melodrama as an aesthetic form, it is because I certainly recognize its "evil" effects, its simplifications, its Manichaean polarities, its inherent violence. Yet if I have also tried hard not to (melodramatically) judge melodrama as the cause of our racial hatreds and resentments, it is because I have started with my own vulnerability to it. Beginning with my own reaction to the "wrong" verdict in the Simpson case, I have tried not to excoriate melodrama but to get inside its logic to see its insidious power. The worst thing we can do to melodrama is to condescend to it. The next worst thing we can do is to ignore it. Faced with the powerful influence of the melodrama of black and white, and with its often regressive influence in American culture, perhaps the best thing we can do is to name and recognize melodrama when we see it, and analytically to recognize the power of its ability to make us feel the aggrieved virtue of racial sufferers, whether as blacks or as whites. The melodrama of black and white is so deeply embedded in the structure of American popular culture that the kind of break Nichols calls for inevitably amounts to a break with the

Conclusion

popular itself. Thus, while I agree with the outraged sentiment of the *New Yorker* critic, and with Nichols's urgent sense of the need to be critical of moralizing identificatory frames, I seriously doubt that it will be possible for popular culture to break with melodrama's obsession with past injury as a way of establishing moral legitimacy. Until we grasp the full extent of the melodramatic imagination of race, and all of our susceptibilities to it, we will continue to be, like Harriet Beecher Stowe, in a profound state of denial as to what we are about.

310

Notes

Preface

1. In addition to the many popular pundits, Shoshana Felman (1997) is one of many scholars to make this claim.

2. Moral legibility is Peter Brooks's (1995, 20) term for melodrama's propensity to reveal the existence of a moral universe behind appearances. I am indebted to Misa Oyama for the phrase "racial legibility," adapted from Brooks.

3. Fiedler (1979, 84) writes about a tradition he likes to call the "inadvertent epic," but which I consider to be better identified as racial melodrama. This tradition oscillates between negrophilic Tom sympathy and negrophobic "anti-Tom" antipathy: "works which long endure win our assent not rationally and logically, like history, philosophy or science, but viscerally, passionately, like rituals in primitive societies or dreams in our own. They tend, that is to say, to reinforce our wildest paranoid delusions, along with our most utopian hopes about the relations of races, sexes and generations: self-indulgent reveries, from which we rouse ourselves in embarrassment, or nightmares from which we wake in terror—but which continue to resonate in our waking heads, whether we be racists, chauvinists, fascists and practicing sadists, or right-minded liberals, pacifists, feminists and twice-born Christians."

Introduction

1. As George Lipsitz has noted, white complaints against blacks could be situated in the present, while black grievances were relegated to distant memory (Lipsitz 1998, 222).

2. Darden said this in the context of objecting to Cochran's goal of inflaming the passions of the jury. In invoking the racially inflaming notion of Simpson's "fetish for blond-haired white women," however, Darden was doing the very thing he was claiming to avoid (Toobin 1996, 293).

3. The lead defense attorney, possibly chosen for *his* race, made the charge once Darden was announced as part of the prosecution team (Darden 1996, 170–71).

4. Eric Lott's chapter on the arrival of *Uncle Tom's Cabin* in the budding American culture industry demonstrates how James's description of the play was also an apt description of the new "melodramatic reproducibility" of a work that was both everywhere and nowhere at once. James's metaphor of the leaping fish referred to a P. T. Barnum oddity, a performing fish. See my discussion of Lott and James in Chapter 2. Susan Gillman's work on American race melodrama is another pioneering study. In a number of remarkable articles covering such seemingly diverse topics as the late writings of Mark Twain, the occult writings of African-American novelist Pauline Hopkins (1996), and the sociology of W.E.B. Du Bois (1992), Gillman discovers a constant thread of melodramatic articulation at the intersection of the literary and the scientific and of high and popular culture. See her forthcoming book *American Race Melodrama, 1877–1915*. Lauren Berlant's ongoing work on sentiment and the "female complaint" is another important influence.

Chapter One

1. The Oxford English Dictionary defines melodrama as follows: "In early 19th century use, a stage-play (usually romantic and sentimental in plot and incident) in which songs were interspersed and in which the action was accompanied by orchestral music appropriate to the situations. In later use the musical element gradually ceased to be an essential feature of the 'melodrama' and the name now denotes a dramatic piece characterized by sensational incident and violent appeals to the emotions, but with a happy ending." It defines melodramatic as "having the characteristics of melodrama. Often in a depreciative sense: Characterized by sensationalism and spurious pathos." Theater historian David Mayer notes that by 1855 in England the term was "on its way to becoming an obsolescent, even taboo, term amongst the middle-class and in theaters that cater to predominantly middle class audiences" (Mayer 1996, 215). Here, as with Stowe, and as I shall argue in much popular American culture, Mayer describes an ongoing tradition of "melodrama by practice if not by name" (215). In the United States, however, the term would, by the end of the century, be fully recognizable as a description of a sensationalizing pathos-filled popular entertainment form.

2. Consider: "[*Happy Together*] is an intoxicating blend of glossy nighttime visuals and loose melodramatic narrative that would give Douglas Sirk pause" (Gill 1997, 33).

3. Andre Bazin first invoked the word classical to describe American directors who had developed a maturity and harmony of style that reflected "the genius of the system" (Bazin 1968, 154). Later, under the influence of both structuralism and ideological criticism of the 1970s, the classical cinema, sometimes also called the classical realist cinema, ceased to be a term of praise and began to describe the dominant form of the "readerly" and "transparent" nineteenth-century realist novel as it had been carried over into the twentieth-century film (Barthes 1977).

4. I am certainly aware that the term *melodrama* carries a lot of baggage; it connotes an archaic form; to some it connotes an old-fashioned "blood and thunder" theatricalism, to others it connotes a feminine pathos. But I argue that the baggage that comes with melodrama is actually less weighty, and more to the point of what the

majority of popular films do for their audiences than the French seventeenth-century baggage of the neoclassical. At the very least I invite a consideration of what we hold on to when we hold on to the term *classical*.

5. Harriet Beecher Stowe wrote that her vocation in writing *Uncle Tom's Cabin* was that of a painter: "There is no arguing with *pictures* and everyone is impressed by them, whether they mean to be or not" (Hedrick 1994, 202).

6. See, for example, Eric Bentley (1964), Peter Brooks (1995), David Grimsted (1987), Geoffrey Mason (1993), Bruce McConachie (1992), Elaine Hadley (1995), and Thomas Postlewait (1996). For the ways cinema appropriated elements of the melodramatic stage, see Nicholas Vardac (1949) and Ben Brewster and Lea Jacobs's important revision of Vardac (1997).

7. With the term melodramatic mode, rather than what theater historians and many film scholars call the genre of melodrama, I am opting for a more general aesthetic term that describes aspects of a wide range of media. I am sympathetic to the historical need to specify the actual emergence and development of a theatrical genre called melodrama, rather than the vaguer application, as in the case of Stowe's disapproving cultivated artist, of the adjectival "melodramatic." But genre denotes a rather large category of texts in theater studies (comedy, tragedy, tragi-comedy, melodrama) and a relatively narrow category in film studies (westerns, musicals, detective stories, thrillers, adventure stories, courtroom dramas, screwball comedies, and, just to confuse matters, what are often called family melodramas). Since the medium of film will prove more central to this study than that of theater, and since part of my argument about melodrama is that it transcends the narrow definition that has traditionally been allowed film melodrama within genre study, I prefer to speak of a more general melodramatic mode. For a discussion of the theatrical genre of melodrama see especially Michael Hays and Anastasia Nikolopoulou's *Melodrama: The Cultural Emergence of a Genre* (1996). For a defense of treating melodrama as a mode see John Belton (1994) and Christine Gledhill's "Rethinking Genre" (2000). For previous discussions of film melodrama as a genre, see the long tradition of feminist theory and criticism interested in the melodramatic genre of family melodrama or "The Woman's Film" in Elsaesser (1975), Doane (1987), Williams (1984), Modleski (1982), Kaplan (1992), and Klinger (1994). For an excellent overview of the history of film studies' approach to melodrama see also Gledhill (1987). And for an early important effort to think about melodrama and race, see Gaines (1993).

8. David Remnick (1996) reports that this reporting was part of a scientific campaign to shape the broadcasts to "a feminine sensibility" since presumably male viewers will watch sports without benefit of empathy for the competitors.

9. This encounter will be discussed at length in the next chapter.

10. Elaine Hadley, writing about nineteenth-century British melodrama, claims that "sympathy superseded in importance all other social feelings. . . . In effect sympathetic identification with an other, often if not always an other of distinct status, confirmed one's personal identity. . . . In these scenarios, sympathy is what might be called the recognition of sameness in difference, the delicate, highly orchestrated, and rigidly predetermined procedure of 'relating' to another who is always both like and unlike oneself" (Hadley 1995, 307).

11. See much of the work cited in note 7.

12. See, for example, Bordwell, Staiger, and Thompson's (1985) assertion of the essential classicism of popular American cinema, or Thomas Schatz's (1988) study of "the genius" of the classical studio system.

13. Critics of fifties family melodrama delighted in the way the repressed emotions of characters seemed to be "siphoned off" onto the vivid colors and mute gestures and general hysteria of the *mise-en-scène*, but they were strangely silent about the emotional reactions of audiences to all this hysteria induced by the *mise-en-scène*. It was almost as if there were a "bad" melodrama of manipulated, naively felt, feminine emotions and a "good" melodrama of ironical hysterical excess thought to be immune to the more pathetic emotions. See, for example, Geoffrey Nowell-Smith, "Minnelli and Melodrama" (1977). Christine Gledhill comments on this division by noting the creation of two audiences for melodrama: "One which is implicated, identifies and weeps, and one which, seeing through such involvement, distances itself. The fact that . . . the first is likely to be female and the other male was not remarked on" (1987, 12).

14. Robert B. Ray (1985), for example, has noted this mythic dimension of the "classic Hollywood cinema," citing it as one of the important elements of what Truffaut once called "a certain tendency of the Hollywood cinema," and relating it to the tradition of American exceptionalism. However, Ray may too quickly subsume this mythic, resolution-seeking nature of popular films to the subordination of style to story, of affects to narrative, typical of the model of the bourgeois realist text derived from the novel (Ray 1985, 32–33; 56–57).

15. I do not mean to negate the important work of feminist critics in carving out an area of critical inquiry devoted to works addressed primarily to female spectators. I wish, rather, to bring some of the insights of this work into conversation with the cinematic mainstream. Film critic Rick Altman (1998) has recently traced the process by which the term melodrama, once used by critics and distributors alike to denote male-dominated movies of action and adventure, became in the 1980s a term designating pathos-filled films aimed primarily at women (74–77). Altman's point is that feminist critics simply reoriented a number of diverse female-oriented cycles of film production located within a variety of different genres (Gothic, romance, and so on) into a category that is now called a genre. He argues that those historians who have understandably balked at the violence done to the original meaning of the term should realize that such is the process of generic transformation. My concern is that we miss something that is basic both to the older, action sense of the term *melodrama* and to the newer emotional female sense of what emerged in the 1930s and 1940s in the "woman's film" or "family melodrama" if we accept the new sense of the term. My goal in refusing the narrow particulars of the term genre, and opting for the general appeal of the melodramatic mode across many genres, is to see how melodramatic pathos and action have worked together in a wide variety of "moving pictures" aimed at constructing the moral legibility of victim-heroes.

16. A glance through the *AFI Catalog of Features, 1921–1930*, reveals an even more astounding proliferation of categories of melodrama: stunt melodrama, society melodrama, mystery melodrama, rural melodrama, action melodrama, crook melodrama, and underworld melodrama, even comedy-melodrama, as well as just plain melodrama. While one might attribute this proliferation of types of melodrama to the predominance of the silent era in this period, a look at a more recent A.F.I. volume—covering 1961–70—shows that many of these categories have persisted at least in the

eyes of archivists and catalogers. In fact, in addition to nine of the above categories, this period even lists a new one, science fiction melodrama. Film scholar Steve Neale has studied the use of the term *melodrama* in the trade journal *Variety* from 1938 to 1959, and confirms this observation that the term continued to mean the same thing that it did in the teens and twenties: "The mark of these films is not pathos, romance, and domesticity . . . but war films, adventure films, horror films, and thrillers, genres traditionally thought of as, if anything, 'male' " (Neale 1993, 69). This persistence, I would argue, points to the continued usefulness of melodrama as a descriptive term that extends beyond the limits of genre. I call this the melodramatic mode.

17. Peter Brooks's conception of melodrama consistently emphasizes the importance of the "loss of the sacred" through the trauma of the French Revolution as its crucial raison d'être. He describes the "moral occult"—"the domain of operative spiritual values which is both indicated within and masked by the surface of reality"—as "the repository of the fragmentary and desacralized remnants of sacred myth" (Brooks 1995, 5). While I find Brooks's identification of the "moral occult" enormously useful as a means of identifying the ethical work melodrama performs, the fundamentally Lacanian notion that melodrama resurrects a lost sacred dictates an approach that perpetually finds melodrama retrieving sacred "remnants" of a prior unity and seems doomed to locate archaic remnants of melodrama in more modern works. Nor is it clear that the sacred so quickly dissipates in the aftermath of the French Revolution, leaving individuals acting out personal feats of resacralization. For these and other reasons I prefer to use the other term Brooks deploys to define melodrama—"moral legibility," instead of the more religious, and vaguely Gothic, "moral occult." The construction of moral legibility in the face of an increasingly secular, atomized, and commodified culture strikes me as a better way to explain the ongoing appeal of melodrama in a secular world than a definitive and traumatic contemplation of "the void" marked by the French Revolution. It also strikes me as a term that will be more useful in discussing the more optimistic and already more secular features of American melodrama.

18. Only certain patented theaters had been allowed the politically dangerous privilege of speech in the pre-revolutionary era. Pantomine accompanied by music was thus developed as an important theatrical form in the late eighteenth century. When the revolution abolished the monopoly on speech of the patented theaters, a flowering of pantomime and musical forms of drama occurred on the French stage, culminating in the dominant form of "melodrames"—dramas with music (Brooks 1995, 62).

19. Brooks points to Guilbert de Pixérécourt's 1818 melodrama *La Fille de l'exilé*, in which a sixteen-year-old Siberian girl travels to Moscow to seek pardon from the czar for her exiled father. On the way she falls into the hands of Ivan, her father's persecutor, himself now threatened by ferocious Tartars. The girl saves Ivan in a sensational scene by holding the cross of her virtuous dead mother over his head. The Tartars shrink back under the power of this holy sign. But the sensation does not end there. Ivan now tells the Tartars that the poor girl who now protects him is actually the devoted daughter of the man he once persecuted: "Ah! such generosity overwhelms me! I lack the words to express. . . . All I can do is admire you and bow my head before you" (24–25). In a "spontaneous movement" the Tartars form a semicircle around the girl and fall on their knees, astonished at her goodness. The sensation so grandiosely

orchestrated here is that of the recognition of virtue. Theatrical melodramatic denoue-ment is typically some version of this public or private recognition of virtue prolonged in the frozen tableau whose picture speaks more powerfully than words. Each play is not only the drama of a moral dilemma, but the drama of a moral sentiment—usually of a wronged innocence—seeking to say its name but unable to speak directly (Brooks 1995, 24–25, 43).

20. The term *attraction* refers both backward to the popular tradition of the fair-ground and carnival as well as forward to an avant-garde subversion (Gunning 1986 and 1989).

21. Janet Staiger argues convincingly, for example, that the notion of a war be-tween working class attraction/sensation on the one hand, and bourgeois cause-effect narrative with a bourgeois constituency on the other, is an over-simplification. Staiger deftly negotiates between those historians who have placed too large a claim on the otherness of cinematic attractions vis à vis the classical narrative and those who, like her former collaborators David Bordwell and Kristen Thompson, have argued that "narrative continuity and clarity are the only means of pleasure [audiences] seek during an evening at the theater or movies" (Staiger 1992, 118). Demolishing claims that even the quite primitive 1903 Edwin S. Porter version of *Uncle Tom's Cabin* was a pure spectacle of unreadable cause and effect—since all classes of audience knew the story that lay behind the tableaux and since even the tableaux were arranged in a cross-cut manner—Staiger asserts that the film "interlaces spectacle with a tight crisscrossing of two subplots for a final, *if melodramatic*, climax. Narrativity and visual spectacle existed as available sites of affective response for all spectators of various classes" (Staiger 1992, 118 [emphasis mine]). Staiger offers an important corrective to the concept of a purely linear cause-effect narrative, noting that narrativity and visual spec-tacle work together to produce affective response. However, as with Brooks and Gun-ning, the notion of excess still lurks in the telling "if melodramatic" in the above quotation, as if *Uncle Tom's Cabin* were not fundamentally a melodrama and as if "affective response" was not what melodrama delivers! We must study melodrama *as melodrama*, not as a form that wants to be something else.

22. Bordwell argues, for example, that melodrama represents an excess that vio-lates the smooth flow of narrative described by the paradigm of the classical. However, he assimilates this excess to its special nature as a genre—a genre that, like comedy and the musical, has an exceptional stylization. Arguing, rightly I think, against those critics who have found such stylization subversive, Bordwell maintains that generic expectation governs and explains stylistic excess. In the same breath, however, he also maintains that melodrama has not been established as an empirically or conceptually coherent genre. If Bordwell is right when he says melodrama cannot be understood as a genre, he cannot also be right when he explains its "excesses" as generically moti-vated. There is a fundamental flaw in the approach to melodrama that sees it only as an exception to a more dominant classical mode.

23. Singer (2000) defines melodrama as a "cluster concept" that combines the following five features: (1) pathos triggered by a perception of moral injustice; (2) overwrought emotion; (3) moral polarization; (4) nonclassical narrative structure (he is especially interested in neglected serials); and (5) sensationalism. The genre consists for him in any combination of two or more of these elements. Thus Hollywood melo-

drama of the studio era combines only the first two, while the serial queen melodramas of the teens that are the special focus of his study lack pathos.

24. "For the time being, classical cinema is still a more precise term because it names a regime of productivity and intelligibility that is both historically and culturally specific, much as it gets passed off as timeless and natural. . . . In that sense, however, I take the term to refer less to a system of functionally interrelated norms and a corresponding set of empirical objects than to a scaffold, matrix, or web that allows for a wide range of aesthetic effects and experiences, that is, for cultural configurations that are more complex and dynamic than the most accurate account of their function within any single system may convey and that require more open-ended, promiscuous, and imaginative types of inquiry" (Hansen, 2000, 339).

25. Gledhill argues further that melodrama's goal of moral legibility asks "how to live, who is justified, who are the innocent, where is villainy at work now." (Gledhill, 2000, 234).

26. Theater historian Thomas Postlewait offers a similar appreciation of the relation between realism and melodrama on the stage. He argues that melodrama's relation to realism is not that of its polarized opposite, and that it is a mistake to see the realist drama of an Ibsen or an O'Neill progressing out of the cruder form of melodrama: "Our initial task, then, is to get beyond the pervasive dichotomies: melodrama distorts, realism reports; melodrama offers escapism, realism offers life; melodrama is conservative, realism is radical; melodrama delivers ideologies. . . . In fact, both melodrama and realism distort and report, conserve and criticize. And both articulate and challenge the ideologies of the time" (Postlewait 1996, 56).

27. I borrow this subtitle from Virginia Wexman's article on D. W. Griffith's *Way Down East* to point to the relation between melodrama's manifestation of suffering and the rights of citizenship that often follow upon suffering.

28. Ben Singer (2000), whose excellent study of melodrama and modernity is cited in note 23 above, has taken issue with me on this point. To Singer, melodrama does not necessarily combine pathos and action. Indeed, the serial melodramas of the teens he so interestingly analyzes are long on action and short on pathos (2000, 20). While Singer may be technically correct to argue that the serials he examines do not have pathos and were in their own era called melodramas, I would argue that a melodrama without pathos tends in the direction of what we would today call a "thriller"—a suspenseful, action-packed narrative of sensational incident. If my definition of the term hinges on an element of pathos that we have seen to be central to the censorious modern artist who chastised Harriet Beecher Stowe for her "melodramatic" taste, it is not because I want to fix melodrama in relation to sentimental forms of pathos but rather that I want to stand back far enough to view the two poles of (feminine) pathos and (masculine) action in tension with one another. Singer is certainly right to note, however, that there have been periods in the history of popular film when the term melodrama primarily meant thrilling action, just as there have been times when it has meant a pathetic display of suffering. If we examine the full history of sensational and moving film in conjunction with its roots on the nineteenth-century stage, however, and if we examine this history as a mode and not simply as a genre, melodrama, whether it is called that or not, will be seen to be a necessary term for the relation between exciting action and sensational emotion.

29. In isolating pathos and action, I am privileging the emotion of sympathy engaged in the pathetic spectacle of suffering and the emotion of suspense engaged in action sequences. Although these emotions certainly need to be better understood theoretically, it is not my purpose in this book to offer that theorization. I do want to assert, however, what seems to me to be the obvious importance of emotional gratification in melodrama and my sense that psychoanalytic models determined by lack and loss do not proceed very far in describing the pleasures of these kinds of second-order experiences of affect. See Ed S. Tan (1996) for a discussion of the interpenetration of cognitive schema and affect, Murray Smith (1995, 5) for a discussion of how "structures of sympathy" work, and Jack Katz (1999) for a remarkable phenomenology of emotions in everyday life. My own discussion of pathos and action below is an attempt to see how two kinds of affect work together in the context of the production of "moral legibility."

30. In a related article I discuss the *Rambo* films (1982, 1985) and *Schindler's List* (1993) as examples of the ongoing, mainstream tradition of melodrama (Williams 1998).

31. Nicholas Vardac's pioneering *From Stage to Screen: Theatrical Origins of Early Film: David Garrick to D. W. Griffith* (1949) is a crucial document of the connection between nineteenth-century stage spectacle and the early films of Porter and Griffith, showing how the development of editing in Porter and Griffith continued a tradition of episodic, melodramatic, stage pictorialism. Yet Vardac sees the rise of cinema as a transcendence of the "old melodrama" arriving at a new cinematic realism. More recently, Ben Brewster and Lea Jacobs (1997) have written a meticulous history of the transformation of the pictorial style from stage to screen. Instead of arguing that cinema represented a rupture with the stage, Brewster and Jacobs show how early filmmakers developed and continued the theatrical pictorial tradition. Implicit in their argument is the notion that melodrama (which they tend to treat as an individual genre rather than a pervasive mode) is sustained and developed by the enduring pictorial tradition.

32. Richard Schickel's biography, *D. W. Griffith: An American Life* (1984), is one of the best examples of the tendency to define what is best in Griffith as what transcends his work's melodramatic theatrical origins. But consider as well Tom Schatz's influential *Hollywood Genres: Formulas, Filmmaking, and the Studio System* (1981). In his section on family melodrama, Schatz refers to Griffith, acknowledging that on some level all film is melodrama. However, like most critics who offer this insight, he immediately drops the point to proceed with the more conventional containment of melodrama as a genre that came of age in the 1950s and then languished there. Robert Lang, who discusses Griffith at some length in his book *American Film Melodrama: Griffith, Vidor, Minnelli* (1989), also assimilates Griffith to a psychoanalytic model of fifties "family melodrama" and its hysterical excesses. (More recently, however, Lang has offered a less fifties-derived understanding of melodrama in his introduction to the continuity script of *The Birth of a Nation*.) Scott Simmon (1993) is another Griffith scholar who retroactively situates Griffith's melodramatic tendencies as an anticipation of the later subgenre of "the woman's film." Although all these critics perceive melodramatic tendencies within Griffith, none is willing to define Griffith's art centrally as melodrama. Tom Gunning's excellent study of Griffith's early Biographs is the only study that comes close to naming melodrama as the continuous, active ingredient in

Griffith's transformation of theatrical codes of representation into film, though even Gunning avoids the term, substituting theatrical whenever possible: "The transformation in filmic discourse which Griffith represents can be seen as the fulfillment of the theatrical ideal" (1991, 40). I would argue, however, that Gunning's meticulous study of how the "cinema of attractions" and other archaic forms of sensationalism became integrated into the "narrator system" is actually a study of the modernization of theatrical melodramatic effects into cinema. Thus where Gunning speaks of "the ambiguous nature of Griffith's debt to melodrama" (1991, 107) in his discovery of more realistic ways to express character psychology, I would argue that Griffith revitalizes stage melodrama through the verisimilar power of cinema.

33. Sarah Kozloff has argued that Hardy's novel and a 1887 stage play, later made into a film by Edwin S. Porter in 1913, formed a part of the material Griffith adapted when he made his film in 1920. Kozloff makes the point that Griffith basically stole the Hardy material, finding evidence in Griffith's personal papers of a typed extract of the baptism scene from the novel (Kozloff 1985, 35–41). However, if we recall Rick Altman's argument regarding the influence of popular theatrical melodrama on silent cinema, we can see that such borrowing is hardly exceptional. Even if Griffith did mark the passage in Hardy's novel, his knowledge of it was most likely through its various dramatizations, which included this scene.

34. Elsaesser (1975) argues that melodrama is a special case from the usual kinetic dynamism of American cinema in which pressure builds upon a victim who then finds an outlet in action. I would suggest, however, that if the focus on victims is central to a melodramatic mode, that it is in no way a special case of a "closed" melodramatic world crushing helpless protagonists in opposition to the "openness" of the action genres. Rather, the victim-hero of melodrama gains an empathy that is equated with moral virtue through a suffering that can either continue in the ways Elsaesser so well describes for family melodrama—or which other critics have described in the woman's film—*or* this victim-hero can turn his or her virtuous suffering into action. Melodrama can go either way.

35. Jack Katz (1999) has also written insightfully about the phenomenon of crying, and on the anomaly that so few scholars have tackled its mysteries. Katz usefully notes that crying is "a finely embodied way of being in tension with speech" (194).

36. Think, for example, of the critical praise heaped on action director Jon de Bont for his kinetic *Speed* (1995) and *Twister* (1996), and on James Cameron for the "sensation" scenes of *Titanic*.

37. There are many more fascinating aspects to the role of time and timing in melodrama. Roland Barthes (1977, 119), writing about the pleasure of suspense, notes its distinct mixture of anxiety and pleasure, its assertion of the independence of discourse from the events it describes. Tom Gunning (1991, 104), writing about suspense in early Griffith Biographs, notes the way suspense invokes spectator expectation, then plays with the possibility of not fulfilling it. In the process, Gunning argues, narration itself is foregrounded by flirting with its own dissolution: "Interrupting an action, delaying its resolution, yet creating a structure in which the outcome approaches inevitably, in which the flow of time and narrative is unstoppable (the fatal hour draws near . . .)—these are at the heart of Griffith's temporal and narrative logic." Commenting on the frequent use of deadlines to structure film narratives, Gunning observes

that the increased role of time and suspense in early Griffith were of a piece with the urban and industrial rhythms of workers who were now punching, and racing against, the clock. Thus Griffith's suspenseful parallel editing "invokes the split-second timing of industrial production and worker's enslavement to an oppressive temporality. . . . On the one hand, the film's climax reinforces the experience of temporal enslavement by allying it with narrative pleasure and even offering a lesson in adjustment to industry's quick demands and rhythms. On the other hand, it exposes the unbearable oppression of clock time and acts out a drama of liberation from it" (105–6). Although Gunning is ambivalent about the role of melodrama in this "new precision of tense" that could imitate more traditional narrative forms (like novels), he allows that this "intensification of time through editing also creates sensational melodrama" (106). I would argue, however, that the melodramatic elaboration of filmic time developed by Griffith's development of parallel editing is at the core of most noncomic, narrative cinema and that the dialectic between the pathos of "too late" and the action of "in the nick of time" is its core structure.

38. Susan McClary describes romantic music as giving the effect of a return to origins. For a discussion of the ways nineteenth-century romantic music patterns were adopted by Hollywood see also Claudia Gorbman, *Unheard Melodies: Narrative Film Music* (1987), and Caryl Flinn, *Strains of Utopia: Gender, Nostalgia and Hollywood Film Music* (1992). Flinn notes, for example, that it is music that connects listeners to an "idealized past, offering them the promise of a retrieval of lost utopian coherence" (50). This is to say that music often carries the burden of making the viewer/listener feel the longing for plenitude that is so important to the melodramatic mode. *Titanic's* Academy Award–winning song, "My Heart Will Go On," provides the melos of this particular melodrama.

39. This ordeal is not unlike the ancient system of trial by ordeal for women accused of adultery. In Mesopotamia women accused of adultery were thrown in a river. If a woman survived the ordeal she was presumed to be judged innocent by the river gods. However, the ordeal itself was obviously already a form of punishment (Lerner 1986, 115).

40. Martha Vicinus (1981, 132) aptly names this wish-fulfilling tendency to bogus solution in nineteenth-century domestic melodrama the "reconciliation of the irreconcilable." We can see, however, that the mechanism persists throughout the form.

41. Monopathy was first named by Robert Heilman (1968, 85). It was linked to Manichaeanism by Brooks (1995, 36) and discussed by Elsaesser (1975) in relation to the "non-psychological" conception of character.

42. One reason family melodrama of the 1950s has been taken as such a memorable example of the melodramatic mode could be that it exemplifies that moment in American moving pictures when popular psychology and the "method" became the reigning form of the assertion of personality, when morality itself became explainable by Oedipus. At this point the eruption of symptoms and unconscious gestures began to substitute for the more straightforward bodily expression of good and evil and everyone became a victim of their unconscious desires. Thus Robert Stack's famously swallowed voice, squeezed frame, and hunched way of holding a martini in *Written on the Wind,* so much commented upon by critics, was typical of a whole generation of Oedipally beset protagonists whose virtue was now revealed in somatic symptoms.

Chapter Two

1. Of course this complaint may be the peculiar despair of a film scholar who has grown accustomed to relying upon singular texts whose preservation of the time and space of performance makes them function like uncanny time capsules.

2. Bruce McConachie (1991, 10) shows, in addition, how the principal stage adaptations have eliminated Stowe's "women of principle" in favor of (white) "men of principle" with no source in Stowe. It could very well be, however, that these altered versions are not so much evisceration of her powers as they are permutations implied, though repressed, in her original version.

3. Though Douglass also suggested that Stowe's personal activism had been less significant than that of many other women abolitionists (Adams 1989, 144).

4. During this period, it is significant that Stowe, who was increasingly supplementing the family income with occasional publications, wrote an essay on Dickens. While she disapproved of his frequent depictions of drinking, and his making light of religion, she appreciated his extension of vision to include the common and the everyday to the "whole class of the oppressed, the neglected, and forgotten, the sinning and suffering" whom he drew with sympathy and interest (Hedrick 1994, 155–56).

5. Karen Sánchez-Eppler (1988, 36) writes that reading sentimental fiction is a "bodily act," the success of which is gauged by the "ability to translate words into pulse beats and sobs." However, she assumes that readings were exclusively private acts when there is good evidence that in many families the reading of the novel was a group activity involving quasi-theatrical stagings in the parlor.

6. Billings drew 115 new pictures, some for heads of chapters, some for the insides of chapters as well as ornamental capitals for the first word of each chapter.

7. "The two gigantic negroes that now laid hold of Tom . . . might have formed no unapt personification of powers of darkness. The poor woman screamed with apprehension, and all rose, as by general impulse, while they dragged him unresisting from the place" (1983, 309). The next time we see Tom he is recovering from his beating.

8. See, for example, her mother-to-mother asides, such as the one to the "mother that reads this" regarding the white mother's donation of a dead child's clothes to a fugitive black mother (1983, 75).

9. In an excellent dissertation on antebellum stage melodrama, entitled *Sympathetic Vibrations*, Mark Mullen argues that sympathy is more than an imaginary relation to an object of feeling, but a deep feeling of social connection to the afflicted. Mullen shows that notions of melodramatic virtue relied upon a literal physiological sense of the vibrations of a sympathetic body feeling connected to another (Mullen 1999, part 1).

10. Stowe writes: "It is impossible to describe the scene, as with tears and sobs, they gathered round the little creature, and took from her hands what seemed to them a last mark of her love. They fell on their knees; they sobbed, and prayed, and kissed the hem of her garment; and the elder ones poured forth words of endearment, mingled in prayers and blessings, after the manner of their susceptible race" (251–52).

11. Fredrickson (1994, 430–35) shows that while romantic racialism was in many ways indistinguishable from conventional racist thought, the attribution of childlike,

feminine feeling to Africans could become a source of moral power if such figures were mistreated by overly aggressive Anglo-Saxons. Romantic racialism was thus fundamental to the establishment of the virtue of the sorrowing slave and thus to Stowe's indictment of the culture of slavery.

12. Eliza even disguises herself as a man, and her son as a girl, during a portion of her journey.

13. Douglass thereby omits having to tell that her money financed his escape (Bergner 1998, 250).

14. This haunting episode, discussed at greater length in Chapter 3, reworks the Gothic convention of the confined "madwoman in the attic" into an instrument of both escape and revenge (Gilbert and Gubar 1979, 534).

15. Augustin Daly's later, 1869 melodrama, *Under the Gaslight*, is the exception. Its déclassé white heroine saves a one-armed Civil War veteran tied to the railroad tracks at the play's climax.

16. We shall see, however, that in covert ways the basic topos of the suffering male slave has a long life in black and white American melodrama.

17. We will see in the next chapter how D. W. Griffith reworks this motif of the white sheet, demonstrating the superstition of the guilty white master into the white sheet that terrifies superstitious former slaves.

18. Their "white blood" is undoubtedly what gives these women the power of action in Stowe's eyes, while Tom's pure "black blood" makes him a docile sufferer. Stowe's romantic racialism is certainly racism *tout court*, but it is interesting nevertheless that the passing woman of color plays such a large part in this, the original melodrama of black and white.

19. Saxton cites a typically licentious, racist, and misogynous "love" song:

> My Susy she is handsome
> My Susy she is young. . . .
> My Susy looms it bery tall
> Wid udder like a cow
> She'd give nine quarts easy
> But white gals don't know how (Saxton 1990, 178).

20. Lott's book, *Love and Theft*, is an especially rich study that argues that white interpretations of black life have formed the backbone of much American popular culture. Lott's book is especially useful in this study for its concentration on the minstrel elements of stage versions of *Uncle Tom's Cabin*. Dale Cockrell's (1997) *Demons of Disorder* follows Lott in analyzing both the love and the theft, concentrating on a few major minstrel songs. Both counter the older, standard interpretation of blackface minstrelsy as simple racist stereotyping.

21. Rogin quotes a telling description of American vaudeville by Fred Allen that lists all manner of performers, from female impersonators to one-armed cornetists to Irish, Jewish, German, Swedish, Italian, and "rube" comedians. But where he should list black comedians, Allen lists "blackface," proving Rogin's point most eloquently (Rogin 1996,1).

22. Karen Sánchez-Eppler (1992) has discussed the "intersecting rhetorics of feminism and abolitionism," noting that for both women and blacks it is their physical differences from the cultural norm of white masculinity that obstructs their claims to

personhood. Both had bodies to be bought and owned. Both grounded resistance in the very difference of these more emotion-prone bodies (28). While these identifications were empowering to each group, they could also gloss over specific differences. Thus the slave woman's sexual vulnerability to white masters was often a proxy for the privately complained-about lack of control of the white woman in marriage. Differences between the married white woman and the slave concubine were thus often strategically omitted (31).

323

23. Lott divides the happy and the sad songs into two musical traditions: the brisk African-derived ("musematic") songs composed of very short units—riffs or shouts—associated with the circularity familiar to the oral tradition, as in a song like "Old Dan Tucker"; and the sad, European-derived ballads like "Old Folks at Home." Lott describes the more African, musematic tradition as encouraging a form of ego loss and dispersal, and the more European ballads as more individualistic and narrative (174). Lott argues that minstrel songs often existed at the intersection of the two traditions. Thus, it is the mixture of these two forms that constitutes the complex hybridity of much popular American music and which paves the way for the popular emergence of African-American musical forms.

24. Though the song was so associated with E. P. Christy, who had purchased the copyright from Foster, that he was for many years thought to be its author, it circulated widely in other, nonminstrel, forms.

25. Foster's hits in the early 1850s included "Nelly Bly," "Camptown Races," and "Old Folks," all published by New York's Firth and Pond (Austin 1975, 26). In addition to the minstrel style songs, a number of sentimental ballads grounded in the Tom story were sold as sheet music. Even before the first dramatic versions of Uncle Tom, all of which included song and dance, popular ballads that were cast in a melodramatic mode sang of the virtuous suffering of both Tom and Little Eva. A Miss Collier wrote a best-selling trio of ballads, "The Death of St. Clare," "Eva's Parting," and "Eva's Flight." And from the Aiken-Howard version of the novel a number of nonminstrel hits, in the category of "sentimental parlor song," were written by the show's producer, G. C. Howard: "Eva to Her Papa" (asking that Tom be set free); "St. Clare to Little Eva in Heaven," and "Uncle Tom's Religion" ("When de whip to me am giben, I'll think of him who' died to save") (Riis 1994, 100).

26. Writing about Victorian England, theater historian David Mayer (1996) shows that "parlor and platform" melodrama flourished in the second half of the nineteenth century due to a number of factors: the still uncertain status of the professional theater, the growing emphasis on private domestic life in middle-class families where social entertainment is carried out in the form of "improving" recreations in the home; and the growing popularity of amateur performances. Mayer's intriguing point is that many of the materials of amateur performance in the home were very much like abridged melodramas or comedies performed on the stage (Mayer 1996, 211–15). Thus even if the term melodrama, as we have seen in Stowe's own reaction to the word in 1854 (see Chapter 1), had fallen into disrepute, it was home-grown forms of melodrama that already formed a major portion of family entertainment.

27. The playbill for the Troy, New York, production of 1853 names the song ("With Words and Music by G. P. Christy," as it was then attributed) along with three others written by manager G. C. Howard (Kesler 1968, 135).

28. Arthur Riis (1994, xvii) cites no fewer than three dozen name-associated songs. He also notes that while the beginnings of acts—reserved for the advancement of the narrative—were frequently without music, all acts concluded with music.

29. Foster's sketchbook for "My Old Kentucky Home" originally ended each stanza with lines addressed directly to Tom, such as "Poor Uncle Tom, Good Night." In addition, a chorus that fits no extant melody also spoke to Tom, adding the lines, "Grieve not for your old Kentucky home/You'r bound for a better land/Old Uncle Tom" (Austin 1975, 233).

30. Though very like sympathy, empathy involves an identification with an emotional state in which the empathic onlooker may attribute to the other his or her own emotional state, thus appropriating the feeling of the other as one's own. Mark Mullen (1999) sees sympathy as a feeling for another that does not necessarily impose one's own emotional state upon that other. However, I find the distinction hard to make, since it is always difficult to tell when this imposition operates.

31. It appears that Foster actually was divided as to whether to write the song in dialect. His original sketchbook had alternative dialect spellings omitted in the final publication (Austin 1975, 233). We shall see in Chapter 6 how this white appropriation of black dialect later figures in the person of Scarlett O'Hara. One of the working titles for Margaret Mitchell's novel was *Tote the Weary Load*.

32. Considering that the play was not performed in the South except in burlesque form, this figure is truly astounding. In Troy, New York, a city of 30,000 where Henry Aiken's version was first performed, 25,000 saw the play during its first season (Mullen, "Nothing to Do with Literature" p. 5).

33. The first consisted of "fairy tale melodramas" in a direct line of descent from the French stage and Guilbert de Pixérécourt. These melodramas dominated the 1820-35 period, and were produced by paternalistically run stock companies and enjoyed primarily by elite gentlemen. The second formation is what McConachie calls "heroic melodramas" dominating the 1830s through the 1850s. These melodramas, typified by the Edwin Forest vehicle *Metamora*, traced apocalyptic events and heroic acts of often-doomed Jacksonian heroes. They were enjoyed by mostly male working-class audiences.

34. This version was first staged in Boston, then later staged in New York by P. T. Barnum. It restored Tom in the end to his "old Kentucky home."

35. McConachie (1992) describes this moral reform melodrama as fully complicit with a capitalist market economy that places its fate in "rational men of principle" who will reform social problems, whether demon rum or bad treatment of slaves. While I do not quarrel with this characterization of *Uncle Tom's Cabin* as moral reformist in orientation, McConachie fits this particular version of the play into too narrow a mold and takes it as typical of all stage versions of the novel. There certainly are "rational men of principle" in this version—George Shelby, Jr., who in this version rescues Tom from Legree, and an added character, Penetrate Partyside, who attempts to save Tom from the slave auction and takes notes throughout the play for a book on slavery—but there are not such men in all versions.

36. McConachie (1991) has also offered a meticulous comparison of the two most influential versions of the Tom play, arguing that both adaptations were antislavery but that they lost the force of Stowe's radical challenge to the dominant culture of market capitalism. While I agree with McConachie's general critique of the "watering down" of Stowe's novel, and rely on his research considerably in what follows, it is

important to understand just what these stage versions did accomplish apart from their literary source.

37. See, for example, Jeffrey Mason's (1993) discussion of *Metamora* (1829) in *Melodrama and the Myth of America*, and Mark Mullen's (1999) discussion of a range of native American melodramas in his dissertation "Sympathetic Vibrations."

38. Here, then, are what McConachie (1992) calls "rational men of principle"— George Shelby, Jr., and Penetrate Partyside—putting their heads together to free the good slave, thus "reforming" the occasional excesses of the institution while at the same time assuring its continuation.

39. Aiken was a cousin of George C. Howard, manager of the Troy Museum Company in Troy, New York. Theaters in this era of reform melodrama were often euphemistically called "museums" to soften the oppositions of the pious. Howard was an actor-manager whose company was very much a family affair. His daughter Cordelia had already been a success as little Dick in Dickens's "Oliver Twist," playing opposite her mother as Oliver. This mother-daughter team would spend the next ten years playing Topsy and Little Eva to one another.

40. The action of the Aiken-Howard version is as follows:

Act I, Scene i: Decision of George Harris to flee told to his wife Eliza
          ii: Discussion of sale of Tom and Harry between Shelby and Haley overheard by Eliza
          iii: Tom's decision to remain
          iv: Escape of Eliza from tavern with aid of Phineas
          v: Pursuit of Eliza by trio of pursuers
          vi: Eliza's crossing the river (Kesler 1968, 253)

Act II, Scene i: Arrival of St. Clare, Eva, Ophelia, and Tom at the plantation
          ii: Introduction of Topsy
          iii: Escape of George from tavern with aid of Wilson and Phineas
          iv: Eva's love for Topsy
          v: Reunion of Eliza and George Harris
          vi: Freedom of Eliza, Harry, and George (Kesler 1968, 255)

Act III, Scene i: St. Clare's challenge to Ophelia
          ii: Eva's premonition
          iii: Tom's foreboding
          iv: Death of Eva (K, 257)

Act IV, scene i: Tom's religion; Ophelia's receipt of Topsy; St. Clare's bereavement
          ii: Interference of St. Clare [in a fight]
          iii: Announcement of St. Clare's wound
          iv: Death of St. Clare (Kesler 1968, 259)

Act V, Scene i: Sale of Tom and Emmeline to Legree
          ii: Ophelia and Topsy in Vermont
          iii: Cruelty of Legree
          iv: Routing of Cute by Topsy (Kesler 1968, 260)

Act VI, Scene i: Tom's witness to Cassy
          ii: Joining of George Shelby, Marks, and Cute
          iii: Guilt of Legree and plot of Cassy and Emmeline
          iv: Death of Legree
          v: Death of Uncle Tom (Kesler 1968, 262)

41. See Gossett (1985, 270) and Fletcher 1958.

42. A reviewer for William Garrison's antislavery *The Liberator* wrote: "O, it was a sight worth seeing those ragged, coatless men and boys in the pit (the very *material* of which mobs are made) cheering the strongest and sublimest anti-slavery sentiments! The whole audience was at times melted to tears, and I own that I was no exception. It was noticeable that the people, after witnessing the death of Uncle Tom, went out of the house as gravely and seriously as people retire from a religious meeting!" (Gossett, 272) This theater review was even more enthusiastic than Garrison's own review of the novel, suggesting that it was the visible effects on audiences as social groups rather than individual readers that had the greatest effect on racial feeling.

43. Thomas Gossett cites a review of the play in the *National Anti-Slavery Standard* that praised the theater for admitting blacks but censured it for segregating them. The review notes, however, that blacks stood a better chance of seeing and hearing the play at the National than they did of seeing and hearing a sermon in most New York churches. (If lucky enough to be admitted to a church, Negroes were usually given the pew "least favorable for sight and hearing") (Gossett 1985, 271).

44. Gossett, however, notes the existence of a black troupe that performed movingly in Davenport, Iowa, in 1902 (Gossett 1985, 381). Not until 1914 would there be a black actor in the role of Uncle Tom in film. See discussion of both below.

45. This seems especially the case given the fact that not only was blackface the norm for representations of blacks on stage, but drag was the norm for representation of black women. The portrayal of Topsy by Mrs. Howard was thus, for all its minstrel stereotype, a highly realistic innovation. Thanks to Lea Jacobs for pointing this out.

46. An interesting case in point is Harriet Beecher Stowe's own dramatic adaptation of her novel *The Christian Slave*, performed in 1855. This three-act dramatization represented a principled attempt to perform the work through the voice and body of an actual black woman, a Mrs. Mary E. Webb, for whom the work was expressly written. Webb was a mulatta "reader" or oral reciter in whose career Stowe took much interest, writing in a letter, "I think the brown of her complexion like that of old paintings preferable to all the lighter tints of the world," and "She is to me a new and beautiful revelation of what womanhood can be" (Wagenknecht 1965, 132, 235–36). This genteel, nontheatrical reading favored precisely the long speeches and didactic sermons that give readers of the novel so much trouble today. Through them, Stowe dramatized the maternal voice that was missing from the stage versions. Indeed, her enthusiasm for Mrs. Webb's reading, in which she seems to have naively, but genuinely, awakened to the beauty and eloquence of a mature black woman, seems to echo something of her narrator's plaintive "Why don't somebody wake up to the beauty of old women?" (1983, 116), in that portion of the novel most celebrated by feminist critics and most regularly omitted on the stage. It might be possible to see this "politically correct" and racially more "authentic" version of Uncle Tom as failing to gain popular acceptance because it eschewed the most familiar elements of both melos and drama; however, we could also see Mrs. Webb's recital as another instance of the many relations between the popular stage and pulpit.

47. "[It] represents Southern Negro SLAVERY AS IT IS embracing all its abhorrent deformities, its cruelties, and barbarities. . . . It exhibits a true picture of Negro life in the South, instead of absurdly representing the ignorant slave as possessed of all the polish of the drawing room, and the refinement of the educated whites."

48. In this version, Tom is not even sold away from Kentucky. Rather, returning from a revival camp meeting he criticizes the dandified pretensions of "free Darkies" and expresses his love for "old Kentuck." In the last act, George and Eliza are joined in a slave "wedding" ceremony consisting of "jumping the broom" (Gossett 1985, 276; Toll 1974, 93).

49. Harry Birdoff (1947, 187) tells of an antebellum Tom troupe stranded in the anti-theater town of Springfield, Illinois, aided in the politically sensitive task of getting their licence fee reduced by a certain "lanky young lawyer."

50. Since the Aiken-Howard convention always had her played by an adult (Mrs. Howard played Topsy to the Little Eva of her own daughter, Cordelia), this was easy to do.

51. We will see in the next chapter how D. W. Griffith will find another way to celebrate this reunion of North and South when he has, as an intertitle puts it, "former enemies of North and South . . . united again in common defense of their Aryan birthright" in the defense of the cabin at the end of *The Birth of a Nation*.

52. The cakewalk is a dance derived from the "walk-around"—a sort of strutting promenade in which couples compete with fancy improvised steps—that concluded many minstrel shows. More distantly, it was derived from Sunday dances performed by slaves who would dress up in their masters's handed-down finery to do a high-kicking, prancing dance (here, the finery is not handed-down: the women wear all-white dresses with elegant parasols; the men wear all-black or all-white tuxedos with top hats). The movements of the dance were an imitation of the high manners of the masters in the "big house," performed for these masters in a contest in which a cake would be awarded to the couple with the "proudest movements" (Sundquist 1993, 277–78).

53. This last is not literally a tableau, suggesting, as Brewster and Jacobs argue, that Porter was already moving away from the stage convention (1997, 57).

54. I have not been able to locate a copy of this version, produced by Imperial.

55. Other black actors had been acclaimed in the role on stage. In 1902, a white actor writes of attending an all-black performance of *Uncle Tom's Cabin* in Davenport, Iowa, in 1902 as a joke. "We went to laugh but remained to pray, for we saw an exquisitely beautiful, dignified and marvelously pathetic and sweet performance given of Uncle Tom by Charles Albins, who afterwards came to New York and played Othello" (Gossett 1985, 381).

56. A print I have seen at the British National Film Archive is missing precisely this scene.

Chapter Three

1. Historian Bruce McConachie (1992, xiii) notes that on the nineteenth-century American stage, popular British melodrama, often derived from French originals, outnumbered successful American ones by five to one. Daniel Gerould (1992, 14) notes that "American melodrama came of age with a purely native-born triumph, *Uncle Tom's Cabin*."

2. According to Kevin Brownlow, what Wilson actually said was, "I congratulate you on an excellent production" (1992, documentary film, *D.W. Griffith, Father of Film*).

3. Chandler, for example, defines the epic form of Scott's "historical romance" as an accurate display of manners against the background of larger historical struggles. In contrast to the "world historical" heroes of the classical epic form who epitomize the unity of nations or peoples, the Scott hero, whom Chandler argues Dixon and Griffith inherit, is an ordinary person caught between two factions. The resolution of his conflict produces the emergent nation for whom this person comes to stand (1990, 230–31).

4. Jane Tompkins (1985) and Nina Baym (1981) are the feminist literary critics who have done the most to champion this reading of the novel as proto-feminist. Michael Rogin's (1984) groundbreaking essay on *The Birth of a Nation* was the first to see Griffith's racism as organically connected to the Oedipal power of a film in which the castrated, weakened, and feminized son of the defeated South reempowers himself, with his father's metaphoric phallic sword, by taking on a new enemy—not the Union soldiers, but the former slaves these soldiers freed. In this formulation the maternal, antiracist melodrama of the abolitionist 1850s can be seen to have been defeated by the paternal, racist melodrama of the Jim Crow teens. See also Kathleen McHugh's (1999, 97–107) discussion of feminine domesticity in the context of Griffith's race melodrama.

5. Some of the titles—like *Life at the South; or "Uncle Tom's Cabin" as It Is; Uncle Tom's Cabin Contrasted to Buckingham Hall;* or *Uncle Robin in His Cabin in Virginia, and Tom without One in Boston*—explicitly take on the Tom tradition; others—like *Yankee Slave-Dealer; or, An Abolitionist Down South; The Master's House; Scenes Descriptive of Southern Life*—simply imply a response (Gossett 1985, 429–31).

6. Romantic racialism, an offshoot of the general tendency in nineteenth-century Europe and American "enthnology" to characterize the inherent differences of races and peoples, contrasted the innate, childlike, feminine gentleness and simplicity of the Negro with the aggressivity and will-to-power of the Anglo-Saxon. As George M. Fredrickson (1994, 430–35) has shown, historians have tended to view it as indistinguishable from the mainstream of racist thought. In naming and distinguishing it, however, Fredrickson points out that in the mid-nineteenth century the attribution of childlike, feminine simplicity was a high compliment and potentially powerful if such figures of goodness were mistreated by the overweening aggressivity of Anglo-Saxons. Romantic racialism was thus fundamental to the establishment of the claim to virtue of the sorrowing slave and, as we saw in the last chapter, to Stowe's indictment of the entire culture of slavery.

7. Recall how easy it was for Karl Brown to conflate these two eras from the later perspective of 1914 in his description of the set-building for *The Birth of the Nation*.

8. Dixon's working title for the novel was *The Rise of Simon Legree* (Dixon 1984, 263).

9. Stowe, after all, had made Legree a Yankee in order not to vilify the South alone. Dixon capitalizes on this Yankee status to illustrate the rapaciousness of northern robber barons.

10. Dixon either forgets Harry's name or gives the son his father's name to enhance his identification with the father.

11. As the Quaker labor leader comments: "The picture of that brute with a whip in his hand beating a Negro caused the most terrible war in the history of the world. Three millions of men flew at each others's throats and for four years fought like

demons. . . . Compare that Legree with the one of to-day, and you compare a mere stupid man with a prince of hell. But does this fiend excite the wrath of the righteous? Far from it. His very name is whispered in admiring awe by millions" (Dixon 1903, 404–5).

12. Interestingly, however, when abundant evidence of a prior racial mixing by white men and black women slaves is brought up in the novel, Dixon's spokespersons are unconcerned. This particular mongrelization is simply the "result of the surviving polygamous and lawless instincts of the white male" (Dixon 1903, 336). Thus Dixon minimizes the scandal of the infusion of white male blood (and semen) into black women while maximizing the horror of the infusion of black blood (and semen) into white women. The mix of "blood" thus only threatens white racial integrity. The black woman has no racial or sexual integrity to violate. As for the white woman: "The South must guard with flaming sword every avenue of approach to this holy of holies" (Dixon 1903, 336).

13. Robyn Wiegman (1995, 198) argues that Tom is released from the confines of his black masculine body in order to be "ushered into Stowe's humanizing agencies of the feminine." We have seen, however, that on the stage there was no release from corporeal presence, and that this was at least one reason for the advanced age of a great many stage Uncle Toms.

14. Michael Rogin (1984; 213–14) notes that the heroines of both *The Leopard's Spots* and *The Clansman* begin as independent New Women but end as old-fashioned helpmates.

15. As Robyn Wiegman argues, to the white supremacist male the threat of masculine sameness posited by the enfranchising of the black man was "so terrifying that only the reassertion of a gendered difference can provide the necessary disavowal" (Wiegman 1995, 90).

16. Jacquelyn Dowd Hall observes that rumors and descriptions of interracial rape became a kind of "acceptable folk pornography" in the heyday of southern lynching (1993, 150). On the evidence of Dixon's novel, it would seem that this folk pornography was much more titillating to viewers in its evocations of the lascivious black male than any picture of his contact with the white woman.

17. This punishment, which often included castration, could be construed as a kind of "communal rape" of the black man by the white crowd (Harris 1984, 23). As Jane Gaines (1993, 53) writes, it was a "uniquely American" phenomenon that did not so much repress the sexual details of its castration and rape of the black man as its economic motives for this abuse: sex was asserted, money was denied.

18. In 1892, 255 persons were killed by lynch mobs (Hall 1993, 130–32; Wiegman 1995, 93).

19. The "romance" of Dixon's subtitle only emerges in the second two hundred pages of *The Leopard's Spots*, in the form of a "modern" love story between the "new South" Charles Gaston, son of a Confederate colonel killed in the war, and Sallie Worth, daughter of a wealthy former general and Democratic politician. Thus a melodramatic saga of young love is told against the historically realistic backdrop of great historical events. In *The Clansman*, romance emerges on the first page of the novel as Elsie Stoneman, daughter of the Radical Republican senator Austin Stoneman, nurses the wounded Confederate colonel Ben Cameron in a Washington hospital. Yet even in this more effective racial melodrama in which the Clan tries Gus and then later

rides to the rescue of Austin Stoneman's son, Phil, sentenced to death for killing a black man who attacked his sister, the last-minute rescue of the white man misses the chance to combine the action of rescue with the foiling of the "beast's" attack on the white woman.

20. Dixon had enrolled in a course in dramatic technique to adapt his novels to the stage (Cook 1968, 136). He efficiently transfers *The Clansman's* novelistic climax from a ride to the rescue of Phil Stoneman to a rescue of Elsie. (The play is not in print but is available from the Harvard Theater Collection.)

21. Before proceeding with plans for the forced marriage, he proclaims, again in the words of his earlier character's incarnation in the first novel, "You've stripped the rags of slavery from a black skin, but what are you going to do with the man. . . . If I could take the stain from this skin, the kink from this hair, I'd bathe in hell fire!" (Dixon 1905b, 27).

22. These cronies, like Charles Sumner, assert a theoretical equality between white and black but cannot "endure physical contact with a negro" (Dixon 1905a, 92).

23. In the play *The Clansman*, Dixon drops the Lydia Brown character, as if he could not handle two mulatto villains in the same work. Dixon must wait for Griffith to combine the two in one work.

24. *The Leopard's Spots* sold over a hundred thousand copies within a few months; *The Clansman* sold more than a million within a few months. Both books established the fortunes of the publishing house that would become Doubleday (Cook 1968, 112; Williamson 1984, 172). Neither book rivaled the success of *Uncle Tom's Cabin* but, as we shall see, the combined novels' "leap" into the new medium of film would accomplish the challenge to Stowe that Dixon had so fervently desired.

25. Reviews in the South were often wildly enthusiastic. However, one Chattanooga editor called it a "riot breeder . . . designed to excite rage and race hatred" and Dixon's own father, upon seeing the play in Shelby, North Carolina, found it "too hard on the Negro" (Cook 1968, 103, 149).

26. In one speech he said the following: "My object is to teach the north, the young north, what it has never known—the awful suffering of the white man during the dreadful reconstruction period. I believe that Almighty God anointed the white men of the south by their suffering during that time immediately after the Civil War to demonstrate to the world that the white man shall be supreme" (Cook 1968, 140).

27. Reviews in the North were decidedly mixed. In his autobiography, D. W. Griffith called the play "a terrible frost." In fact, it did respectable business. It so happened that the New York run of *The Clansman* coincided with a mass fund-raiser for Booker T. Washington's Tuskegee Institute, held at Carnegie Hall. Newspapers reportedly made much of the melodramatic opposition between the crowds gathered to cheer the negrophobic play and the crowds at Carnegie Hall gathered to support the uplift of Negroes. Dixon sent Washington a note offering to donate ten thousand dollars to the institute if Washington would declare at the meeting that he did not seek social equality and that his school was opposed to racial amalgamation. Washington declined to answer and Dixon continued his attack in a speech the following week: "We must remove the negro or we will have to fight him. He will not continue to submit to the injustice with which we treat him in the North and South. The negro makes a magnificent fighting animal. . . . When the negro smashes into your drawing

room . . . his flat nostrils dilated, his yellow eyes and teeth gleaming, you will make good on your protestations of absolute equality or he will know the reason why" (Cook 1968, 147).

28. Indeed, when a shark attack killed the leading man when the company was swimming at a beach in North Carolina, Dixon eagerly took over the role of Ben Cameron with some success.

29. Variations of the phrase occur repeatedly in his novels. For example, the "ark of the covenant of American ideals rests [in] the South. . . . From these poverty stricken homes, with their old fashioned, perhaps medieval ideas, will come forth the fierce athletic sons and sweet-voiced daughters in whom the nation will find a new birth!" (Dixon 1903, 337).

30. Cedric Robinson (1997, 174) has also argued, against Thomas Cripps, for the continuity of the grotesque representation of blacks between nineteenth-century minstrelsy and Griffith's film and for the importance of Griffith's contribution to the birth of a new "virile American whiteness."

31. Both these writers, however, tend to locate this greater hatefulness in Griffith through an analysis of what Griffith adds to the novel, without examining the important intertext of Dixon's play version of *The Clansman*.

32. It is also possible to make the claim that African-American reaction to Griffith could only take place, as in the work of Oscar Micheaux, on the terrain of racial melodrama. In this sense D. W. Griffith's role as the (white) "legitimate" "father" of film in reaction to Stowe's negrophilia can be seen to have spawned the reaction of Micheaux, who refashions the themes and techniques of both. See Gaines (2000).

33. Recall the critic who noted how even a happy-ending Tom play threatened the "peace of the whole country" (Gossett 1985, 273).

34. Gaines and Lerner are expounding on research by Martin Marks (1997).

35. Elsie, for example, is introduced in Dixon's novel playing a minstrel tune on a banjo; she is later implored to give up that African-associated instrument for the guitar (Griffith keeps the banjo). And just before a mother and daughter commit suicide after being raped by a black man, they are haunted by "the music of a banjo in a negro cabin, mingled with vulgar shout and song and dance." A verse of the "ribald senseless" music drifts into their hearing and seems to mock them: "Chicken in de bread tray, picin'up dough;/ Granny will your dog bite? No, chile, no!" (Dixon 1905a, 306–7).

36. According to Seymour Stern, portions of this prologue were among the first that Griffith cut after protests were registered against the film. During the first five weeks of the Liberty Theater run, an opening sequence of the original prologues supposedly showed Yankee "kidnappers raiding African villages and bringing the slaves to New England in chains, and then tracing the rise of the Abolitionist movement to the hypocrisy of the slave-raiders' descendants who, as a *subtitle* [sic] explained, had 'no further use of the slaves themselves' " (Stern 1965, 66). See discussion of Stern below.

37. Rogin writes: "By cutting back and forth, Griffith juxtaposed events separated in time (the flashback) and space (the cutback) and collapsed the distinctions between images in the head and events in the world. By speeding up, reversing, and stopping time, he brought the past into the present. . . . By juxtaposing events widely separated

in space, he overcame barriers of distance (barriers overcome in the film plot by the ride to the rescue). Griffith created an art of simultaneities and juxtapositions rather than traditions and continuities" (Rogin 1984, 199).

38. The character Nelse does much the same thing at the end of Act 2 of the play *The Clansman,* but the act does not serve to rescue any white characters. Instead, it is a pointed gag played upon the scalawag governor, Shrimp, who had just arrested Dr. Cameron and made a speech that blacks were the equal of any man. Nelse, the Cameron family's "faithful" servant, asks, as Jake in the film does, "Is I yo equal?" and then follows it with a blow: "Den take dat from yo equal." In Dixon, the gag turns the tables on the governor by showing whites how claims for black equality will backfire. The blow is rhetorical, however, and simply provides punctuation to bring down the curtain. In Griffith the rhetorical point is lost in the excitement of the ongoing rescue that Jake's blow enables. In effect, Griffith displaces the potentially disturbing instance of Jake's black-on-white violence, which fails to make its rhetorical point that blacks will use violence against whites if granted equality, with the misogynist minstrel comedy of Mammy's crushing body, described in this chapter.

39. Griffith had already sketched the pathos side of this updating of the Tom-like "faithful soul" portrait in his Biograph two-reeler, *His Trust* and *His Trust Fulfilled* (1911). The two-part film tells the story of a (blackface) slave who pledges his trust to protect the family of a master who goes off to fight the Civil War. Faithful to his trust, he cares for the mother and daughter, giving the daughter a ride on his back like a horse and caring for their every need. When the father is killed and Union soldiers burn and loot the house, he risks his life to save first the daughter and then the father's sword. He then offers his "little cabin" as their home, sleeping on its doorstep like a guard dog. In the film's second part, "emancipation" shows all the slaves but George running away. When the daughter's mother dies, George becomes her only protector, sacrificing all his "savings" to place her in a nice home, paying a lawyer who pretends the money comes from the girl's estate. When George offers to shake the lawyer's hand, the lawyer refuses, making the exchange of money replace the handshake. Later, when the daughter wants to go away to school, George gives "the last of his savings." Now in rags, George is tempted to steal from the lawyer for the girl. Thinking better of it, he is nevertheless caught and chastised by the lawyer. When the girl finally marries, George, still in rags, and not a guest at the wedding, congratulates her, hobbles home to his cabin, and strokes the white father's sword. His only reward for a life of sacrifice is the arrival of the lawyer at his cabin who now offers the hand that was earlier refused. George smiles.

40. The abolitionist senator Charles Sumner, portrayed visiting Austin Stoneman in Griffith's film, once said that without *Uncle Tom's Cabin* there would have been no Lincoln in the White House (Whicher 1963, 563; Hanne 1994, 77).

41. Griffith was a Kentuckian whose autobiography is suffused with nostalgia for the good Kentucky home and the pastoral beauty of its countryside dotted with (former) slave cabins. He cites one spring morning in which he felt a "luminous glow of joy" while walking near a double log cabin where two of his family's former slaves lived, and of "Aunt Easter," who cooked him hoecakes that, as for young Master George, tasted better than those of his own mother (Hart 1972, 28–29).

42. Kathleen McHugh (1999, 99) points out that no black families are represented in the film (Mammy and Jake only seem related, as do Mammy and Prissy in

Gone With the Wind, because they are black and "coupled" in the cabin). Mammy is asexual and exists only in relation to the masters she serves.

43. We have also seen that many of the theatrical Uncle Tom's simply ignore this problem and make Kentucky home.

44. See Russell Merritt's (1978–79) insightful analysis of the spatial incoherence of this set.

333

45. We first see Elsie in the Union Hospital, for example, playing the banjo.

46. Lindsay (1915, 152–53) writes that "white leader, Col. Ben Cameron . . . enters not as an individual, but as representing the white Anglo Saxon Niagara. . . . The wrath of the Southern against the blacks and their Northern organizers has been piled up through many previous scenes. As a result this rescue is a real climax, something photoplays that trace strictly personal hatreds cannot achieve."

47. It is possible that this, too, is the result of cuts made in the film after its release. Seymour Stern asserts that a scene showing "the actual rape of *Flora* by *Gus*, on the rock" was eliminated, along with scenes of Negro rapists whisking white women into doorways and back alleys of Piedmont. Eliminated also, according to Stern, was the indirectly depicted castration of Gus (discussed below), an epilogue featuring Lincoln's statement opposing racial equality, and images of the deportation of masses of Negroes from New York Harbor to the jungles of Africa. In all, Stern claims that the film was cut from 1,544 shots in the first Liberty Theater run to the 1,375 shots of the 12 ½ reels in the present version (Stern 1965, 66). I am inclined to doubt that Griffith ever showed an "actual rape" on the rock, though he may have intimated this rape by indirect means. See below for further discussion of Stern.

48. Critics have understandably made much of actor Walter Long's portrayal of Gus, citing his unnatural hunched-over, bestial walk and run and his frothing lips caused by swilling hydrogen peroxide, during his pursuit of Flora (see Rogin 1984, Taylor 1991, Robinson 1997). Despite the bestial pose, however, there is nothing in the scene as now played that insinuates his sexual intentions toward Flora. The Lynch/Elsie scene, on the other hand, is remarkably lascivious.

49. In that film, a woman's body is slashed because it is female—obsessive castration is enacted as a kind of overkill by a psychopath who has lost all connection with civilization. Here, the body is mutilated because it is black and male and because it has come too close to the white woman.

50. Walker says this as an old man in an on-camera interview in Kevin Brownlow and David Gill's 1992 documentary, *D. W. Griffith, the Father of Film*. We do not know what precise version of the film Walker saw.

51. For a fascinating discussion of the Gothic dimension of Stowe's novel, and indeed, of the Stowe family, see Halttunen (1985).

52. Recall that Stowe herself never killed off Legree, though most stage versions did. She seemed to consider Legree's haunting punishment enough.

53. He would prove it again, even more memorably, in *Intolerance* (1916) and, as we have seen in Chapter 1, in *Way Down East* (1920).

54. This was also part of the Conway version that originated at the Boston Museum and which rivaled Aiken's version at P.T. Barnum's Museum in New York in the early 1850s.

55. Thomas Gossett reports, however, that Gilpin may also have been drunk (1985, 384).

56. In a letter to her publisher in 1862, Stowe wrote that she was going to Washington "to have a talk with 'Father Abraham' himself" to determine how serious he had been about the Emancipation Proclamation (Gossett 1985, 314). It was at this meeting that Lincoln reportedly referred to Stowe as the "little lady who made this big war."

Chapter Four

1. See, for example, Michael Rogin's pioneering study, *Blackface, White Noise: Jewish Immigrants in the Hollywood Melting Pot* (1996), and Susan Gubar's study of the fluid relations between black and white, *Racechanges: White Skin, Black Face in American Culture* (1997).

2. The great exception is Lauren Berlant's magisterial essay, "Pax Americana: The Case of *Show Boat*"(1996), to which I will be referring.

3. Anthropologist Renato Rosaldo has offered the following explanation of the dynamics of this process: "A person kills somebody, and then mourns the victim. In more attenuated form, someone deliberately alters a form of life, and then regrets that things have not remained as they were prior to the intervention. At one more remove, people destroy their environment, and then they worship nature. In any of its versions, *imperialist nostalgia* uses a pose of 'innocent yearning' both to capture people's imaginations and to conceal its complicity with often brutal domination" (Gubar 1997, 69–70; emphasis mine).

4. Culture critic Susan Gubar (1997), for example, has applied Rosaldo's notion of "imperialist nostalgia" to the slave system that first destroyed African culture and then committed the further "spirit-murder" of minstrel shows and blackface films. Film critic and political scientist Michael Rogin (1996) has similarly emphasized the role of blackface in eradicating authentic forms of African-American culture. In what follows I will be more interested in understanding the impure, contaminated hybridities enabled by the activation of a melodramatic "space of innocence" within this Jazz Age blackface tradition.

5. Examples include *The Singing Fool* (Bacon, 1928), *Applause* (Mamoulian, 1929), and *Broadway Melody* (Beaumont, 1929). The first is father-son, the second mother-daughter, and the third is sister-sister family melodrama.

6. See, for example, Martin Gottfried's *Broadway Musicals*, which argues that *Show Boat* represented the first serious, adult merger of song and dramatic stage sense (1979, 161). Ethan Mordden (1989, 79) has also argued that *Show Boat* is the ancestor of all serious American musical theater as distinguished from musical comedy. The operettas, written by the likes of Victor Herbert, Sigmund Romberg, and Rudolph Friml, were integrated but they did so in escapist, exotic contexts and in musical idioms derived from Europe. It could be that "show business" substituted for the exotic kingdoms of many an operetta.

7. As Susan Gubar has explained, if white people have attempted to sympathize with African Americans in ways that have distorted and usurped their proper perspective, it is nevertheless fruitless to presume within the context of so many cross-racial entanglements that there can even be an actual "proper" perspective (Gubar 1997, 246).

8. This comedian had presumably once hidden his Irishness under similar circumstances. This man passed the tricks of the trade to a new generation of predominantly Jewish performers who would soon rework blackface to "jazzier" ends.

9. Although Raphaelson had based his work on Jolson's Mammy-singer persona, he had already once declined to have Jolson star in it on Broadway once Jolson had made it clear that his vision of the work was a hammed-up musical revue in the manner of *Robinson Crusoe Jr.* (Carringer 1979, 12). It is no wonder, then, that he was not pleased with Warner Brothers' decision at the last minute, after a script had been written for the play's star George Jessel, to make the film a musical vehicle for the work's actual inspiration, superstar Al Jolson.

10. Speaking in an oral history transcription Raphaelson vented his anger: "Jolson didn't have any comedy dialogue. The man's a terrific comedian—and a lousy actor. He's a not-actor. They gave him 'dramatic' scenes—that is, 'straight' scenes—terribly written synopsis dialogue. . . . It was embarrassing. A dreadful picture. . . . They put a lot of songs in that were bad, and badly placed. . . . The corny part was overdone" (Columbia Oral History Transcription, quoted in Carringer 1979, 21). Raphaelson is actually objecting here to the transformation of his play into an integrated musical melodrama, precisely the source, I argue, of its significance.

11. As Pearl Sieben, one biographer, put it: "He needed applause the way a diabetic needs insulin" (Pleasants 1974, 49). Jolson had runways built into theaters in order to put him in closer contact with the audiences who fed him his characteristic energy.

12. Rogin reminds us that in the shooting script Yudelson called them "nigger songs" (1996, 95).

13. "Shuffle Along" was the title of an all-black musical that had taken Broadway by storm in 1921. Its success marked the beginning of the new vogue for all things Negro that marked the Harlem Renaissance. Playing for nearly two years, and acting as a showcase for the black talent that would mark the decade (Paul Robeson, Adelaide Hall, and Josephine Baker were in the chorus), the show marked the beginning of the end of blackface (Woll 1989, 60–70).

14. Coffee Dan's in San Francisco was an actual cafe where an up-and-coming Jolson once sang twenty songs in a row standing on a table (Goldman 1988, 44).

15. The song resembles the following year's even more pathos-filled Jolson hit, "Sonny Boy," from the film *The Singing Fool.*

16. The song assumes the persona of a shiftless wanderer singing an affectionate farewell to a girlfriend in a carefree mood that belies the pathos of parting: "Toot, Toot, Tootsie goodbye/Toot, Toot, Tootsie don't cry. . . . Watch for the mail, I'll never fail/ If you don't get a letter then you'll know I'm in jail."

17. Jolson first spoke this line at a World War I fundraising drive in which his act followed that of Enrico Caruso, one of the greatest tenors in opera history. Caruso had just sent the audience into a patriotic frenzy with a performance of George M. Cohan's "Over There." Partly self-deprecating, partly serious, Jolson introduced himself with this line (Goldman 1988, 98). Thereafter, he would only use it to surpass himself. Of course, the line is important in other ways as well. When Jolson prophesied, "You ain't heard nothin' yet," "he turned out to be talking about more than just his next number. Out of *The Jazz Singer* sprang the Hollywood musical" (Mast 1987, 89).

18. The song originally scheduled to be sung here, "It All Depends on You," was actually recorded but scratched at the last minute and replaced by "Blue Skies."

19. Rogin is right to argue, however, that such ethnicity is "whitewashed" out of the later tradition of popular American film. Moreover, if Jewish ethnicity is not actually eradicated it is placed within an intergenerational conflict between father and son that displaces the more overt conflict between gentile and Jew.

20. Rogin points out the sexual nature of this slapping: "The sexual origins of the word *jazz*—in copulation—have never been more spectacularly, or inappropriately, present" (1996, 83).

21. The song was actually introduced in 1920 by the vaudeville tenor William Frawley ("Fred Mertz" of *I Love Lucy* fame). It was Jolson, however, who made it a hit when he interpolated it into his 1921 Broadway Show, *Bombo*; his face was printed on the sheet music (liner notes for *Al Jolson: The Best of the Decca Years*).

22. The song was first introduced in the 1918 opening of *Sinbad*, and reprised in *Bombo* (1922), and in the 1926 Vitaphone short that launched sound film in advance of *The Jazz Singer* (Goldman 1988, 94).

23.   Rock-a-bye your baby with a Dixie melody
        When you croon, croon a tune, from the heart of Dixie
        Hang that cradle, Mammy mine,
        Right on that Mason-Dixon Line
        And swing it from Virginia
        To Tennessee with all the soul that's in ya.
        "Weep No More My Lady"
        Mammy sing it again for me
        And *"Old Black Joe"* just as though
        You had me on your knee.
        A Million baby kisses I'd deliver
        If you would only sing that *"Swanee River"*
        Rock-a-bye your rock-a-bye baby with a Dixie melody!

24. This quiet passing in which Jakie simply fails to mention his racial origins is more overt in Raphaelson's short story, "The Day of Atonement," where he clearly desires the non-Jewish qualities of his gentile girlfriend and is frankly ashamed of, for example, his natural ability to dance in a more rhythmic, whole-body fashion.

25. Rogin notes that one of the early Vitaphone shorts that introduced movie audiences to sound was tenor Giovanni Martinelli's performance of the aria "Vesti la giubba" from Leoncavallo's opera *Pagliacci*. Rogin suggests that the popularity of this original showstopping, sad clown routine may well have influenced Warner Brothers to make *The Jazz Singer* and *The Singing Fool* (1996, 147).

26. It is not quite accurate to say, however, as Rogin does, that this mask hides Jewishness. In a remarkable way it also permits its expression. Jewishness is seen, heard, and celebrated. And it is only at the moment Jakie puts on blackface that he confesses his "race" to Mary. Rogin is right to argue, however, that blackness is only celebrated as black*face*, that is, as an absence.

27. The mother of this blackface "Mammy" song is neither the southern Mammy of minstrel tradition, nor the Yiddish Mama of the Jewish ghetto tradition. Rather, she is the sentimentalized mother of English-Irish tradition. If you close your eyes and

listen to this song you can almost hear a brogue. It is thus not in the music and lyrics of this song, but in its image of the pathetic son singing of the primal emotion of mother love that the traditional black Mammy is evoked.

28. Significantly it was this moment that author Samson Raphaelson most hated in the Warner Brothers musical adaptation of his story and play: "Lord Almighty, the one thing that I wouldn't have him sing was a song about *mother*. There's a limit" (Carringer 1979, 21). Yet it was precisely a song about a black mother, "Dixie Mammy," that Raphaelson did have his character sing in his play. What Raphaelson seems to object to here is precisely the link between Jewish mother and Dixie Mammy. That is, he resists the blatant melodrama of the appeal to primal familial emotions without the cultural protection of singing to a mammy rather than a mother.

29. Susan Gubar (1997, 72) argues that Jolson's blackface seems to "stage a mourning over precisely the injust spirit-murder it repeatedly enacts." Michael Rogin (1996, 73–129) had earlier argued much the same thing specifying that the supposed sympathy for blacks is also an eradication. While mourning and eradication seem apt descriptions of the sins of blackface, it is important to realize that this particular black-face film created a space for the articulation of the felt similarities between Jewish and black suffering that are both basic to the American "genealogy of entertainments" and a continuation of the Tom tradition of black/white racial sympathy.

30. *Variety* commented that May McAvoy was "smothered on footage with no love theme to help" (October 12, 1927).

31. When Jack tries to convince Mary, and himself, that his career means more to him than anything, Mary asks, "More than me?" Jack's nod of assent is distinctly out of place in a conventional backstage romance. However, were Jack to confess undying love for Mary at the very moment he first speaks of his race, it would raise the specter of their racial differences. Blackface thus diverts attention from the difference between gentile and Jew by raising the more dramatic and visible specter of black and white racial difference that, by contrast, minimizes the more subtle differences between them. More profoundly, however, the blackface "mammy song" plunges the Jew back into a pre-Oedipal state of maternal thrall where sexual desires do not matter.

32. *The Singing Fool* repeats this effect when its character, named Al, twice re-prises the song "Sonny Boy," originally sung as a lullaby to his young son. The first reprise is in the hospital on the child's deathbed; the second is in blackface on stage where the now bereft father poignantly sings, "I still have you, Sonny boy," to a giant image of his son superimposed over the audience.

33. Theologically, Kol Nidre is something of an anomaly in Orthodox Jewish service. Written in Aramaic, not Hebrew, it appears to be a legal text about the annul-ment of vows and has worked its way into the liturgy as a kind of prayer. What matters, however, is that it is a lugubrious, popular melody, going back to the 1500s, which has attached itself to the Day of Atonement. It opens the Yom Kippur service and signifies a Jew asking to be released from any vows made to God, not to others. It constitutes a kind of wiping-the-slate-clean at the start of the year but is not an actual plea for forgive-ness (Elbogen 1993; Deborah Malmud, personal communication).

34. Rogin does not condemn all black-inflected music of urban Jews. Noting that the second-generation ethnic vitality of Tin Pan Alley, Broadway, and the Lower East Side often found newly expressive ways of being Jewish, he nevertheless argues that the Hollywood homogenization of this culture typified by *The Jazz Singer* screened

out both actual black jazz and Jewish ethnicity (Rogin, 1996, 100). I am arguing, however, that *The Jazz Singer* was actually an exceptional film in its willingness to bring (certain) issues of race to the forefront, in advance of the mainstream whitewashing of Hollywood.

35. For an extensive discussion of the full extent of this mongrelization see Ann Douglas (1995).

36. Arguing against the conventional view that jazz was born out of the musical amalgamation of the American Negro and the American Jew, Rogin asserts that assimilation to whiteness, not the speaking of any specific Jewish or black woe, and certainly not the making of "jazz" music, is what crucially takes place in this film (Rogin 1996, 73–120). Thus, Al Jolson's Jewish "jazz" singer, Jakie Rabinowitz, assimilates to the American melting pot, shedding his Jewishness to become "Jack Robin." He paints himself black, as Rogin puts it, "to wash himself white" (102). The embrace of blackface thus allows Yoelson-Jolson/Rabinowitz-Robin to erase the stereotype of the ambitious, rootless, cosmopolitan Jew with the substitute stereotype of the darkie still pining (like Uncle Tom and other rootless white Americans) for the fantasized good Kentucky (or Virginny or Alabammy) home. Instead of the dynamic cosmopolitan and free-roaming accents of actual jazz, which were a mix of musical influences presided over by actual African-American musicians, Rogin argues that Jack Robin dons blackface to sing a sad song about home and mother. It is precisely the pathos of this moment, however, that I argue needs more scrutiny.

37. Rogin, for example, criticizes the acceptance of Whiteman as the King of Jazz in his famous 1924 concert at Aeolian Hall in New York and later in the film *The King of Jazz*. Both of these events told an implicit story of the evolution of a "discordant" early jazz (depicted as black) toward the heights of George Gershwin's "Rhapsody in Blue" (Rogin 1996, 138–39).

38. Certainly violence is done to the real black men and women whose own performances of blackness are erased from this representation, but the fact that this violence simultaneously brought a new form of African-American pathos to the very center of popular American entertainment with the "invention" of sound needs recognition.

39. This word is emphasized in Raphaelson's stage play. When Jack and Mary each try to explain who their "people" (76–77) are to one another, Mary uses the term in the sense of family, while Jakie uses the term in a more racial sense. It is only later that Mary understands that Jakie is a cantor's son.

40. Indeed, they very much resembled the kind of disparate collection of variety acts that one sees in the show being rehearsed by Jakie and Mary in *The Jazz Singer*—a hodgepodge of songs and dances that contrasts sharply with the much-more motivated songs sung in the film itself. Only in the European-derived and exotically set romantic operettas did songs develop out of character and situation (as in the previous year's *The Desert Song* by Sigmund Romberg, for which Oscar Hammerstein II wrote the book and lyrics).

41. Gerald Mast writes that *Show Boat* became the first American musical to translate the operetta's romantic attachment to historical settings into a moral question about history. It translated the operetta's romantic attraction to the class structure into a moral concern with American class distinctions (Mast 1987, 59).

42. Examples include, the musical bars of "I Got Shoes," the lyrics of "Deep River," and "All God's Chillun' Got Wings."

43. Indeed, it is the origin of the tradition that would eventually lead, after the hiatus of the Depression and the passing of Kern, to the more "mature" melodramatic musicals represented by Oscar Hammerstein II's late works deploying similar "tragic" plots and subplots of race: *South Pacific* (1949), *The King and I* (1951), *The Sound of Music* (1959), as well as *West Side Story* (1957), *Miss Saigon* (1989), and *Ragtime* (1996). Although these musicals follow the pattern of the tragic racial subplot initiated by *Show Boat*, it would not be until *West Side Story* that a popular musical would once again place racial melodrama in an American context.

44. Significantly, unlike the text of subsequent Broadway musicals, *Show Boat* has no fixed script and is subject to radical change from one production to the next.

45. I am indebted to Miles Kreuger's lovingly produced *Show Boat: The Story of a Classic American Musical* (1977a) for much of the production history. For the sake of clarity let me here acknowledge the important productions detailed in Kreuger's study. In chronological order they are the 1927 Ziegfeld version; the 1928 London version, the first to include Paul Robeson as Joe; a 1929 Universal film version, originally shot as a silent film, to which sound sequences and some music—not always Kern and Hammerstein's—was added and from which the miscegenation subplot was deleted; a 1932 Ziegfeld revival on stage with Paul Robeson; the 1936 Universal film version, directed by James Whale, with Irene Dunne, Alan Jones, Helen Morgan, Paul Robeson, and Hattie McDaniel; a 1946 postwar stage revival that, according to Miles Kreuger, reportedly excised the word "nigger" unless spoken with hostility by a bad guy and changed the line "Niggers all work on de Mississippi" in the opening chorus to "Colored folks work on the Mississippi" (this version contains a great many new dances); a 1951 MGM film directed by George Sidney, with Kathryn Grayson and Ava Gardner, that condenses the work's timespan and seems deeply afraid of its racial theme. I also rely upon the 1993 revival that originated in Toronto, directed by Harold Prince, which played New York for an extended run and toured major cities. I have seen the Toronto and Los Angeles versions of this production.

46. "Mrs. Hawks, bustling into the show-boat kitchen with her unerring gift for scenting an atmosphere of mellow enjoyment, and dissipating it, would find Magnolia perched on a chair, both elbows on the table, her palms propping her chin as she regarded with round-eyed fascination Queenie's magic manipulations [of a stuffed ham]. Or perhaps Jo, the charming and shiftless, would be singing for her one of the Negro plantation songs, wistful with longing and pain; the folk songs of a wronged race, later to come into a blaze of popularity as spirituals" (Ferber 1994, 90).

47. Ferber's enthusiasm for this black folk music goes so far as to reprint the musical notation for "I Got Shoes" (91) and to reproduce the lyrics of "Deep River" (83), the spiritual that was the model for Kern and Hammerstein's "Ol' Man River." *Deep River* was also the name of an all-black musical produced the previous year on Broadway. Though it failed, running only four weeks, it is remembered as a musically ambitious "native opera" and forerunner to Gershwin's *Porgy and Bess* (1935). See Bordman (1978, 417).

48. For ten cents extra Cap'n Andy's patrons could stay for an "olio," a postmelodrama variety show.

49. In the 1936 film black audiences enter the show boat to the left and up to the balcony while white audiences go to the main floor. Simultaneously humble and grand, democratically inclusionary and brutally segregated, the Cotton Blossom is an idealized extrapolation of the Old South, a contradictory mix of racial amity and rigid segregation. As a floating plantation unmoored from the historic horrors of slavery, its crucial points of reference remain the sorrows of slaves that had become so basic a part of American national identity since *Uncle Tom's Cabin*. We do well to remember how iconographically embedded riverboats themselves had become in the theatrical and film "Tom" tradition. Stowe's novel included a scene in which Tom rescues Eva when she falls overboard from a riverboat. Though the Aiken stage version includes no such scene, other stage versions and most film versions include the scene and play up the local color of riverboat lore. Both the overboard scene and a narratively extraneous race between the *Natchez* and the *Robert E. Lee*—enacted by tiny models in an obvious tank in the 1903 Edison film version—attest to the importance of riverboat iconography in the Tom tradition continued in all subsequent film versions (e.g., World 1910, Daly 1914, Pollard 1927).

50. Indeed, in a world in which a "genealogy of entertainments" has replaced the events of history (Berlant 1996, 401), the public place where entertainment is produced is equated with the private place of home. Backstage musicals, as we have seen, tend to privilege this equation ("Broadway—Home—MOTHER"). For Magnolia, this equation is there almost from the beginning and reachieved near the end of the novel when, alone and abandoned, she seeks work at Jopper's Varieties, in a basement theater in Chicago, and suddenly realizes "a feeling of security, of peace, of homecoming" in the dingy stage and crude paint and in a "coon song full of mah babys and choo-choos and Alabam's" (Ferber 1994, 273).

51. This number is severely truncated in the 1936 film version. I rely here on Miles Kreuger's (1977a) description of the Ziegfeld production and my notes on the 1993 staging.

52. In 1904 Will Marion Cook's *The Southerner* included black and white talent in a musical without adverse incident. By the mid-twenties it was not unheard of for a few black performers to appear in predominantly white shows, but they did so cordoned off from the rest of the numbers, like the later MGM musicals featuring Lena Horne in glorious isolation. It was still rare to mix black and white talent in both leading roles and chorus (Vincent Youman's 1929 *Great Day* reportedly did so). It was unprecedented, however, for black talent to star in the context of a narrative premised upon the problem of racial difference (Woll 1989, 211). There had, of course, been occasional black performers in predominantly white musical reviews, most famously Bert Williams, who was a major attraction in Ziegfeld's Follies from 1910 through 1919. But Williams was an exception and his numbers were not integrated with the rest of the cast (Woll 1989, 48).

53. Africanist is the term used by Toni Morrison (1992) to designate what people of African descent have meant in the imaginary fears and desires of whites.

54. Gardella later played opposite the black Jules Bledsoe (and then opposite Paul Robeson on stage in the 1932 revival. She was not replaced until one of the Jubilee Singers, Angeline Lawson, took over her role in a touring company of the 1932 revival. Alberta Hunter, however, had already played the role opposite Robeson in the intervening 1928 London production (Kreuger 1977a, 104).

55. It seems unthinkable today, for example, but before George Gershwin wrote *Porgy and Bess* for black performers, Al Jolson had wanted Jerome Kern and Oscar Hammerstein II to adapt the Dubose Heyward story for him.

56. By contrast, in Ferber's novel this conflict erupts suddenly, with no preparation, and disappears just as suddenly, with no aftermath.

57. I refer mostly to the 1936 film's staging and performance in this discussion, and thus to Robeson's performance.

58. The low-key quietness of the performance is somewhat offset in the film by James Whale's busy camera, which immediately cranes behind and above Joe as he starts to sing.

59. See my discussion of this notion in Chapter 3.

60. Spirituals often encourage resignation to the cares of the world in exchange for the peace of an otherworldly "beyond." But they may also express coded forms of complaint.

61. Spirituals, in contrast, were composed out of much simpler, sixteen-bar, AB structures. "Go Down Moses," for example, simply alternates between an eight-bar A verse ("When Israel was in Egypt land") and an eight-bar B refrain ("Go down, Moses"). Minstrel songs imitated this simpler form. Compare, for example, Stephen Foster's "Old Black Joe."

62. Miles Kreuger (1977a, 54) was the first to point out this simplicity of the short lines and the limited use of rhyme. Lauren Berlant (1996) makes the further observation that the single rhyme "cotton" and "forgotten" echoes the most infamous of all minstrel songs, "Dixie."

63. In the 1936 film, the two parts of the song run together. Perversely, the 1951 film version, with William Warfield in the part of Joe, cuts out this stevedore chorus entirely.

64. As with Joe, however, the vigor in Whale's version is considerably softened by the fact that all sing entirely from a seated posture. All post–civil rights era versions of the song, and even the 1951 version that is otherwise so unconscious of racial tension, present it from a much more virile standing position.

65. At least it did in the performances of this production I saw in 1993 in Toronto and in 1996 in Los Angeles. Of course, the filmed performance of Robeson in Whale's 1936 production can have none of the interaction of the live audience. In addition, as Lauren Berlant has noted, Whale's often expressionist mise-en-scène, with its montages of Robeson toting barges, lifting bales, and landing, in a high-angle shot, "in jail," tends to augment the sense that the black realities depicted in these highly contained montages are "estranged" by the very expressionism of its style from the rest of the white narrative (Berlant 1996, 412). At the same time, however, Whale's version does considerably more than earlier and later stage versions to bring Joe's story into the white narrative, giving him the task of rowing to shore to bring Gaylord to Magnolia when she gives birth. It also adds a casual and markedly unexpressionist new song ("I Still Suits Me") of self-satisfied laziness that is not at all estranged by expressionism but is fully consistent with lazy darky stereotypes, thus contributing further to the incoherence of Joe's character.

66. The 1951 film version of *Show Boat* seems to want to rectify this passivity by having William Warfield deliver the song standing on the boat as it is casting off, just after the expulsion of Julie and Steve from the acting troupe. The song is thus interest-

ingly repositioned to become a commentary on the Julie-Steve troubles rather than on Magnolia's insipid infatuation with Gaylord. The progressiveness of this repositioning is undercut, however, by the total absence of the stevedore chorus in this song and the absence of an interracial context for the subsequent "Can't Help Lovin' Dat Man." The ultimate effect is the emasculation of serious racial content from this version.

67. For example, when the stevedores join him to reprise the song, the scene shifts from the Natchez levee to a black-and-white backdrop of cotton fields that looks for all the world like the theatrical cotton field backdrop in Edwin S. Porter's 1903 film of *Uncle Tom's Cabin*. This version builds to an even more rousing conclusion unsoftened by any smile and rendered considerably ironic by the fact that the shift to the next scene of the musical is accomplished by these same cotton picker/stevedores whose job it is to "tote" out the next set.

68. Over the years Robeson would gradually change the words, extending its references to oppression, shifting its meaning from ultimate resignation to ongoing struggle, and omitting all traces of Negro dialect. For example, the original line expressing envy of the river, "Dat's de ol' man dat I'd like to be," becomes rejection, "That's the old man I don't like to be," and the original "Git a little drunk an' you land in jail" becomes the more combative "Show a little grit and you land in jail" (Dyer 1986, 105-107). These changes attest to Robeson's own grit and perseverance over the years, but they are changes enabled by the song itself.

69. One white cartoonist in *Sketch* portrayed Robeson with the caption, "Despite ragtime and jazz music, poor old Joe sings 'Ole Man Ribber' right through the years from 1880 to 1928" (in Duberman 1989, 115). Even this anger demonstrates the extent to which the song, and Robeson's mere presence on stage, raised expectations for putting the African American into history.

70. Indeed, it would not be until the 1996 musical *Ragtime*, produced very much in the wake of the 1993 revival of *Show Boat*, that a narrative would be spun out of an American story that could put not only the black man, but the black American family, front and center in its narrative. Unfortunately, however, *Ragtime*'s melos has very little of the power of *Show Boat*'s.

71. Once again my discussion relies upon the 1936 film for staging and performance details that seem to be the closest to the 1927 Ziegfeld Theater original.

72. In the 1993 Toronto production, Julie was played by Lonette McKee, a light-skinned African American who plays the role with great feeling. Unlike Helen Morgan, however, her over-the-top bluesy rendition of the song is an instant giveaway to her mixed-race identity. We know Julie for black the moment she starts to sing. While Julie's black pride and pleasure in the song may be the only way it can now be performed in a post–civil rights era, McKee's bravura performance subverts the more complex tensions between the melodrama of passing as white and posing as black played out by Morgan.

73. In the 1993 revival references to gin were excised. In the 1951 film there are also no references to gin, but neither is there any black-white interaction in the course of the number beyond that between Julie (Ava Gardner) and Magnolia (Kathryn Grayson). In this rigorously segregated version Julie and Magnolia sing on the upper deck of the show boat while the darkies undulate below, leaving the number utterly eviscerated of its integrating and miscegenational excitement.

74. "Bill" was actually written years earlier by Jerome Kern and P. G. Wodehouse for a show entitled *Oh, Lady, Lady* (1918), about a girl in love with a boy named Bill. Pulled from the earlier musical, Kern inserted it in *Show Boat*'s second act when he needed a torch song for Julie. The musical success of the song, which became an instant hit and is, indeed, lovely, has tended to obscure discussion of why Kern choose to borrow an old song with no blues influence rather than write a new torch song more appropriately tailored to Julie's narrative and musical situation. I suggest that to write a new, narratively appropriate torch song—perhaps one entitled "Steve"—would have been to flirt too overtly with the miscegenational fantasy that is at the root of the Julie-Steve subplot.

75. One important difference, however, is that while all the principals except Parthy are sympathetic to Julie and Steve's plight in the musical, this is true only of Cap'n Andy and Magnolia in the novel.

76. On stage the word was "nigger"—a word more in keeping with the language of a turn-of-the-century Mississippi sheriff, but a word impossible to utter in film due to the proscriptions then in place under the Hollywood Production Code. See discussion below.

77. In *Hollywood's Fantasy of Miscegenation*, a 1997 doctoral dissertation, Susan Courtney traces the history of the ban on miscegenation in the Motion Picture Producers and Distributors of America's first list of "Don'ts and Be Carefuls," adopted in 1927, through the formalized Production Code of 1930, the more strictly enforced code of 1934, and the final lifting of the ban in 1956. Courtney brilliantly shows that what is at stake in the code's rules on miscegenation, and in the negotiations between studios and the Production Code Administration, is not only "who could be seen doing what with whom on screen, but how spectators would be cinematically prompted to read 'race' " (170). Hollywood's ban on the representation of miscegenation might seem to have precluded the representation of the Julie-Steve subplot in *Show Boat*. Indeed, the Julie-Steve relation is entirely excised from the first, 1929, Universal production. However, the very centrality of miscegenation, both in the white fantasy of "anti-Tom" racial melodrama depicting the white woman endangered by the "black beast" and in the more historically based representation of black women impregnated by white masters in the "Tom" tradition, made the official Hollywood ban on the representation of miscegenation difficult to sustain. As Courtney has shown, representations of the figure of the mulatto or mulatta were often unavoidable. For example, the 1939 reissue of the 1927 version of *Uncle Tom's Cabin* came smack up against the new taboos against miscegenation in the inference of Legree's past sexual relations with Cassy and his overtures toward Eliza (Courtney 1997, 195). Cuts were made to soften the sexual force of the relation but Simon Legree's leering pursuit of his mulatta servants (always played, of course, by white women) was such a fixture of American racial melodrama throughout the second half of the nineteenth and well into the early twentieth century that it could not be completely excised.

78. Interestingly, considerably more worry was expressed over the miscegenational overtones of white and black cast members playing a married couple. Tess Gardella, the white musical performer who played Queenie in blackface on Broadway, was originally scheduled to play opposite Paul Robeson's Joe in the film. Joseph Breen of the Production Code Administration responded to Universal's concern about this

form of miscegenation—at the level of performance rather than at the level of the performer's fictional characters—with the following advice: "It is our judgment that there can be no serious objection to our casting Robeson, the negro, to play the part he played on the stage, and, at the same time, to cast the white woman, Aunt Jemima [Gardella's stage name], for the part of Robeson's wife. *I think you should be extremely careful, however, not to indicate any physical contact* between the white woman and the negro man *for the reason that many people know Aunt Jemima is a white woman and might be repulsed by the sight of her being fondled by a man who is a negro*" (Courtney 1997, 240). One wonders what would have happened to the line "I even love him/When his kisses got gin" had Gardella played Queenie. The problem was rendered moot, of course, by the casting of Hattie McDaniel in the role of Queenie and the effective end of blackface performance in the film, but this very decision may have been influenced by the realization that the song "Can't Help Lovin' Dat Man," as we have seen, deflected attention away from the narrative-level miscegenation of Julie and Steve precisely through a refocus on the "down and dirty" sexual relation of Joe and Queenie.

79. Susan Courtney (1997) reports that in the file dated the same day that the code certificate of approval for *Show Boat* was sent to the studio, notice is made of accusation of miscegenation against the "two leads in Capt. Hawks [sic] show," but approval is granted with no further comment.

80. In Reconstruction, miscegenation law internalized the feudal economy the Civil War had supposedly ended. It used blood to control the legal legitimation of social unions and the legal disposition of property to the children of these unions. The possession of white blood allowed courts to conceive all whites as members of a family sharing race as property. Tracing a defendant's genealogy became the equivalent of a title search. If traced back far enough, this metaphorical title to blood revealed the actual historical fact of legal title: the title in a Negro that could be sold.

81. That tie, of course, does not last, for reasons that neither the novel nor any of the musical forms, stage or film, explore. The next time we see Julie she is again posing as white, this time without Steve. No explanation for his absence is given in this narrative about the inconstancy and "shiftlessness" of men.

82. In Whale's film Magnolia's adoption of black characteristics is especially pronounced in the addition of a blackface number from the show boat's "olio" not included in the original stage production. Called "Gallivantin' Around," it is an overt, comic "coon song" with banjo, woolly wig, and chorus of blackface men. A brief shot from the balcony's "nigger heaven" displays the backs of several Negroes looking down on the blackface antics below.

83. This 1929 version of the film, however, does include a brief reference to the Negro audience in the balcony of the show boat, shot, as in Whale's film, from behind their backs. The expulsion of Julie and Steve in the stage version, however, would have a particular resonance with the newly integrated audience and performers of the Ziegfeld Theater. The substitution of integration for miscegenation as the crime for which Julie and Steve are banished would have permitted even those audiences who might have been offended by a story that rendered sympathetic the crime of miscegenation to displace this offense onto the sheriff's intolerance of integration. This blurring of the cause of Julie and Steve's expulsion may have allowed sophisticated New York

audiences of the stage musical to condemn the backwards ways of a turn-of-the-century Mississippi town without having to come to terms with feelings that were very likely more conflicted.

84. Whale's film does, however, utilize a storm on the river to give a moment of heroism associated with the river to Joe, who rows to shore in a storm to fetch Gaylord when Magnolia gives birth to Kim.

85. In the 1936 film, Kim is seen performing in a show that looks for all the world like an updated minstrel show sans blackface.

Chapter Five

1. See James Baldwin (1949, 578) and Leslie Fiedler (1982, 173) and the discussion of both in Chapter 2.

2. The rehabilitation of sentimental literature has sometimes been achieved at the expense of segregating the female-domestic-maternal-sentimental from the rest of American popular culture. The great interest of the home-embracing melodrama of black and white is that it is not a female-centered ghetto of overwrought emotion, but, as Mark Mullen puts it, describing the nineteenth-century stage, a "place of commonality between men and women" (Mullen 1998, 54).

3. Compare, for example, the two great set pieces of *The Birth of a Nation* and *Gone With the Wind*: Ben Cameron's and Scarlett O'Hara's returns to their ravaged plantation homes after or during the Civil War.

4. Of course this image of African-American fixity was itself a myth. The first two decades of the century were a time of unprecedented migration by African Americans to the industrial cities of the north (Baker 1993, 75).

5. Edward D.C. Campbell, Jr., for example, notes that the reason for the success of both Mitchell's and Selznick's works was that in each "the South was portrayed as an uncomplicated society" in contrast to the complexity and confusion of the postwar era. A conservative ideal of the past is thus held up against the encroaching urban, commercial, and racial despair that followed the South's demise (1981, 127).

6. The best of the historians is David Thomson's (1993) magnificent biography of Selznick. The best of the buffs is Gavin Lambert's (1973) loving account of the film's making and Aljean Harmetz's lushly illustrated (1996) version of the same.

7. For example, David Cook's (1990) well-respected textbook mentions the film in passing five times and always for purely technical (its use of Technicolor) or economic reasons. David Bordwell, Janet Staiger, and Kristin Thompson (1985) mention it three times, but never to discuss its thematic importance. Recently, however, historian Mathew Bernstein (1999) has begun to attend to the film's reception in the South.

8. During the postwar era, critics increased their disdain as the reputations of writers like William Faulkner, who seemed more at odds with the "horror" of the patriarchal past, grew. More recently, critics like Darden Pyron, whose 1991 biography of Mitchell is a landmark, have taken Mitchell more seriously. Helen Taylor's groundbreaking *Scarlett's Women: Gone With the Wind and Its Female Fans* (1989), based on interviews with the book's female lovers in both England and the United States over the past five decades, is exemplary.

9. Cowley did, however, acknowledge the power of the book as a popular culture phenomenon and the fact that it moved him: "She makes us weep at a deathbed (and really weep), exult at a sudden rescue and grit our teeth at the crimes of our relatives the damnyankees. I would never, never say that she has written a great novel, but in the midst of triteness and sentimentality her book has a simple-minded courage that suggests the great novelists of the past" (1983, 20).

10. Joel Williamson notes that at the peak of lynch law, between 1889 and 1899, one person on average was lynched every other day, and two of three of these were black. In the first decade of the century, one was lynched every fourth day, with nine of ten of these blacks—a ratio that would continue. In the teens the figure was one in five and in the twenties it was one every nine days. By the thirties, however, lynching had declined significantly. Nineteen forty-six is usually accepted as the year that marked the end of the lynching era (Williamson 1984, 117–18).

11. As evidence that Mitchell was consciously working in the anti-Tom Dixonian tradition, many critics have cited her correspondence with Thomas Dixon, who wrote to her immediately after the novel's publication, praising it and promising to write an extended study of it. Mitchell returned the compliment, telling Dixon that she had been raised on his writing and had even dramatized one of his novels while still a girl. However, Mitchell wrote flattering letters to everyone important who praised the novel. Leslie Fiedler's argument that *Gone With the Wind* constitutes a subversive "feminization" of the anti-Tom novel is compelling in its assertion that her work does not simply extend the Dixon model but displaces both it and the Tom model of Stowe as well. In other words, Mitchell finally did what Dixon only dreamed of doing: rivaling in the popular American consciousness the appeal of the Tom story with a more appealing and modern version of the anti-Tom story. However, Fiedler, like Cowley and a great many other critics, is vague about what he means by feminization. At times it seems to refer to the fact that the "good nigger" of Mitchell's novel is no longer a desexed male Uncle Tom but a female Mammy. At other times, he begins to confront the question of what it means to place a rebellious daughter in the place of the southern belle in need of rescue by the white patriarchs. I take my lead from this latter inclination while attempting to understand Scarlett's role as a "morally legible" hero of black and white melodrama.

12. For all the stated love of Tara and home, Scarlett leaves it during the initial stages of the war to seek diversion in Atlanta and only returns when Atlanta burns. She then leaves it again to seek a husband able to pay its taxes and only returns once more for a brief visit.

13. In 1991 a much-debated sequel was finally written by Alexandra Ripley and adapted into a television miniseries (1994).

14. Publisher Latham, for example, recalls a "tiny lady sitting on a divan beside the biggest manuscript he had ever seen" (Lambert 1973, 24). Ralph McGill's 1962 essay, "Little Woman, Big Book: The Mysterious Margaret Mitchell," also works this image. Recall, also, Thomas Dixon's mixture of anger and condescension in his reference to Stowe, "a little Yankee woman wrote a crude book. The single act of that woman's will caused the war, killed a million men, desolated and ruined the south" (Dixon 1903, 264).

15. As this is written, *GWTW* is once again in theaters, garnering praise for its digitally remastered Technicolor version that preserves the original aspect ratio instead

of forcing it into wide screen. In a June 28, 1998, review in the *New York Times*, Vincent Canby wrote, " 'Gone with the Wind' has always had an alarming ability to enchant millions of people who know better, as well as millions of people who don't."

16. Selznick even contemplated hiring D.W. Griffith for some of the second unit work showing the evacuation of Atlanta (Selznick 1972, 184). His many memos constantly compare the scope and innovation of the two films.

17. See Michael Rogin (1996), who makes the intriguing argument that there are four transformative moments in the history of American film—moments that combine box office success, critical recognition of revolutionary significance, formal innovations, and shifts in the cinematic mode of production—all of which are organized "around the surplus symbolic value of blacks" (14). These works are Edwin S. Porter's *Uncle Tom's Cabin* (1903), *The Birth of a Nation* (1915), *The Jazz Singer* (1927), and *Gone With the Wind* (1939) (Rogin 1996, 15). While I think Rogin overemphasizes the transformative nature of the Porter and the Selznick films, which are not on a par with the transformations wrought by *The Birth of a Nation* and *The Jazz Singer*, the fact that these changes are linked to representations of African Americans (and to black and white melodrama) is, indeed, striking. Rogin's observation asks us to move beyond the oft-noted similarities of the two Civil War epics (*Birth* and *GWTW*) to a deeper connection between race, cultural transformation, and media.

18. Of course this apparent African-American "family" constitutes no family at all to one another: though Pork was Gerald O'Hara's personal slave and Mammy was Ellen's, they are not related to each other, nor to Prissy, who is the daughter of Dilcey, a significant slave character entirely omitted from the film.

19. This scene is adapted with some significant racial changes in the film. I will defer most discussion of the film version, however, to the second half of this chapter.

20. Leslie Fiedler notes that Scarlett is no helpless belle, that even in this instance she is armed and shoots, and that ultimately Mitchell is gently subverting Dixon with this figure of the sadomasochistic Scarlett, at one moment the sexual victim, at another moment the Sadean woman (1982, 205–6). However, his focus on "inter-ethnic rape" as the fantasy driving the Tom/anti-Tom tradition leads him to stretch a point when the only actual rape of this work is the intraracial marital one carried out by Rhett on Scarlett.

21. Kenneth O'Brien notes other differences between this attack on the white woman and the conventional attack of the plantation legend novels: its biracial nature; its use of Shantytown as a place of criminal—and not necessarily racially motivated—activity; and the fact that the attackers are strangers rather than former slaves, as they are in "plantation legend tradition" (O'Brien 1983, 161).

22. Helen Taylor's reception study of the novel and the film's impact among primarily British women readers and viewers in the period since the novel and the film's release offers an excellent picture of the many ways the work has impacted on their lives. While American critics have tended to focus on the novel's impact in the era of the Great Depression, Taylor's English-centered study offers an especially compelling description of the image of the survival of home during a cataclysmic war for a nation whose homes "were under nightly threat of bombing" (Taylor 1989, 99).

23. It is precisely this world of unbridled competition and unprotected ambitious women that Thomas Dixon most feared. It is obvious that his reading of Mitchell was not very tuned in to Scarlett's impatience with the limitations of southern belle-hood.

24. Molly Haskell calls her "a forerunner of the career woman, with her profession-obsession (the land), her business acumen," and the energy of perpetual sexual repression (1973, 125).

25. Cora Kaplan explains, for example, "All of Scarlett's moral, sexual and emotional awakening 'come too late' " (1986, 118). Yet despite these delays, countless readers and viewers have hoped right along with Scarlett that there is still time to set things right and achieve her desires; "after all, tomorrow is another day" (1024). It is the tension between Scarlett's forward-looking embrace of the future and nostalgia for the rapidly disappearing past that gives the work its special energy.

26. Jakie Rabinowitz sings "in the nick of time" in the synagogue to please his dying father, but this performance makes him temporally "too late!" to please the public in the theater. The performance in the synagogue is the performance that brings him emotionally "home" to the world of his fathers. Later, his delayed performance of "Mammy" in the theater refunctions the patriarchal Jewish home as the maternal, rural, black-inflected American home of the tradition of racial melodrama. The tension between one home and the next is ultimately the racially inflected question of where true virtue can best be recognized. Thus, *The Jazz Singer* combines the sad melodrama of "too late!" with the happy melodrama of "in the nick of time!" in an ambivalent ending that both gains the father's love and loses his life, that misses opening night, but regains a later one.

27. In the musical version of *Show Boat*, for example, the emotional force of the music itself forges the logic, against the novel's more realistic awareness that he is an inconstant lover, of Gaylord's return, "in the nick of time," to the show boat home of his and Magnolia's youth.

28. "Oh, Ashley, you should have known, years ago, that you loved her and not me! . . . But you wait till now, till Melly's dying, to find it out and now it's too late to do anything. Oh, Ashley, men are supposed to know such things—not women!" (1002).

29. Margaret Mitchell's biographer Darden Pyron argues convincingly that the figure Mitchell herself sought, and with whom she associated her harrowing journey on the road to Tara, was her own mother. Mitchell's mother's death, when she was away at college in the North, caused her to return home permanently to care for her father and brother. In the novel this virtuous maternal figure, who dies taking care of poor "white trash" neighbors, consistently eludes Scarlett, who loves and wants to please her mother but whom, as the rebellious bad girl, she can never please. Pyron also interestingly argues that many of the liberal ideas of Mitchell's mother have been placed in the mouth of Rhett Butler, thus giving resonance to the recognition, too late!, that it is Rhett she has always loved.

30. "She was as forthright and simple as the winds that blew over Tara and the yellow river that wound about it, and to the end of her days she would never be able to understand a complexity" (29).

31. As Grace Hale (1998) and both of Mitchell's biographers, Finis Far (1965) and Darden Pyron (1991), have noted, Mitchell did escape from the traditional confines of the woman's role as homemaker but, rather paradoxically, these escapes usually brought her back to a southern home and a southern conventionalism with which she could never entirely break. Initially breaking with southern tradition to attend college in the East, she returned home after a single tumultuous year to care for her father

after her mother's death. Marrying young and rashly to a man who could not support her, she was forced to earn a living as a reporter on the *Atlanta Journal*'s Sunday magazine. Yet her society news beat kept her close to the local doings of Atlanta's former debutantes. Finally, a second marriage to a staid insurance agent made her the housewife with the leisure to write her book.

349

32. Hale (1998, 112–13) writes that the mammy "both eased and marked the contradiction at the heart of that new home-based white womanhood, its dependence on a gendered influence and yet possession of a racial authority, its masking of the new with a conscious celebration of the old."

33. In an intriguing psychoanalytic analysis of the mammy figure in general and Scarlett's Mammy in particular, Maria St. John (1999) argues that the ample figure of this Mammy is fantasmatically taken as the mother whom Scarlett always needs and that she is crucial to the construction of the whiteness of the white heroine.

34. Rhett is initially present with Scarlett and others at Melanie's home. When he sees Scarlett seek out Ashley after her last meeting with Melanie, he seems to leave out of pure jealousy. But as soon as Scarlett recognizes her lack of interest in Ashley, she notices that Rhett is absent and runs home after him. Thus the suspense of her slow recognition does not build through the action of running toward an initially undefinable destination, but is all too simply a more purposeful chase after the absent Rhett. Scarlett simply hurries home through a fog to find Rhett packing. The prolonged reevaluation of her life and loves that takes place first as she panics and runs home, then as she and Rhett talk, is mostly absent.

35. According to Selznick, this montage of voices was his own invention (1972, 259).

36. As we have seen, Malcolm Cowley's much-quoted review of the novel is deeply affronted by its revival of the plantation legend. More recently, two feminist music critics reading the film through its music have asserted that the ideological project of reinscribing the "idealized mythic status of the antebellum plantation narrative" and to induce regret for its destruction is "easily read in the lushness of the visual images that represent the Old South" (Dagle and Kalinak 1994, 17). I hope to show that though such readings are easier in the film than the novel, they are not the whole story.

37. In the novel she also has her own son, Wade Hamilton, in tow. This son is eliminated in the film.

38. Significant, also, is the fact that Scarlett's elemental connection with the land takes place, not, as in the film, at Tara, but in the burnt-out ruins of the more elegant Twelve Oaks, the apotheosis of the plantation legend. This plantation's utter destruction seems linked, in both novel and film, to Ashley's fond memories of the "old days" and "old ways" imbued with this idealized picture of singing and laughing slaves. In contrast, Scarlett derives new strength not from dwelling on this idyllic happy past but from groveling in the dirt associated with the sweat and toil of slave labor. For example, in a late conversation between Ashley and Scarlett that takes place in the mill, Scarlett resists his continuing tendency to "look back" at these pretty pictures that include, in this late instance, Ashley's memory of "high soft laughter from the quarters!" (912).

39. This is not the only moment in the novel when a "nigger smell" comes to the forefront. During Melanie's childbirth Scarlett notes that the sweating Prissy "smelled so abominably Scarlett would have sent her from the room had she not feared

the girl would take to her heels if once out of sight" (361). Ironically, this statement suggests that the supposedly useless Prissy might have some unmentioned use to Scarlett after all.

40. Even in the corset-lacing scene Scarlett cannot keep her food down—she burps and complains that she will not be able to get through the day without belching. See St. John (1999, 17).

41. Pork does, however, win Scarlett's respect by learning to steal food.

42. Dilcey, who is eliminated from the film, is the one slave with the capacity to adapt to new circumstances and, like Scarlett, to shoulder the load of hard work in the fields as well as the house. Dilcey's greater humanity and good sense, however, is attributed to her mix of Indian blood.

43. Only Steiner's own musical compositions were more numerous (Ussher 1983, 160).

44. As we saw in Chapter 2, Foster's song originally contained lyrics addressed directly to Uncle Tom. Though these lyrics were eventually cut, the song itself speaks directly to the situation of the weary and dying Tom, separated from the Kentucky home figured not as the big house of the plantation but as the humble cabin home, where the sun once shone bright. We also saw how this song, written after Foster's earlier hit "Old Folks at Home," which immediately attached to the Aiken-Howard stage version, seemed to shift emphasis from a home figured as plantation ("Still longing for the old plantation") to the home figured as cabin, specifically associated after 1852 with Uncle Tom.

45. In the film, which omits the singing in the parlor, we first hear Prissy singing "My Old Kentucky Home" as she returns from failing to fetch Dr. Mead to deliver Melanie's baby. We are told that "the song grated on Scarlett" (343). Later, when Scarlett goes in Prissy's place to find the doctor and encounters the mass of wounded and dying soldiers at the depot, with the camera's dramatic pullback to reveal Scarlett standing in the midst of such extensive misery, Steiner switches to the other Foster favorite, "The Old Folks at Home," giving it the full symphonic treatment.

46. Although both novel and film admire the strength and courage of so young a girl performing so difficult a function, neither acknowledges the injustice of the expectation that Prissy (who in the novel is only twelve years old—in the film the twenty-eight-year-old Butterfly McQueen played her as a thirty-year-old going on twelve) should be expected to have the same strength and courage. The novel is more understanding than the film, however, in explaining that the basis of her claim to know is her mother, Dilcey, eliminated from the film, who is both an experienced midwife and who becomes wet nurse to the baby once born. As Helen Taylor notes, we hate Prissy precisely because she is not Mammy and cannot be left to do all the tasks whites would rather not do for themselves (Taylor 1989, 179).

47. Noel Ignatiev's (1995) *How the Irish Became White* tells the story of the Irish assimilation into "whiteness" and white supremacy in nineteenth-century America at the expense of African-Americans.

48. The other titles were *Another Day, Bugles Sang,* and *Not in Our Stars* (Lambert 1973, 24).

49. Indeed, of the works we have so far examined in this study of black and white melodrama, *Gone With the Wind* is the work that has most perfectly continued to live simultaneously in its dual form. The novel continues as a perennial best-seller in this

country and around the world; the film is one of the handful of Hollywood films to be regularly revived both theatrically and on television. While *The Birth of a Nation* is much better known than either its source novel or Dixon's play, and while *Show Boat* and *The Jazz Singer* have similarly assumed their most "definitive" forms in the "leap" away from literature (to stage and film for *Show Boat*; to film exclusively for *The Jazz Singer*), *Uncle Tom's Cabin* lived during the long period James describes (the entire latter part of the nineteenth century) most intensely on both page and stage.

50. Although the 1991 sequel written by Alexandra Ripley generated quite a bit of publicity, it never approached the popularity of the original. Nor did the television special made from it. I count neither as important contributors to the tradition of racial melodrama I am tracing.

51. It remains to be seen, of course, whether GWTW will continue to live as vitally in its two forms. *Uncle Tom's Cabin* did not continue to do so in the twentieth century, where, despite numerous film versions, it has mostly reverted to its original, literary form.

52. The city fathers, in an effort to recreate the "old days," had asked participating whites and performing blacks to wear period attire. On stage at this charity ball the facade of Tara had been recreated and a young debutante impersonated Scarlett. At the theater, the facade was decorated with false pillars to resemble Twelve Oaks (Branch 1988, 55; Hale 1998, 283).

53. The historical text of the civil rights movement is too complex and vast, and too much beyond my powers as a culture critic, to analyze. Nevertheless, it is worth noting that its efficacy as a social movement was due almost entirely to its ability to activate the moral Manichaeanism, the racialized recognition of virtue and pathos and action that we have seen to be the hallmarks of a deep-seated national tradition of black and white racial melodrama. For an intriguing visual documentation of the "racial symbolics" of Jim Crow segregation as it came to be pictured through the perspective of the "moral supremacy" of its victims, see Elizabeth Abel's study of bathroom doors and drinking fountains (1999).

Chapter Six

1. Haley was still completing the book as the television writers were beginning to draft the script. The book was published in October 1976. The miniseries aired in January 1977. The confluence of these dates meant that promotion for the book was simultaneously promotion for the miniseries and vice versa.

2. Leslie Fiedler writes that this broadcast represented the first moment in American popular culture that an African-American writer had succeeded "in modifying the mythology of Black-White relations *for the majority audience*" (Fiedler 1979, 71).

3. Writing about nineteenth-century stage melodrama, feminist critic Martha Vicinus notes how frequently the home becomes the scene of a "reconciliation of the irreconcilable" more in keeping with what is desirable than with what is possible or actual (Vicinus 1981, 202).

4. Recall Peter Brooks's notion that melodrama employs a dramaturgy that tends toward "spectacular moments of public homage to virtue" where the ethical evidence of virtue is recognized in a moment of astonishment (Brooks 1995, 26).

5. Peter Brooks describes nomination as the grand moment in melodrama when the good or evil person is finally revealed and named ("I am the man . . .") (Brooks 1995, 39). Interpellation is defined by Louis Althusser (1971, 174) as the process by which an individual recognizes himself or herself in the discourse that names him or her. Interpellation thus represents the insidious, apparently unforced way a culture imposes its ideological values on individuals. Racial interpellation is described by Franz Fanon (1967, 112) as the process by which a racial group (as in the phrase, "Look, a Negro!") is named as such and thus made to correspond to preexisting racial stereotypes. Haley's version of interpellation is a melodramatic nomination designed to undo the previous negative effects by restoring the black father who had been so ruthlessly written out of African-American juridical identity.

6. Leslie Fiedler, for example, argues that Kunta Kinte is an "anti-anti-Tom"—a noble African who is predominantly determined by Alex Haley's internalization of Malcolm X's critique of the passive Tom. After a symbolic castration and a happy marriage he becomes a "good bad nigger," modeled, Fiedler believes, on Malcolm X himself, passing on the hope of freedom but running away no more. Fiedler's insight is productive and explains many aspects of Haley's book, particularly Kunta Kinte's black Moslem-like sexual abstinence modeled on Malcolm's twelve-year self-imposed celibacy. But even an "anti-anti Tom" is, by the logic of the double negative, still a Tom. And indeed, Fiedler's chapter on *Roots*, subtitled "Uncle Tom Rewrites *Uncle Tom's Cabin*," concentrates on Haley himself, who played the "Tom" role opposite Malcolm's Black-Power "good/bad" African. In contrast to this provocative, though sometimes glib, reduction of the melodramatic power of *Roots*, I offer in the first part of this chapter a more systematic exploration of the way *Roots* the book rewrites *Uncle Tom's Cabin*.

7. Toni Morrison points out that in the history of American fiction, "whatever popularity the slave narratives had. . . . [they] did not destroy the master narrative. The master narrative could make any number of adjustments to keep itself intact" (Morrison 1990, 50–51). By master narrative, Morrison means the dominant narrative of the white supremacist tradition. The example of *Roots* might seem to prove Morrison wrong since here, finally, is a slave narrative that is a "response from the Africanist persona" that sets out to set straight both the Tom and the anti-Tom master narratives. Yet as Helen Taylor has argued, such a setting straight does not supplant either its Tom or its anti-Tom antecedents; it adopts and adapts the rules of the genre rather than destroying them. Whether this is good or bad depends a lot on whether one believes it is possible within popular culture to perform the kind of "destruction" of popular myths and forms that Morrison seems to wish for, and actually seems to have succeeded in carrying out in her own great novel of slavery and its aftermath, *Beloved*.

8. As we shall see, once children are born in this "home," the return to Africa can only be a symbolic matter of pride for African Americans; it cannot be a real home.

9. Recall that in the Aiken-Howard version of the play, this comic ignorance is expanded into the song "Oh! I'se So Wicked," in which Topsy sings of never being born, and simply being raised "on de corn" (Riis 1994, 64–67).

10. Arthur Riss (1994, 513) argues that Stowe's notion of the integrity of the family is not based on the fact that the children are related to the parents, but on the fact that the parents are biologically related to one another.

11. As we shall see below, even Alex Haley's Afrocentric version, which works so hard to locate virtue in the good African home, cannot ultimately overcome this tradition.

12. One of the biggest effects of the book and miniseries's popularity was the creation of a genealogy craze among Americans of all races and ethnicities, all seeking the "farthest back" ancestor.

13. Novelist and folklorist Harold Courlander, for example, writes that Haley grossly overdoes the "noble savage" nature of his hero, making him ignorant of all sorts of objects, tools, and concepts—ships, muskets, sexual relations—with which a man of his situation would have been familiar. Courlander is particularly tough on Haley's decision to keep his hero a virgin until his thirty-ninth year, when nothing in his Mandinka culture or Islamic teachings dictated sexual abstinence (Courlander 1986, 299). Michael Steward Blayney (1986) also criticizes the book from this perspective. (Courlander is the novelist who sued Haley for copying eighty passages from his own 1967 novel, *The Slave*. He received a $650,000 out-of-court settlement.)

14. Spillers argues that gender, as a sign of humanity, was withheld from African-American subjects and that the only route toward the recognition of human worth was, in fact, through white patriarchy. Though she ultimately aims at understanding the American tradition of pathologizing the matriarchal black family, the force of her argument is to leave us with few tools for understanding the exaggerated marks of gender that circle around the black body in the antebellum and postbellum eras. Since my analysis depends on the exaggerated marks of masculinity and femininity as they take on moral power in race melodrama, I cannot dismiss the importance of gender in conjunction with the signs of race.

15. See Daniel Patrick Moynihan, "The Negro Family and the Case for National Action." Moynihan's famous report, originally published in 1965, had argued that slavery had its most profound effects on "the Negro family" in the pathology of matriarchy. According to Moynihan, the black mother was now the figure most responsible for the "degendering" of her sons. The absence of paternal discipline in the family was perceived as the pathological heritage of slavery used by Moynihan to explain the failure of a black male work ethic and the search for more immediate forms of gratification.

16. As we shall see below, this motif of father rescue represents the work's flip anti-Tom side aligned with the heroic rescue of patriarchy so familiar in *The Birth of a Nation*.

17. Kizzy resolves, for example, that however light her baby would be, whatever name would be forced upon him, she would "never regard him as other than the grandson of an African" (438). It is worth noting the significance of the indefinite article, which seems a dead giveaway of Haley's much-discussed fabrication of genealogy: that Kizzy's child is the grandson of *an* African is without doubt; at issue for many readers is the question of whether this grandson who is known, like Kizzy herself, in the family history of Haley's ancestors is the grandson of *the* African, the historical Kunta Kinte. His history, because of the erasures of connection to Africa effected by the Middle Passage, cannot be known the same way Kizzy's and her descendants' are known. The deeper issue in this debate over the definite and the indefinite article is how firmly the black family can be reconnected with its ancestral black African father. The fantasy of *Roots* is that this father-centered home can be recovered.

18. Helen Taylor (1993) has noted how *Roots*'s tripartite structure corresponds to the plantation legend's "master narrative," which is itself patterned on the structure of Paradise/Paradise Lost/Paradise Regained.

19. In the plantation legend, "darkies" are happy to serve their white masters and find big house and lowly cabin their true home. In *Roots*, African slaves in Africa are described as often indistinguishable from free men. Kunta Kinte's father explains that some of these slaves became slaves due to starvation, others are taken as prisoners, but all are guaranteed the "right" to food, clothing, land, and wife or husband (Haley 1976, 52–53).

20. Taylor (1993, 51–52) draws these parallels to show that Haley does not escape the structure and parameters — as well as the ideological power — of the white-authored "master narrative."

21. Moreover, as we have also already seen, *Gone With the Wind* itself was an important, gynocentric revision of many of the patriarchal aspects of the plantation legend tradition relying on black virtue to give its selfish heroine moral fiber.

22. We shall see below, however, that *TV Roots*, having abandoned the Haley part of the narrative, would attempt to compensate for this loss by bringing something of the excitement of this last-minute rescue to its concluding episode.

23. Each time the members of the Kunte clan leave one of these homes they make a point of not looking back. And while the "good" masters are acknowledged, they are never thanked.

24. Numerous critics have noted the lack of historical correspondence between the idyllic Juffure Haley describes, where whites are mere rumors and Africans do not collaborate in the slave trade. David Gerber, for example, has argued that Haley succumbed to the "temptation to create an Africa beyond history's and indeed humanity's stain" (Gerber 1977, 100). Leslie Fiedler notes that although the Moslem culture Haley represents was polygamous, Haley cannot bring himself to portray Kunta Kinte's father in such a relationship. The father thus remains monogamous and Kunta Kinte himself, as we have already seen, remains an unlikely virgin until his thirty-ninth year (Fiedler 1982, 225).

25. See again Leslie Fiedler (1982, 213–45) and David Gerber (1977, 100).

26. In Leslie Fiedler's Tom/anti-Tom racial shorthand, Alex Haley played the Uncle Tom "good, good nigger," first to Malcolm X's initial "bad bad nigger" of Malcolm's early days as a hoodlum in Detroit, and then to the revised "good bad nigger" who emerged after Malcolm's conversion to the Nation of Islam. The role continued even more after Malcolm's trip to Mecca and his break with Black Muslim leader Elijah Muhammad (Fiedler 1982, 224–25).

27. Fiedler points out, for example, that Haley's vivid scene of the rape of Kizzy by her white master seems to be modeled on one of Malcolm's standard speeches recorded in the *Autobiography* about the rape of "our great-grandmothers and our great-great-grandmothers" by the "white rapist slavemaster" (Haley 1976, 226).

28. Rescued from a crowded holding dormitory at the Jedda airport, where he was waiting for permission to go to Mecca, by an urbane, educated, and quasi-royal Saudi Arabian family, Malcolm is dazzled by the existence of a Muslim world not trapped by the stark binaries of black and white. In Mecca itself, he encounters "thousands upon thousands of praying pilgrims, both sexes, and every size, shape, color, and

race in the world" and is impressed by the "color-blindness of the Muslim world's religious society" (338).

29. Paul Gilroy uses the term "black Atlantic" to refer to the hybridity of the many homes of the African diaspora. His book of the same name focuses on the importance of a black Atlantic culture that cannot be pinned down to specific race, ethnicity, and nationality. Interestingly, for our purposes, he works the image of ships in motion across the spaces between Europe, America, Africa, and the Caribbean to work against the fantasy of a hermetically enclosed, authentic, stable, and "rooted" identity that has proved so crucial to various forms of black nationalism (Gilroy 1993, 4, 30–31).

30. Haley settled one large claim out of court with author Harold Courlander, whose novel *The Slave* was the basis for some of Haley's passages (Taylor 1993, 53). Philip Nobile (1993, 32), who studied the many charges of plagiarism, concludes that Haley "was a writer of modest talents . . . who required enormous editorial support." In addition, he summarizes the case of the many historians, journalists, and ethnographers who have checked his "facts" and found them wanting. David Chioni Moore (1994, 5) notes, for example, that as of 1994 the Modern Language Association's comprehensive database indicates that not a single scholarly article on Haley's book had been published since 1986.

31. Stowe wrote a *Key to Uncle Tom's Cabin*, citing her sources to prove the authenticity of her picture of slavery; Thomas Dixon offered to pay a thousand dollars to anyone who could find error in *The Clansman*; Margaret Mitchell spent the rest of her life writing letters to readers and critics upholding the historical truth of her novel (Taylor 1993, 52).

32. Both Helen Taylor (1993) and David Chioni Moore (1994) have discussed, and themselves broken, this silence in penetrating articles that tackle the phenomenal popularity of the work.

33. Before the book was published Broadway producer David Merrick attempted to purchase the rights (Wolper and Troupe 1978, 45). *Roots*, the musical, was certainly not an outlandish possibility. Similarly, one can easily imagine a blockbuster film version being produced a year or two after the book's publication. By 1977, however, neither the *Show Boat* nor the *Gone With the Wind* model was appropriate to the immense popularity of the *Roots* phenomenon. Only a "new" medium—or more exactly a recent medium whose seriousness and legitimacy remained to be proven—could fit the bill.

34. We might recall that theater manager George Howard's decision to combine the two separately performed short versions of *Uncle Tom's Cabin*—the first depicting only the death of Little Eva, the second depicting the death of Uncle Tom—into one "Grand Combination" exceeding the length of most previous stage melodramas anticipates producers Wolper and Silverman's decision to extend *TV Roots* over an unprecedented eight consecutive nights. In both cases the dramatic power of novel objects of empathy, upsetting previously dominant modes of minstrelsy, seemed to command the new form and extraordinary length.

35. Wolper got his start making television documentaries like *The Race for Space*, *The Making of the President*, and a documentary on John F. Kennedy. He had undergone something of a baptism of fire when he had attempted a film based on William Styron's *The Confessions of Nat Turner* in the late sixties. Black power advocates who

objected to the sometimes less-than-heroic portrait of Nat Turner raised enough of a fuss to give the producing company cold feet. The project was never made, but Wolper seems to have learned from the experience how to listen to the objections of African Americans about representations of their race. He went on to produce a series of recreated trials for television (e.g., the Rosenbergs, Lt. William Calley). Actor Ossie Davis told Wolper about *Roots* while it was being written. Wolper eventually met Haley, was dazzled by his storytelling ability, and bought an option to produce it for television.

36. Indeed, only one of the series' several directors was an African American.

37. General Motors and McDonald's were the two primary sponsors.

38. Brandon Stoddard, vice president for novels for television at ABC, explained the policy of adaptation as getting out of Africa and to America as soon as possible: "In *Roots*, we got out of Africa as fast as we could. I kept yelling at everyone, 'Get him to Annapolis'. . . . I knew as soon as we got Kunta Kinte to America we would be okay" (Quoted in Fishbein 1983, 280).

39. The first, second, sixth, and eighth programs were each two hours, each corresponding in format to a typical made-for-TV movie comprising seventy-five minutes of actual drama.

40. In Chapter 7 we will see how Simpson's dual role as victim and/or villain of the media "trial of the century" thickened the plot of yet another version of the melodrama of black and white.

41. The first episode, the best in the series, was directed by David Greene. None of the other episodes has the vitality and originality of this one.

42. *Bonanza* was a weekly western television series, set on a ranch in Nevada, popular in the late sixties and seventies. In it a wise patriarch presides over the life lessons of his sometimes hotheaded sons.

43. Recall that Ben Cameron received his "inspiration"—as an intertitle calls it—on a hill where he agonizes over the fate of his people. Upon seeing some white children below frighten some black children with a sheet that makes them appear as ghosts, he suddenly understands that the white-sheeted Clan will be the instrument for the salvation of the South. *TV Roots*'s "inspiration" holds on only to the need for anonymity to cloak the perpetrators of white-on-black violence. The hoods do not have the distinctive points of KKK hoods.

44. When Tom seems to pass out, George claims there is no more point to beating him once he is senseless, and the night riders buy the argument. After the beating, Tom's family—which had previously taken umbrage to Ol' George's elevation above them—shows its gratitude.

Chapter Seven

1. As Kimberlé Crenshaw and Gary Peller note, it was an "easy event for the entire mainstream of American culture to abhor; it didn't present any of the 'hard questions' of the 1990s controversies over race—like the 'dilemma' of affirmative action" (Crenshaw and Peller 1993, 57).

2. This is not to say that there have not been many intervening examples of police brutality and use of excessive force. Most recently in New York the case of the Haitian immigrant Abner Louima, brutally beaten by police, as well as the inexplicable forty-one shots fired into the unarmed body of Amadou Diallo, demonstrate that such in-

stances are all too common. In the case of the King beating, however, the existence of the videotape, played repeatedly on television, made public reaction to the spectacle of the beating itself inevitable.

3. King answered his plea in the affirmative, plaintively noting that there was no real alternative: "We all can get along. We've just got to, just got to. We're all stuck here for awhile" (*Los Angeles Times*, 2 May 1992, 3). Even if these words were "ventrilo-quized" by King from his white lawyer, as Houston Baker argues, the fact of his moral authority is undiminished (Baker 1993, 45).

4. Both the president of the United States, George Bush, and the police chief in charge of the L.A.P.D. issued initial condemnations, though the police chief, Daryl Gates, would soon backpedal on his. A similar racial and sectional consensus was reached about an equally repellent spectacle—this one not televised—of white-perpe-trated racial violence in Jasper, Texas, in 1999. A mixed-race jury tried and convicted John William King for dragging a black man, James Byrd, Jr., over three miles of road until his body fell apart in pieces. This trial, unlike that of the police in the beating of Rodney King and unlike the O. J. Simpson murder trial, seemed to unite blacks and whites in opposition to the crime.

5. For a discussion of the comparative mediatizations of these two videos, along with that of the videotaped beating of white trucker Reginald Denny, see John Fiske (1996, 125–90).

6. "Riot" connotes a relatively unplanned, spontaneous reaction of rage, while "rebellion" connotes a greater level of organization and direction, as well as the history of a class basis of action. Riot is sometimes assumed to derogate the motives of the rioters, though not necessarily; rebellion is sometimes assumed to elevate the motives of the rebels, though not necessarily. Socialist urban critic Mike Davis contends that the events constituted a rebellion for the youths who started it, since some L.A. gangs actually used the term. He notes, however, that riot could also be applicable (Davis 1993, 142). Cornel West, on the other hand, dismisses both terms, arguing that it was a "multiracial, trans-class, and largely male display of justified social rage" (West 1993, 255). I choose riot somewhat by default because I believe "events" or "unrest" are both too neutral, "uprising" implies a knowledge of what one is rising up to, and "rebellion" confers planning and organization on what was still a spontaneous reaction. Race riot recalls a long history of black/white antinomies reaching back to the late-nineteenth-century institution of Jim Crow. Although this particular riot was also multiracial, with Hispanic rioters joining African Americans and with Asian store owners often as targets, its flashpoint was nevertheless the traditional black/white antinomy of previous Ameri-can riots. See Jewelle Taylor Gibbs (1996, 66–67) for another discussion of these terms.

7. For example, the white judge who sentenced Soon Ja Du appeared unmoved by Korean/black violence. The white jury in the King beating was unmoved by the attack on King. Response to the verdict was thus actually a response to a black/white opposition already colored by other kinds of racial oppositions. Similarly, the riot itself was hardly a black/white conflict. Mike Davis reports, for example, that in contrast to the Watts riot of 1965, 52 percent of the first five thousand people arrested were Latino (Davis 1993, 144).

8. In a poll published in *Newsweek* before the trial began, for example, African Americans tended to believe Simpson was guilty. Only 12 percent of African Ameri-cans thought at that time that Simpson had been framed (July 25, 1994). Near the end

of the trial a majority of African Americans thought he had been framed and 75 percent thought so in L.A. (Bugliosi 1996, 65).

9. This was, of course, the perspective of the prosecution as elaborated in trial books by both Marcia Clark (1997) and Christopher Darden (1996), as well as of the majority of commentators on the case. It was also the opinion voiced by defense attorney Robert Shapiro, even though he appeared to be the author of the defense's police conspiracy theory. It was also the opinion of Jeffrey Toobin, whose *New Yorker* article, "An Incendiary Defense," first disclosed this police conspiracy theory. Toobin's book (1996) on the Simpson trial similarly develops this thesis, as does a popular book by Los Angeles prosecutor Vincent Bugliosi (1996). Even Lawrence Schiller and James Willwerth's "inside story" of the defense, while resolutely presenting the defense's point of view on the case, manages to hint at a growing belief in Simpson's guilt on the part of some members of the defense team as the case wore on (Schiller and Willwerth 1996).

10. The June 27, 1994, cover of *Time* darkened by several shades the natural color of Simpson's skin and accompanied it with the title, "An American Tragedy." Given the already bleak and vilifying genre of the mug shot itself, the darkening immediately made Simpson's race appear to be a factor in his alleged crime. The NAACP and other civil rights groups were quick to protest. *Time* defended itself by saying that the doctoring was properly labeled and that magazines regularly enhance photos for dramatic effect. It is unlikely that anyone would have noticed the darkening had not *Newsweek* featured an unaltered version of the same mug shot on its cover that same week (Toobin 1996, 71).

11. This jury was drawn from the Ventura County town of Simi Valley, where the trial was moved after a request for a change of venue from Los Angeles. Ventura County has a population that is 65.9 percent white and 2.2 percent black (Dumm 1993, 192).

12. The jury that began the trial was composed of six African-American women, two African-American men, and four whites. By the end of the trial, after several alternates had taken the place of dismissed jurors, it was composed of eight African-American women and one African-American man, one Hispanic man, and two white women. The jury pool for this trial came from the central, "downtown," district of Los Angeles, a district that has a disproportionate number of African Americans (31.3 percent) compared to the general population. The district attorney would come under much criticism for changing the venue of the trial from Santa Monica (the western district near where the crime took place and where blacks are only 7 percent of the population) to downtown.

13. Ann Ducille cites this list as the forms of "white riot" against blacks, though she does not include the end of affirmative action as one of its forms (1997, 337).

14. The A. C. Nielson Company reported that a 91 percent share of the viewing audience watched the verdict. A survey commissioned by CNN found that 142 million Americans listened to the verdict on radio or watched it on television (Bugliosi 1996, 354). *TV Roots* (1977), the previous television "event" to hold the record (after *Gone With the Wind*'s 1976 broadcast) had garnered between 60 and 70 percent of the audience share (Wolper and Troupe 1978, 151).

15. Gates writes: "In the aftermath of the Simpson trial the focus has been swiftly displaced from the verdict to the reaction to the verdict and then to the reaction to the

reaction to the verdict and, finally, to the reaction to the reaction to the reaction to the verdict" (1995, 56). A verdict that many already perceive to be a reaction to the white justice of *California v. Powell* thus generated a veritable series of reactive aftershocks.

16. *Trial of the century* is, of course, a term used all too freely by popular pundits, often out of all proportion to the importance of the trial. Yet the very overuse of the term points to the growing importance that trials occupy in popular culture. Even the scholars who resist the claim with respect to the Simpson trial end up making it in a backhanded sort of way. Consider arts editor and critic Armond White, who writes, "Calling the Simpson trial 'the trial of the century' is . . . a grotesque, ignorant tabloid conceit. Yet in its unwieldy way it is our great racial drama, our fin-de-siècle *Birth of a Nation* or Death of a Republic. This new culture industry habit of fomenting consensus by turning movie houses or TV rooms into courts of public opinion (horrendous concept) only means one thing: keeping people in the dark" (White 1997, 349). It is clear from this vehement disavowal that, as Shoshana Felman (1997, 741) has noted, there is a recognition of the relevance of the law to larger cultural and political issues to which the law itself remains professionally blind.

17. Raymond Williams first introduced this term to describe the effect of immediacy and presence offered by broadcast television in which program, commercials, and news all blend together. Television, to Williams, is ultimately a never-ending flow in which it is impossible to separate out individual texts. I will be treating the Simpson trial as an individual text but one in which "flow"—especially its seemingly endless, live unfolding—is crucial.

18. One of the first Court TV celebrity trials was, in fact, successfully prosecuted by Marcia Clark as early as the fall of 1991. It concerned an actress, Rebecca Schaeffer, stalked and murdered by a male fan. This case helped establish Clark's reputation as a fierce prosecutor of crimes involving women victims (Toobin 1996, 77).

19. I will be basing much of the following discussion of the trial of the officers on a Court TV one-hour-and-fifty-six-minute videotape condensation of these 150 hours, entitled *The "Rodney King" Case: What the Jury Saw in California v. Powell* (1992), but also on more detailed *Court T.V.* segments of the trial.

20. Fiske cites the difference between the Rodney King beating and the beating death of Malice Green, a black motorist in Detroit whose beating was not videotaped and whose death therefore did not matter in the same public way (Fiske 1996, 2). George Lipsitz similarly cites the difference between mediated celebrity O. J. Simpson and Geronimo Pratt, Johnny Cochran's other client, also accused (and convicted) of a double murder with a white woman victim. Pratt was incarcerated for more than twenty-five years before his conviction was overturned. His story, every bit as dramatic as Simpson's, could not be sold on television because Pratt was no celebrity (Lipsitz 1998, 99–104).

21. If they cannot be "cut" in the sense of conventional shot-counter-shot or other forms of montage, they can, of course, be captioned in ways that produce an editorializing effect, as when Court TV provides boxed information about a witness during testimony.

22. Damien Williams was accused of attempted murder and eventually convicted of mayhem and assault with a deadly weapon. His trial, along with that of Henry Watson, took place in the summer of 1993 after the second, civil rights, trial of the

police officers in the beating of King in which most of the officers were found guilty, and after the federal judge had imposed extremely light sentences on Officers Koon and Powell. Because he was not convicted of the crime for which he was originally charged, the perception by many was that Williams had gotten off. However, his sentence of ten years (maximum sentence) was a far cry from not-guilty and a remarkable contrast to the thirty months (minimum sentence) received by Koon and Powell (Bugliosi 1996, 282; Gibbs 1996, 92–107).

23. Many commentators, arguing after the fact, have maintained that the prosecution in the Simpson trial should have resisted this temptation. Even if the physical demonstration was deemed necessary, it would have been possible, as prosecutor Christopher Darden requested in a sidebar, to have Simpson try on a new glove, but the same size and brand. The sight of Simpson apparently struggling to get them on became one of the key icons of the defense's case, summed up in final argument by Johnny Cochran's mantra: "If they don't fit, you must acquit." According to Marcia Clark—somewhat conveniently since blame for this miscalculation goes to Darden—this is the moment the prosecution lost the case (Clark 1997, 405–7).

24. Peter Brooks argues that melodrama's dramaturgy of gesture and inarticulate cry places faith in the ability of mute signs and gestures to recover a truth and presence that is lost in language. Brooks calls this faith "the text of muteness" and points to numerous examples in French theatrical melodrama of mute characters or pantomimes that reveal a truth exceeding traditional codes of expression (Brooks 1976, 66–67).

25. Some news stations even used a distinctively soap opera–style music to introduce its coverage of the trial, thus adding the all-important "melos" of melodrama. For useful analyses of the melodramatic form of television soap operas see Tania Modleski (1982), Cantor and Pingree (1983), and Robert Allen (1995).

26. I am deeply indebted to Carol J. Clover for allowing me to look at portions of her forthcoming book on the jury trial as a popular entertainment form, provisionally entitled *Trials, Lies, and Movies* (Princeton University Press, forthcoming). Although Clover's book concentrates on the trial movie, her observations on the "adversarial imagination" so basic and so unique to Anglo-American jurisprudence have been extremely helpful in my thinking about the trial form of American racial melodrama and contemporary trial mania. In what follows I will be referring to her 1998 published essay "God Bless Juries!" and to some portions of the forthcoming manuscript.

27. Janet Malcolm's study of an attorney, Sheila McGough, who was almost constitutionally incapable of spinning stories in her client's—and eventually in her own—defense is a case in point. In defending an embezzler and guilelessly holding some of his assets in her own bank account, McGough laid herself open to charges that she was a greedy lawyer who collaborated with her con-man client. The greedy lawyer story seemed more plausible than the guileless one and so McGough went to jail (Malcolm 1999).

28. Recalls Peter Brooks: "The desire to express all seems a fundamental characteristic of the melodramatic mode. Nothing is spared because nothing is left unsaid; the characters stand on stage and utter the unspeakable, give voice to their deepest feelings, dramatize through their heightened and polarized words and gestures the whole lesson of their relationship. . . . We might say that the center of interest and the

scene of the underlying drama reside within what we could call the 'moral occult,' the domain of spiritual values which is both indicated within and masked by the surface of reality" (Brooks 1995, 4–5).

29. The multiple trials of the nine Scottsboro Boys convicted by all-white Alabama juries of raping two white women while riding the rails in Alabama in 1931 had, for the first time in American jurisprudence, dramatically raised the issue of the "whiteness" of American justice. Even after one of the allegedly raped women had recanted her testimony, and even after the U.S. Supreme Court had twice overturned the Alabama court's verdicts, all-white Alabama juries continued to find them guilty. One of the Supreme Court rulings in the case (*Norris v. Alabama*) dismissed the verdict (and its accompanying death sentence) against Clarence Norris on the grounds that Negroes had been illegally excluded from the jury rolls making up the pool of the juries that tried the Scottsboro Boys (Goodman 1994, 243–44). This landmark decision, which addressed the de facto discrimination against black jurors as a violation of the Fourteenth Amendment, represented the first time since Reconstruction that African Americans were acknowledged in the South as deserving to make up a "jury of peers."

30. Darden introduced this term during argument for a motion to exclude "remote, inflammatory and irrelevant character evidence" about detective Mark Fuhrman's past history of using racial slurs against African Americans, in particular the word "nigger." Darden argued that introduction of the term "nigger" would blind the jury to the point that "they won't be able to discern what is true and what is not," bringing "extreme prejudice" to the case: "Mr. Cochran wants to play the ace of spades and play the race card. . . . If you allow Mr. Cochran to use this word and play this race card, not only does the direction and focus of the case change, but the entire complexion of the case changes. It's a race case then. It's white versus black" (Bugliosi 1996, 66).

31. Defense attorney Robert Shapiro would reinvoke this metaphor after the verdict to imply that lead defense attorney Johnny Cochran had used this card to cheat— dealing it "from the bottom of the deck." Shapiro did not note, however, that this card, in the form of the defense's theory that racist cop Mark Fuhrman had planted evidence, had been introduced by Shapiro himself.

32. Johnny Cochran, lead defense attorney, possibly chosen for *his* race to appeal to the predominantly black jury, charged that Darden was chosen for his race (Darden 1996, 170–71). Schiller and Willwerth call Darden's argument "disingenuous" (1996, 321). Vincent Bugliosi calls it an overstatement, but agrees that the "complexion" of the case did change (Bugliosi 1996, 66). Kimberlé Crenshaw argues, most convincingly, that Darden was caught between the "institutional expectations that he would perform 'as if' color-blindness and constitutional proceduralism prevailed and on the other hand, a profound and troubling recognition that there were dimensions of this case that clearly belied this claim" (Crenshaw 1997, 129).

33. Kimberlé Crenshaw forcefully argues that under the official ideology of "the color blind paradigm" racism is represented as isolated, aberrational, and relegated to the distant past. "The 'race card' . . . presumes a social terrain devoid of race until it is (illegitimately) introduced. Racism in this vision remains relevant primarily as an historical concept, relevant only to mark the contrast between an enlightened present

and a distant and unfortunate past. Within this racially enlightened era, not only are whites expected to adopt a color-blind performance, but African-Americans are expected to approach the occasional discovery of racist actors or actions with cool rationality rather than with hysteria or paranoia" (Crenshaw 1997, 104).

34. As Peggy Pascoe (1999, 482) puts it in a study of the history of miscegenation law, "In a society newly determined to be 'color blind,' granting public recognition to racial categories [seems] to be synonymous with racism itself."

35. Prosecutor Darden alluded to it, however, with every photo of a battered Nicole and, once, with presumed irony, when he rambled on about how "outrageous" it would be were he to claim that O. J. Simpson had a "fetish" for "blond-haired white women" (Toobin 1996, 293).

36. Butler uses this term to argue that the black male body is "always already performing within a white racist imaginary" prior to the production of the video (Butler 1993, 19). While this is entirely true, it is important to see that this imaginary was also capable of perceiving the beaten black male body as the desexualized "Tom" victim—as indeed so many had done before the trial. The lesson is thus not that the field of the visible is inherently racist but that viewers can be led to read into it radically different melodramatic scenarios. Had the prosecution played its "race card" successfully, it is arguable that the jury could have been led to see King as a victim.

37. Consider, for example, the following obsessive attention paid to demeanor in this description of Monica Lewinsky's videotaped testimony played in the Senate during the impeachment trial of President Clinton: "Her appearance, voice and vocabulary said she was all grown up and even a little bit hard. Wearing a sensible suit, pearls, heavy makeup and a semi-lacquered hairdo, Ms. Lewinsky was well-spoken, used no slang and showed only trace evidence of the Valley Girl of her taped phone conversations. . . . Even her voice seemed different now, more modulated, less high pitched and breathy. . . . Widening her eyes and then narrowing them to slits, she conveyed both ennui and contempt for the questioners. Once she sighed and raised her eyebrows to indicate that she did not understand why she was being asked a question twice. Still, her expressions—looking up, frowning, pouting, even exhaling dramatically while contemplating—had the cumulative effect of presenting her as a credible witness" (New York Times, February 7, 1999). Clearly, demeanor goes far beyond the simple matter of determining whether a witness lies, extending to an entire fascination with external evidence of who they really are in the context of the stories that get woven around them. Even raced demeanor came to play a role in the impeachment trial. It was widely speculated, for example, that Republican senators failed to call Betty Currie, the president's secretary and the person who was most privy to his relations with Lewinsky, because they wanted at all costs to avoid the spectacle of white men interrogating a sympathetic and loyal black woman.

38. Clover writes: "One can't help supposing that the Americanness of the lie detector has something to do with the Americanness of the jury . . . and that these two things in turn have something to do with a structure (the adversarial structure) that not only does not discourage lying, but actually works to produce it" (Clover, forthcoming, chapter entitled "Polygraphic Camera").

39. In the impeachment trial of President Clinton, the Republican prosecutors' fondest hope was that the demeanor of live witnesses would do what written testimony, argument, and evidence had not—present the president in a harsh enough light to

convict him in the Senate. The hope was futile as far as the floor of the Senate was concerned, since in a venue so large (with its hundred "jurors") no senator could read the witnesses' demeanor close-up. The compromise that presented videotaped clips from an earlier deposition lacked the power of live drama, but actually was able to provide the closer view needed to allow for the inspection of the tiniest of facial gestures. See note 37 for the fascination with Monica Lewinsky's demeanor.

40. Simpson's Hollywood career never made him an actual star. He had hoped to be cast in the Coalhouse Walker role in the film version of *Ragtime* and actively campaigned for the part. Instead, he found roles in lesser films, often comedies, or mere cameos, as in *TV Roots*.

41. This was the title of the *Time* cover that famously darkened Simpson's face. It would also become the title of the Schiller and Willwerth book chronicling his defense.

42. Consider, for example, former prosecutor Vincent Bugliosi's uncontained fury at the spectacle of the smirking and confident Simpson demeanor throughout the trial: "The straw that broke the camel's back was Simpson's demeanor throughout the case and in the wake of the verdict. I've seen many murderers in my life, but none even approached Simpson for audacity. . . . In fact, his entire demeanor and body language indicated that he felt he was being put out by the trial. . . . After all, he was *still* O. J., wasn't he?" (Bugliosi 1996, 23).

43. Carol Clover (forthcoming) argues that for trial movies which picture jurors, the audience often occupies the position of the jury—the one position in the courtroom that is never seen. In televised trials this unseen point of view becomes literal.

44. This enactment of the trial took place on the *E! Entertainment* channel. The program commented upon and acted out portions of the previous day's testimony. It also had viewers call in votes on the credibility of testimony.

45. Brown reported with regard to one of these incidents, for example, that "his whole facial structure changed. . . . The eyes got real angry. . . . It wasn't as if it was O. J. anymore" (Court TV, February 6, 1995).

46. It is worth noting, however, that this inversion is not complete because the racial and gendered power structures are not equivalent. There is a false perception of equivalence here.

47. Ruth Wilson Gilmore (1993, 29) discusses Koon's "rescue" of Singer in similar terms, suggesting that the gesture of protecting white womanhood is a reassertion of race/gender in the national hierarchy, making King stand in for Willie Horton *and* for Singer herself, who threatens to do a man's job.

48. While I cannot say for sure that Stacey Koon saw the film to which he alludes—though he is old enough—it is clear that with this reference he conjures up a highly ambivalent fascination with "the sexual prowess of blacks" not only as objects of fear and horror but, as the film itself reveals, as objects of desire.

49. In her testimony in the first trial, Singer's empathy for King's suffering is given less drama. Though she recounts expressing a need for an ambulance for King and later at the hospital describes pulling a towel over his eyes when the lights hurt him, she does not exhibit the overtly feminized empathy of her weeping in the second trial.

50. It is worth noting the relative insignificance of Ron Goldman, the white male victim, in this scenario. Goldman, who had kindly retrieved Juditha Brown's glasses,

and was apparently returning them to Nicole Brown when they were both attacked, was surely a victimized innocent bystander, but because there was no prior history of deploying a white male as privileged victim, his victimization never figured as prominently as that of Nicole in the prosecution's case.

51. The very fact that everyone refers to this event as the low-speed chase, when, strictly speaking, it was not a chase at all but a respectful police escort, suggests the degree to which the media have imposed on the Simpson case the excitement of melodrama and the implicit comparison with King's high-speed parallel.

52. Simpson and Cowlings turned around and headed north after finding the cemetery in Orange County where Simpson's wife had been buried swarming with reporters.

53. Shoshana Felman refers to the reverberation of one famous legal case with another as "cross-legal resonance." The Simpson case, and its chase, thus inevitably called up the Rodney King chase and beating, which in turn called up Dred Scott. "In its simultaneous gesture of commemoration and of forgetfulness of what in effect it repeats," the Simpson trial becomes a site of "traumatic repetition" (Felman 1997, 767).

54. Arguably, Simpson's celebrity status and friendliness with police, who frequently hung out at his home and swam in his pool, contributed to police unwillingness to be tough with him in the no fewer than eight times they were called to his house for incidents of spousal abuse. During the only one of those incidents that had any repercussions for Simpson—a New Year's morning in 1989—police responding to a call from Nicole found her bruised and half-naked, hiding in the bushes outside her house. They permitted Simpson to go upstairs to change out of his bathrobe before being taken to the station. Instead of complying, Simpson got in his car and drove away, with a police car in brief and unsuccessful pursuit. Because Nicole Simpson was unwilling to prosecute him and settled for informal mediation, Simpson only received a mild punishment of community service. However, this event precipitated an inquiry into the previous eight times police had been called to the house. Only one officer was willing to submit a report. This man recalled a 1985 incident in which Simpson had smashed the window of his own car with a baseball bat. That man was Mark Fuhrman, the officer whose testimony was so discredited due to having lied about having uttered racist remarks (Toobin 1996, 50–58). That the only officer willing to submit a follow-up report on Simpson's spousal abuse was the infamous racist cop is a sad commentary on the failure of the L.A.P.D. to fulfill its obligation to serve and protect citizens.

55. This is the title of the *New Yorker* journalist Jeffrey Toobin's book on the trial (1996).

56. In the predominantly black city of Compton, Toobin reports that a small crowd gathered to watch. By the time the Bronco reached Inglewood and the edge of Watts, African Americans were cheering. Hundreds lined the overpass at Venice Boulevard as the Bronco headed into the West Side. Predominantly middle-class white communities, like Torrence, did not cheer, however, and when the car reached Sunset at the edge of Bel Air, near its Brentwood destination, only a handful of people were there to cheer (Toobin 1996, 107–8). However, this portrait of immediately polarized black and white response is entirely too schematic. As a resident of Orange County at

the time who watched much of the "chase" on television, I can attest that a great many enthusiastic young white men participated in this cheering. Patricia Williams's account of the chase confirms my perception (Williams 1997, 275).

57. Earlier, in a news conference after Simpson had disappeared, Garcetti had spoken of his "empathy" toward Simpson: "We saw, perhaps, the falling of an American hero" (Toobin 1996, 94).

58. Simpson's flight, combined with what seemed to be a farewell suicide note, were both damning pieces of evidence that the prosecution failed to present.

59. Henry Louis Gates, Jr., writes that the entire nation remains captive to a "binary racial discourse of accusation and counter-accusation, of grievance and counter-grievance, of victims and victimizers . . . a discourse in which everyone speaks of payback and nobody is paid. The result is that race politics becomes a court of the imagination wherein blacks seek to punish whites for their misdeeds and whites seek to punish blacks for theirs, and an infinite regress of score-settling ensues" (Gates 1995, 65).

60. Recall Thomas Dixon's frequently uttered question: "*Can you hold in a Democracy a nation inside a nation of two hostile races?* We must do this or become mulatto, and that is death" (Dixon 1903, 244). If the two "hostile races" were to become friendly and the nation to be one nation of racially mixed people, then Dixon's worst nightmare would be realized. Black men would be "at home" with white women, and white patriarchs would have to face their family line ending in what Dixon frequently called a "brood of mulatto brats." Griffith, in contrast to Dixon, would use the presence of the black "good souls" to redefine the good home as white sovereignty with black servitude.

61. Though the trail of blood allegedly led to Simpson's Rockingham home, it was not the scene of the crime. Simpson would later claim surprise that tourists flocked to Rockingham, not Bundy, Nicole's condominium and the scene of the crime. "Nothing bad happened at Rockingham," he said (*San Francisco Chronicle*, July 30, 1998). The prosecution's case against Simpson depended on the jury believing that some very bad things did indeed happen there.

62. When after some renovation it went on the market to help pay Simpson's debts after he lost the civil suit, the realtor showing the house described it as a "grandly cozy cottage," luxurious but "not that regal. . . . "It's not supposed to be an 'Oh-my-God' house. It's supposed to be a warm house" (*Los Angeles Times*, November 16).

63. At another time he explained that his use of force against her was an attempt to get "her out of my bedroom" (Toobin 1996, 239).

64. During jury selection of his first trial, Simpson, in the course of arguments about whether Simpson should be let out on bail, Simpson held forth to the judge that he had not been running away: "I was headed back home" (Toobin 1996, 205).

65. In 1976 Simpson announced he would retire if he was not traded to a West Coast team. He reversed field, however, when Buffalo upped his salary considerably (*Playboy*, December 1976). Longing for home and family—at this point it was his black family with wife Marguerite—was always given as the reason. Leola Johnson and David Roediger argue that Simpson's famous longing for home, and the "rescue O. J. from Buffalo" melodrama, portrayed him as a stable family man in contrast to the

familiar paradigm of absent fathers (Johnson and Roediger 1996, 214–15). That Simpson *was* absent, in fact, did not seem to matter so much as his desire to be home.

66. "Willie didn't give me no discipline rap; we drove over to his place and spent the afternoon talking sports. He lived in a great big house in Forest Hill and he was exactly the easygoing, friendly guy I'd always pictured him to be" (*Playboy*, December 1976, 94).

67. Except for the fires in the fireplaces, which Judge Ito ordered extinguished, and except for the flag, which was forgotten, the house was transformed as planned.

68. For example, Schiller's novelistic style of journalism has Kardashian, who has consistently been portrayed as none too quick, undergo an eleventh-hour change of heart: "Standing there, watching O. J. shout at the TV set, Bob realizes that if Simpson has withheld and hidden and disguised so much of himself for so many years, he must be hiding still more now. Bob started out believing in O. J.'s innocence. But over the months, he has begun to doubt. . . . Kardashian knows his doubts will never leave him, his friendship with O. J. will never be the same" (Schiller and Willwerth 1996, 682–83).

69. A *People* magazine profile of the post-conviction family life portrayed Simpson as trying to be a good father, baking cookies with the children, living with his sister and her husband. Yet the life depicted, with a housekeeper, a gardener, a pool man, and two bodyguards inside the increasingly isolated gates of the mansion, cut off from the Brentwood community that once frequented his home, was full of pathos, and Denise Brown is quoted as saying she is afraid for Simpson's daughter, Sydney, who is like Nicole: "I'm afraid of what might happen if she starts mouthing back and behaving the way she sometimes does" (*People*, January 13, 1997, 56).

70. This same reporter also notes an odd sign hanging in a cabana by the tennis court, apparently once hung at Wimbledon but given, in this context, a snide racial twist: "Wimbledon Tennis Club—Mixed Doubles Are Only Allowed 5 Mins. Knocking Up Time on the Center Court."

71. For an excellent assessment of the meaning of this decision, see the essays collected in Robert Post and Michael Rogin (1996). See also Cheryl Harris's "Whiteness as Property" (1993) and George Lipsitz (1998, 36).

72. William Pizzi, a former federal prosecutor, writes, for example, that "inexperienced fact finders with no professional training are brought in for a single case, important categories of citizens are deselected from jury service, lawyers are permitted the most adversarial arguments and behaviors, and the judge renders the least amount of help in reaching the verdict. Is it any wonder that confidence in the jury is weak and that many verdicts seem driven by raw emotionalism and not by an attempt to apply the law to the facts?" (Pizzi 1999, 219).

73. And even the theatrical icon of Eliza never provided the figure of a black woman but only the figure of a white woman actress impersonating a mulatta passing for white.

74. From *The Birth of a Nation* on, the white woman emerged as the only woman, and the black woman became the comic or pathetic Mammy. In *Show Boat* she made a brief appearance—played of course by white women—in order to cede her role as suffering woman to the white female protagonist. If she surfaces briefly in *Roots* in the character of Kizzy, daughter of the "African" patriarch and mother of Chicken George who eventually leads his people out of bondage, it is only as the

bearer of the seed of the patriarchal "African." Women are more consistently portrayed in Haley's "faction" as the betrayers of African identity and black men as its upholders.

75. Wendy Brown examines how injury has become the basis for political identity in contemporary life, resulting in a politics in which the desire for freedom devolves into (melodramatic) moralization (Brown 1995). Lauren Berlant (2000), revising Brown, investigates how this injury-based identity strategically plays itself out in popular culture and politics. Robin Wiegman investigates the anatomical iconicity of the narratives of black suffering and white supremacy from the perspective of the intersection of race and gender (Wiegman 1995).

367

Conclusion

1. As Sharon Willis (1997) has noted with respect to the contemporary incarnation of the crossracial buddy film (the *Die Hard* and *Lethal Weapon* series), the inability to directly thematize race, the need to pass over in silence racial differences that were once noted and mentioned in an earlier film tradition (e.g., *The Defiant Ones*), has meant that white masculinity has taken on a particularly fraught relation to black masculinity, miscegenation, and homoerotic desire. Explaining why the battered body of the white hero of countless action films of the 1980s needed to be found, at the conclusion of the film, cradled in the arms of the black buddy, Willis notes that where women and men of color once did the "work of embodiment," now in these black and white buddy action films it is the mutilated white man who is spectacularly embodied as good, and bad white guys battle it out before the appreciative gaze of the black man (Willis 1997, 31). But perhaps a better explanation of such unthematized but intensely affective tableaux of "racial legibility" lies in the deeply felt but verbally unmentionable legacy of the Tom and anti-Tom melodramas of black and white in which the melodramatic "text of muteness" recognizes a racially constituted virtue and villainy.

2. These include Dion Boucicault's popular play about a tragic mulatta, *The Octoroon*, and a number of significant musicals before and after *Show Boat*, from the little known *Deep River* (1926) to *Ragtime* (1997), the first American musical hit to actually center its narrative on a black character, Coalhouse Walker.

3. Colin McArthur (1972) first employed this phrase in discussing the genre of the gangster film. Cycles of popular film can be viewed as forms of contemporary mythmaking that seek imaginary forms of resolution to real social problems that have urgency and currency in the present moment.

4. Carol Clover, as discussed in the last chapter, has pointed out how the adversarial structure of Anglo-American law has combined with the entertainment form of the trial movie to make Americans see conflict from the perspective of a jury. This is the case even in what Clover calls "courtroomless" courtroom dramas—dramas in which trials do not take place but the audience is still treated like jurors (Clover 1998 and forthcoming).

5. Lewis M. Steel, one of Carter's lawyers, argues that the film's failure to depict both the much more elaborate process of racially motivated framing by the prosecutor's office, which included the misuse of a lie detector test and the attribution of racial revenge to Carter and Artis's motives for the murder, is an example of the systemic reasons African Americans have for suspecting the fairness of American justice (*Nation*, January 2, 2000, 23–24).

Notes to Conclusion

6. We are also privileged to see the deeper villainy of how the murderer-rapist kept each of the two girls silent during their abduction by threatening the life of the other. To save her sister, each was quiet. As Coffey puts it, "He killed them with their love." It is this misuse of love that Coffey punishes when he orchestrates the murder of the guilty man. Now, placed in the ideal position from which to judge, we know, as the white racist court did not, that it was the black man's love for the suffering white that motivated the circumstantial evidence of crime.

Bibliography

Abel, Elizabeth. 1999. "Bathroom Doors and Drinking Fountains: Jim Crow's Racial Symbolic." *Critical Inquiry* 25 (Spring): 435–81.

Adams, John R. 1989. *Harriet Beecher Stowe*. Boston: G. K. Hall.

Affron, Charles. 1982. *Cinema and Sentiment*. Chicago: University of Chicago Press.

Agee, James. 1969. *Agee on Film*. 1958. Reprint, New York: Gosset and Dunlap.

Alexander, Nikol G., and Drucilla Cornell. 1997. "Dismissed or Banished? A Testament to the Reasonableness of the Simpson Jury." In Toni Morrison and Claudia Brodsky Lacour, eds., *Birth of a Nation'hood: Gaze, Script, and Spectacle in the O. J. Simpson Case*. New York: Pantheon.

Allen, Robert C. 1995. *To Be Continued: Soap Operas around the World*. New York: Routledge.

Althusser, Louis. 1971. *Lenin and Philosophy and Other Essays*. Translated by Ben Brewster. London: New Left Review.

Altman, Rick. 1987. *The American Film Musical*. Bloomington: Indiana University Press.

———. 1989. "Dickens, Griffith and Film Theory Today." *South Atlantic Quarterly* 88:2, 331. Reprinted in Jane Gaines, ed., *Classical Hollywood Narrative: The Paradigm Wars*. Durham, N.C.: Duke University Press, 1992.

———. 1998. "Reusable Packaging: Generic Products and the Recycling Process." In Nick Browne, ed., *Refiguring Film Genres: Theory and History*. Berkeley: University of California Press.

Ammons, Elizabeth, ed. 1994. *Uncle Tom's Cabin*. New York: W. W. Norton.

Appiah, Anthony, and Amy Gutman. 1996. *Color Conscious: The Political Morality of Race*. Princeton: Princeton University Press.

Arvidson, Linda. 1969. *When the Movies Were Young*. 1925. Reprint, New York: Dover Publications.

Austin, William W. 1975. " 'Susanna,' 'Jeanie,' and 'The Old Folks at Home' ": The Songs of Stephen C. Foster from His Time to Ours. New York: Macmillan.

Baker, Houston. 1993. "Scene . . . Not Heard." In Robert Gooding-Williams, ed., *Reading Rodney King/Reading Urban Uprising*. New York: Routledge.

Baldwin, James. 1949. "Everybody's Protest Novel." *Partisan Review* 16 (June): 578–90.

Bibliography

Barthes, Roland. 1977. *Image, Music, Text.* Ed. and trans. Stephen Heath. New York: Hill and Wang.

Baym, Nina. 1981. "Melodramas of Beset Manhood: How Theories of American Fiction Exclude Women Authors." *American Quarterly* 33.

Bazin, Andre. 1968. "La Politique des auteurs." In Peter Graham, ed., *The New Wave*, New York: Doubleday.

Belton, John. 1994. *American Cinema/American Culture.* New York: McGraw-Hill.

Benjamin, Walter. 1968. *Illuminations.* Ed. Hannah Arendt. Trans. Harry Zohn. New York: Schocken.

Bentley, Eric. 1964. *The Life of the Drama.* New York: Applause Theatre.

Bergner, Guen. 1998. "Myths of Masculinity: The Oedipus Complex and Douglass's 1845 *Narrative.*" In Christopher Lane, ed., *The Psychoanalysis of Race,* 241–60. New York: Columbia University Press.

Berlant, Lauren. 1991. "National Brands/National Body: Imitation of Life." In Hortense J. Spillers, ed., *Comparative American Identities: Race, Sex, and Nationality in the Modern Text,* 110–40. New York: Routledge.

———. 1996. "Pax Americana: The Case of *Show Boat.*" In Dierdre Lynch and William B. Warner, eds. *Cultural Institutions of the Novel.* Durham, N.C.: Duke University Press.

———. 1997. *The Queen of America Goes to Washington City.* Durham, N.C.: Duke University Press.

———. 1998a. "Poor Eliza." *American Literature* 70: 3. 635–68.

———. 1998b. "The Female Complaint." *Social Text: Theory/Culture/Ideology.* 9/20: 237–58.

———. 2000. "The Subject of True Feeling: Pain, Privacy, and Politics." In Jodi Dean, ed., *Cultural Studies and Political Theory.* Ithaca: Cornell University Press.

Bernardi, Daniel, ed. 1996. *The Birth of Whiteness: Race and the Emergence of U.S. Cinema.* New Brunswick: Rutgers University Press.

Bernstein, Mathew. 1999. "Selznick's March: Hollywood Comes to White Atlanta." *Atlantahistory, A Journal of Georgia and the South* 43, 2: 7–33.

Birdoff, Harry. 1947. *The World's Greatest Hit: Uncle Tom's Cabin.* New York: S.V. Vanni.

Blayney, Michael Steward. 1986. "*Roots* and the Noble Savage." *North Dakota Quarterly* 51:1 (winter): 1–17.

Bogle, Donald. 1989. *Toms, Coons, Mulattoes, Mammies, and Bucks: An Interpretive History of Blacks in American Films.* New York: Continuum.

Bordman, Gerald. 1978. *American Musical Theatre: A Chronicle.* New York: Oxford University Press.

———. 1980. *Jerome Kern: His Life and Music.* New York: Oxford University Press.

Bordwell, David, Janet Staiger, and Kristen Thompson. 1985. *The Classical Hollywood Cinema: Film Style and Mode of Production to 1960.* New York: Columbia University Press.

Brakhage, Stan. 1977. *Film Biographies.* Berkeley: Turtle Island.

Branch, Taylor. 1988. *Parting the Waters: America in the King Years, 1954–1963.* New York: Simon and Schuster.

Brantlinger, Patrick. 1990. *Crusoe's Footprints: Cultural Studies in Britain and America.* New York: Routledge.

Brewster, Ben, and Lea Jacobs. 1997. *Theater to Cinema: Stage Pictorialism and Early Feature Films.* London: Oxford University Press.

Brooks, Peter. 1995. *The Melodramatic Imagination.* 1976. Reprint, New Haven: Yale University Press.

Brown, Karl. 1973. *Adventures with D. W. Griffith.* London: Martin Secker and Warburg.

Brown, Wendy. 1995. *States of Injury: Power and Freedom in Late Modernity.* Princeton: Princeton University Press.

Brownlow, Kevin, and David Gill. 1992. *D. W. Griffith, Father of Film.* American Masters Documentary Film.

Bugliosi, Vincent. 1996. *Outrage: The Five Reasons Why O. J. Simpson Got Away with Murder.* New York: W. W. Norton.

Burch, Noel. 1990. *Life to Those Shadows.* Trans. Ben Brewster. Berkeley: University of California Press.

Burgoyne, Robert. "National Identity, Gender Identity, and the 'Rescue Fantasy' in *Born on the Fourth of July.*" *Screen* 35:3 (Fall): 211–34.

Butler, Judith. 1993. "Endangered/Endangering: Schematic Racism and White Paranoia." In Robert Gooding-Williams, *Reading Rodney King/Reading Urban Uprising,* 15–22. New York: Routledge.

Byers, Jackie. 1991. *All That Hollywood Allows: Re-Reading Gender in 1950s Melodrama.* Chapel Hill: University of North Carolina Press.

Campbell, Edward D.C., Jr. 1981. *The Celluloid South: Hollywood and the Southern Myth.* Knoxville: University of Tennessee Press.

Cantor, Muriel, and Suzanne Pingree. 1983. *The Soap Opera.* Beverly Hills, Calif.: Sage Publications.

Carby, Hazel. 1992. "The Multicultural Wars." In Gina Dent, ed., *Black Popular Culture.* Seattle: Bay Press.

Carringer, Robert L., ed. 1979. *The Jazz Singer.* Madison: University of Wisconsin Press.

Cawelti, John. 1991. "The Evolution of Social Melodrama." In Marcia Landy, ed. *Imitations of Life: A Reader on Film and Television Melodrama.* Detroit: Wayne State University Press.

Chandler, James. 1990. "The Historical Novel Goes to Hollywood: Scott, Griffith and Film Epic Today." In Gene Ruoff, ed., *The Romantics and Us: Essays on Literature and Culture.* New Brunswick: Rutgers University Press. Reprinted in Robert Lang, ed., *The Birth of a Nation: D.W. Griffith, director.* New Brunswick: Rutgers University Press, 1993.

Cheng, Anne. 2000. *The Melancholy of Race: Psychoanalysis, Assimilation, and Hidden Grief.* New York: Oxford University Press.

Clark, Marcia, with Teresa Carpenter. 1997. *Without a Doubt.* New York: Penguin Books.

Clover, Carol J. 1998. "God Bless Juries!" In Nick Browne, ed., *Refiguring American Film Genres: Theory and History.* Berkeley: University of California Press.

———. Forthcoming. *Trials, Lies, and Movies* (working title). Princeton: Princeton University Press.

Cockrell, Dale. 1997. *Demons of Disorder: Early Blackface Minstrels and Their World.* New York: Cambridge University Press.

Connolly, William. 1991. *Identity/Difference: Democratic Negotiations of Political Paradox.* Ithaca: Cornell University Press.

Cook, David. 1990. *A History of Narrative Film.* New York: W.W. Norton.

Cook, Raymond Allen. 1968. *Fire from the Flint: The Amazing Careers of Thomas Dixon.* Winston-Salem, N.C.: John F. Blair.

Courlander, Harold. 1986. "Kunta Kinte's Struggle to Be African." *Phylon: A Review of Race and Culture* 47:4 (December): 294–302.

Courtney, Susan. 1997. "Hollywood's Fantasy of Miscegenation." Ph.D. dissertation, University of California, Berkeley.

Cowley, Malcolm. 1983. "Going with the Wind." In Darden Asbury Pyron, ed., *Recasting Gone With the Wind in American Culture.* 1936. Reprint, Miami: University Presses of Florida.

Crary, Jonathan. 1988. "Modernizing Vision." In Hal Foster, ed., *Vision and Visuality* 29–44. Seattle: Bay Press.

Crenshaw, Kimberlé Williams. 1997. "Color-Blind Dreams and Racial Nightmares: Reconfiguring Racism in the Post–Civil Rights Era." In Toni Morrison and Claudia Brodsky Lacour, ed., *Birth of a Nation'hood: Gaze, Script, and Spectacle in the O. J. Simpson Case,* 97–168. New York: Pantheon.

Crenshaw, Kimberlé, and Gary Peller. 1993. "Reel Time / Real Justice." In Robert Gooding-Williams, ed., *Reading Rodney King / Reading Urban Uprising,* 56–70. New York: Routledge.

Cripps, Thomas. 1983. "The Winds of Change." In Darden Asbury Pyron, ed. *Recasting Gone With the Wind in American Culture,* 143–59. Miami: University Presses of Florida.

———. 1993a. *Slow Fade to Black: The Negro in American Film, 1900–1942.* 1977. Reprint, New York: Oxford University Press.

———. 1993b. *Making Movies Black: The Hollywood Message Movie from World War II to the Civil Rights Era.* New York: Oxford University Press.

Dagle, Joan, and Kathryn Kalinak. 1994. "The Representation of Race and Sexuality: Visual and Musical Construction" in *Gone With the Wind.*" *Post Script* 13/2 (Winter-Spring): 14–27.

Darden, Christopher, with Jess Walter. 1996. *In Contempt.* New York: HarperCollins.

Davis, Mike. 1993. "Uprising and Repression in L.A." In Robert Gooding-Williams, ed., *Reading Rodney King / Reading Urban Uprising.* New York: Routledge.

Dayan, Daniel, and Elihu Katz. 1992. *Media Events: The Live Broadcasting of History.* Cambridge: Harvard University Press.

Denby, David. 1998. Capsule Film Review of *American History X. New Yorker* (December 21): 24.

Dershowitz, Alan. 1986. *Reversal of Fortune: Inside the von Bulow Case.* New York: Pocket Books.

Deutsch, Linda, and Michael Fleeman. 1995. *Verdict: The Chronicle of the O. J. Simpson Trial.* Kansas City: Universal Press Syndicate.

Dixon, Thomas Jr. 1903. *The Leopard's Spots: A Romance of the White Man's Burden.* New York: Doubleday.

———. 1970. *The Clansman: An Historical Romance of the Ku Klux Klan.* 1905. Reprint, Lexington: University Press of Kentucky.

———. 1905. *The Clansman.* Manuscript. Harvard Theater Collection.

————. 1984. *Southern Horizons: The Autobiography of Thomas Dixon*. Alexandria, Va.: I.W.V. Publishing.

Doane, Mary Ann. 1987. *The Desire to Desiree: The Women's Film of the 1940s*. Bloomington: Indiana University Press.

Donovan, Josephine. 1991. *Uncle Tom's Cabin: Evil, Affliction, and Redemptive Love*. Boston: Twayne Publishers.

Dorman, James. 1967. *Theater in the Ante-Bellum South*. Chapel Hill: University of North Carolina Press.

Douglas, Ann. 1977. *The Feminization of American Culture*. New York: Avon.

————. 1995. *Terrible Honesty: Mongrel Manhattan in the 1920s*. New York: Noonday Press.

Douglass, Frederick. 1972. "The Heroic Slave." In Ronald T. Takaki, ed., *Violence in the Black Imagination: Essays and Documents*, 37–77. New York: G.P. Putnam.

Drummond, A. M., and Richard Moody. 1952. "The Hit of the Century: *Uncle Tom's Cabin* — 1853–1952." *Educational Theatre Journal* 4: 315–22.

Du Bois, W.E.B. 1989. *The Souls of Black Folk*. 1953. Reprint, New York: Bantam Books.

Duberman, Martin, 1989. *Paul Robeson: A Biography*. New York: W. W. Norton.

DuCille, Ann. 1996. *Skin Trade*. Cambridge: Harvard University Press.

————. 1997. "The Unbearable Darkness of Being: 'Fresh' Thoughts on Race, Sex, and the Simpsons." In Toni Morrison and Claudia Brodsky Lacour, eds., *Birth of a Nation'hood: Gaze, Script, and Spectacle in the O. J. Simpson Case*. New York: Pantheon.

Dumm, Thomas. 1993. "The New Enclosures: Racism in the Normalized Community." In Robert Gooding-Williams, ed., *Reading Rodney King/Reading Urban Uprising*, 56–70. New York: Routledge.

Dyer, Richard. 1981. "Entertainment and Utopia." In Rick Altman, ed., *Genre: The Musical*, 175–89. London: Routledge and Kegan Paul.

————. 1986. *Heavenly Bodies: Film Stars and Society*. New York: St. Martin's Press.

Eisenstein, Sergei. 1949. "Dickens, Griffith and the Film Today." In Jay Leyda, ed., *Film Form: Essays in Film Theory*, 195–255. Trans. Jay Leyda. New York: Harcourt, Brace and World.

————. 1974. "Montage of Attractions." Trans. Daniel Gerould. *Drama Review* 18 (March): 78–79.

Elbogen, Ismar. 1993. *Jewish Liturgy: A Comprehensive History*. Trans. Ismar Elbogen. Philadelphia: Jewish Publication Society.

Elias, Tom, and Dennis Schatzman. 1996. *The Simpson Trial in Black and White*. Los Angeles: General Publishing Group.

Elsaesser, Thomas. 1975. "Tales of Sound and Fury: Observations on the Family Melodrama." *Monogram* 4: 1–15. Reprinted in Christine Gledhill, ed., *Home Is Where the Heart Is*, 43–69. London: British Film Institute, 1987; and in Marcia Landy, ed., *Imitations of Life: A Reader on Film and Television Melodrama*, 68–91. Detroit: Wayne State University Press, 1991.

Ewen, David. 1964. *The Life and Death of Tin Pan Alley: The Golden Age of American Popular Music*. New York: Funk and Wagnalls.

Fanon, Frantz. 1967. *Black Skin, White Masks*. New York: Grove Press.

Farr, Finis. 1965. *Margaret Mitchell of Atlanta, The Author of* Gone With the Wind. New York: Morrow.

Felman, Shoshana. 1997. "Forms of Judicial Blindness, or the Evidence of What Cannot Be Seen: Traumatic Narratives and Legal Repetitions in the O. J. Simpson Case and Tolstoy's *The Kreutzer Sonata.*" *Critical Inquiry* 23 (Summer):738–88.

Ferber, Edna. 1994. *Show Boat.* 1926. Reprint, New York: Penguin Books.

Feuer, Jane. 1983. "The Concept of Live Television: Ontology as Ideology." In E. Ann Kaplan, ed., *Regarding Television: Critical Approaches—An Anthology.* Frederick, Md.: University Publication of America.

Fiedler, Leslie. 1966. *Love and Death in the American Novel.* 1960. Reprint, New York: Stein and Day.

———. 1971. "Come Back to the Raft Ag'in, Huck Honey!" *The Collected Essays of Leslie Fiedler.* Vol. 1. New York: Stein and Day: 142–51.

———. 1979. *The Inadvertent Epic.* New York: Simon and Schuster.

———. 1980. "Harriet Beecher Stowe's Novel of Sentimental Protest." In Elizabeth Ammons, ed., *Critical Essays on Harriet Beecher Stowe.* Boston: G. K. Hall.

———. 1982. *What Was Literature: Class Culture and Mass Society.* New York: Simon and Schuster.

Fishbein, L. 1983. "*Roots*: Docudrama and the Interpretation of History." In J. O'Connor, ed., *American History, American Television: Interpreting the Video Past,* 279–305. New York: Frederick Ungar.

Fisher, Philip. 1985. *Hard Facts: Setting and Form in the American Novel.* New York: Oxford University Press.

Fiske, John. 1996. *Media Matters: Everyday Culture and Political Change.* Minneapolis: University of Minnesota Press.

Fletcher, Edward G. 1958. "Illustrations for Uncle Tom." *Texas Quarterly* 1: 166–80.

Flinn, Caryl. 1992. *Strains of Utopia: Gender, Nostalgia and Hollywood Film Music.* Princeton: Princeton University Press.

Fluck, Winfried. 1992. "The Power and Failure of Representation in Harriet Beecher Stowe's Uncle Tom's Cabin." *New Literary History* 23: 319–38.

Foner, Eric. 1988. *Reconstruction: America's Unfinished Revolution, 1863–1877.* New York: Harper and Row.

Foster, Stephen. 1975. *Stephen Foster Sesqui-Centennial Song Book: July Fourth 1826–July Fourth 1976.* Carlstadt, N.J.: Ashley Publications.

Foucault, Michel. 1979. *Discipline and Punish: The Birth of the Prison.* Trans. Alan Sheridan. New York: Random House.

Franchot, Jenny. 1990. "The Punishment of Esther: Frederick Douglass and the Construction of the Feminine." In Eric Sundquist, ed., *New Literary and Historical Essays on Frederick Douglass,* 141–65. New York: Cambridge University Press.

Fredrickson, George. 1994. "Uncle Tom and the Anglo-Saxons: Romantic Racialism in the North." In Elizabeth Ammons, ed., *Uncle Tom's Cabin.* New York: W. W. Norton. 1994.

Gaines, Jane. 1993. "Fire and Desire: Race, Melodrama, and Oscar Micheaux." In Manthia Diawara, ed., *Black American Cinema.* New York: Routledge.

———. 1996. "*The Birth of a Nation* and *Within Our Gates*: Two Tales of the American South." In Richard King and Helen Taylor, eds., *Dixie Debates: Perspectives on Southern Cultures.* New York: New York University Press.

—. 2000. *Fire and Desire: Mixed Race Movies in the Silent Era*. Chicago: University of Chicago Press.

Gaines, Jane, and Neil Lerner. 2000. "The Orchestration of Affect: The Motif of Barbarism in Breil's *The Birth of a Nation* Score." In Richard Abel and Rick Altman, eds., *The Sounds of Early Cinema*. Bloomington: Indiana University Press.

Garrow, David. 1978. *Protest at Selma: Martin Luther King, Jr., and the Voting Rights Act of 1965*. New Haven: Yale University Press.

Gates, Henry Louis, Jr. 1995. "Thirteen Ways of Looking at a Black Man." *New Yorker* (October 23): 56–65.

Geduld, Harry, ed. 1971. *Focus on D. W. Griffith*. Englewood Cliffs, N.J.: Prentice-Hall.

Gerber, David A. 1977. "Haley's Roots and Our Own: An Inquiry into the Nature of a Popular Phenomenon." *The Journal of Ethnic Studies* (53): 87–111.

Gerould, Daniel C., ed. 1992. *American Melodrama*. New York: Performing Arts Journal Publications.

Gibbs, Jewelle Taylor. 1996. *Race and Justice: Rodney King and O. J. Simpson in a House Divided*. San Francisco: Jossey-Bass.

Gilbert, Sandra, and Susan Gubar. 1979. *The Madwoman in the Attic: The Woman Writer and the Nineteenth-Century Literary Imagination*. New Haven: Yale University Press.

Gill, Brendan. 1997. Capsule Film review of *Happy Together*. *New Yorker* (November 17): 33.

Gillman, Susan. 1992. "The Mulatto, Tragic or Triumphant? The Nineteenth-Century American Race Melodrama." In Shirley Samuels, ed., *The Culture of Sentiment: Race, Gender and Sentimentality in Nineteenth-Century America*, 221–43. New York: Oxford University Press.

—. Forthcoming. *American Race Melodramas, 1877–1915*. Chicago: University of Chicago Press.

Gilmore, Glenda Elizabeth. 1996. *Gender and Jim Crow: Women and the Politics of White Supremacy in North Carolina, 1896–1920*. Chapel Hill: University of North Carolina Press.

Gilmore, Ruth Wilson. 1993. "Terror Austerity Race Gender Excess Theater." In Robert Gooding-Williams, ed., *Reading Rodney King/Reading Urban Uprising*, 23–37. New York: Routledge.

Gilroy, Paul. 1993. *The Black Atlantic: Modernity and Double Consciousness*. Cambridge: Harvard University Press.

Gish, Lillian. 1969. *The Movies, Mr. Griffith and Me*. New York: Avon.

Gledhill, Christine. 1978. "Recent Developments in Feminist Film Criticism." *Quarterly Review of Film Studies* 3:4. Revised and reprinted in Mary Ann Doane, Patricia Mellencamp, and Linda Williams, eds., *Re-Vision: Essays in Feminist Film Criticism*, Frederick, Md.: University Publication of America, 1984.

—. 1986. "Dialogue." *Cinema Journal* 25:4 (Summer): 44–48.

—. 1987. "The Melodramatic Field: An Investigation." In *Home Is Where the Heart Is: Studies in Melodrama and the Woman's Film*, 5. London: British Film Institute.

—. 1988. "Pleasurable Negotiations." in E. Deidre Prioram, ed., *Female Spectators*. New York: Verso, 1988.

Bibliography

Gledhill, Christine. 1991. "Signs of Melodrama." In Christine Gledhill, ed., *Stardom: Industry of Desire*. New York: Routledge, 1991.

———. 1992. "Between Melodrama and Realism: Anthony Asquith's *Underground* and King Vidor's *The Crowd*." In Jane Gaines, ed., *Classical Hollywood Narrative: The Paradigm Wars*, 129–67. Durham, N.C.: Duke University Press.

———. 2000. "Rethinking Genre." In Christine Gledhill and Linda Williams, eds., *Reinventing Film Studies*. London: Edward Arnold.

Goldberg, David Theo. 1993. *Racist Culture: Philosophy and the Politics of Meaning*. Oxford: Basil Blackwell.

Goldman, Herbert G. 1988. *Jolson: The Legend Comes to Life*. New York: Oxford University Press.

Gooding-Williams, Robert, ed. 1993. *Reading Rodney King/Reading Urban Uprising*. New York: Routledge.

Goodman, James. 1994. *Stories of Scottsboro*. New York: Vintage Books.

Gorbman, Claudia. 1987. *Unheard Melodies: Narrative Film Music*. Bloomington: Indiana University Press.

Gossett, Thomas F. 1965. *Race: The History of an Idea in America*. Reprint, New York: Oxford University Press, 1997.

———. 1985. *Uncle Tom's Cabin and American Culture*. Dallas: Southern Methodist University Press.

Gottfried, Martin. 1979. *Broadway Musicals*. New York: Harry N. Abrams.

Grieveson, Lee. 1998. "Fighting Films: Race, Morality, and the Governing of Cinema, 1912–1915." *Cinema Journal* 38: 1 (fall): 40–72.

Grimsted, David. 1987. *Melodrama Unveiled: American Theater and Culture, 1800–1850*. Berkeley: University of California Press.

Gubar, Susan. 1997. *Racechanges: White Skin, Black Face in American Culture*. New York: Oxford University Press.

Gunning, Tom. 1986. "The Cinema of Attraction." *Wide Angle* 8:3/4.

———. 1989. "An Aesthetics of Astonishment: Early Film and the (In)Credulous Spectator." *Art and Text* 34 (spring). Reprinted in Linda Williams, ed., *Viewing Positions: Ways of Seeing Film*. New Brunswick: Rutgers University Press, 1995.

———. 1991. *D. W. Griffith and the Origins of American Narrative Film*. Urbana: University of Illinois Press.

Hadley, Elaine. 1995. *Melodramatic Tactics: Theatricalized Dissent in the English Marketplace, 1800–1885*. Stanford: Stanford University Press.

Hale, Grace Elizabeth. 1998. *Making Whiteness: The Culture of Segregation in the South*. New York: Pantheon.

Haley, Alex. 1964. *The Autobiography of Malcolm X*. New York: Random House.

———. 1976. *Roots*. Garden City, N.Y.: Doubleday.

Hall, Jacquelyn Dowd. 1993. *Revolt against Chivalry: Jessie Daniel Ames and the Women's Campaign against Lynching*. New York: Columbia University Press.

Halttunen, Karen. 1985. "Gothic Imagination and Social Reform: The Haunted Houses of Lyman Beecher, Henry Ward Beecher, and Harriet Beecher Stowe." In Eric Sundquist, ed., *New Essays on Uncle Tom's Cabin*. New York: Cambridge University Press.

———. 1998. *Murder Most Foul: The Killer and the American Gothic Imagination*. Cambridge: Harvard University Press.

Hanne, Michael. 1994. *The Power of the Story: Fiction and Political Change*. Providence: Berghan Books.

Hansen, Miriam. 2000. "The Mass Production of the Senses: Classical Cinema as Vernacular Modernism." In Christine Gledhill and Linda Williams, eds., *Reinventing Film Studies*. London: Edward Arnold.

Harmetz, Aljean. 1996. *On the Road to Tara: The Making of* Gone With the Wind. New York: Harry N. Abrams.

Harris, Cheryl. 1993. "Whiteness as Property." *Harvard Law Review* 106, 8 (June): 1709–91.

Harris, Trudier. 1984. *Exorcising Blackness: Historical and Literary Lynching and Burning Rituals*. Bloomington: Indiana University Press.

Hart, Thomas, ed. 1972. *The Man Who Invented Hollywood: The Autobiography of D. W. Griffith*. Louisville: Touchstone Publishing.

Haskell, Molly. 1973. *From Reverence to Rape: The Treatment of Women in the Movies*. Chicago: University of Chicago Press.

Hays, Michael, and Anastasia Nikolopoulou. 1996. *Melodrama: The Cultural Emergence of a Genre*. New York: St. Martin's Press.

Hazen, Don, ed. 1992. *Inside the L.A. Riots: What Really Happened—and Why It Will Happen Again*. New York: Institute for Alternative Journalism.

Hedrick, Joan D. 1994. *Harriet Beecher Stowe: A Life*. New York: Oxford University Press.

Heilman, Robert. 1968. *Tragedy and Melodrama: Versions of Experience*. Seattle: University of Washington Press.

Hoberman, J. 1991. *Bridge of Light: Yiddish Film between Two Worlds*. New York: Schocken.

Jacobs, Lea. 1993. "The Woman's Picture and the Poetics of Melodrama." *Camera Obscura* 31: 120–47.

Jacobs, Lewis. 1968. *The Rise of the American Film*. 1939. Reprint, New York: Teacher's College Press.

James, Henry. 1941. *A Small Boy & Others*. 1913. Reprint, New York: Charles Scribner's Sons.

Jeffords, Susan. 1989. *The Remasculinization of America: Gender and the Vietnam War*. Bloomington: Indiana University Press.

———. 1994. *Hard Bodies: Hollywood Masculinity in the Reagan Era*. New Brunswick: Rutgers University Press.

Johnson, Leula, and David Roediger. 1997. " 'Hertz, Don't It?' Becoming Colorless and Staying Black in the Crossover of O. J. Simpson." In Toni Morrison and Claudia Brodsky Lacour, eds., *Birth of a Nation'hood: Gaze, Script, and Spectacle in the O. J. Simpson Case*. New York: Pantheon.

Jordan, Winthrop D. 1968. *White over Black: American Attitudes Toward the Negro, 1550–1812*. Chapel Hill: University of North Carolina Press.

Kaplan, Ann E. 1992. *Motherhood and Representation: The Mother in Popular Culture and Melodrama*. London: Routledge

Kaplan, Cora. 1986. "The Thorn Birds: Fiction, Fantasy, Femininity." In *Sea Changes: Essays On Culture and Feminism*. London: Verso.

Katz, Jack. 1999. *How Emotions Work*. Chicago: University of Chicago Press.

Bibliography

Kern, Jerome, and Oscar Hammerstein II. 1927. *Show Boat* (vocal score). New York: T. B. Harms Company.

Kesler, William Jackson II. 1968. *The Early Productions of the Aiken-Howard Version of Uncle Tom's Cabin*. Ph.D. dissertation, University of Texas, Austin.

Klinger, Barbara. 1994. *Melodrama and Meaning: History, Culture, and the Films of Douglas Sirk*. Bloomington: Indiana University Press.

Koon, Stacey C., and Robert Deitz. 1992. *Presumed Guilty: The Tragedy of the Rodney King Affair*. Washington, D.C.: Regnery Gateway.

Kozarski, Richard. 1990. *An Evening's Entertainment: The Age of the Silent Feature Picture, 1915–1928*. New York: Charles Scribner's Sons.

Kozloff, Sarah. 1985. "Where Wessex Meets New England: Griffith's *Way Down East* and Hardy's *Tess of the D'Urbervilles*." *Literature/Film Quarterly* 13:1: 35–41.

Krafft-Ebing, Richard von. 1965. *Psychopathia Sexualis*. New York: Stein and Day.

Kreuger, Miles. 1977a. *Show Boat: The Story of a Classic American Musical*. New York: Oxford University Press.

——— 1977b. *Souvenir Programs of Twelve Classic Movies, 1927–1941*. New York: Dover.

Lahr, John. 1996. "Heaven Can Wait." *New Yorker* (September 16): 101–2.

Lambert, Gavin. 1973. *The Making of* Gone With the Wind. New York: Bantam.

Landy, Marcia, ed. 1991. *Imitations of Life*: A Reader on Film and Television Melodrama. Detroit: Wayne State University Press.

Lane, Anthony. 1997. "Titanic." *New Yorker* (December 15): 156–57.

Lang, Robert. 1989. *American Film Melodrama: Griffith, Vidor, Minnelli*. Princeton: Princeton University Press.

———, ed. 1993. *The Birth of a Nation: D. W. Griffith, Director*. New Brunswick: Rutgers University Press.

Lerner, Gerda. 1986. *The Creation of Patriarchy*. New York: Oxford University Press.

Lindsay, Vachel. 1915. *The Art of the Moving Picture*. New York: Macmillan.

Lipsitz, George. 1998. *The Possessive Investment in Whiteness: How White People Profit from Identity Politics*. Philadelphia: Temple University Press.

Lott, Eric. 1993. *Love and Theft: Blackface Minstrelsy and the American Working Class*. New York: Oxford University Press.

Malcolm, Janet. 1999. *The Crime of Sheila McGough*. New York: Knopf.

Maltin, Leonard. 1999. *Movie and Video Guide*. New York: Penguin.

Marks, Martin. 1997. *Music and the Silent Film: Contexts and Case Studies, 1895–1924*. New York: Oxford University Press.

Mason, Jeffrey D. 1993. *Melodrama and the Myth of America*. Bloomington: Indiana University Press.

Mast, Gerald. 1987. *Can't Help Singin': The American Musical on Stage and Screen*. Woodstock, N.Y.: Overlook Press.

Mattuck, Farid. 1996. "What about the Victims?" Unpublished manuscript, University of California, Irvine.

Mayer, David. 1996. "Parlour and Platform Melodrama. In Michael Hays and Anastasia Nikolopoulou, eds., *Melodrama: The Cultural Emergence of a Genre*. New York: St. Martin's.

McArthur, Colin. 1992. *Underworld USA*. New York: Viking Press.

McConachie, Bruce, A. 1991. "Out of the Kitchen and into the Marketplace." *The Journal of American Drama and Theater* 3 (Winter): 5–28.

————. 1992. *Melodramatic Formations: American Theatre and Society, 1820–1870.* Iowa City: University of Iowa Press.

McDowell, Deborah E. and Arnold Rampersad, eds. 1989. *Slavery and the Literary Imagination: Selected Papers from the English Institute, 1987.* Baltimore: Johns Hopkins University Press.

McGill, Ralph. 1962. "Little Woman, Big Book." In Richard Harwell, ed., *Gone With the Wind as Book and Film.* Columbia: University of South Carolina Press, 1983.

McHugh, Kathleen Anne. 1999. *American Domesticity: From How-to Manual to Hollywood Melodrama.* New York: Oxford University Press.

Merritt, Russell. 1978–79. "On First Looking into Griffith's Babylon: A Reading of a Publicity Still." *Wide Angle* 3 (winter): 12–21.

————. 1983. "Postmortem for a Phantom Genre." *Wide Angle* 5, 3: 24–31.

Michaels, Walter Ben. 1987. *The Gold Standard of the Logic of Capitalism.* Berkeley: University of California Press.

Miesel, Martin. 1980. "Speaking Picture." In Daniel Gerould, ed., *Melodrama,* 58–59. New York: New York Literary Forum.

————. 1983. *Realizations: Narrative, Pictorial, and Theatrical Arts in Nineteenth-Century England.* Princeton: Princeton University Press.

Mitchell, Margaret. 1993. *Gone With the Wind.* 1936. Reprint, New York: Warner Books.

Modleski, Tania. 1982. *Loving with a Vengeance: Mass-Produced Fantasies for Women.* New York: Methuen.

Moore, David Chioni. 1994. "Routes." *Transition: An International Review* 64: 4–21.

Mordden, Ethan. 1989. " 'Show Boat' Crosses Over." *New Yorker* (July 3): 79–94.

Moretti, Franco. 1983. "Kindergarten." In *Signs Taken for Wonders: Essays in the Sociology of Literary Forms* 159–62. London: Verso.

Morrison, Toni. 1990. *Playing in the Dark: Whiteness and the Literary Imagination.* New York: Random House.

Morrison, Toni, and Claudia Brodsky Lacour, eds. 1997. *Birth of a Nation'hood: Gaze, Script, and Spectacle in the O. J. Simpson Case.* New York: Pantheon.

Moynihan, Daniel Patrick. 1967. "The Negro Family and the Case for National Action." In Lee Rainwater and William Yancey, eds., *The Moynihan Report and the Politics of Controversy.* Cambridge: MIT Press.

Mullen, Mark. 1999. "Sympathetic Vibrations: The Politics of Antebellum Melodrama." Ph.D. dissertation, University of California, Irvine.

Mulvey, Laura. 1975. "Visual Pleasure and Narrative Cinema." *Screen* 16:2 (Autumn): 6–18. Reprinted in Mulvey, *Visual and Other Pleasures,* 14–26. Bloomington: Indiana University Press, 1989.

————. 1977–78. "Notes on Sirk and Melodrama." *Movie* 25: 53–56. Reprinted in Christine Gledhill, ed., *Home Is Where the Heart Is,* 75–79. London: British Film Institute, 1987.

————. 1986. "Melodrama In and Out of the Home." In Colin MacCabe, ed., *High Theory/Low Culture: Analyzing Popular Television and Film.* Manchester: Manchester University Press.

Bibliography

Musser, Charles. 1990. *The Emergence of Cinema: The American Screen to 1907*. New York: Charles Scribner.

Nash, Gary. 1990. *The American People: Creating a Nation and Society*. New York: Harper and Row.

Neale, Steve. 1986. "Melodrama and Tears." *Screen* 27:6 (November-December): 8.

————. 1993. "Melo Talk: On the Meaning and Use of the Term 'Melodrama' in the American Trade Press." *Velvet Light Trap* 32 (Fall): 66–89.

Nichols, Bill. 1994. *Blurred Boundaries: Questions of Meaning in Contemporary Culture*. Bloomington: Indiana University Press.

Nietzsche, Friedrich. 1956. *The Birth of Tragedy* and *The Genealogy of Morals*. Trans. Francis Golffing. New York: Doubleday.

Nobile, Phillip. 1993. "Uncovering *Roots*." *Village Voice* (February 23): 30–33.

Nowell-Smith, Geoffrey. 1977. "Minnelli and Melodrama." *Screen* 18:2 (summer): 113–18. Reprinted in Christine Gledhill, ed., *Home Is Where the Heart Is*, 70–74. London: British Film Institute, 1987 and in Marcia Landy, ed., *Imitations of Life: A Reader on Film and Television Melodrama*, 268–74. Detroit: Wayne State University Press, 1991.

O'Brien, Kenneth. 1983. "Race, Romance, and the Southern Literary Tradition." In Darden Asbury Pyron, ed., *Recasting* Gone With the Wind *in American Culture*, 153–173. Miami: University Press of Florida.

Omi, Michael, and Howard Winant. 1986. *Racial Formation in the United States: From the 1960s to the 1980s*. New York: Routledge.

————. 1993. "The Los Angeles 'Race Riot' and Contemporary U.S. Politics." In Robert Gooding-Williams, ed., *Reading Rodney King/Reading Urban Uprising*, 97–114. New York: Routledge.

Pascoe, Peggy. 1999. "Miscegenation Law, Court Casey, and Ideologies of 'Race' in Twentieth-Century America." In Martha Hodes, ed., *Sex, Love, Race: Crossing Boundaries in North American History*. New York: New York University Press.

Petro, Patrice, and Carol Flinn. 1985. "Dialogue." *Cinema Journal* 25:1 (Fall): 50–54.

Pierpont, Claudia Roth. 1996. "The Strong Woman." *New Yorker* (November 11).

Pizzi, William. 1999. *Trials without Truth: Why Our System of Criminal Trials Has Become an Expensive Failure and What We Need to Do to Rebuild It*. New York: New York University Press.

Pleasants, Henry. 1974. *The Great American Popular Singers*. New York: Simon and Schuster.

Post, Robert, and Michael Rogin, eds. 1996. "Race and Representation: Affirmative Action." *Representations* 55 (Summer): 1–12.

Postlewait, Thomas. 1996. "From Melodrama to Realism: The Suspect History of American Drama." In Michael Hays and Anastasia Nikolopoulou, eds., *Melodrama: The Cultural Emergence of a Genre*, 39–600. New York: St. Martin's Press, 1996.

Pudovkin, V. I. 1970. *Film Technique and Film Acting*. New York: Grove Press.

Pyron, Darden Asbury, ed. 1983. *Recasting* Gone With the Wind *in American Culture* Miami: University Presses of Florida.

————. 1991. *Southern Daughter: The Life of Margaret Mitchell*. New York: Oxford University Press.

Rahill, Frank. 1967. *The World of Melodrama*. University Park: Penn State University Press.

Raphaelson, Samson. 1925. *The Jazz Singer.* New York: Brentano's Publishers.

Ray, Robert B. 1985. *A Certain Tendency of the Hollywood Cinema, 1930–1980.* Princeton: Princeton University Press.

Remnick, David. 1996. "Inside-out Olympics." *New Yorker* (August 5): 26–28.

Riis, Thomas, ed. 1994. *Uncle Tom's Cabin.* New York: Garland.

Riss, Arthur. 1994. "Racial Essentialism and Family Values in Uncle Tom's Cabin." *American Quarterly* 46:4 (December): 513–44.

Robinson, Cedric J. 1997. "In the Year 1915: D. W. Griffith and the Whitening of America." *Social Identities: Journal for the Study of Race, Nation and Culture* 3: 2, 161.

Roediger, David R. 1994. *Towards the Abolition of Whiteness: Essay on Race, Politics, and Working Class History.* London: Verso.

Rogin, Michael. 1984. "The Sword Became a Flashing Vision': D.W. Griffith's Birth of a Nation." In *Ronald Reagan, the Movie, and Other Episodes in Political Demonology*, 190–235. Berkeley: University of California Press, 1987.

———. 1996. *Blackface, White Noise: Jewish Immigrants in the Hollywood Melting Pot.* Berkeley: University of California Press.

Rose, W. L. 1979. *Race and Region in American Historical Fiction: Four Episodes in Popular Culture.* Oxford: Oxford University Press.

Rosen, Jeffrey. 1996. "The Bloods and the Crits: O. J. Simpson, Critical Race Theory, the Law and the Triumph of Color in America." *New Republic* (December 9): 27–42.

Rosen, Phillip. Forthcoming. "Change Mummified: Historical Times and Media Times."

Saks, Eva. 1988. "Representing Miscegenation Law." *Raritan* 8:2 (fall): 39–69.

Sánchez-Eppler, Karen. 1988. "Bodily Bonds: The Intersecting Rhetorics of Feminism and Abolition." *Representations* 24 (fall): 28–59. Reprinted in Shirley Samuels, ed., *The Culture of Sentiment: Race, Gender and Sentimentality in Nineteenth-Century America.* New York: Oxford University Press, 1992.

Saxton, Alexander. 1990. *The Rise and Fall of the White Republic: Class Politics and Mass Culture in Nineteenth-Century America.* London: Verso.

Schatz, Thomas. 1981. *Hollywood Genres: Formulas, Filmmaking, and the Studio System.* New York: Random House.

———. 1988. *The Genius of the System: Hollywood Filmmaking in the Studio Era.* New York: Henry Holt.

Schickel, Richard. 1984. *D. W. Griffith: An American Life.* New York: Simon and Schuster.

Schiller, Lawrence, and James Willwerth. 1996. *American Tragedy: The Uncensored Story of the Simpson Defense.* New York: Random House.

Selznick, David O. 1972. *Memo from: David O. Selznick.* New York: Viking Press.

Silva, Fred. 1971. *Focus on* The Birth of a Nation. Englewood Cliffs, N.J.: Prentice-Hall.

Silverman, Kaja. 1992. *Male Subjectivity at the Margins.* New York: Routledge.

Simmon, Scott. 1993. *The Films of D. W. Griffith.* Cambridge: Cambridge University Press.

Simonett, John E. 1966. "The Trial as One of the Performing Arts." *American Bar Association Journal* 62: 1145–47.

Singer, Ben. 1990. "Female Power in the Serial-Queen Melodrama: The Etiology of an Anomaly." *Camera Obscura* 22 (January): 91–129.

———. 2000. *Melodrama and Modernity*. New York: Columbia University Press.

Smith, Murray. 1995. *Engaging Characters: Fiction, Emotion and the Cinema*. Oxford: Oxford University Press.

Southern, Eileen, ed. 1983. *Readings in Black American Music*. New York: W.W. Norton.

Spelman, Elizabeth V. 1988. *Inessential Woman: Problems of Exclusion in Feminist Thought*. Boston: Beacon.

Spillers, Hortense J. 1987. "Mama's Baby, Papa's Maybe: An American Grammar Book." *diacritics* (summer): 65–81.

Staiger, Janet. 1992. *Interpreting Films: Studies in the Historical Reception of American Cinema*. Princeton: Princeton University Press.

Stern, Seymour. 1965. "Griffith I—'The Birth of a Nation.'" *Film Culture* 36 (spring-summer): 114–32.

St. John, Maria. 1999. "Cinematic and Fantasmatic Contours of Mammy: A Psychoanalytic Exploration of Race, Fantasy, and Cultural Representation." *fort da: The Journal of the Northern California Society for Psychoanalytic Psychology* 4: 2 (fall): 6–21.

Stowe, Charles Edward. 1911. *Harriet Beecher Stowe: The Story of Her Life*. New York: Houghton-Mifflin.

Stowe, Harriet Beecher. 1983. *Uncle Tom's Cabin; or, Life Among the Lowly*. Ed. Ann Douglas. 1852. Reprint, New York: Penguin American Library.

———. 1854. *Sunny Memories of Foreign Lands*, vol 2. Boston: Phillips, Sampson and Co.

Studlar, Gaylin. 1988. *In the Realm of Pleasure: Von Sternberg, Dietrich and the Masochistic Aesthetic*. Urbana: University of Illinois Press.

Sundquist, Eric J. 1988. *New Essays on Uncle Tom's Cabin*. New York: Cambridge University Press.

———. *To Wake the Nations: Race in the Making of American Literature*. Cambridge: Belknap Press of Harvard University Press.

Tan, Ed S. 1996. *Emotion and the Structure of Narrative Film*. Mahwah, N.J.: Lawrence Erlbaum.

Taylor, Clyde. 1991. "The Re-Birth of the Aesthetic in Cinema." *Wide Angle* 13: 3–4 (July-October): 12–30.

Taylor, Helen. 1989. *Scarlett's Women: Gone With The Wind and Its Female Fans*. London: Virago.

———. 1993. " 'The Griot from Tennessee': The Saga of Alex Haley's Roots." *Critical Quarterly* 37:2 (spring): 46–62.

Thomson, David. 1993. *Showman: The Life of David O. Selznick*. London: Andre Deutsch.

Toll, Robert C. 1974. *Blacking Up: The Minstrel Show in Nineteenth-Century America*. New York: Oxford University Press.

Tompkins, Jane. 1985. *Sensational Designs: The Cultural Works of American Fiction 1790–1860*. New York: Oxford University Press.

Toobin, Jeffrey. 1996. *The Run of His Life: The People v. O. J. Simpson*. New York: Random House.

Tucker, Lauren R., and Hemant Shah. 1992. "Race and the Transformation of Culture: The Making of the Television Miniseries *Roots.*" *Cultural Studies in Mass Communication* 9: 325–36.

Uffen, Ellen Serlen. 1980. "Edna Ferber and the 'Theatricalization' of American Mythology." Midwestern Miscellany 8: 82–93.

Ussher, Bruno David. 1983. "Max Steiner Establishes Another Film Music Record." In Richard Harwell, ed., Gone With the Wind *as Book and Film.* Columbia: University of South Carolina Press.

Vardac, Nicholas. 1949. *From Stage to Screen: Theatrical Origins of Early Film: David Garrick to D. W. Griffith.* Cambridge: Harvard University Press.

Vicinus, Martha. 1981. "Helpless and Unfriended: Nineteenth-Century Domestic Melodrama." *New Literary History* 13: 1 (autumn): 132.

Wagenknecht, Edward. 1965. *Harriet Beecher Stowe: The Known and the Unknown.* New York: Oxford University Press.

Watts, Gevry G. 1993. "Reflections on the Rodney King Verdict and the Paradoxes of the Black Response." In Robert Gooding-Williams, ed., *Reading Rodney King/Reading Urban Uprising.* New York: Routledge.

West, Cornel. 1993. "Learning to Talk of Race." In Robert Gooding-Williams, ed., *Reading Rodney King/Reading Urban Uprising.* New York: Routledge.

———. 1994. *Race Matters.* New York: Vintage Books.

Wexman, Virginia Wright. 1993. *Creating the Couple: Love, Marriage, and Hollywood Performance.* Princeton: Princeton University Press.

Whicher, George. 1963. "Literature and Conflict." In Robert Spiller, ed., *The Literary History of the United States.* Third edition. London: Macmillan.

White, Armond. 1997. "Eye, the Jury." In Toni Morrison and Claudia Brodsky Lacour, eds., *Birth of a Nation'hood: Gaze, Script, and Spectacle in the O. J. Simpson Case.* New York: Routledge.

Wiegman, Robyn. 1991. "Black Bodies/American Commodities: Gender, Race and the Bourgeois Ideal in Contemporary Film." In Lester Friedman, ed., *Unspeakable Images: Ethnicity and the American Cinema,* 308–28. Urbana: University of Illinois Press.

———. 1995. *American Anatomies: Theorizing Race and Gender.* Durham, N.C.: Duke University Press.

———. 1998. "Race, Ethnicity and Film." In John Hill and Pamela Church Gibson, eds. *The Oxford Guide to Film Studies,* 158–60. London: Oxford University Press.

———. 1999. "Whiteness Studies and the Paradox of Particularity." *boundary* 2, 26 (3) (fall): 115–50.

Wilder, Alec. 1972. *American Popular Song: The Great Innovators, 1900–1950.* New York: Oxford University Press.

Williams, Linda. 1984. " 'Something Else Besides a Mother': Stella Dallas and the Maternal Melodrama." *Cinema Journal* 24:1 (fall): 2–27. Reprinted in Christine Gledhill, ed., *Home Is Where the Heart Is,* 299–325. London: British Film Institute, 1987.

———. 1991. "Film Bodies: Gender, Genre, and Excess." *Film Quarterly* 44:4 (summer): 2–13.

Williams, Linda. 1998. "Melodrama Revised." In Nick Browne, ed., *Refiguring American Film Genres: Theory and History,* 42–88. Berkeley: University of California Press.

Bibliography

Williams, Patricia. 1997. "American Kabuki." In Toni Morrison and Claudia Brodsky Lacour, eds., *Birth of a Nation'hood: Gaze, Script, and Spectacle in the O. J. Simpson Case.* New York: Pantheon.

Williamson, Joel. 1984. *The Crucible of Race: Black-White Relations in the American South Since Emancipation.* New York: Oxford University Press.

Willis, Sharon. 1997. *High Contrast: Race and Gender in Contemporary Hollywood Film.* Durham, N.C.: Duke University Press.

Woll, Allen. 1989. *Black Musical Theatre: From Coontown to Dreamgirls.* Baton Rouge: Louisiana State University Press.

Wolper, David, and Quincy Troupe. 1978. *The Inside Story of TV's "Roots."* New York: Warner Books.

Young, Robert. 1991. *White Mythologies: Writing History and the West.* London: Routledge.

Index

388

Index

Index

401